Volume I

A Girl's Guide to a *Princess's Pathway*

A Teen Christian's Guide to God, Self-Worth, and Inner Beauty

Volume 1: A Girl's Guide to a Princess's Pathway...Walk in Worth

 **Coming Soon**

A Girl's Guide to a Princess's Pathway...

♥ <u>Volume 2</u>
A Teen Christian's Guide to Relationships, Dating and Finances.

*Topics include relationships, abuse,
sex, dating, marriage, finances and so much more!*

"To acquire wisdom is to love yourself; people who cherish understanding will prosper."
Proverbs 19:8

For more information, visit <u>www.princesspathway.com</u>.

Такава горѣ-долу е программата на „Соц.-Демократъ". Колкото за съдържанието на всѣка статия отдѣлно, ще кажемъ по нѣколко думи само за по-главнитѣ. На първо мѣсто стоятъ статиитѣ: „Н. Г. Чернишевский" отъ Г. Плеханова (№ I, II, III, и IV), които по обема (300 ст.) и съдържанието си съставляватъ едно прѣвъсходно критическо съчинение въ областьта на политическата економия.

Въ първата си статия за Чернишевски, Плехановъ разглежда философскитѣ взглядове на Чернишевски, неговото отношение къмъ литературата и искуството, неговото участие въ приготовляющата се въ петдесетитѣ и въ началото на шестдесетитѣ години реформа въ Руссия. Ученикъ на Фейербаха, Чернишевски е материалистъ въ крѫга на биологията, диалектикъ до нейдѣ въ искуството и литературата. Но благодарение на обстоятелството, че въ врѣмето, когато сѫ се образували неговитѣ взглядове, гениалнитѣ наслѣдници на Фейербаха—Марксъ и Енгелсъ *едва току що бѣхѫ* захванали да продължаватъ наченатото отъ него дѣло: да снематъ диалектиката на Гегеля отъ облацитѣ и да я поставятъ надъ реалнитѣ материални условия на живота, което Фейербахъ бѣше почти направилъ въ биологията и въ особенность въ психологията, но което на Маркса и Енгелса прѣдстоеше да направятъ въ социологията и историята, Чернишевски, както и всичкитѣ социалисти утописти, си остава идеалистъ по своитѣ взглядове върху философията на историята. Подобно на Фурйо, на Овена, въобще на социалиститѣ-утописти и на философитѣ въ XVIII-я вѣкъ, Чернишевски гледа на всичкитѣ сѫществующи обществени и економически отношения, а тъй сѫщо и на тѣзи, които прѣзъ всичкото си сѫществувание до днесъ человѣчеството е имало, като на неимеющи никакъвъ смисълъ, „неотговоряющи на здравата теория", и които хората търпятъ, защото не сѫ биле достатъчно просвѣтени, защото не сѫ имали никаква разчетливость, за да могѫтъ да видятъ и разберѫтъ, че не тъй, а друго-яче, „съобразно съ трѣбванията на разума" трѣбва да уредятъ живота си. А щомъ като сегашнитѣ економически и обществени учрѣждения сѫ недобри, неразумни, то нѣма защо и да изучаваме тѣхната сѫщность, тѣхнитѣ отличителни свойства, тѣхния характеръ. Главната ни работа трѣбва да е насочена да покажемъ какви трѣбва да бѫдѫтъ тѣзи учрѣждения съгласно съ разума и да дадемъ на всички да разбератъ, че тѣ до сега сѫ се лъгали и че е врѣме вече да устроятъ живота си разумно, рационално. Чернишевски е социалистъ-утопистъ. Въ втората и третата си статии Плехановъ, слѣдъ като излага въ общи чърти принципитѣ на научния соци-

нение, само когато се измѣнятъ послѣднитѣ, които пъкъ отъ своя страна се развиватъ и видоизмѣняватъ по логиката на самата своя сѫщность, механически, по строго опрѣдѣлени закони,—тѣ, отъ друга страна, прилагатъ тѣзи общи принципи къмъ русския общественъ и економически животъ. Тѣ показватъ, че исчезванието на руската община, която по своята примитивность не може по никой начинъ да служи за основа на едно социалистическо общество, е било неминуемо. Че, както наврѣдъ, тъй и въ Руссия, капиталистическото производство, основано на размѣната, експлуатацията и конкурренцията, истиква отъ общественната сцена първобитния начинъ на производството, билъ той индвидуаленъ или общественъ и го замѣня съ новъ, по усъвършенствуванъ, по-рационаленъ. Но прѣдъ това неминуемо разложение на общината ний не трѣбва да плачемъ, а да се радваме, казватъ тѣ; на капитализма у насъ да не гледаме като на реакционно развращающе явление, а напротивъ, като на нѣщо прогрессивно, тъй като той, отъ една страна, като разлага общината, като експроприира дребнитѣ собственници, като съсрѣдоточава богатствата въ сè помалко и по-малко рѫцѣ, приготвя материалнитѣ условия за бѫдѫщето социалистическо общество, а отъ друга, като обръща секенитѣ и занаятчиитѣ въ пролетарии и като ги организира, той приготвя и революционната сила, която ще извърше социалната революция. Прочее, въ Руссия, както и въ Западна Европа, може да има дума за социализмъ до толкозъ, до колкото е развитъ капитализма, до колкото има пролетариатъ. Пролетариата е единственния общественъ елементъ, който може и ще направи социалната революция. Всичкото внимание на руската младежь, на рускитѣ революционери трѣбва да бѫде отправено къмъ тази точка. А има ли въ Руссия капитализмъ, има ли пролегарпатъ? —Има го, отговорятъ редакторитѣ на *Социалъ-демократъ*. Руссия е взела и отъ день на день се по-вече и по-вече взема видъ на западно-европейска буржуазна държава. Задачата на руската революционна интеллигенция е—да се слѣе съ русския пролетариатъ, да му разясни (като прѣдварително сама го разбере, разбира се) начина, по който ще се освободи отъ експлуатацията на капитала; да му покаже историческата роль, която положението му налага да играе при трансформацията на днешния общественъ и економически строй; съ една дума, да го поведе на борба съ капитализма въ всичкитѣ му проявления, на борба съ буржуазията. Но тази борба е немислима при сѫществующия днесъ въ Руссия абсолютизмъ, слѣдователно, тя трѣбва да го поведе, прѣди всичко, на борба съ деспотизма.

Volume I

A Girl's Guide to a *Princess's Pathway*
A Teen Christian's Guide to God, Self-Worth and Inner Beauty

Chrystal Epps-Bean

Anchored Redemption, LLC
2020

Volume 1: A Girl's Guide to Princess's Pathway…A Teen's Christian Guide to God, Self-Worth and Inner Beauty

Copyright © 2019 by Chrystal Epps-Bean

All rights reserved. This book, illustrations, or any portion thereof may not be reproduced or used in any manner whatsoever without the express written permission of the publisher.

First Printing: 2020
Printed in the United States of America
ISBN 978-1-7347310-0-2

Anchored Redemption, LLC
PO Box 1031
Cordova, TN 38088

www.anchoredanew.com

Ordering Information: Special discounts are available on quantity purchases. For details, contact the publisher at the above listed address.

Library of Congress Cataloging-in-Publication Data
Epps-Bean, Chrystal
   A Girl's Guide to a Princess's Pathway, Volume 1 and 2 other works

Unless otherwise indicated, all Scripture quotations are taken from the Holy Bible, New Living Translation, copyright © 1996, 2004, 2015 by Tyndale House Foundation. Used by permission of Tyndale House Publishers, a Division of Tyndale House Ministries, Carol Stream, Illinois 60188. All rights reserved.

Scripture quotations marked (AMP) are taken from the Amplified Bible, Copyright © 1954, 1958, 1962, 1964, 1965, 1987 by The Lockman Foundation. Used by permission. All rights reserved.

Scripture quotations marked (ESV) are taken from The ESV® Bible (The Holy Bible, English Standard Version®), copyright © 2001 by Crossway, a publishing ministry of Good News Publishers. Used by permission. All rights reserved.

Scripture quotations marked (GNT) are taken from the Good News Translation - Second Edition © 1992 by American Bible Society. Used by permission.

Scripture quotations marked (GW) GOD'S WORD are a copyrighted work of God's Word to the Nations. Quotations are used by permission. Copyright 1995 by God's Word to the Nations. All rights reserved.

Scripture quotations marked (NASB) are taken from the New American Standard Bible, Copyright © 1960, 1962, 1963 1968, 1971, 1972, 1973 1975, 1977, 1995 by The Lockman Foundation. All rights reserved. Used by permission. http://www.Lockman.org

Scripture quotations marked (NIV) are taken from the Holy Bible, New International Version®, NIV®. Copyright © 1973, 1978, 1984, 2011 by Biblica, Inc.™ Used by permission of Zondervan. All rights reserved worldwide. www.zondervan.com The "NIV" and "New International Version" are trademarks registered in the United States Patent and Trademark Office by Biblica, Inc.®

Scripture quotations marked (NKJV) are taken from the New King James Version®. Copyright © 1982 by Thomas Nelson. Used by permission. All rights reserved. Scripture quotations marked (KJV) are taken from the King James Version.

Rev.2

Dedication

This book is dedicated to my beloved husband, son and my *bea*utiful mother, Bea. Thank you for your continued support and encouragement. Son, I appreciate your heartfelt patience and understanding with me while writing this book. I know I committed a great deal of time to this endeavor that reduced our quality time together, but God is a redeemer of time. Additionally, I dedicate this book to my family, friends, mentors, future generations, and all the beautiful daughters/princesses in Christ who will rise and take their rightful place in the world.

Contents

Preface vii
Introduction viii
    Social-Eternity Knowledge Model™ (SEKM) x
    Summary Steps xii
    Poetic Princess xiii

Chapter 1: Tormented Teen 1
Learn about a torment to triumph journey — a true story

Chapter 2: Paved Pathway 5
Learn the truth about yourself, your Creator, and the world

Chapter 3: Flawless Foundation 35
Learn how to make yourself divinely beautiful

Chapter 4: Validated Value 63
Learn who you are and your extraordinary value

Chapter 5: Predestined Princess 85
Learn the traits of a true princess and your pre-determined royal inheritance

Chapter 6: Qualified Queen 147
Learn how to become elevated as royalty

Chapter 7: Faithful Father 159
Learn about your Daddy — first Father

Chapter 8: Evil Enemy 174
Learn about your evil enemy and how to defeat him

Chapter 9: Perfect Path 208
Discover divine direction to the Princess's Pathway — the path to success

Chapter 10: Powerful Prayer 222
Learn how to talk to your Father and invoke His blessings and promises

Chapter 11: Endless End 268
Learn about infinite endings and the 'Books' that reveal your infinite destiny

    Poetic Princess and the MVP (Most Valuable Prayer) 276

Preface

Being a teen can be hard. I personally remember how hard it was when I struggled with low self-esteem, peer pressure, and teen dating violence. My struggles were a direct result of me not knowing my identity in Christ and who God created me to be. Many young girls do not understand their full intrinsic value which far exceeds the price of rubies or gold (Proverbs 31:10).

Oftentimes, when girls are little, their parents give them princess parties, tiaras, dolls, princess books, princess room decor, and may even call their little girl "princess". Their goal in doing this is to boost their child's confidence and build a self-awareness of being valuable, priceless, beautiful, significant, and special. The moral to this lesson is to convey that being a princess is not about having fancy things, clothes, a kingdom, or a crown, but more about a mind-set as it relates to who you are and your royal inheritance which can only be truly found in Christ Jesus – the King of kings.

A Girl's Guide to a Princess's Pathway: A Teen Christian's Guide to God, Self-worth and Inner Beauty teaches teen girls that being a princess is no fairytale. It is no dream that you should wish for. If you are guided correctly and choose the proper path to life (Deuteronomy 30:19), you will learn that you are born a princess through Christ Jesus. And as you mature in the love of God, you will grow to be elevated as a queen.

Growing up, the most idiotic cliché or catchphrase I heard was, *"What you don't know can't hurt you."* This is undoubtedly one of the most untrue statements ever made. The truth of the matter is, what you do not know can hurt you; in fact, what you do not know can destroy you. How do I know? Because what I did not know almost destroyed me. This book aims to bring awareness, knowledge, and wisdom to rescue and heal those who do not know. Sadly, people perish for a lack of knowledge (Hosea 4:6). This book will help combat this societal ill by teaching you what life's experiences taught me; and sharing and spreading knowledge abroad to prevent perishing, pain, and pointless mistakes.

*"...how much more will those who receive God's abundant provision of grace and of the gift of righteousness **reign in life** through the one man, Jesus Christ!"* Romans 5:17

Disclaimer: This book is for <u>mature</u> teens and young adults and may include explicit terms and analogies (straight talk) for the purpose of bringing understanding to engender proper decision making. The content is not believed to be inappropriate, but straight-forward to combat the stream of illicit influences and information taught in the world today via television, music, social media, online media/content, video games, peers, and secularism—which all work together to take you off course and lead you in the wrong direction.

Introduction

Life is not a fairy tale, yet many girls live their lives in a world of deception and make-believe created by peer pressure, false doctrines, false love and ill illusions that are perpetuated by music, television, social media and secular culture – while other girls battle the real world and its real life issues, struggling with abuse, abandonment, poverty, relational dysfunction, rejection, self-hate and low self-esteem, but soon too succumb to the world of make-believe for comfort and escape. Both worlds seek to entangle and ensnare, aiding in the destruction of identity, self-worth, purpose, and destiny. This book introduces a new world, a kingdom of truth, which seeks to expose the lies while uncovering the princess from within and the promises that supersede every problem.

"A Girl's Guide to a Princess's Pathway" collection is founded on biblical principles and provides a comprehensive in-depth review of real-life issues that often deter, discourage, and devalue teen girls and young adults. This book serves as a reference guide, a toolkit, for educating girls on various challenges and life skills to galvanize hope, encourage positive decision making, and foster a healthy sense of identity, esteem, and self-worth. This guide works to transform the reader holistically, sowing seeds by digging deep into their organic state, to provide a total mental makeover that alters negative behaviors, illuminates natural inner beauty and God sanctioned regal power. A Girl's Guide to a Princess's Pathway provides purpose, direction, and the ability to break free to S.T.A.N.D.* and walk into destiny wearing a crown of greatness.

*"**I will guide you along the best pathway for your life**. I will advise you and watch over you."* Psalm 32:8

*"...**make known to me the path of life**; you will fill me with joy in your presence, with eternal pleasures at your right hand."* Psalm 16:11

God and His infinite wisdom are your Guide to a Princess Pathway.
Wisdom is your compass to the crown of life.

"Learn to be wise, and develop good judgment. Don't forget or turn away from my words. Don't turn your back on wisdom, for she will protect you. Love her, and she will guard you. Getting wisdom is the most important thing you can do! And whatever else you do, get good judgment.
If you prize wisdom*, she will exalt you. Embrace her and she will honor you. She will place a lovely wreath on your head;* **she will present you with a beautiful crown.*"*** Proverbs 4:1-9

***S**et Yourself Apart, **T**ake your place, **A**ffirm your Identity, **N**ullify your past, **D**emonstrate your purpose

There are many experiences that lead you to your destiny; but there is only one right path and one wrong path. When you start the journey of life, your choices will take you there.

Social-Eternity Knowledge Model™

For each chapter, there are guideposts that indicate and convey each component of the model.

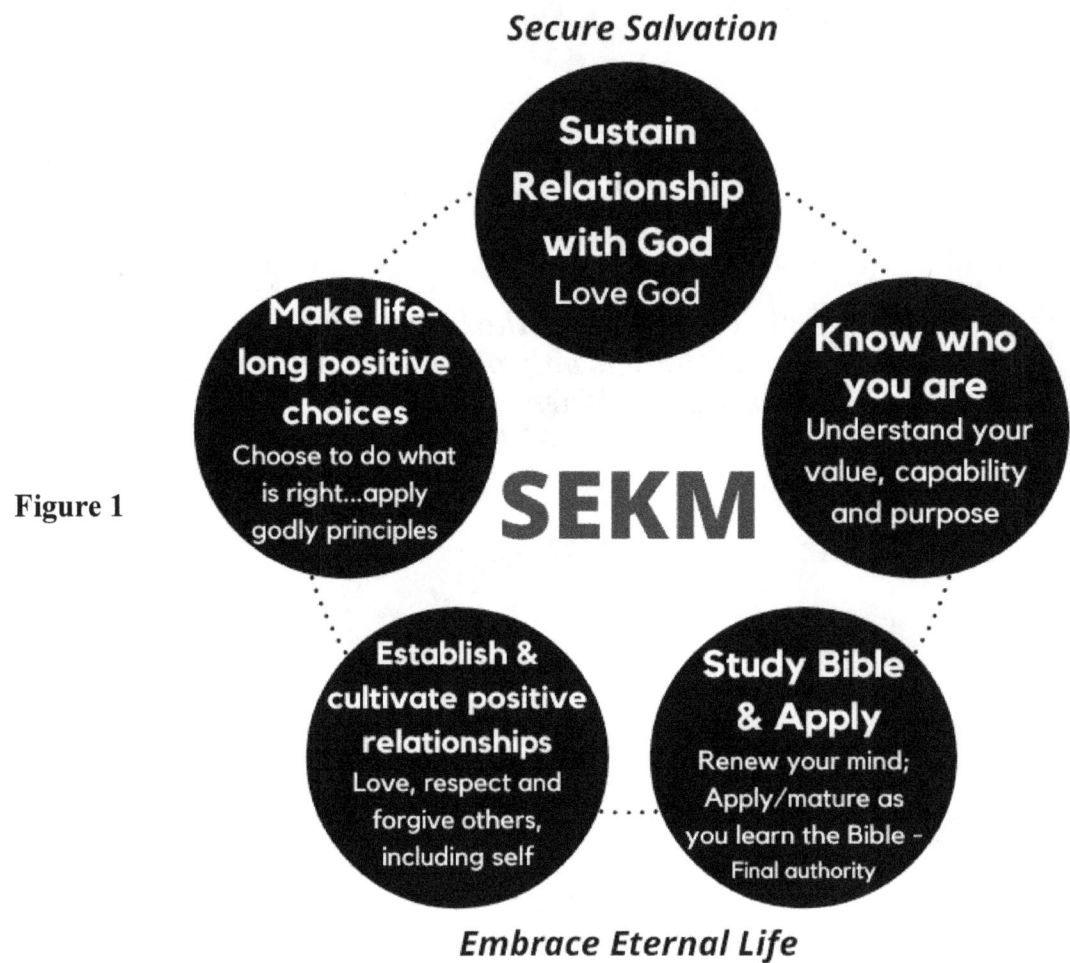

Figure 1

How to Use this Book

This book is written as an integrated whole with each chapter building upon each other. To get the most out of this book, read each chapter sequentially and focus intently on the supporting scriptures (emphasized in *italic* and "quotations") preceding and/or succeeding the content. There are also scripture reference(s) provided at the end of some sentences for you to reference in your Bible to gain additional understanding.

It is important to know that this book, *"A Girl's Guide to a Princess's Pathway"*, is not the guide, in and of itself, but will lead you to 'The Guide' – the Bible (God's Guidebook), its wisdom and the Spirit who inspires its principles.

Royal Legend

The following legend labels are listed throughout the book to highlight significant content and to underscore its meaning.

- ♛ **Action Activity** – An activity that requires the reader to respond either by thought, action, word, or deed.

- ♛ **Candid Clarification** – An explanation provided to clear up misinterpretation(s).

- ♛ **Fast Fact** – A quick statement consisting of statistics or facts.

- ♛ **Minute** (mī-noot′) **Memoir** – A brief autobiography written about the author's personal experience(s).

- ♛ **Purpose Point** – Key points, navigational nuggets and trajectory tips that are significant to the chapter and content.

- ♛ **Supporting Scriptures** – Key scriptures that support the preceding/succeeding content (may be cited with or without legend label). Scriptures taken from the New Living Translation, unless otherwise noted.

- ♛ **Text Term** – An important term included in the text and succinctly defined.

 Summary Steps

*The first step to walking in worth is to know who you are
and whose you are.*

Worth (definition): the value of something measured by its qualities or by the esteem in which it is held; deserving of; of substantial or significant value or merit – e.g., a woman's worth
Source: Merriam-Webster

Volume 1
"Walk in Worth"
"...walk in a manner worthy of the calling to which you have been called," Ephesians 4:1 ESV
For your Journey...Steps to the Princess Pathway

1. Know who you are, whose you are and why you were created
2. Be honest about your pain
3. Seek proper help to foster healing
4. Accept Jesus as your Lord and Savior
5. **S**et yourself Apart
6. **T**ake your place
7. **A**ffirm your Identity
8. **N**ullify your Past
9. **D**emonstrate your Purpose
10. Understand your true worth and walk in it
11. Love and respect yourself
12. Do not allow anyone or anything to devalue you
13. Know that you are beautifully and wonderfully made
14. Enhance your inner beauty with the Word of God
15. Be pure and humble in heart
16. Behave and speak like a lady
17. Grow, mature, acquire knowledge/wisdom and apply <u>the truth</u> to your life
18. Gain a new perspective of your Heavenly Father and know His great love for you
19. Be wary of the evil enemy who seeks to war against you
20. Choose the right way, the Highway of Holiness/Righteousness Road (Perfect Path)
21. Be a woman of prayer, praise, and worship
22. Know the "end" is inevitable – endless; live with the *end* in mind

Now, let's embark on the journey. Take my hand as you are guided to the Princess Pathway.

Poetic Princess

PREMEDITATED PLAN for a PRINCESS

The wicked demon started the attack in the womb.
"This one is special", he said, "I must act soon."
"Let me whisper in her parents' ear with anxiety and fear, aborting is the solution,
yes, yes this proves to be a resolution."
The father said "Yes", and the mother said "No"
But the guardian Spirit said, "I AM in control,
she will live, it is so."
A precious beautiful *Princess* was
born, so innocent, so sweet.
Little did she know the wicked demon was after her,
following her every beat.
"I will work through her family, friends and boyfriends,"
he said. "I will even work through her.
I will make her wish she was dead.
I will get her off the right path and
take her down the rocky road.
I will make her think she has found her prince,
but it will be a demonic toad."
As time went on, these things surely came to past
but thanks to the guardian Spirit, they didn't last.
The precious princess…hurt, rejected, misused, and abused
must find it in herself to move on,
although she feels so damaged and alone.
She must look to the guardian Spirit
for guidance and restoration.
She must study her instruction manual
from Genesis to Revelation.
Regardless of all the attacks and her mess,
She <u>must believe</u> that she is a beautiful *Princess*.

"You did your best to kill me, O my enemy, but the Lord helped me.
The Lord is my strength and my song; he has become my victory" Psalm 118:13-14

Poetic Princess

GO AWAY WITH ME

Go away with me
Imagine this girl bent down low - hurt, sad, confused, rejected, misused, and abused.
She has so many dreams, but a low self-esteem.
"Why doesn't anyone love me?" she asks, "I've done nothing wrong;
I am always left feeling hurt and alone."
She is tangled up in chains of pain and depression.
Someone sees and yells, "I can help, all I need is for you to believe and a confession.
I want to set you free from these chains that have held you bound.
Stop struggling, be still, don't make a sound.
Trust me, take my hand, I am the man you have been waiting for.
Hurry, Hurry I am knocking, open the door.
I can bring your dreams to reality, my precious princess.
Behind you will find so much more, and nothing less.
Wear your crown, don't frown or be down,
I can turn everything around."
The Savior is saying, "Take my hand, I'll be your man;
I am all you need, believe and understand."
The girl struggles as she makes her way to open the door.
The King enters and bends down to the tear-soaked floor.
He untangles the chains and lifts her up.
"Here", He says, "you can drink from my cup"
Go away with me
Now imagine this girl where happiness and peace cover her like an umbrella.
No, this girl is not Cinderella.
She is beautiful, amazing, precious, priceless, royalty…
can you guess?
It is you, a beautiful princess.
Show your beauty, exercise your duty–
your Savior, your King awaits you!

"I will lift up a cup symbolizing his salvation;
I will praise the Lord's name for saving me." Psalm 116:13

*"…**Stand up** and praise the Lord your God, for he lives from everlasting to everlasting!"*
Nehemiah 9:5

"Be still and know that I am God!" Psalm 46:10

Chapter 1
Tormented Teen (Purposed Pain)

Minute Memoir: At the age of 10 I felt drawn to carnal pleasures. There was a gravitational force within me pulling me to a forceful secular mechanism. While most girls this age play house and watch popular children television programs, I often stayed up late watching adult channels, engulfed with explicit scenes, scenarios, and situations.

I lived in the same house with both my parents when they were together, but when they separated, I sometimes stayed with my mother and other times with my father. My mother was a very sweet and nice lady. I never recall her yelling or spanking me. My father, on the other hand, was a different story. He was often moody and angry, and other times he was caring and giving. I was afraid of him and felt that I was not pleasing to him. It seemed as though everything I did was wrong or not enough. I remember saying, *"I can't wait until I get grown."*

My teen years were the worst times of my life. My precious childhood was robbed from me as a result of my own disobedience. The rebellion started at the age of 12 while staying with my mother in the 7th grade. I loved the middle school I was attending and was hoping to remain there until my transition to high school. My mother and I, however, moved to a different part of town. As a result, I had to transfer to another school. I was so angry that I had to switch schools and leave my friends, so I rebelled in every kind of way from fights at school to skipping classes. As time went on, still angry and discontented over losing my best friends coupled with carnal consciousness, my chasteness was compromised. Something so precious, so priceless was given away without any thought or hesitation. Something that was meant to be for my king (husband) was given away to a peasant.

Purpose Point: God's plan is for us to remain a virgin until we get married. This may not be popular, but it is His principle. *"This explains why a man leaves his father and mother and is joined to his wife, and the two are united into one."* Genesis 2:24

As a result of my rebellious activities while staying with my mother, it was decided that I should move with my father. I absolutely didn't want that, but I was forced to move in with him. Once again, I had to transfer to another school that was closer to my father's house.

It was then that I met the devil himself, not my father, but this boy I had begun dating who was 18 years of age. Legally, he was considered an adult and I was a young teen who was still in middle school. I dated him for four years – four years of torment, trauma, and abuse.

Fast Fact: When an adult (generally 18 years of age or older) has a non-forceable sexual relationship with someone who is below the age of consent such as a young teenager, this is often called *"Statutory Rape"** which is a crime (illegal). *State laws are dependent upon the aspects and nuances of the situation and may vary in terms of starting adult age, age of consent, the age of the minor in relation to the age of the perpetuator and the nature of the crime which determines the ultimate charge(s).

The young man I had begun dating was very disturbed. He did every foul act to me you can think of, including: abusing me physically, verbally and sexually; kidnapping me and throwing me into the trunk of his car while threatening to leave me in the middle of nowhere; attempting to push me down the stairs and throw me over a balcony; assaulted me with a gun; harassed my friends and family; stalked me; strangled me to a point where I almost passed out, and sexually assaulted me. There were so many times that he said, "I'll change", "It won't happen again" – yeah right! Lies, lies, and more lies. The abuse occurred throughout the entire course of four years. The most life-threatening attack I can remember is when he threw a chair across the room and it struck me on the head. This resulted in a swollen black eye the next day. The doctor said that the chair was so close to striking a major artery, if it had, I would have died. I was still in middle school at the time and told my classmates that a bee had stung me.

My mom tried to keep me from seeing my boyfriend, but I rebelled, making excuses for him. My father only told me, *"You should never let a man put his hands on you"* – what good that did me. My self-esteem and self-confidence were too damaged for me to help myself. I felt that it was something that I had done wrong or deserved. One night, I remember lying in the bed and writing a prayer to God. I later gave the prayer to my mom and she kept it.

It reads,

Oh Lord I pray…
Please give me the strength to see another day.
I love you with all my heart.
I will always believe in you and pray to be with you someday and never apart.
I ask you for another chance—free me from my sins.
Without you, I couldn't win.
I'm begging for hope and forgiveness.
Free me from all diseases.
My life is going very bad at this age.
I hope and pray that I live to see the next stage.
I pray, and pray, and ask for your blessing.
Believe it or not, I've learned my lesson.
Lord, I Love You—Amen
6-20-94

Even at a young age, in my early teens, I knew that God was my only hope. But although this prayer came from the heart, the truth was I had not learned my lesson – not yet anyway. No matter what my boyfriend did to me, I still stayed with him. Some people may call this stupid, but I call it hurt, confused and *'all tied up'*. I often rebelled against my parents just to see him. One day my father got so fed up that he asked me if I wanted him (referring to himself) in or out my life. Being the teen that I was, I told my father that I did not want him in my life. I knew this way I would have more freedom to do what I wanted to do. As a result, my father was no longer a part of my life. We had no communication whatsoever during the latter part of my teen years. My boyfriend, however, remained. There were so many times I wanted to get out of the relationship with him, but I lacked the strength and courage to do it.

Purpose Point: Unhealthy bonds are developed when you have premarital sex (sex before marriage). You do not have to have sex with a boy just because you call him your 'boyfriend' or just because he claims to be your boyfriend. In other words, you do not have to give your body away to acquire, sustain or get over a relationship.

I prayed almost every day, asking God to help me and He did. My boyfriend was later arrested for aggravated robbery and assault. These charges were due to him robbing a lady at gunpoint at a bank and attacking her. His capture finally freed me from his harassment, obsession, and abuse. God knew that I did not have the strength to do it on my own, so He did it for me. He allowed him to get caught and arrested. God will always provide a way of escape (1 Corinthians 10:13); only seek Him and trust Him for your deliverance. It was only then that my boyfriend (ex-boyfriend) was completely out of my life.

Through all the torment and violence, someone was watching over me…protecting and preserving my life. This someone was God. And because of God, I was able to move from *torment to triumph.* God is your hope. Hope in Him, and you will not be disappointed (Romans 10:11).

Most people think of God as a high power seated in heaven with lots of rules and regulations, ready to punish anyone who does wrong. Instead, God is slow to anger, merciful and a loving Father who protects His children from harm (Psalm 145:8-9). Yes, it is true that He is a higher being in heaven with commandments, but He is not happy with punishing us. All His commands are meant to protect us. For example, one of God's commands is not to have sex before you are married (1 Corinthians 6:18). If I had only obeyed this command, I would have never experienced what my ex-boyfriend did to me or all the pain and turmoil I endured in my teenage years.

Nevertheless, everything I went through in my early years was purposeful and very much worth it – the abuse, hurt and torment. Yes, it was all worth it! If this book helps you in anyway, if my pain releases your pain, if my experiences prevent you from having the same experiences, it was worth it! I heard a saying once, *"You can't teach what you don't know and you can't lead where you won't go".* I say, **you can't comprehend where you haven't been.** In other words, the best teacher is experience – oftentimes the evaluated experience of others. If you can learn from someone else's experiences without going through them, you are exceedingly fortunate. It has been said, *"smart people learn from their mistakes, but wise people learn from the mistakes of others."*

Irrespective of the cliché catchphrases and platitudes, no one really knows your pain or how you feel unless they have had the same experiences. No one can teach you what they don't know. If I had not been in an abusive relationship, how can I really understand the way you feel or give you advice on the matter? If I had never experienced teen pregnancy and single parenting, how can I understand the struggle?

Purpose Point: Pain can have purpose and it can be pretty if it helps you or someone else.

As a teen, I went through immense pain and torment that even most adults never go through; however, there are millions of young girls in the world today who are experiencing something similar or worse. Many girls have been molested, raped, prostituted/trafficked, abused, abandoned, abducted, and neglected; they are trying desperately to escape, recover and find their way.

The purpose of this book(s) is to encourage, inspire and inform mature teen girls, and even young adults about various matters and challenges that affect many today; and to guide readers to the solutions to overcome these challenges.

Stay tuned for more upcoming books and related volumes that address these matters in more detail. No matter how hopeless a situation may seem, there is always hope and this book(s) will help you tap into it! *"Commit yourself to instruction; attune your ears to hear words of knowledge."* Proverbs 23:12

Chapter 2
Paved Pathway (Important Intro)

"So we fix our eyes not on what is seen, but on what is unseen, since what is seen is temporary, but what is unseen is eternal." 2 Corinthians 4:18 NIV

We must not be concerned with the things we see, for the things we see are only temporary. The unseen things are more important. For example, we could not live without air. We cannot see air, but it is vital to our existence; without it we would die. God is the same way; He is crucial to our existence. We cannot see Him but without God we will surely die. You might say, 'But everyone dies' – this is true. But people who die physically will live again, if they believe and obey God, just as Jesus died and lived again (1 Corinthians 15).

God is the Creator of all things. He created the world and everything in it, including you. Everything that you see around you was created by God. You may think, well, my mother and father created me, or Apple created my I-phone and Mac computer. These people assisted in the creation, but God is the ultimate Creator. God created humans and gave them the capability to produce children, and the knowledge, ingenuity, and resources to make things like your home, TV, bed, clothing, phone, and computer. God is in control of everything that exists; nothing can exist without God allowing it to exist. You would not be here today reading this book, if God did not allow you to be born. He was the one who breathed life into your body when your parents conceived you. He made all the delicate parts of your body and formed you while you were in your mother's womb.

Secure Salvation

Sustain Relationship with God
Love God

"The Lord, your Redeemer and Creator, says: "I am the Lord, who made all things. I alone stretched out the heavens. By myself I made the earth and everything in it." Isaiah 44:24

"You made all the delicate inner parts of my body and knit me together in my mother's womb. Thank you for making me so wonderfully complex! Your workmanship is marvelous and how well I know it. You watched me as I was being formed in utter seclusion as I was woven together in the dark of the womb. You saw me before I was born. Every day of my life was recorded in your book. Every moment was laid out before a single day had passed." Psalm 139:13-16

There is only one true and living God. People of other religions, outside of Christianity, worship gods and idols that they have created, or individuals that died long ago, but the God of the Bible is the only real God that lives. *"I am the Lord, and there is no other God. I am the Lord, and there is no other…"* Isaiah 45:5

Minute Memoir: When I was young (before all the hell broke loose in my life), I went to church with my mother. I heard about God and Jesus while there, but no one ever sat down to teach me about Him and His will for my life. All I knew was that Jesus died on the cross for my sins with nails in his hands. For me, church was just a time to talk to the other kids, flirt with boys, play tic-tac-toe and eat at the church luncheons. The Bible seemed like a foreign book written in another language, boring and unimportant. I thought life was just about living and being afraid of dying. My thinking was totally wrong, and it almost killed me! There is more to Jesus than a cross and nails; church is not a recreational center and the Bible is the most important book in the world. Most importantly, life is not just about living and being afraid of dying.

*"Because God's children are human beings – made of flesh and blood – Jesus also became flesh and blood by being born in human form. For only as a human being could he die, and only by dying could he break the power of the Devil, who had power over death. **Only in this way could he deliver those who have lived all their lives as slaves to the <u>fear of dying</u>**."* Hebrews 2:14-15

Purpose Point: If we believe in Jesus and obey him, we no longer have to fear dying because after we die a physical death we transition to our heavenly home and will later rise to live again by God's power (1 Thessalonians 4:15-17; 1 Thessalonians 5:10).

"For we know that when this earthly tent we live in is taken down (that is, when we die and leave this earthly body), we will have a house in heaven, an eternal body made for us by God himself and not by human hands." 2 Corinthians 5:1

I am sure you have heard about Jesus too, maybe while in Sunday school, at church with your parents or on TV and radio. But hearing about Jesus is not enough, he wants you to know him, and most importantly he wants you to know you. He wants you to know why you were created, your value and your purpose in life.

Purpose Point: The Trinity is comprised of the Father (God), the Son (Jesus) and the Holy Spirit (the Spirit that lives in you when you become saved). We are a three-part being (spirit, soul, and body) just as God also functions as a three-part being – the Father, the Son and the Holy Spirit…one great God in three different dimensions. Therefore, when we refer to God, we are also referring to Jesus and His Spirit. When we refer to Jesus, we are also referring to

God and His Spirit; and when we refer to His Spirit, we are also referring to God and Jesus – they are all one.

The truth about Jesus
Jesus is a real person and is still alive today. He resides in heaven seated on the throne, on the right side of God. 2000 years ago, Jesus lived on earth. His mother's name was Mary, who was a virgin when she became pregnant with him. Now, you may ask, how can a virgin, a person who has never had sex, become pregnant. Many people wondered this, including Mary and the man she was supposed to marry. The truth is that God made her pregnant with Jesus, not through sex, but through His mighty power – His Holy Spirit.

How did Mary become pregnant?
God sent an angel, Gabriel, to Mary to tell her she will become pregnant with a son, and she should name him Jesus. Mary was confused by his remark because she was a virgin. How could this happen she wondered, given the fact that I have never had sex with a man. The angel said, God's Spirit (power) will come upon you and overtake you. The baby will be holy as God is holy and will be called the Son of God (Luke 1:26-35).

Why did God send Jesus?
I am sure we all know or have heard of The Ten Commandments given by God to Moses, such as: "Do not lie, Do not steal, Do not worship any other gods, Do not murder…" God gave Moses these commandments so that people could know the difference between right and wrong and know the ways of God. God also gave Moses additional instructions for the people to live by and obey. *"When Moses had announced to the people all the teachings and commandments the Lord had given him, they answered together, 'We will do everything the Lord has told us to do.' Then Moses carefully wrote down all the Lord's instructions (Exodus 24:3-4 NLV).* These instructions were known as "The Book of Covenant". But although the people said that they will do everything the Lord told them to do, they did not. I am sure we all can relate to this because how many times have we told our parents that we would do something, but didn't do it. When someone does not do what God tells them to do, this is called 'SIN', and the wages of sin is eternal death. So in order to avoid the wages of sin, which is spiritual death, God had to establish a system where people could take responsibility for their sins and receive forgiveness. This system included priests and sacrificial offerings made to God. Priests served as mediators between God and man. When someone sinned, it was required for them to take an animal or offering to the priest for them to sacrifice it to God. *"In this way, the priest will make atonement for those who are guilty, and they will be forgiven."* Leviticus 6:7

Examples of sacrificial offerings include the following:

"…bring to the Lord a young bull with no physical defects…Slaughter it in the Lord's presence….take some of the animal's blood into the Tabernacle and dip your finger into the blood, and sprinkle it seven times before the Lord…The priest will put some of the blood on the horns of the incense altar…The priest must remove all the fat around the bull's internal organs, the two kidneys with the fat around them near the loins, and the lobe of the liver. Then he must burn them on the altar of burnt offerings…" Leviticus 4:3-10

"...they must confess their sin and bring to the Lord as their penalty a female from the flock, either a sheep or goat. This will be a sin offering to remove their sin, and the priests will make <u>atonement</u> for them." Leviticus 5:5-6

Some examples of sin that required a sacrifice include, but are not limited to, adultery, murder, stealing, homosexuality, fornication, lying, disobedient to parents, idolatry, and witchcraft.

Text Terms:

- A <u>*covenant*</u> is a formal binding agreement between two or more parties, where everyone involved agrees to do their part.
- <u>*Atonement*</u> is making things right for a wrong that was done. In an effort to make things right with God because of sin, people sacrificed animals because only by shedding blood can sin be forgiven (Hebrews 9:22).
- <u>*Mediators*</u> are people who help to settle differences between two or more individuals or groups.

Moreover, God found fault with the system of priests, and considered it weak and useless (Hebrews 7:18). Due to the many disadvantages of this system, God established a new system, His Son Jesus Christ. Jesus was made the perfect High Priest and gave his life as the ultimate sacrifice when he died on the cross. With this new system there is not one disadvantage; it is perfect, just as our Lord Jesus Christ is perfect. *"...God qualified him [Jesus] as the perfect High Priest, and he became the source of eternal salvation for all those who obey him."* Hebrew 5:9

The only way sin can be forgiven is through the shedding of blood. This law was established by God and cannot be changed. Since the old priestly system was weak and useless, God created Jesus in human form and required that he be crucified on the cross for the sins of the world. Therefore, God allowed cruel and evil people to kill Jesus so that all people could receive forgiveness for their sins and receive the gift of eternal life without performing repetitive animal sacrifices. Although Jesus died for our sins, receiving forgiveness is not automatic. People are required to confess their sins, repent, believe and acknowledge Jesus as their Lord and Savior to receive forgiveness and eternal life.

Purpose Point: *"...Without the shedding of blood, there will be no forgiveness of sins."* Hebrews 9:22

Purpose Point: Remember, sin is disobedience, doing what God your Creator told you not to do. It is easy to disobey God when you don't have Jesus in your life, but when you truly accept Jesus Christ, His Holy Spirit will come to live in you and will help you obey. He will exchange your desires for His desires. Bad or sinful things you once liked doing, you will not want to do anymore.

Evil Entry – How Sin Entered the World

Sin entered the world through one man, Adam. Adam was the first man to be created on earth. God gave Adam a specific commandment to not eat from the Tree of Knowledge (Genesis 2:16-17, 3:6). But as you may know, Adam sinned and disobeyed God by eating the apple from the tree that God told him not to eat from. Although his wife Eve encouraged him, God held Adam – the man (the head of the family) responsible. It was through this one act that sin entered the world. *"When Adam sinned, sin entered the entire human race. Adam's sin brought death, so death spread to everyone, for everyone sinned...Because one person disobeyed God, many people became sinners."* Romans 5:12,19

The *good news* is when Jesus Christ obeyed God by never sinning and dying on the cross for our sins, he canceled out the power of sin in the world. As a result, all humanity has an opportunity to become right with God and live forever. Jesus' obedience and blood sacrifice made final atonement for our sins…making us right with God. But remember, this is not automatic. We are required to confess our sins, repent, believe and acknowledge Jesus as our Lord and Savior to receive forgiveness and eternal life.

Purpose Point: The devil (an evil angel or demon) encouraged Adam and his wife to sin. He is behind all evil and sin in the world. Refer to the 'Evil Enemy' chapter for more information.

Below is a comparison chart of the priestly system versus the new system of Jesus with its respective disadvantages or advantages.

Old System – Priests (Disadvantages)	New System – Jesus (Advantages)
"There were many priests…when one priest died, another priest had to take his place." Hebrews 7:23	Jesus became the one and only High Priest; he died a physical death but later rose again by God's power and lives in heaven pleading to God on our behalf. He will never die; therefore, no one can ever take his place (Romans 8:34).
Priests had to offer sacrifices every day or once a year on the Day of Atonement for the forgiveness of sins. First, they had to offer sacrifices for their own sins and then offer sacrifices for the sins of the people. These sacrifices required the death and blood of animals because **"without the shedding of blood, there will be no forgiveness of sins."** Hebrews 7:27, Hebrews 9:22, Leviticus 23:26-44	Jesus was the Lamb of God. He was the ultimate sacrifice. He shed his blood on the cross for us so that our sins could be forgiven. *"For the wages of sin is death, but the free gift of God is eternal life through Christ Jesus our Lord."* Romans 6:23 Because of what Jesus did, we do not have to worry about taking a bull or sheep to priests to be slaughtered and presented to the Lord because Jesus paid the penalty for our sins. Thank God! Note: The average cost for a bull is around $2,500. If we had to go to a priest every day with a sacrificial sin offering, that is approximately $17,500 a week, $70,000 a month and $840,000 a year. **Jesus sacrificed himself for us once and for all! Our debt was paid in full!!** *"He was oppressed and treated harshly, yet he never*

Old System – Priests (Disadvantages)	New System – Jesus (Advantages)
	said a word. He was led as a lamb to the slaughter. And as a sheep is silent before the shearers, he did not open his mouth. From prison and trial, they led him away to his death. But who among the people realized that he was dying for their sins—that he was suffering their punishment? He had done no wrong, and he never deceived anyone. But he was buried like a criminal; he was put in a rich man's grave." Isaiah 53:7-9 Jesus only had to die once to forgive the sins of many but priests had to make sacrifices often (yearly)—Hebrews 9:24-28. But remember, the forgiveness of sin(s) is not a free ticket to sin but an opportunity to rise above sin with God's mercy, grace, and power. And when we mess up, we should confess our sin(s) to Jesus as he is faithful and just to forgive us (1 John 1:8-10).
"Those who were high priests under the Law of Moses were limited by human weakness…" Hebrews 7:28	The priests were weak and sinned too which limited their effectiveness as mediators between God and man. Jesus was without sin. He never sinned; therefore, he was able to be the perfect example of how we should live, as a true High Priest should.
"…For the gifts and sacrifices that the priests offer are not able to cleanse the consciences [mind, heart, soul] of the people who bring them." Hebrews 9:9	A person's conscience is how one thinks about what is right or wrong as it relates to their behavior. Although the people presented sacrifices to the priests for the forgiveness of their sins, many still believed that it was okay to sin, so their conscience or way of thinking was still wrong and unclean. Presenting the sacrifices to the priests did not cleanse or change their way of thinking for the better. However, when Jesus sacrificed himself for us, God supernaturally put His laws in our minds so we would understand them; and in the same way he wrote His laws on our hearts so we could obey them. Everyone from the least to the greatest already knows God's law. (Hebrews 8:10) The truth about God is known to everyone naturally and instinctively without being taught. God has put this knowledge in our hearts (Romans 1:19) which means we are able to know the difference between right and wrong. *"Even when the Gentiles who did not have God's written law, instinctively followed what the law said, they show that in their hearts they know right from wrong. They demonstrate that God's law is written within them, for their own consciences either accuse them or tell them they are doing what is right. The day will surely come when God, by Jesus Christ, will judge everyone's secret life."* Romans 2:14-16

Supporting Scriptures:

"...a high priest is a man chosen to represent other human beings in their dealings with God. He presents their gifts to God and offers sacrifices for sins. And because he is human, he is able to deal gently with the people, though they are ignorant and wayward. For he is subject to the same weaknesses they have. That is why he has to offer sacrifices, both for their sins and for his own sins. And no one can become a high priest simply because he wants such an honor. He has to be called by God... That is why Christ did not exalt himself to become High Priest. No, he was chosen by God..." Hebrews 5:1-5

"... we have a great high priest who has gone to heaven, Jesus the Son of God. Let us cling to him and never stop trusting him. This High Priest of ours understands our weaknesses, for he faced all the same temptations we do, yet he did not sin." Hebrews 4:14-15

Now let's review. Before Jesus, those who did not obey the laws of God given to Moses were required to go to the priests to receive forgiveness of their sins by sacrificing animals. Priests served as mediators between God and man. God saw this system to be weak and useless, so He sent His precious son Jesus to die for us and to be the ultimate sacrifice for our sins. The wages of sin is death and without the shedding of blood there would be no forgiveness of sins, so somebody had to die – it was either Jesus or us. Jesus courageously and gracefully took our place and hung on the cross as he was nailed to it and shed his blood for us – reconciling us to God and making us right with Him (Colossians 1:20). Jesus is unlike any man – he is the only one who lived on this earth without sin, yet he died for our sins. It is important to know that Jesus did not come to give us a free will to sin*; he came to offer repentance and salvation (forgiveness of sins) and the gift of eternal life to anyone who <u>believes</u>, <u>trusts</u> and <u>obeys</u> him.

Purpose Point: Obedience is key to receiving and maintaining your salvation. As you have read, many years ago people sacrificed animals to receive forgiveness for their sins, but scripture says that obedience is better than sacrifice. In other words, if people obeyed, there would be no need for a sacrifice because most sacrifices were made when people disobeyed. It is not enough to just believe in God, we must also obey His commands.

*"This is what the Lord Almighty...says: Away with your burnt offerings and sacrifices! Eat them yourselves! ...it was not burnt offerings and sacrifices I wanted... **Obey me**, and I will be your God, and you will be my people. Only do as I say, and all will be well!"*
Jeremiah 7:21

"...Obedience is far better than sacrifice. Listening to him is much better than offering the fat of rams. Rebellion is as bad as the sin of witchcraft, and stubbornness is as bad as worshipping idols." 1 Samuel 15:22-23

Jesus says, "Don't misunderstand why I have come. I did not come to abolish the Law of Moses or the writings of the prophets. No, I came to fulfill them. I assure you, until heaven and earth disappear, even the smallest detail of God's law will remain until its purpose is achieved."
Matthew 5:17

Some might say that it is difficult to obey Jesus. The actions to obey may be challenging at times, but the knowing of what is right is already within you. When we know better, we should always strive to do better. Jesus will help you to obey when you surrender and trust him.

Supporting Scriptures:

"They demonstrate that God's law is written within them, for their own consciences either accuse them or tell them they are doing what is right." Romans 2:15

"For the truth about God is known to them instinctively. God has put this knowledge in their hearts. From the time the world was created, people have seen the earth and sky and all that God made. They can clearly see his invisible qualities – his eternal power and divine nature. So they have no excuse whatsoever for not knowing God." Romans 1:19-20

The primary reason that God sent Jesus was because of His great love for you! God loves you unconditionally, beyond measure. He wants to forgive you for all your sins and offer you the gift of eternal life. It is not required that you go to a priest or pastor for forgiveness of sins, you can go to God directly for yourself because of what Jesus did for you. He only requires that you **believe** in your heart that Jesus Christ died for your sins, **confess** with your mouth that God raised Jesus from the dead, and **trust** and **obey** Him. *"...it is this Good News that saves you if you firmly believe it..."* 1 Corinthians 15:2

*"For God so loved the world that he gave His only Son, so that everyone who **believes** in him will not perish but have eternal life. God did not send his Son into the world to condemn it, but to save it."* John 3:16

*"For if you **confess** with your mouth that Jesus is Lord and **believe** in your heart that God raised him from the dead, you will be saved. For it is believing in your heart that you are made right with God, and it is by confessing with your mouth that you are saved."* Romans 10:9-10

*"Anyone who denies the Son [Jesus] doesn't have the Father [God] either. But anyone who **confesses** the Son has the Father also."* 1 John 2:23

*"And all who **believe** in God's Son have eternal life. Those who don't **obey** the Son will never experience eternal life, but the wrath of God remains upon them.* John 3:36

*"...Jesus said...I assure you, anyone who **obeys** my teaching will never die!"* John 8:51

How does eternal life work? When Jesus comes back to earth from heaven, all Christians who have died a physical death will rise from their graves first. *"Then, together with them, we who are still alive on earth will be caught up in the clouds to meet Jesus and remain with him forever and ever."* 1 Thessalonians 4:15-17

"But those who die in the LORD will live; their bodies will rise again! Those who sleep in the earth will rise up and sing for joy! For your life-giving light will fall like dew on your people in the place of the dead!" Isaiah 26:19

Upon Jesus' return, people who believe in him will be transformed, given new bodies and will live forever (1 Corinthians 15).

If you want God to forgive you for your sins, you must accept Jesus Christ as your Lord and Savior. **Jesus is the only one who can save you from your sins and give you eternal life**

(life after natural death). He can also give you so much more such as love, peace, joy, wisdom, prosperity, protection, healing, deliverance, and restoration. Accepting Jesus Christ as your Lord and Savior is the most important decision you will ever make.

Just pray this simple prayer:

"Dear God, I believe in my heart that Jesus died for my sins and that you raised him from the dead. I repent of my sins; cleanse me and make me as white as snow. Come into my heart and live in me. I accept you as my Lord and Savior." If you prayed this prayer, you are SAVED!! THANK JESUS for what he has done!

Although it may seem as though nothing happened to you in the natural, something extraordinary happened in the supernatural. Your spirit is being transformed and the angels are celebrating in heaven! God's Spirit comes to live in you to help you obey. Now put Jesus in the driver seat and let him control your life. He is your Savior, Lord, Master, friend, brother, teacher, healer, counselor, helper, deliverer, provider, or whatever you need him to be (aligned with God's will). You can trust him with your life because he is the essence of life. Jesus loves you so much that he died for you. What greater love is there than that! *"But let the Lord Jesus Christ take control of you, and don't think of ways to indulge your evil desires."* Romans 13:14

The Lord said, **"And I will put my Spirit in you so that you will follow my decrees and be careful to obey my regulations."** Ezekiel 36:27

"So letting your sinful nature control your mind leads to death. But letting the Spirit control your mind leads to life and peace." Romans 8:6

Jesus said, *"If anyone acknowledges me publicly here on earth, I will openly acknowledge that person before my Father in heaven. But anyone who denies me here on earth, I will deny that person before my Father in heaven."* Matthew 10:32-33

Purpose Point: Begin to learn about Jesus Christ, your Lord and Savior, by reading your Bible and attending a Bible-based church. Suggested readings include the books of Matthew, Mark, Luke and John (commonly known as the Gospels). Attending church is an important part of your Christian life. God gives pastors and preachers special knowledge and understanding on how to help the people of God. These pastors and preachers in turn share this special knowledge with the church – you. Additionally, God wants us to attend church so that we can fellowship with other Christians and encourage each other.

"And let us not neglect our meeting together, as some people do, but encourage and warn each other, especially now that the day of his coming back again is drawing near." Hebrews 10:25

"How then will they call on Him in whom they have not believed? How will they believe in Him whom they have not heard? And how will they hear without a preacher?" Romans 10:14 NASB

Purpose Point: It is also important for you to **get baptized**. Jesus commands us to be baptized to demonstrate receiving new life and the forgiveness of sins. Jesus said, *"Anyone who believes and is baptized will be saved."* Mark 16:16 When we believe and confess Jesus as Lord our spirit is transformed…we become a new creature and are **born again** spiritually (John 3).

I know this seems difficult to understand, but Jesus said, *"Just as you can hear the wind but can't tell where it comes from or where it is going, so you can't explain how people are born of the Spirit."* John 3:8

Baptisms demonstrate our old sinful spirit dying and our new spirit becoming alive or rising. When we are emerged in water it is symbolic of our old sinful life being buried; and when we come up out of the water it is symbolic of our new spirit life being born, rising and becoming alive, similarly to Jesus. He was crucified and buried, and later his new body rose again with God's power. Like so, *"Our old sinful selves were crucified with Christ so that sin might lose its power in our lives..."* Romans 6:6. Jesus was also baptized during his time on earth. You can read about his baptism in Matthew 3:13-17.

Purpose Point: You must be born again spiritually to receive salvation and eternal life. When you are born again you do not receive a new body (this will happen during the resurrection–Rev.20:6), but you do receive a new spirit. You become a new person inside. However, when Jesus comes back, he will fully complete us by giving us a new body along with our new spirit.

Jesus said, *"I assure you, unless you are born again, you can never see the Kingdom of God. What do you mean? exclaimed Nicodemus. How can an old man go back into his mother's womb and be born again? Jesus replied, the truth is that no one can enter the Kingdom of God without being born of water and the Spirit. Humans can reproduce only human life, but the Holy Spirit of God gives new life from heaven. So don't be surprised at my statement that **you must be born again.**"* John 3:3-7

"...those who become Christians become new persons. They are not the same anymore, for the old life is gone. A new life has begun. All this newness of life is from God, who brought us back to himself through what Christ did...For God made Christ, who never sinned, to be the offering for sin, so that we could be made right with God through Christ."
2 Corinthians 5:17-18, 21

"For you have become born again. Your new life did not come from your earthly parents because the life they gave you will end in death. But this new life will last forever because it comes from the eternal, living word of God." 1 Peter 1:23

Purpose Point: Your parents assisted with channeling life to your earthly body when you were born, but this physical body will die one day. When you accept Jesus and obey him, God gives you a new spirit that will never die. However, although God gives you a new spirit, you must then aim to make your soul (mind, thoughts, will and emotions) new by renewing your mind with the Word of God – allowing Him to change the way you think. You do this by studying the Bible and seeking understanding of His will. Just like the world requires you to be educated from kindergarten to 12th grade and even beyond that, from college undergrad to the doctorate level, God also demands that you educate your mind with His Word. Although it is important to get educated in the world to learn basic life skills and career disciplines, it is equally important to get educated in God by learning godly principles derived from the wisdom of God and how to apply those principles.

Education may improve your life, but only wisdom can save it. Life and career skills are temporary, but God's Word and His rewards are eternal. *"Wisdom and money can get you almost anything, but only wisdom can save your life."* Ecclesiastes 7:12

"Wisdom is more precious than rubies; nothing you desire can compare with her. She offers you long life in her right hand, and riches and honor in her left." Proverbs 3:15-16

*"Don't copy the behavior and customs of this world, but **let God transform you into a new person by changing the way you think.** Then you will know what God wants you to do, and you will know how good and pleasing and perfect his will really is."* Romans 12:2

Minute Memoir: One day my son asked me, *"Momma, when people die are they born again?"* I was unsure about how to answer him. Not because I didn't know the answer but because both cannot happen at the same time. You cannot be born again after you die. You must be born again <u>before</u> you die. If you die and did not accept Jesus while you were living, then you were not born again and did not receive a new spirit. Therefore, you would not have eternal life but instead eternal death (eternal separation from God) in hell forever.

Purpose Point: Only while we are alive can we be born again and saved. Being saved means Jesus has saved us from our sins and eternal death.

ONCE SAVED ALWAYS SAVED - NOT ENTIRELY SO

Many people believe that once saved always saved. After much consultation and studying of scripture, I do not believe that this is entirely so. It is true that a person who has truly accepted Jesus Christ (becomes a genuine follower of Christ) and remains in the faith to the end will never perish and is sealed forever by God's Holy Spirit. Therefore, once you accept Jesus Christ as your Lord and Savior, you are saved and your sins are forgiven once and for all; however, you can negate or give up your salvation by turning away from the faith (i.e. abandoning your belief in God/Jesus – apostasy; worshiping an idol god – idolatry or no god at all – atheism).

One important component of salvation is *repentance* – a turning away from sin(s) because of your decision to turn to Jesus and give your life to him. Repentance does not mean that you will never sin or struggle with sin, but it means you have changed your mindset towards sin by believing that it is not the right thing to do. After you have truly accepted Jesus as your Lord and Savior (made a conscious decision to turn from your sins) Jesus will come to live in you through his precious Holy Spirit and give you the desire to obey Him. You will eventually become repulsed by sin and will no longer want to do the sinful things you once did.

Jesus said, *"I have not come to call the righteous, but sinners to repentance."* Luke 5:32 NIV

"...Repent and be baptized, every one of you, in the name of Jesus Christ for the forgiveness of your sins. And you will receive the gift of the Holy Spirit." Acts 2:38 NIV

Purpose Point: Like the Holy Spirit, *repentance* is a gift from God – a gift that leads to life. Just think of how terrible it would be if we were sentenced to death physically and eternally with no hope, no meaning, and no one to save us from eternal damnation. God sent Jesus to give us hope, to give us meaning, value and significance, and to offer us eternal life through the wonderful gift of repentance unto salvation. To receive this gift, we must simply repent – turn away from our sins and accept Jesus as our Lord and Savior. In Acts 11:18 NIV it says, *"When they heard this, they had no further objections and praised God, saying, 'So then, even to Gentiles **God has granted repentance that leads to life.**'"*

Purpose Point: True salvation is indicative of *repentance* and the *redeemer* (Jesus Christ). When you reject these two fundamentals, you reject the way to life.

"For the kind of sorrow God wants us to experience leads us away from sin and results in salvation. There's no regret for that kind of sorrow. But worldly sorrow, which lacks repentance, results in spiritual death." 2 Corinthians 7:10

Purpose Point: If you backslide (go back to your old way of life) or become saved and later decide to live a life of habitual disobedience and sin, Jesus still loves you and longs for you to return to him. Recognize your sins, confess them and trust that God will help you to overcome (2 Chronicles 7:14; 1 John 1:8-10).

Read about the parable narrated by Jesus in Luke 15:11-32 to help you better understand how happy God would be to have you back again. Many people believe that once they meet the requirements for salvation by believing and confessing Jesus as Lord according to Romans 10:9 that they can continue to live the sinful lives they were living before—not true. You may struggle with sin or sin from time to time but since you have been born again, a change should have taken place within you to the extent that you no longer want to live the sinful life you once did. In the beginning you may struggle with sin, but deep-down sinning is not something you want to do. You must go all the way with God and not halfway. If you believe and confess Jesus as Lord, you must also obey His commands and trust Him to carry out His will for your life. What if God only went halfway with you? What if He only allowed Jesus to be born, but did not allow him to die for your sins and be raised from the dead – resulting in the forgiveness of your sins and the gift of eternal life? God went all the way with us, so we should also go all the way with Him. It is not enough to just believe in God, you must also obey Him. *"Do you still think it's enough just to believe that there is one God? Well, even the demons believe this, and they tremble in terror. Fool! When will you ever learn that faith that does not result in good deeds is useless? Don't you remember that our ancestor Abraham was declared right with God because of what he did when he offered his son Isaac on the altar? You see, he was trusting God so much that he was willing to do whatever God told him to do. His faith was made complete by what he did – by his actions. And so it happened just as the Scriptures say: 'Abraham believed God, so God declared him to be **righteous**.' He was even called "the friend of God." **So you see, we are made right with God by what we do, not by faith alone.** Rehab a prostitute is another example of this. She was made right with God by her actions – when she hid those messengers and sent them safely away by a different road. Just as the body is dead without a spirit, so also faith is dead without good deeds."* James 2:19-26

Purpose Point: It is important to know, however, that performing good deeds alone will not make you saved, and simply believing that there is a God will not save you either. You must accept Jesus as your Lord and Savior, confess him as Lord and obey his commands (repent) to *exhibit* true salvation – an expression of your faith. You do not perform good deeds to earn God's love, salvation, and acceptance, you perform good deeds because you love God and have accepted Jesus and what he has already done for you. *"Prove by the way you live that you have repented of your sins and turned to God."* Matthew 3:8

Standards and Sacrifice - What would you think about a police officer who murdered people and stole from them? You would not expect a policeman to do these things, right? If the policeman was really a true police officer at heart, he wouldn't have the desire or will to do these evil acts. You would probably feel as though the man who calls himself a policeman does not have the right to be a police officer because of his negative behavior and lack of standards. You may also feel that he should be in jail, or you may become very angry or develop a strong sense of resentment because the officer violated his oath to protect and serve the community. It would have not been enough for the police officer to make a verbal oath to protect and serve, he must also live up to this oath by his actions of protecting, serving, and representing the police department well. His actions of murder and theft did not line up with his oath to protect and serve so no one would actually consider him to be a true officer of the law. In the same way, we are expected to represent God well and live by His standards when we take an oath to accept and confess Jesus as our Lord and Savior. Again, this doesn't mean that you will never mess up, make mistakes, or engage in wrong behaviors because you don't know any better…it just means that when we know better we should do better (repent) so that we can represent God in a way that will bring Him glory and protect the name we claim. God is a loving God and has drawn you to Himself through His loving-kindness and tender mercies.

Moreover, there are also instances where a person knows they are doing wrong and has a sincere desire to stop but struggles to get out of that situation. In this case, God knows your struggle and does not condemn you because He knows that you have a heart to change. It is when you habitually and continually do wrong without any conviction after receiving the truth about God's Word that you lack repentance. It all boils down to a person's heart. If you reject God's commands, enjoy doing wrong and do not care about doing right then your salvation comes into question because repentance is lacking, even if you claim to have accepted and confessed Jesus as Lord. But if you enjoy doing right and feel bad or struggle with doing wrong and have a desire to change, then God lives in you and gives you the desire to obey Him. He will help you to change and do right as you depend on Him. You do not have to feel guilty and condemned; you are secure in Jesus. None of us are perfect…we all make mistakes, but what separates Christians from non-Christians are for one, we believe that Jesus Christ is our Lord and Savior and that he died for our sins, and two, we have a heart to obey His commands and change our ways if we see that we are not obeying Him or living up to His standards. When we mess up, God is faithful to forgive us of our wrong doings and cleanse us from all unrighteousness. <u>If we fall down by doing something wrong, we must get back up by confessing the wrong that we have done and turning away from it.</u> Everyone will fall, but the question is will they get back up. When we confess Jesus and become a Christian, we do not become sinless (live without ever sinning), but we do and should sin less (less often and less deliberately). Again, it is the habitual sinning without any conviction or feeling of sorrow that blocks a relationship with Jesus.

*"…This is what the Lord says: '**When people fall down, don't they get up again**? When they start down the wrong road and discover their mistake, don't they turn back? Then why do these people keep going along their self-destructive path, refusing to turn back, even though I have warned them? I listen to their conversations and what do I hear? Is anyone sorry for sin? Does anyone say, "What a terrible thing I have done?" No! All are running down the path of sin as swiftly as a horse rushing into battle!"* Jeremiah 8:4-6

"If we say we have no sin, we are only fooling ourselves and refusing to accept the truth. But if we confess our sins to him, he is faithful and just to forgive us and to cleanse us from every wrong. If we claim we have not sinned, we are calling God a liar and showing that his word has no place in our hearts." 1 John 1:8-10

"For all have sinned; all fall short of God's glorious standard." Romans 3:23

So you see, it is not enough for you to just believe and confess, you must also act by obeying God's statutes and represent Him well. When you confess Jesus as Lord and profess to be a Christian, God expects you to live a life that reflects Jesus. You are expected to be kind, gentle, modest, respectful, and loving. God, and people, do not expect you to curse someone out, sleep around, disobey parents and authority, participate in bullying and gangs, or fight a girl over a boy…just like you would not expect a policeman to murder people. Our words must line up with our actions. It is absolutely wrong to confess Jesus as Lord and then continue living a sinful life while believing Jesus died so that you could live that way. **Jesus did not sacrifice himself so that you could continue living a sinful life. There is no such sacrifice for a person who continues and deliberately sins** (Hebrews 10:26).

Just think about it, hypothetically speaking and considering these three options: (1) Would you give your life for someone who would continue to do wrong and evil in the world? (2) Would you give your life for someone who does evil but eventually would probably turn from evil and do good in the world? (3) Or, would you give your life for someone who never did anything bad and always did good?

The truth is most people would probably say that they would not give their life for anyone (Romans 5:6-7). It is sad, but true, that most people are only concerned with themselves. On the other hand, many might say that they'll give their life for a family member such as a child, parent or spouse; and some might consider giving their life for someone who never did anything bad and always did good in the world…while never considering to give their life for someone who presently does evil, regardless of the off chance of them later choosing to do good.

If we are completely honest, we all know that very few people would say that they would give their life for someone who lived to do evil. But Jesus, on the other hand, was one of the few. He died for us while we were yet sinners (knowing that one day we would be born with a sinful nature). He died with the hope of us wanting to change our evil ways (repent), live for him and do good in the world. It was not guaranteed that people would want to turn from their evil ways and do good, but he sacrificed himself anyway.

As a matter of fact, if Jesus knew that you would be the only person in the world with the potential of doing good, he would have died just for you. Again, he did not die for us just so we could keep sinning and doing evil in the world. *"But God showed his great love for us by sending Christ to die for us while we were yet sinners."* Romans 5:8

Jude 1:4 says, *"…some godless people have wormed their way in among you, saying that God's forgiveness allows us to live immoral lives. The fate of such people was determined long ago, for they have turned against our only Master and Lord, Jesus Christ."*

Purpose Point: Many false religions imply or require people to sacrifice themselves (die physically) or kill for the cause via terroristic activities, suicide bombings, living sacrifices, etc. Jesus, on the other hand, the one and only Savior of the world, the true and living God gave his life for many – for you. He only requires that you die to self (deny your sinful/selfish nature and wrong behaviors). Doing so, exemplifies true devotion, allegiance, and sacrifice.

"But Samuel replied, "What is more pleasing to the LORD: your burnt offerings and sacrifices or your obedience to his voice? Listen! ***Obedience is better than sacrifice****, and submission is better than offering the fat of rams."* 1 Samuel 15:22

Purpose Point: Jesus was the ultimate sacrifice for your sins, but there are sacrifices that you must also make if you want to receive everything God has planned for you. You must give up your sinful lifestyles and desires and let your sinful nature die. It is in this way that you are truly living.

Paul, a servant of God, stated: *"My old self has been crucified with Christ. It is no longer I who live, but Christ lives in me. So I live in this earthly body by trusting in the Son of God, who loved me and gave himself for me."* Galatians 2:20

"Those who are dominated by the sinful nature think about sinful things, but those who are controlled by the Holy Spirit of God think about things that please the Spirit. If your sinful nature controls your mind, there is death. But if the Holy Spirit controls your mind, there is life and peace. For the sinful nature is always hostile to God. It never did obey God's laws, and it never will. That's why those who are still under the control of their sinful nature can never please God." Romans 8:5-8

Repentance and obedience allow you to experience the full package of salvation – peace, joy, love, favor, blessings, protection, prosperity, wisdom, provision, long life, healing/health, and so much more. But how can you obey God if you don't believe Him? And how can you say you trust Him if you do not obey Him? That is why it is important for you to first believe, and secondly to trust God so that you can obey.

Purpose Point: Everything that God commands us to do is for our good and protection. **Obeying God does not mean that your life will be *boring*, it only means that your life will be *better*. Obeying God does not mean bondage to deprivation – (depriving yourself of the things you like to do), but freedom from sin.**

When we accept Jesus as our Lord and Savior, we take an oath to trust, believe, and obey him. Jesus then becomes our Lord and Master. All slaves have masters, and we know that slaves are required to obey their master. But unlike a slave master, Jesus doesn't consider us as slaves, instead he sees us as his own family – his brothers and sisters which means God is our Father, and we are His daughters…special princesses and sanctified queens. Jesus wants us to obey him by living according to the Word of God – the Bible, as the Bible tells us how we should live and serves as the infallible guide to a prosperous Princess's Pathway. Therefore, it's so important to read your Bible to strengthen yourself in the Word and remain on the right path.

If you choose not to obey by sinning habitually and blatantly without conviction after you have received the truth and have no desire to turn from your sin(s), the benefits of repentance are far from you.

Supporting Scriptures:

"You are not slaves; you are free. But your freedom is not an excuse to do evil. You are free to live as God's slaves." 1 Peter 2:16

*"…**if we deliberately continue sinning after we have received a full knowledge of the truth, there is no other sacrifice that will cover these sins**. There will be nothing to look forward to

but the terrible expectation of God's judgment and the raging fire that will consume his enemies. Anyone who refused to obey the law of Moses was put to death without mercy on the testimony of two or three witnesses. Think how much more terrible the punishment will be for those who have trampled on the Son of God and have treated the blood of the covenant as if it were common and unholy. Such people have insulted and enraged the Holy Spirit who brings God's mercy to his people." Hebrews 10:26-29

"Well then, should we keep on sinning so that God can show us more and more kindness and forgiveness? Of course not! *Since we have died to sin, how can we continue to live in it? Or have you forgotten that when we became Christians and were baptized to become one with Christ Jesus, we died with him? For we died and were buried with Christ by baptism. And just as Christ was raised from the dead by the glorious power of the Father, now we also may live new lives."* Romans 6:1-4

"Dear children, don't let anyone deceive you about this: When people do what is right, it is because they are righteous, even as Christ is righteous. But **when people keep on sinning, it shows they belong to the Devil, who has been sinning since the beginning.** *But the Son of God came to destroy these works of the Devil."* 1 John 3:7-8

"Those who have been born into God's family do not sin, because God's life is in them. **So they can't keep on sinning, because they have been born of God.** *So now we can tell who are children of God and who are children of the Devil. Anyone who does not obey God's commands and does not love other Christians does not belong to God."* 1 John 3:9-10

"This is the message he has given us to announce to you: God is light and there is no darkness in him at all. So **we are lying if we say we have fellowship with God but go on living in spiritual darkness.** *We are not living in the truth. But if we are living in the light of God's presence, just as Christ is, then we have fellowship with each other, and the blood of Jesus, his Son, cleanses us from every sin."* 1 John 1:5-7

"But God's truth stands firm like a foundation stone with this inscription: **'The Lord knows those who are his',** *and* **'Those who claim they belong to the Lord must turn away from all wickedness.'"** 2 Timothy 2:19

"And how can we be sure that we belong to him? By obeying his commandments. *If someone says, "I belong to God," but doesn't obey God's commandments, that person is a liar and does not live in the truth. But those who obey God's word really do love him. That is the way to know whether or not we live in him.* **Those who say they live in God should live their lives as Christ did."** 1 John 2:3-6

Jesus *"...became the source of eternal salvation for all those who* **obey** *him."* Hebrews 5:9

"...Jesus said...I assure you, anyone who **obeys** *my teaching will never die!"* John 8:51

Purpose Point: Jesus did not come to give us a free will to sin; he came to offer salvation and the gift of eternal life to anyone who believes, trusts, and obeys him.

Purpose Point: The grace of God should not be mistaken as a free ticket to do whatever you want to do. God is so patient with us. His grace gives us time to turn away from our sins. We, however, do not know when this grace will run out so it would be best to turn away from your sins as soon as possible. While we are living, we still have a chance to repent and make things right with God; but when we die, we have no chance. Your destination of eternal life or death, heaven or hell will be set – FINAL.

"Don't you realize how kind, tolerant, and patient God is with you? Or don't you care? Can't you see how kind he has been in giving you time to turn from your sin? But no, you won't listen. So you are storing up terrible punishment for yourself because of your stubbornness in refusing to turn from your sin. For there is going to come a day of judgment when God, the just judge of all the world, will judge all people according to what they have done. He will give eternal life to those who persist in doing what is good, seeking after the glory and honor and immortality that God offers. But he will pour out his anger and wrath on those who live for themselves, who refuse to obey the truth and practice evil deeds. There will be trouble and calamity for everyone who keeps on sinning..." Romans 2:4-9

Purpose Point: Conviction is a symptom of a God-conscience; in other words, conviction is realizing that you have done wrong, feeling bad about it, and desiring to turn away from evil or change wrong behaviors. If you do not get convicted when you do wrong, when you know that it is wrong, then there may be a disconnect. Please do not misunderstand; salvation is not complicated. *The Bible clearly says that when you confess Jesus as Lord and believe in your heart that God raised him from the dead you are saved (Romans 10:9). Therefore, the steps to true salvation can be summed up in two steps: (1) Believe/Repent (2) Confess. And follow-up actions include (a) get baptized – Acts 2:38; (b) renew your mind (let God change the way you think so your behaviors can change – Romans 12:2); (c) move forward in your God-given purpose with the Holy Spirit as your guide – Ephesians 1:11.*

Salvation requires that the mouth and heart work together to make it effective. *"For it is with your heart that you believe and are justified, and it is with your mouth that you profess your faith and are saved."* Romans 10:10 NIV   Therefore, when you confess and genuinely believe [1, 2, a.], God's Spirit will come to live on the inside of you to help you overcome temptations and trials (Isaiah 41:10). This does not mean that you will be perfect; you will, like everyone, make mistakes. But the difference is that since God now lives on the inside of you, you will sense conviction when you do wrong by God's Spirit working in you through your conscience and be convinced to change any wrong behaviors. Remember, conviction convinces to bring positive change.

God will give you the strength to turn away from doing wrong. You cannot do it in your own strength, and you do not have to. It is only when you choose to ignore His voice and your conscience that you hinder God from working in you and through you. Sin can then take control of your life when *you* limit God.

Purpose Point: The scripture below tells us to *work out* our salvation. We do not *work for* our salvation by performing good deeds and behaviors, but we *work it out* by repenting and changing our heart (renewing our mind) which in turn compels us to do good deeds and do what is right as an expression of our faith in what Jesus has done for us.

"So then, my dear ones, just as you have always obeyed [my instructions with enthusiasm], not only in my presence, but now much more in my absence, continue to work out your salvation [that is, cultivate it, bring it to full effect, actively pursue spiritual maturity] with awe-inspired fear and trembling [using serious caution and critical self-evaluation to avoid anything that might offend God or discredit the name of Christ]. For it is [not your strength, but it is] God who is effectively at work in you, both to will and to work [that is, strengthening, energizing, and creating in you the longing and the ability to fulfill your purpose] for His good pleasure." Philippians 2:12-13 AMP

Now let's review!

1. When you genuinely accept Jesus and continually believe in Jesus with all your heart your eternal salvation is secure – you are saved, even when you mess up or do not always get it right or do what is right.

   For example, when David, a servant of God, sinned and messed up, he repented and said, *"Restore to me the joy of your salvation and grant me a willing spirit, to sustain me."* Psalm 51:12 NIV

   "For it is by grace you have been saved, through faith--and this is not from yourselves, it is the gift of God--" Ephesians 2:8 NIV

2. You can nullify or give up your salvation and the gift of eternal life by turning away from God (denying Him/apostasy) – not remaining faithful to the faith (when you stop believing the truth about Jesus/God and reject or deny Jesus' work on the cross). Some people argue that you can't ever lose your salvation. You cannot lose it, but you can give it up by turning away from God as previously mentioned. Salvation is a gift that is always available (as long as a person lives on earth–activated per Romans 10:9) because God is faithful (people are not). So no one really loses salvation; they choose to give it up or reject it. Losing implies that it was taken away or lost – unable to be found.

Supporting Scriptures: Jesus referred to people who turn away from him as cowards.

*"**But cowards who turn away from me**, and unbelievers, and the corrupt, and murderers and the immoral, and those who practice witchcraft, and idol worshipers, and all liars – their doom is in the lake that burns with fire and sulfur. This is the second death."* Revelations 21:8

*"Now the Holy Spirit tells us clearly that in the last times **some will turn away from what we believe**; they will follow lying spirits and teachings that come from demons."* 1 Timothy 4:1

*"And who is the great liar? The one who says that Jesus is not the Christ. Such people are antichrists, for they have denied the Father and the Son. **Anyone who denies the Son doesn't have the Father either. But anyone who confesses the Son has the Father also. So you must remain faithful to what you have been taught... If you do, you will continue to live in fellowship with the Son and with the Father. And in this fellowship we enjoy the eternal life he promised us.**"* 1 John 2:22-25

*"Sin will be rampant everywhere, and the love of many will grow cold. **But those who endure to the end will be saved.**"* Matthew 24:12-13

"By this gospel you are saved, if you hold firmly to the word I preached to you. Otherwise, you have believed in vain." 1 Corinthians 15:2 NIV

*"If we die with him, we will also live with him. If we endure hardship, we will reign with him. **If we deny him, he will deny us.** If we are unfaithful, he remains faithful, for he cannot deny who he is."* 2 Timothy 2:11-13

Purpose Point: People reject salvation when they choose to deny Jesus and His truth – the Word of God. For example, some people believe Jesus existed, but they do not believe that Jesus is the Son of God, was born of a virgin, lived in the flesh, was raised from the dead and is the ONLY Savior of the world. Anyone who denies these truths are essentially denying Jesus and rejecting God. Some churches and denominations teach Jesus incorrectly by denying certain truths about him and God's Word.

"Many deceivers have gone out into the world. They do not believe that Jesus Christ came to earth in a real body. Such a person is a deceiver and an antichrist. Watch out, so that you do not lose the prize for which we have been working so hard. Be diligent so that you will receive your full reward. For if you wander beyond the teaching of Christ, you will not have fellowship with God. But if you continue in the teaching of Christ, you will have fellowship with both the Father and the Son." 2 John 1:7-9

Purpose Point: You must continue believing the infallible truths about Jesus and refuse to be tricked into believing something else. Your spiritual destination, relationship and fellowship with God will be based on what you believe. *"But I fear that somehow you will be led away from your pure and simple devotion to Christ, just as Eve was deceived by the serpent. You seem to believe whatever anyone tells you, even if they preach about a different Jesus than the one we preach, or a different Spirit than the one you received, or a different kind of gospel than the one you believed. But I don't think I am inferior to these "super apostles." I may not be a trained speaker, but I know what I am talking about."* 2 Corinthians 11:3-6

Purpose Point: Do not be deceived. Study God's Word and know the truth when it comes to the truth about God – His Word, will and ways. Make sure the church you attend or the one you choose to listen to teaches in line with the Word of God (the Bible). Note that many people claim that they believe in God but their god could be anyone or anything (i.e. nature, universe, moon, stars, statue, animals, idols, or a person living or decease). Jesus is the determining factor when it comes to salvation, truth, and authentic Christianity.

Purpose Point: Those who deny God and His truth can reconcile with God if they *confess*, *repent* (humble themselves…turn away from evil) and obey the commandments of God.

"Then if my people who are called by my name will humble themselves and pray and seek my face and turn from their wicked ways, I will hear from heaven and will forgive their sins and heal their land." 2 Chronicles 7:14; *"But if we confess our sins to him, he is faithful and just to forgive us and to cleanse us from every wrong."* 1 John 1:9

"Put all your rebellion behind you, and find yourselves a new heart and a new spirit. For why should you die...? I don't want you to die, says the Sovereign Lord. Turn back and live!"
Ezekiel 18:31-32

"For if you confess with your mouth that Jesus is Lord and believe in your heart that God raised him from the dead, you will be saved." Romans 10:9

"The Lord isn't really being slow about his promise to return, as some people think. No, he is being patient for your sake. He does not want anyone to be destroyed, but wants everyone to repent."
2 Peter 3:9

Jesus said, *"I have not come to call the righteous, but sinners to repentance."* Luke 5:32 NIV

Redemption + Reverence = Repentance

Jesus was beaten, whipped, nailed to the cross and died just for you – redeeming you from the effects of sin (death) and providing eternal life, bountiful blessings, and prosperous promises *(redemption)*. When you truly value what Jesus did on the cross for you…when you honor and respect God for sending His one and only Son to die for you…when you love God because He first loved you…when you are thankful for who God is and what He has done…and when you truly appreciate His love, kindness, tender mercies and amazing grace *(reverence)*, you will change your mind about sin – turn away from it *(repentance)*.

Repentance is a part of believing. If you are to believe that Jesus died for your sins and was raised from the dead, you must also believe why he died – why he came in the first place. Jesus came to call sinners to repentance (Luke 5:32). He did not come for people to keep loving and believing in their sin(s)–and to keep sinning (Hebrews 10:26; Acts 20:21), but to love and believe in him and turn away from their sins. *"…Can't you see that his kindness is intended to turn you from your sin?"* Romans 2:4

It is by God's grace that you believe (Acts 18:27), and this same grace will keep you as you continue to believe and walk on the path Jesus has paved for you (Hebrews 10:19-22). You might slip up and sin, when you do, simply get back up (repent) and keep moving forward (Jeremiah 8:4-7; 2 Timothy 4:7-8).

Purpose Point: Salvation should be a joyful experience and not just something you feel compelled to do because you do not want to go to hell. Simply going through the motions of receiving salvation will not spark enthusiasm and could result in a dismal and possible disconnected experience. David said, "Restore to me the *"joy"* of my salvation and make me willing to obey you." (Psalm 51:12) And Luke 15:10 says, *"There is "joy" in the presence of God's angels when even one sinner repents."*

Purpose Point: "Sin" seems to be a taboo word – a word that many perceive as judgment and condemnation or a word that should be avoided in modern day society. But how can we discuss the right way without discussing the wrong way; how can we discuss the path of light without discussing the path of darkness? How can we discuss the path of life without discussing the path of death and how can we share a cure without talking about the disease? To defeat any enemy, we must first recognize it, know its strategy, how it operates, and its weaknesses. See sin as the enemy (the target) and not yourself. Jesus loves you so much – that's why He died for your sins to protect you from the enemy. When you separate yourself from sin by not becoming a practicing partner with it and know that you can live a fulfilled life without being a slave to sin, you become everything Jesus died for and created you to be. Sometimes, recognizing and understanding the *negative* (the opposite) is what puts you on a *positive* path to success. Knowing the enemy and how it operates empowers us to defeat it. Of course, we will slip up from time to time, and get stuck struggling to get out, but the grace of God catches us every time – during every misstep. However, we must keep fighting to get away from the very enemy that aims to ensnare, entangle, and entrap us. Remember: This book, replete with scripture(s), is not intended to condemn but to cultivate positive change by exposing the enemy and its behaviors. This book is not meant to beat you down but to help you <u>break free</u> (John 8:32). Only God truly knows a person's heart.

DON'T BEAT YOURSELF UP!

The Bible says that **all have sinned and fall short (Romans 3:23)** which means no one is perfect. When you get saved, you will sin from time to time and may struggle with situations such as bad habits, lustful desires, and negative or ungodly thinking and behaviors.

This is not uncommon. I struggled with sin for most of my life, although I loved God wholeheartedly and wanted to please Him. When you truly trust, believe and desire to please God there will be an inner conviction --- a sense of wrong doing and a desire to change or come out of that negative situation *(...for their own consciences either accuse them or tell them they are doing what is right.* Romans 2:15). Additionally, there will be a focus on positive change despite sinful actions and you will not be content with wrong living or what the world deems as acceptable. It may take years to finally get free, but through the process, you choose to acknowledge and admit what is wrong, work towards becoming better and doing better, and aim to be aligned with God's will for your life.

This chapter simply states TRUTH, God's truth, and is not meant to judge or condemn anyone. **Where sin abounds, grace more abounds (Romans 5:20).** But we must accept God's truth and work towards becoming more and more like Him every day through His wonderful grace.

I recently heard someone repeat a saying that he heard: **"Grace is not the freedom to do what we want but the power to do what we ought according to the Creator's guidebook for our life."**

Change is sometimes a process and will not always be instantaneous. So don't beat yourself up when you do wrong, just continue to do your best, and trust God with the rest. Believe that He can deliver you from every wrongdoing and temptation.

Just like you wouldn't give up on your child if they did wrong, God will not give up on you.

Aim to do what is right, and base what is right on the Word of God.

If you miss it or mess up, keep trying, keep pushing and get back up until you get it right. Remember, we are not saved by our works or good deeds, but we are saved and made right with God by our faith, belief, and trust in Jesus Christ *alone* (Romans 3:22; Romans 4:1-5). So even when we mess up, our salvation is secure. Continue to pray and talk to God about every struggle every day. Ask Him to help you. Remember, we all have issues, but the question is will you recognize it and allow God to deliver and direct you through them.

God's Spirit lives in you to enable you to behave right.

You are the righteousness of God through Christ Jesus; you are accepted and justified in Christ. The Lord said, *"And I will put my Spirit in you so that you will follow my decrees and be careful to obey my regulations."* Ezekiel 36:27

"He made Christ who knew no sin to be sin on our behalf, so that in Him we would become the righteousness of God [that is, we would be made acceptable to Him and placed in a right relationship with Him by His gracious loving kindness]." 2 Corinthians 5:21 AMP

Understanding the Struggle: *"The law is good, then. The trouble is not with the law but with me... I don't understand myself at all, for I really want to do what is right, but I don't do it. Instead, I do the very thing I hate. I know perfectly well that what I am doing is wrong, and my bad conscience shows that I agree that the law is good...It seems to be a fact of life that when I want to do what is right, I inevitably do what is wrong. I love God's law with all my heart. But there is another law at work within me that is at war with my mind..."* Romans 7:14-23

"And I am sure that God, who began the good work within you, will continue his work until it is finally finished on that day when Christ Jesus comes back again." Philippians 1:6

The Lord brought me out, and He will do the same for you! God loves you! By His nature and through His marvelous grace, He is patient and merciful. He only wants the best for you.

The truth about the Bible. Who wrote the Bible? Is the Bible accurate?
A common acronym for the Bible is, "**B**asic **I**nstructions **B**efore **L**eaving **E**arth." This one phrase says it all. The Bible is an instruction manual for life. When we buy something new, such as a car, cell phone, computer, or TV, it comes with an instruction manual provided by the company who manufactured or created the product. The purpose of the manual is to give instructions on how to operate, describe the features that are included and explain the product's capabilities. Although we might think we know it all sometimes, without an instruction manual we would be lost – we would not fully know how to operate the product or understand all its capabilities.

For example, for Christmas one year I asked my mother to buy me a digital camera with a camcorder built into it. When Christmas came, I unwrapped my gift, and it was exactly what I had asked for; a camera with a camcorder built into it. Assuming that there were no other features besides the camera and camcorder capability, I did not open the package and stored it in my room until I was ready to use it. Three months went by and I never opened it, but during that time I remember thinking that it would be nice to have a MP3 player (this was before Ipods, smartphones and tablets). One day, I was cleaning my room and found the camera in a bag where I had stored it. I took the camera out and read the instruction manual which explained all its features and capabilities. Sure enough, the camera not only had camcorder capability, but it was also a MP3 player. Something that I had thought would be nice to have was already in my possession, if I had only taken the time to read the package and the instruction manual.

Likewise, we are the product of God only more special; He manufactured us. Don't just assume or think you are only what you see; you are so much more than that – simply read your instruction manual (the Bible) to find out. God created us and provided the Bible as our instruction manual. It tells us how we were created, why we were created, who we are, whose we are, and our features and capabilities. It tells us how to activate the power in our lives and operate everything God put inside of us. The Bible is so important. If you think it is boring, falsified, hard to understand and insignificant, you will never come to know your full potential, features and capabilities. You might as well put yourself in a bag and place yourself on a shelf somewhere because without Bible knowledge, God's truth, you will not fulfill your purpose. You cannot view the Bible in a negative way, you must change the way you think. I once viewed the Bible negatively, thinking that it was written in a way that I could not understand. And since I chose not to read it for this reason, my life was miserable. It was only until I read and understood my instruction manual (the Bible) that my life began to change.

Unlike the typical instruction manual, which lists a step by step process with several diagrams, the Bible (the Word of God) is far from boring. It's entertaining with drama, suspense, parables, and plenty of love stories. It is better than any novel, soap opera, movie or reality series, from a wife allowing her husband to have sex with her maid just to get her pregnant, to a king sleeping with another man's wife and then killing her husband, to a man getting swallowed by a giant fish, to three men being put in a scorching fire without getting burned, to a woman turning in to a pile of salt, and so much more. These are all true events that happened many years ago and were recorded to teach us vital principles. But unlike a soap opera or movie, the purpose of the Bible is not to entertain, but to teach us who we are, how we should live and to show us what would happen if we lived God's way and what would happen if we lived the world's way. Essentially, the Bible was written to give us hope.

"...And the Scriptures give us hope and encouragement..." Romans 15:4

Purpose Point: The Bible is not boring. Read the Bible (your instruction manual and guide) daily. Before reading, ask God to speak to your heart and bring knowledge, revelation and understanding.

Purpose Point: The older version of the Bible, such as the King James Version, uses words like, "thou", "shall", "hath", "ye" and "thee" which may not be easy to understand; however, there are newer versions of the Bible such as the New Living Translation, New International Version, Amplified, and New King James Version that makes bible reading easier to understand.

You can see the palpable difference between two versions by reading the scriptures below:

King James Version (KJV) *– "Say not thou, What is the cause that the former days were better than these? For thou dost not inquire wisely concerning this. Wisdom is good with an inheritance: and by it there is profit to them that see the sun. For wisdom is a defence, and money is a defence: but the excellency of knowledge is, that wisdom giveth life to them that have it."* Ecclesiastes 7:10-12

New Living Translation (NLT) *– "Don't long for the good old days, for you don't know whether they were any better than today. Being wise is as good as being rich; in fact, it is better. Wisdom or money can get you almost anything, but it's important to know that only wisdom can save your life."* Ecclesiastes 7:10-12

Do you see the difference in your level of understanding? To most people, the NLT version is easier to understand than the KJV. There are several Bible apps and websites that list scriptures in every version for you to easily pick your preference.

Action Activity: If you have a smartphone or tablet, download the Bible app 'YouVersion' provided by Life.Church. It provides reading plans, devotionals, videos, and multiple versions of scripture in text and audio. Pick and choose the version that works best for you.

Purpose Point: It is important for you to read the Bible on a regular basis (daily) to get the Word of God deep in your heart and to become wise. *"...the Word of God is full of living power...sharper than the sharpest knife, cutting deep into our innermost thoughts and desires."* Hebrews 4:12 True wisdom only comes from God (James 3:17). Reading God's Word will help you to obey Him. It is in this way that you are beautifying your heart. Reading the Bible will also help you to know God. I recommend that you read your Bible every day in a version that is easy for you to understand such as the New Living Translation or other translations and study Bibles that are geared towards young teens and adults.

God versus the world
Anything that is not of God is of the world and anything that is not of the world is of God. You might ask, "Didn't God create the world"? Yes, He did. He created the world and everything in it, but just because He created it does not mean it is of Him. For example, imagine having an older brother, born of your mother and father. Your brother is very cruel and evil; he assaulted and murdered people. Your mother and father, on the other hand, are very loving, kind, and respectable people. Although your parents gave birth to your brother, we can see here that your parents and brother are totally different; their ways are not the same. Your brother's ways are cruel, hateful, and atrocious (world's way); and your parent's ways are kind, loving and meek (God's way). In a similar manner, God gave birth to the world so to speak (He created it), but there is no comparison – they are totally opposite. It is not guaranteed that a living creation will have the same morals, values, and actions of their creator. Why? Because we all have a choice. We are free moral agents, free to do and choose whatever we want. We can choose to love or choose to hate, choose to have a positive attitude or choose to have a negative attitude, choose to live or choose to die. Whatever we choose, it will either be the world's way or God's way, there is no in between.

But with our freedom of choice, comes responsibility and consequences for our actions. Any loving parent will advise you of the right choices and warn you about the negative ones. And like a loving parent, God tells us in our instruction manual which choices to make and the consequences of not making those choices. He tells us we should choose His way, "Life", …which includes love, faith, hope, peace, patience, kindness, meekness, gentleness, godliness, humility, marriage, obedience to parents, forgiveness, and respect – all roads to a Princess's Pathway. Love is the most important (1 Corinthians 13:13). These traits lead us to experience a prosperous life while on earth and eternal life after physical death.

Purpose Point: God loves the world and <u>all</u> people in the world; however, He does not love the sinful ways of the world. *"For this is how God loved the world: He gave his one and only Son, so that everyone who believes in him will not perish but have eternal life."* John 3:16

The World's Way
The world's way is opposite of God's way and involves removing God's way of doing things in the world and replacing it with mankind's way of doing things in the world. Some of the world's ways include hatred, fear, fighting, strife, pride, selfishness, deceit, manipulation, malice, retaliation, lust, murder, stealing, jealousy, lying, fornication, adultery, homosexuality, idolatry, rebellion, violence, unforgiveness, etc. The world is the devil's domain as he walks the earth seeking who he can devour (1 Peter 5:8); hence, the devil is not in hell. He is in the world on earth, and he wants to kill and destroy you. He can accomplish this if he can get you to live out his ways – the world's way. Majority of the TV programs, movies, music, and peers promote the world's way to the extent that they encourage people to think that it is okay to have sex before marriage and okay to hate, lie, disobey parents, cheat on their wife or husband, kill, steal, fight, etc. This is a LIE. It is absolutely NOT okay to do these things. If you live the world's way, the Bible (our instruction manual) says we will surely reap horrible consequences along the way. Supporting Scripture: *"...Don't you realize that friendship with this world makes you an enemy of God? I say it again, that if your aim is to enjoy the world, you can't be a friend of God...so humble yourselves before God. Resist the Devil and he will flee from you. Draw close to God, and God will draw close to you..."* James 4:4; James 4:7-8

Purpose Point: What you don't know can hurt you, or even kill you. The world will seek to make you ignorant about the ways of God. *The Lord says, "My people are being destroyed because they don't know me."* Hosea 4:6

If I had lived God's way, I would have never experienced the pain and torment I suffered in my teen years. For example, God's way is marriage not fornication. The only reason that my boyfriend was interested in me was because I was having sex. If I were not interested in boys or sex, I would have never got that close to him. If I had only known God's way and what he wanted for me, I believe that I would have maintained my virginity. But the truth of the matter is I did not know, and what you don't know can hurt you, or even kill you. I lived what I knew—what the world taught me through TV, music, and friends. I was disobedient to parents, fornicating, lustful, rebellious, smoking, and cursing. I loved the world and the world only hated me in return through abuse, hurt, pain, sadness, oppression, and depression. **Listen girls, the world's way does not work!** I tried it and as you know it almost killed me! Well, you might say, because it happened to you does not mean it will happen to me, or all guys are not abusive. Don't be naive! What happened to me may not happen to you, but I guarantee something bad will happen if you live the world's way. A boy almost killed me, but other things or situations can bring death, devastation, and destruction too, such as sexual transmitted diseases, human trafficking, addictions, etc. If you love the world, it will only hate you in return. But if you love God and His ways, He has already loved you back and will show Himself mighty in your life.

If you are reading this book, then you are coming to know God's truth. So, if you are thinking about living the world's way **DON'T** and if you are already living the world's way **STOP**.

"Stop loving this evil world and all that it offers you, for when you love the world, you show that you do not have the love of the Father [God] in you. For the world offers only lust for physical pleasure, the lust for everything we see, and pride in our possessions. These are not from the Father. They are from this evil world. And this world is fading away, along with everything it craves. But if you do the will of God, you will live forever." 1 John 2:15-17

Purpose Point: The world hated Jesus, and it will hate you too, especially when you start to stand for Christ and live a life that is pleasing to God. Jesus said that the world *"...hates me because I testify that its works are evil."* John 7:7 NIV Regardless of how the world felt about Jesus, Jesus knew who he was. He leaned on God and drew strength from God's Word.

Like God, the Bible (the Word) is full of living power and gives life and health to us (Hebrews 4:12). The Bible is God's Word and the Word is God (John 1:1). In other words, when you read the Bible you are reading God because the Bible is God's Word and God's Word is God. The Bible tells us how we should live, the rewards of living that way and the consequences of not living the way God commands us. The rewards are called promises and the negative consequences are considered punishment. For example, God says that children should obey their parents because this is the right thing to do. This commandment is the first of the Ten Commandments that ends with a reward or promise for obeying it. *"And this is the promise: If you honor your father and mother, you will live a long life, full of blessing."* Ephesians 6:3

Disobeying God's commandments could result in not getting the thing that was promised and receiving possible punishment – executed by the inherent power of sin. For example, if a teenager did not honor and obey their mother and father then they are not entitled to the promise of long life, and the punishment could be early death. Like any good parent, God desires to give you the promise, but when His commands are not followed it hurts Him to allow negative consequences. Note, however, that it is not necessarily God punishing us, but a natural law that becomes fulfilled. For instance, what you sow, you will reap (Galatians 6:7); every action creates an equal and opposite reaction. This is a natural law.

Some of God's promises include:

- Deliverance
- Eternal Life
- Forgiveness
- Healing/Health
- Joy
- Long life
- Peace
- Prosperity
- Protection
- Restoration
- Salvation

"...God has given us both His promise and oath. These two things are unchangeable because it is impossible for God to lie...for we can hold on to his promise with confidence."
Hebrews 6:18

"Beloved, I pray that you may prosper in all things and be in health, just as your soul prospers." 3 John 1:2 NKJV

Is God's Word true? Who wrote the Bible?
God's Word is the only truth because God's Word is God. It is impossible for God to lie. How do we really know all the formulas in an Algebra book are correct? We know because the formula gives you the right answer – proven results. God's Word is the same way; it is true for two important reasons:

1. The Bible was written by many prophets and servants of God long ago. Everything written in the Bible, all scripture, was <u>inspired</u> by God (2 Timothy 3:16); and since all scripture is inspired by God, we can conclude that God actually wrote the Bible. Since it is impossible for God to lie because there is no deceit or bad in Him, then the Bible must be true.

   "Above all, you must understand that no prophecy in Scripture ever came from the prophets themselves or because they wanted to prophesy. It was the Holy Spirit who moved the prophets to speak from God." 2 Peter 1:20-21

2. God's Word gives us the formula for life and has proven results; it gives us the right answer. Many of the prophecies and predictions in the Bible have already come true and are still coming true today. Additionally, everything the Bible tells us to do and not

to do reaps similar results and consequences that are stated in the Bible. For example, the Bible says to give, and it shall be given unto you, which means that if you give to others, others will give to you (Luke 6: 38). This principle works every time if you are giving for the right reason. If you give to someone just to get something in return or for people to talk about how good you are, then the true benefit/reward of this scripture will not work. People may give to you, but it will only be because they feel indebted or want something in return. But if you give to someone out of the generosity of your heart and do not expect anything in return, I guarantee that you will receive your reward from God, and someone will soon be genuinely giving unto you. Try it!

Purpose Point: There can only be one truth in everything, anything else is a lie. For example, if a light is on in a room, one can say the light is on and another person can say the light is off, but there can only be one truthful answer. The person who sees the light on will know the truth, but another person who is blind that says the light is off will not know the truth but will think that they know the truth. It is the same way with God's Word; some people can see with their hearts that God's Word is true, and others cannot see - they are blind in their hearts. We know God's Word, the Bible, is true because of faith and fact.

"Every word of God proves true..." Proverbs 30:5

"All scripture is inspired by God and is useful to teach us what is true and to make us realize what is wrong in our lives. It straightens us out and teaches us to do what is right. It is God's way of preparing us in every way, fully equipped for every good thing God wants us to do." 2 Timothy 3:16

"Such things were written in the Scriptures long ago to teach us. They give us hope and encouragement as we wait patiently for God's promises." Romans 15:4

Text Term: The appropriate meaning of "inspire" in the text is to guide or control by divine influence [Source: dictionary.com].

Accept the promise (covenant) – Avoid the punishment (consequence)!

How to Accept God's Promise and Avoid Punishment:

1. **Love God with all your heart, mind, and strength, and love your neighbor as you love yourself – Luke 10:27**

   Your neighbors are all the people you encounter, or anyone outside of yourself such as your family, friends, teachers, people you pass by, and even your enemies. God wants you to be kind to people, respect and love them as you love yourself.

   Candid Clarification: Loving your neighbor(s) doesn't mean that if someone is trying to harm you physically or if you think someone is trying to harm you that you should be quiet and kind. You do whatever you need to do to protect yourself. Depending on the situation, sometimes this means walking away, defending yourself, telling an adult, or running away from a stranger who is trying to get you to do something inappropriate.

Jesus says, *"If you love me, obey my commandments."* John 14:15

"Love means doing what God has commanded us, and he has commanded us to love one another, just as you heard from the beginning." 2 John 1:6

2. **Believe, trust, and obey God in all things**

"Trust in the Lord with all your heart; do not depend on your own understanding. Seek his will in all you do, and he will direct your paths." Proverbs 3:5

If you do these things (love, believe and obey), God promises that you will receive His blessings and avoid punishment. But note this doesn't mean that nothing bad will ever happen to you, it only means that if something bad does happen it will not be as a result of a wrong that you did.

For example, if a person gets drunk, drives, and gets into a car accident he or she will be punished for their crime with jail time and a suspended license. But if this person just happened to get into an accident without drinking alcohol and the other driver was at fault, then there will be no punishment for this person because they did nothing wrong. However, being involved in an accident even though it wasn't their fault may be perceived as something bad that happened. Another example is when a person pays the light bill and the lights still get cut off. Not only was the bill paid, but it was paid on time but somehow the person is stuck sitting in the dark. This person did nothing wrong; it was not their fault the lights cut off. There was an outage in the area – it was out of their control. Outages, inconveniences, and trouble in life will happen because we live in an imperfect world. It does not matter how good you think you are or if you do everything right, things will happen. Hopefully, this brings some clarity around the proverbial question, **"Why do bad things happen to good people?"** The important thing to understand is that doing right helps you to avoid negative consequences and instead receive the promises of God. God never promised us that nothing bad will ever happen in our life. He did promise, however, that when it does happen, He will be with us and bring us through victoriously. Loving God, believing and obeying Him, brings blessings into your life and grace to endure and overcome the bad. God knows that if you love Him first, you will also love yourself and others. Remember, it is through keeping God's commands that we show we love Him (John 14:15).

Supporting Scriptures:

God requires you to love and obey him. *"He requires you to fear him, to live according to his will, to love and worship him with all your heart and soul, and to obey the Lord's commands and laws that I am giving you today for your own good."* Deuteronomy 10:12-13

"The Lord your God is the God of gods and Lord of lords. He is the great God, mighty and awesome, who shows no partiality and takes no bribes. He gives justice to orphans and widows. He shows love to the foreigners living among you and gives them food and clothing. You, too, must show love to foreigners...You must fear the Lord your God and worship him and cling to him...He is your God, the one who is worthy of your praise..." Deuteronomy 10:17-21

"You must love the Lord your God and obey all his requirements, laws, regulations, and commands." Deuteronomy 11:1

"Today I am giving you the choice between a blessing and a curse! You will be blessed if you obey the commands of the Lord your God...You will receive a curse if you reject the commands of the Lord your God..." Deuteronomy 11:26-28

"God will judge us for everything we do, including every secret thing, whether good or bad". Ecclesiastes 12:14

"Remember, it is better to suffer for doing good, if that is what God wants, than to suffer for doing wrong!" 1 Peter 3:17

"...be careful to obey every command I am giving you today, so you may have strength to go in and occupy the land you are about to enter. If you obey, you will enjoy a long life in the land the Lord swore to give to your ancestors and to you, their descendants – a land flowing with milk and honey.[*]" Deuteronomy 11:8-9 *PROMISE

Jesus says, *"If you love me, obey my commandments."* John 14:15

Purpose Point: Listen girls! Everything you do has a consequence – either good or bad. We refer to this as seed time and harvest time, or what you sow you will reap. What you do today, will affect your tomorrow, no matter how young you are. **Disaster has no age limit.** God's mercy and forgiveness is everlasting to everlasting, but the laws of nature are not that way.

Nature is explicitly defined by the 'what you sow you will reap' concept. For example, if you sleep with any and every body, nature will set its course and sexually transmitted diseases and/or unwanted pregnancies will come, or if you jump off a 500-ft building without any apparatuses or support, based on the law of gravity, you will fall to your death.

Purpose Point: God is a loving God, but He is also a Man of His Word...His Word is true. If you live a life of disobedience, negative consequences can follow.

"Do not be deceived: God cannot be mocked. A man reaps what he sows. Whoever sows to please their flesh, from the flesh will reap destruction; whoever sows to please the Spirit, from the Spirit will reap eternal life. Let us not become weary in doing good, for at the proper time we will reap a harvest if we do not give up. Therefore, as we have opportunity, let us do good to all people..." Galatians 6:7-10 NIV

Candid Clarification: God loves you and does not expect for you to be perfect. We all make mistakes, and when we do, God is not sitting around waiting to punish us. He instead, gives us grace while we are struggling and striving to change. However, you must work (put forth effort through faith, obedience, and the attainment of wisdom, knowledge and understanding) to get it right with a *sense of urgency and deep reverence for God, as stated in Philippians 2:12.

"Therefore, my dear friends, as you have always obeyed--not only in my presence, but now much more in my absence--continue to work out your salvation with fear and trembling," *
Philippians 2:12 NIV

Remember, the first and greatest commandment from God is to love Him with all your heart, soul, and mind, <u>AND</u> secondly to love your neighbor as yourself. The way you show God that you love Him is to keep His commandments (John 14:15).

Jesus said, *"'You must love the Lord your God with all your heart, all your soul, and all your mind. This is the first and greatest commandment. A second is equally important: 'Love your neighbor as yourself.' The entire law and all the demands of the prophets are based on these two commandments."* Matthew 22:37-40

"Therefore, brothers and sisters, since we have confidence to enter the Most Holy Place <u>by the blood of Jesus, by a new and living way opened for us through the curtain, that is, his body, and since we have a great priest over the house of God, let us draw near to God with a sincere heart</u> and with the full assurance that faith brings, <u>having our hearts sprinkled to cleanse us from a guilty conscience</u> and having our bodies washed with pure water."
Hebrews 10:19-22 NIV

Purpose Point: Through Jesus' sacrifice he paved a pathway for you – opening a new and living way to receive complete forgiveness of your sins and to have a relationship with God – the Father – that leads to eternal life with Him forever (John 11:25-26). How *awesome* and *amazing* is this!

"May God give you more and more grace and peace as you grow in your knowledge of God and Jesus our Lord. By his divine power, God has given us everything we need for living a godly life. We have received all of this by coming to know him, the one who called us to himself by means of his marvelous glory and excellence. And because of his glory and excellence, he has given us great and precious promises. These are the promises that enable you to share his divine nature and escape the world's corruption caused by human desires." 2 Peter 1:2-4

Chapter 3
Flawless Foundation

"You should clothe yourselves instead with the beauty that comes from within..."
"...let your adorning be the hidden person of the heart with the imperishable beauty of a gentle and quiet spirit, which in God's sight is very precious." 1 Peter 3:4 NLT/ESV

Liquid or powder makeup used to apply on the skin to cover up blemishes, spots and even out skin tone is often called *"foundation"*. Although the title of this chapter is Flawless Foundation, it is not about beauty cosmetics or facial makeup. It is important to know that it is not how you look on the outside that matters, but it is how you look on the inside that really counts. Instead of dealing with making your outward appearance look pretty, this chapter will teach you how to make your heart beautiful – inward appearance. God's Word infused with the knowledge of Jesus Christ is the true foundation and without flaw.

For no one can lay any foundation other than the one we already have—Jesus Christ."
1 Corinthians 3:11

"Nevertheless, God's solid foundation stands firm, sealed with this inscription: "The Lord knows those who are his,"... 2 Timothy 2:19 NIV

Purpose Point: When we talk about the heart, we are not talking about the organ in your chest that beats and pumps blood. Instead, we are referring to the inner being inside of us that makes us who we are. The inner being of your heart includes your will, thoughts, personality, character, moral qualities, emotions, and attitude. Your heart is what makes you do the things you do and say the things you say (Matthew 15:18-19).

Supporting Scripture: *"Don't be concerned about the outward beauty that depends on fancy hairstyles, expensive jewelry, or beautiful clothes. You should be known for the beauty that comes from within, the unfading beauty of a gentle and quiet spirit, which is so precious to God. That is the way the holy women of old made themselves beautiful. They trusted God and accepted the authority of their husbands."* 1 Peter 3:3-5

Study Bible & Apply
Renew your mind; Apply/mature as you learn the Bible - Final authority

Sustain Relationship with God
Love God

Purpose Point: The secret to authentic beauty is trusting God. Beauty is commonly associated with the outward appearance or complexion, but true beauty comes from within. If you can make your heart beautiful, everything else will fall into place.

Contrary to popular opinion that asserts beauty is only skin deep, beauty goes much deeper than the skin. True beauty is formed from the inner layer of the heart and not from the exterior epidermis. Authentic beauty is not solely dependent on facial features or body shape, but on beliefs/behaviors and heart state. If you really want to change the appearance of your face, consider the state of your heart.

"A happy heart makes the face cheerful, but heartache crushes the spirit." Proverbs 15:13 NIV

Purpose Point: Outer beauty does not last, but a woman who obeys the Word of God shall be praised and live forever.

"Charm is deceptive, and beauty does not last; but a woman who fears the Lord will be greatly praised." Proverbs 31:30

Purpose Point: People look at the outward appearance, but God looks at the heart. God will not judge you based on your looks. He will judge you based on your heart – your thoughts, intentions, actions, and motives.

The Lord said, "Don't judge by his appearance or height, for I have rejected him. The Lord doesn't make decisions the way you do! People judge by outward appearance, but the Lord looks at a person's thoughts and intentions [heart]." 1 Samuel 16:7

"The human heart is most deceitful and desperately wicked. Who really knows how bad it is? But I know! I, the Lord, search all hearts and examine secret motives. I give all people their due rewards, according to what their actions deserve." Jeremiah 17:9-10

Purpose Point: Your motives are why you do what you do. When you try to fool people, lie, get over, get revenge, and use people for what you can get, people may not see it, but God does. He sees and knows the secret motives of your heart.

"You want what you don't have, so you scheme and kill to get it. You are jealous for what others have, and you can't possess it, so you fight and quarrel to take it away from them. And yet the reason you don't have what you want is that you don't ask God for it. And even when you do ask, you don't get it because your whole motive is wrong – you want only what will give you pleasure." James 4:2-3

When you apply facial makeup, you need a mirror, a good foundation or powder (makeup) and a brush or sponge. We also need these three important things when we apply makeup to our heart. Except the mirror, foundation and sponge are all the Word of God – the active instrument and ingredient. See yourself and apply it to your heart!

"For the word of God is living and active, sharper than any two-edged sword, piercing to the division of soul and of spirit, of joints and of marrow, and discerning the thoughts and intentions of the heart. And no creature is hidden from his sight, but all are naked and exposed to the eyes of him to whom we must give account." Hebrews 4:12-13 ESV

Mirror - The Word of God serves as the mirror by revealing our flaws – imperfections, blemishes, bumps, bruises, and all. When we read or hear the Word of God, it shows us how wrong we have been. *"God's law was given so that all people could **see** how sinful they were."* Romans 5:20

For example, the Bible says in Exodus 20:15, *"You must not steal"*; therefore, if a person steals before or after reading this scripture, they see how wrong they have been. What do you see when you look in the mirror…when you look in God's Word by reading your Bible? Do you like what you see?

Purpose Point: God's Word exposes us to help us, not to hurt us, because God wants us to reflect Him. You cannot change a reflection without changing the source of its appearance and attributes.

Moreover, God's Word not only serves as a mirror by helping us to see ourselves, but it also serves as a mirror by allowing us to see God – the beauty of His ways, will and wisdom. If you want to know what God really looks like, look in His Word. If you want to glance upon His heart, study His Word. His magnificence, splendor and radiance are shown in His Word. The essence of His beauty is reflected in His behavior which is described all throughout the Bible, just like the essence of your beauty is reflected in your behavior all throughout your life.

"Read His Word until you know His face." - Dr. Myles Munroe
Dr. Munroe read the entire Bible by age 16.

"for the LORD revealed himself…by the word of the LORD." 1 Samuel 3:21 ESV *"One thing I ask from the LORD, this only do I seek: that I may dwell in the house of the LORD all the days of my life, to **gaze on the beauty of the LORD** and to seek him in his temple."* Psalm 27:4 NIV

Remember, reading God's Word on a regular basis will get the Word of God into your heart and enable transformation to take place; it will also help you to obey God and worship Him as He deserves. It is in this way that you are beautifying your heart by exposing all the imperfections and allowing God's Word to make you over with a solid, firm, and flawless foundation.

Purpose Point: Whatever flaws you have, they are not permanent. Since God is beautiful, we too were made to be beautiful because *we were created in His image* (Genesis 1:26). God's Word can perfect your imperfections, heal the bruises, laser love the scars, work through the wrinkles, torch sagging sin, and give you a facial heart lift like never before. Jesus restores our heart and renews our youth. Psalms 103:1 and 103:5 says, *"Let all that I am praise the LORD; with my whole heart, I will praise his holy name…He fills my life with good things. My youth is renewed like the eagle's!"*

Candid Clarification: The end goal of God's Word is not to show us what we look like or how wrong we have been, but to show us who we are. In other words, you may have flaws, but you are the righteousness of God, beautifully and wonderfully made (2 Corinthians 5:21; Psalm 139:14).

You may have failed, but you are not a failure – you are more than a conqueror through Christ Jesus (Romans 8:37). You may have made mistakes, but you are forgiven (1 John 1:9). Accept who you are in Christ and embrace His grace. *"But by the grace of God I am what I am, and his grace to me was not without effect."* 1 Corinthians 15:10 NIV

"Well then, should we keep on sinning so that God can show us more and more of his wonderful grace? Of course not! Since we have died to sin, how can we continue to live in it?" Romans 6:1-2

Broken Mirrors

If you are not using the Word of God as your mirror, you are looking into a broken one. Some broken mirrors include worldly views/ideologies, false doctrines, self-loathing/hate, lies, deception, negative past experiences, and people who do not see your potential and value. When you try to adjust your appearance by looking into a shattered mirror that does not accurately reflect who you are, your image becomes distorted and you remain broken yourself. Only God's Word can repair your soul and transform your entire being whole and anew. *"...Now we see things imperfectly as in a poor mirror, but then we will see everything with perfect clarity. All that I know now is partial and incomplete, but then I will know everything completely, just as God knows me now."* 1 Corinthians 13:12

Purpose Point: I cannot put on my makeup with my eyes closed. In other words, I want to like who I see when I look in the mirror; if I do not, I would probably be quick to close my eyes and just walk away. The only way for me to like who I see (me) is when I choose to live right, do right and be right; when I choose to please God and live my life for Him. I could go to the best make-up artist in the world and she could make up my face beautifully, but if I lack character, integrity and godliness, I absolutely would hate who I see when I look in the mirror every day. Conversely, I could wake up in the morning and look at my bare, pimpled, and blemished face and love who I see because I live for God and aim to live right each and every day. And because of this confidence, I trust God when He says that I am fearfully and wonderfully made (Psalm 139:14), regardless of how I look or feel. If I am beautiful on the inside, no amount of makeup can make me beautiful on the outside because I am already beautiful.

Foundation – The Word of God serves as the foundation by improving our appearance, changing us from the inside out. But in order for our appearance to be improved, we must obey the Word of God. When we obey God's Word, it beautifies our heart, enhances our appearance and changes our behaviors for the better. To the contrary, when we do not obey or believe God's Word, sin and disobedience defiles our heart and does nothing to improve our appearance.

"And remember, it is a message to obey, not just to listen to. If you don't obey, you are only fooling yourself. **For if you just listen and don't obey, it is like looking at your face in a mirror but doing nothing to improve your appearance.** *You see yourself, walk away, and forget what you look like. But if you keep looking steadily into God's perfect law – the law that sets you free – and if you do what it says and don't forget what you heard, then God will bless you for doing it."* James 1:22-25

Jesus said, *"everyone who hears these words of mine and puts them into practice is like a wise man who built his house on the rock. The rain came down, the streams rose, and the winds blew and beat against that house; yet it did not fall, because it had its foundation on the rock.*

But everyone who hears these words of mine and does not put them into practice is like a foolish man who built his house on sand. The rain came down, the streams rose, and the winds blew and beat against that house, and it fell with a great crash." Matthew 7:24-27 NIV

"When the foundations are being destroyed, what can the righteous do?" Psalm 11:3 NIV

"Study this Book of Instruction [the Bible] continually. Meditate on it day and night so you will be sure to obey everything written in it. Only then will you prosper and succeed in all you do." Joshua 1:8

To prepare for the day ahead, when I wake up in the morning, I brush my teeth, wash my face, look in the mirror and then apply make-up. Before applying any cosmetic foundation, you should always cleanse your face first. Like so, God's Word isn't only the mirror, foundation, and application, but it is also the cleanser used to make our hearts holy and clean to support the foundation of His Word. Ephesians 5:26 states in part, *"...to make her holy and clean, washed by the cleansing of God's word."*

Jesus replied, "Unless I wash you, you won't belong to me." John 13:8

Action Activity: Pray this, *"Create in me a clean heart, O God. Renew a right spirit within me...Restore to me again the joy of your salvation and make me willing to obey you. Then I will teach your ways...." Psalm 51:10-13*

Purpose Point: God has already laid the foundation; you must simply choose to do your part.

Sponge - The Word of God serves as a sponge by applying or planting the substance (wisdom/knowledge) of God's Word into our heart. Allow it to soak deep! *"So get rid of all the filth and evil in your lives, and humbly accept the message God has planted in your hearts, for it is strong enough to save your souls." James 1:21*

Allow your spirit and mind to absorb the life-changing Word of God—allow His Word to be firmly implanted and established in your heart. The Word of God specializes in fixing our inner flaws, such as hate, rebellion, selfishness, greed, pride, anger, jealousy, unbelief, and unforgiveness.

God's Word has the power to *transform your flaws into fruits* of His Spirit. This fruit includes peace, joy, kindness, gentleness, patience, love, and faith. God's fruit is what makes your heart beautiful – which in turn produces good fruit (results/behaviors) in our lives.

"But when the Holy Spirit controls our lives, he will produce this kind of fruit in us: love, joy, peace, patience, kindness, goodness, faithfulness, gentleness, and self-control."
Galatians 5:22-23

One day while driving down the street, I noticed the license plate frame of the car in front of me. It read, *"Pretty girls wear pearls."* This may seem true to some, but beautiful girls wear the fruit of the Spirit.

"Never let loyalty and kindness get away from you! Wear them like a necklace; write them deep within your heart. Then you will find favor with both God and people, and you will gain a good reputation" Proverbs 3:3-4

"People are like grass that dies away; their beauty fades as quickly as the beauty of wildflowers. The grass withers, and the flowers fall away. But the word of the Lord will last forever." 1 Peter 1:24-25

Purpose Point: God wants your heart – He treasures it. He wants to help you keep your heart on the right path…glowing beautifully radiant like never before on the Princess's Pathway.

*"O my son [daughter], give me your **heart**. May your eyes delight in my ways of wisdom."* Proverbs 23:26

*"My child, listen and be wise. Keep your **heart** on the right course."* Proverbs 23:19

"Dear children, keep away from anything that might take God's place in your hearts." 1 John 5:21

*"My child, pay attention to what I say. **Listen carefully to my words. Don't lose sight of them. Let them penetrate deep into your heart, for they bring life to those who find them, and healing to their whole body. Guard your heart above all else, for it determines the course of your life.**"* Proverbs 4:20-23

Purpose Point: Your heart will either lead you to Heaven or Hell…it will ultimately determine your eternal destination. Remember, your heart reflects who you are; it also determines your level of value. *"The tongue of the righteous is choice silver, but the heart of the wicked is of little value."* Proverbs 10:20 NIV

Purpose Point: Your heart controls everything you do – the bad and the good. And since God only really knows a person's heart, only He knows what their end will be.

*"…humbly accept the message God has planted in your **hearts**, for it is strong enough to save your souls."* James 1:21

Heart's Treasure…what is your treasure?
Whatever you love, whatever you spend most of your time doing, whatever you focus all your attention on is your treasure. For instance, if you love wild parties, spend most of your time at parties/clubs and focus all your attention on partying, drinking, and having fun, then parties are your treasure…wild living has your heart. Or, if a person loves money and spends most of their time gambling, hustling, and stealing, then money has their heart. God wants to be your treasure. He wants your desires and behaviors to align with His principles and purpose. God knows the moment He becomes your treasure is the moment He has your heart. David, a servant of God, said to Him: *"Your decrees are my treasure; they are truly my heart's delight."* Psalm 119:111

*"Don't store up treasures here on earth, where moths eat them and rust destroys them, and where thieves break in and steal. Store your treasures in heaven, where moths and rust cannot destroy, and thieves do not break in and steal. **Wherever your treasure is, there the desires of your heart will also be.**"* Matthew 6:21

"A good person produces good things from the treasury of a good heart, and an evil person produces evil things from the treasury of an evil heart. What you say flows from what is in your heart." Luke 6:45

Purpose Point: The wrong things can twist your heart into something ugly. An infected heart is indicative of wrong choices and behaviors that manifest in your character/personality, and disable the person God created you to be. Your outer life reflects your inner self (heart).

What makes an ugly heart?
A person's heart is built around three elements: thoughts, beliefs and will. A person's actions and words spoken reflect these three elements and reveal if a person's heart is beautiful or not. All actions and words spoken begin with a thought. What a person thinks and then does and/or says displays a heart of beauty or a beast. Some aspects of an ugly heart include wrong motives, hate, deception/lying, pride, haughtiness, vile/perverse speech, divination, evil/wickedness, manipulation, lust, perversion, malice (ill intent), bitterness, jealousy, resentment, selfishness, greed, unforgiveness, rebellion, vindictiveness, disrespect, ungratefulness, and unbelief.

"When you follow the desires of your sinful nature, the results are very clear: sexual immorality, impurity, lustful pleasures, idolatry, sorcery, hostility, quarreling, jealousy, outbursts of anger, selfish ambition, dissension, division, envy, drunkenness, wild parties, and other sins like these. Let me tell you again, as I have before, that anyone living that sort of life will not inherit the Kingdom of God." Galatians 5:19-21

Jesus said, *"It is the thought-life that defiles you. For from within, out of a person's heart, come evil thoughts, sexual immorality, theft, murder, adultery, greed, wickedness, deceit, eagerness for lustful pleasure, envy, slander, pride, and foolishness. All these vile things come from within [heart]; they are what defile you and make you unacceptable to God."*
Mark 7:20-23

So, you see, it really does not matter how pretty you are on the outside; if you are ugly on the inside you are said to be unclean and unacceptable to God. Therefore, an evil thought-life followed by evil actions and words are what makes an ugly heart.

Imagine sitting at a dinner table in a fancy restaurant waiting to be served. The table is already set with plates, utensils, and wine glasses. You noticed that the glasses are sparkling on the outside but are dirty in the inside. You call your waiter and tell him about the dirty glasses. He says, '*We only clean the outside of our glasses and dishes, we don't clean the inside.*' How crazy would that sound? How would you respond?

Well, as crazy as it may sound, many people treat their body and hearts the same way. They clean and beautify the outside but fail to clean the inside. Many people pretend to be good outwardly, but inwardly they are selfish, sinful, jealous, hateful, unforgiving, and bitter. Our heart is more valuable than any dish or glass. You should first clean your inside by beautifying your heart with God's Word – this will help to control the way you think and act. The inside will then reflect on the outside and make it beautiful and clean also.

Jesus said, *"...you are so careful to clean the outside of the cup and the dish, but inside you are filthy – full of greed and self-indulgence...First, wash the inside of the cup and the dish, and then the outside will become clean, too."* Matthew 23:25-26

A Heart soft as a sponge that cultivates change versus
A Heart hard as a rock that calcifies your core...

Essentially, how you live your life, and how you treat God and others reflect the state of your heart. When you see the negative state of your heart through your thoughts, actions, attitude, and God's Word, and you refuse to change (repent), your heart is hard and not easily broken. One sign that you have genuinely believed in Jesus and accepted his gift of salvation is an overall change of heart. In Romans 2:29, it says that a true person of faith is one whose heart is right with God. It's not merely by obeying the letter of God's law; *"rather, it is a change of heart produced by the Spirit [of God]. And a person with a changed heart seeks praise from God, not from people."* Therefore, when your heart is humble before God, receptive to His will and aims to please Him, it is soft, pliable, tender, and contrite – your heart is right before God. Your thinking, actions, and lifestyle will change as your heart changes for the better.

Supporting Scriptures: *"Their minds are full of darkness; they wander far from the life God gives because they have closed their minds and hardened their hearts against him."* Ephesians 4:18

This is what God desires: *"The sacrifice you desire is a broken spirit. You will not reject a broken and repentant heart, O God."* Psalm 51:17

When you give your heart to God and accept Jesus as your Lord and Savior, God will help you to live the life He has planned for you by initiating a heart transplant procedure...giving you a new heart supernaturally – a heart to follow Him. God said, *"And I will give you a new heart, and I will put a new spirit in you. I will take out your stony, stubborn heart and give you a tender, responsive heart. And I will put my Spirit in you so that you will follow my decrees and be careful to obey my regulations."* Ezekiel 36:26-27

Purpose Point: When you repent and change from a hard heart to a soft heart you may experience feelings of guilt, regret, shame and condemnation because of your past (the things you have done or use to do) and the present (the things you still struggle with). In this case, your heart is condemning you, even after you have repented, confessed it to God and asked for forgiveness. When this happens, you must not allow your heart to hate or despise its master – you, or the main Master – God. You must know that God is greater than your heart, and He forgives you; therefore, you must forgive yourself and keep moving forward on your journey. *"If our hearts condemn us, we know that God is greater than our hearts, and he knows everything."* 1 John 3:20 NIV

"He who believes in Him is not condemned; but he who does not believe is condemned already, because he has not believed in the name of the only begotten Son of God." John 3:18 NKJV

"But if we confess our sins to him, he is faithful and just to forgive us our sins and to cleanse us from all wickedness." 1 John 1:9

Bootyful vs. Beautiful…
Please understand young ladies that you are more than just your butt, breasts, and hips. Boys often lust after you because you are bootyful, or in other words have a big booty or nice shapely figure. Your buttocks, breasts, and other physical characteristics are all a part of your outward appearance/anatomy; however, having a big booty, breasts, hips and thighs, obviously, will not get you into heaven, but being beautiful inwardly will. Furthermore, when you use your beauty for selfish reasons or to fulfill lusts, promote temptation (entice others) and acquire material things, you defile and diminish the full beauty God gave you. You become polluted by your own vanity and pride. Remember, God created you. No matter how beautiful you are on the outside, you are <u>not</u> your own.

"Your heart was filled with pride because of all your beauty. Your wisdom was corrupted by your love of splendor…" Ezekiel 28:17

This is what the Lord said to the people of Jerusalem about their vanity and unfaithfulness – their practice(s) of idolatry: *"…You looked like a queen, and so you were! Your fame soon spread throughout the world because of your beauty. I dressed you in splendor and perfected your beauty, says the Sovereign Lord. But you thought your fame and beauty were your own. So you gave yourself as a prostitute to every man who came along. Your beauty was theirs for the asking…On every street corner you defiled your beauty, offering your body to ever passerby in an endless stream of prostitution…What a sick heart you have, says the Sovereign Lord, to do such things as these, acting like a shameless prostitute."*
Ezekiel 16:13-15, 25, 30

"for God bought you with a high price. So you must honor God with your body"
1 Corinthians 6:20

Purpose Point: The Bible often uses figurative speech – analogies and metaphors to explain important matters. For instance, we know prostitution involves the selling of one's body for sexual gratification in exchange for money and/or material things. However, the Lord also refers to prostitution as being unfaithful to God by embracing and worshipping other gods and idols (lovers). Therefore, when you use your exterior beauty to worship fame, acquire things, embrace ungodly cultures or worldly views, manipulate people and gain the attention of men to fulfill lusts and the hidden desires of your heart, you are also prostituting yourself, so to speak, by not being faithful to God and His ways.

Purpose Point: Guys who only lust after the physical aspects of you are not interested in your inherent beauty and heart; they are more concerned with your body than with your brain (intellect), feelings, interests, thoughts, values and beliefs. It is impossible for them to know your full value because they are only interested in a portion of you (the outside, exterior) and not the complete package (outside and inside). We as God's special princesses should desire a person who is more concerned with our inward appearance than with our outward appearance…at the proper age of course.

Purpose Point: Injections, inserts, implants, and invasive cosmetic surgery may modify your outward appearance, but they do nothing to improve your heart like God's Word. They may temporarily make you feel better about yourself, but they absolutely will <u>not</u> make you a better person.

Unlike people, God cares little about how attractive your physical characteristics are. He is not surprised, smitten or seduced, because He created you. More than anything, He instead wants your heart to be beautiful (inward appearance). When you allow God to make you over, **His Glory will make you gorgeous.**

It costs to look good outwardly, but God's spiritual transformation to achieving magnificent inward beauty is <u>free</u>, a gift to all who accept and believe in Him.

*** To make yourself truly Gorgeous…Glow and Grow in God.
Godliness always outshines glamour…seek to be a godly girl rather than a glamour girl.***

Purpose Point: Never compare your outward beauty to anyone; this will only make you feel bad about yourself, especially if it appears that you don't measure up. God created you just the way He wanted you. Any outer flaws you think you have are God's way of making you unique and special. As you grow older and experience physical changes to your body, you may have to put forth the effort to lose weight or keep it off, but for the most part, your physical characteristics and facial features are a part of God's creative design.
So be you…"BeYOUtiful".

To the contrary, comparing yourself inwardly to others who possess positive attributes such as kindness, love and patience could motivate you to possess these same godly attributes, if you do not already. I think about my mom and how beautiful she is inwardly. She is one of the most open-hearted, patient, and caring persons I know. She inspires me in so many ways.

Purpose Point: Be inspired but be yourself. Sing a song; sing their song – but find your voice.

It is perfectly okay to be inspired by inward beauty because this is something you can change. However, you must be extremely careful about comparing yourself to someone's outward beauty/appearance (facial features or unique physical characteristics) because this is something that you cannot readily change, nor should you.

For example, consider three (3) girls:

1. JILL - a girl who was always told that she was ugly because she had a big forehead and big lips; she also has a bad attitude and loves to fight.
2. TINA - a girl who is perceived as very beautiful on the outside because she has pretty silky skin, long hair and a nice shapely figure; however, she is very mean, stuck-up and disrespectful.
3. SUE - a girl who is perceived as ugly because she has a big nose and large eyes; however, she is very kind and treats others with respect.

Q: How could Jill and Sue who are perceived to be ugly benefit from comparing themselves to Tina who is perceived to be beautiful outwardly?

A: The girls cannot benefit or gain anything if they compared themselves outwardly or inwardly to Tina; they would most likely only end up feeling bad about themselves because they are not thought to be beautiful. They would begin to belittle and tear themselves down and would probably start wondering why they were not created like Tina. Additionally, jealousy and envy may kick in and they may start to mistreat Tina. Comparing themselves inwardly to Tina could also do them no good since Tina is so mean.

Q. On the other hand, how can Jill and Tina benefit from comparing themselves inwardly to Sue?

A. Jill and Tina could learn how to be kind and respectful by observing or analyzing the way Sue behaves compared to their negative behavior. Although Sue may not have attractive features according to the world's standards, she possesses a profound inner beauty due to her kindness and respect for others. Comparing themselves to Sue inwardly could motivate or help them to possess these same traits.

Purpose Point:
- *Constructive Comparison* could help someone to become better.
- *"If you listen to constructive criticism, you will be at home among the wise. If you reject criticism, you only harm yourself; but if you listen to correction, you grow in understanding."* Proverbs 15:31-32
- *"Valid criticism is as treasured by the one who heeds it as jewelry made from finest gold."* Proverbs 25:12
- *Critical Comparison* could influence someone to become worse and/or make someone feel bad about his or herself.

Purpose Point: When you criticize how you look, you are criticizing God – your Creator, because He made you.

Purpose Point: A person is not truly beautiful unless they possess inward beauty comprised of positive/godly attributes, and act becomingly as a young lady.

Q. If a girl is pretty on the outside, but steals, fights, has sex with multiple boys, and disrespects her parents, is she really beautiful?

A. The answer is No. True beauty is reflected in the behavior…not on the body.

Purpose Point: It is important to be happy with who you are, if you do not you will allow anything or anyone to upset you. Part of the reason why Jill may have had a bad attitude was because she was probably letting what people said about her make her angry and unhappy with herself. She may have released that anger by fighting and being rude to others.

Purpose Point: When you are happy with yourself, you act becomingly. For example, regardless of what people thought about Sue and her looks, she remained kind and treated others with respect.

Purpose Point: If you are perceived as beautiful on the outside, never allow your outer beauty to make you stuck-up, snooty, arrogant, or conceited. If you do, you are not truly beautiful because inwardly you are full of vanity and pride. Although Tina was perceived to have outward beauty by others, she did not possess true inward beauty because she was mean and disrespectful to others.

Purpose Point: Your outer beauty diminishes greatly and becomes eroded with negative behaviors and a bad attitude.

Remember, *"You should clothe yourselves instead with the beauty that comes from within, the unfading beauty of a gentle and quiet spirit, which is so precious to God."* 1 Peter 3:4

Purpose Point: When you apply God's Word and trust Him, you will possess a joyful countenance with a dazzling disposition. You will have a sparkle in your eyes and exhibit a memorable smile with a radiant glow. Kindness, meekness, respect, faith, and love will "make up" your actions.

Purpose Point: Regardless, if you have a big forehead, big nose, short hair, kinky hair or no hair, you are beautiful. No matter your race, skin color, complexion, size, or shape, you are beautiful! Just make sure the inside reflects the outside.

Purpose Point: Many people do not believe they are beautiful until someone tells them that they are. You must believe that you possess outer beauty regardless of what you see or what anyone tells you because this is what God says about you – *"You are fearfully and wonderfully made"* (Psalm 139:14).

Action Activity: If no one ever tells you that you are beautiful, say it to yourself and allow these words to root deep into your heart. Let's try it. Say this ten (10) times out loud, *"I am beautifully and wonderfully made. Marvelous are all of the Lord's works."*

Purpose Point: Remember, God determines genuine beauty, not the world. We may not look like the model on the magazine cover, but we are beautiful in God's eyes.

Purpose Point: You are beautiful on the outside because God says you are. You are beautiful on the inside because you choose to be.

Misunderstood, Misconstrued, Misjudged, Mistaken
When you share the good news of Jesus, stand your ground, demand to be treated fairly with respect, set standards and limits, or assert feelings of injustice or inequality, you may be *misunderstood* as being weird, uptight, sour, mean, difficult, funny acting, ill-tempered or hard to get along with. You are not responsible for how others perceive you, but you are responsible for how you treat them. A person may think that you are mean, but if you have not done anything mean to them or others, does it really matter what they think? One important aspect of heart transformation is not being overly concerned about what people think about you. If you know in your heart of hearts that you have done nothing wrong, and you are being obedient to God, do not worry about it. *"To thine own self be true."* - Polonius – Hamlet

Another important aspect of true heart transformation is to be honest or real with yourself. Many women, young and old, try to be the heroines of their lives, mainly because they cannot trust or depend on anyone else to do it. As a result, they put on capes to cover pain and masks [falsehoods] to hide behind the hurt, abuse, rejection, low self-esteem, bitterness, fears, insecurities, secrets, and shame. They are *mistaken* to believe that they must do everything on their own and hold themselves up in their misery. They believe no one can save, help, or protect them, so they zealously pretend and defend to protect themselves. For God to truly transform you, heal your heart and rescue you from rejection and resentment, you must take off your mask and stop trying to be the *she*ro of your life. You must FACE yourself. Be honest about your issues, pray about it, talk to a counselor – seek therapy, if necessary. Putting on make-up, dressing up, looking cute, fulfilling voids through self-gratifying pleasures such as shopping, sex, drugs, alcohol and/or hanging out with friends will not save you or stop you from dying inside. Allow God to be the real hero of your life because you cannot do it in your own strength. When you add God's super to your natural, you gain supernatural power to overcome and succeed. *Break free, gain your freedom and be the real-life Wonder Woman God has called you to be.*

Superheroes – Pain/Purpose > Passion > Pain Point: When I was younger, I loved to watch superhero movies. I recall Batman's superhero powers were motivated by the violent death of his parents. Clark Kent's (Superman) and Peter Parker's (Spiderman) powers were motivated by their refusal to live a mundane and mediocre life with the inherent and acquired powers they knew they possessed. *Super-strength power is derived from inner pain and a sense of purpose; it then moves to passion to addressing a pain point in someone else's life or a wound in the world. But only until you confront your inner pain can you gain power from within and become passionate about helping someone with their pain – thus becoming a superhero in their world.* Will you activate your super strength to do good in the world? What will motivate you – an unfortunate or traumatic event that occurred in your life or your refusal to live in mediocrity and complacency? Do you sense the greatness within you? I do, and God definitely does. Will you use the power God has bestowed upon you through Jesus Christ?

Purpose Point: When you seek to obtain and maintain salvation by the things you do or work to save yourself from inner turmoil, you attempt to make yourself the savior of your life and limit the work of the one and only Savior, our Lord Jesus Christ.

Purpose Point: Don't live your life as a *Cover Girl* – as one who *covers* up her sins, inner flaws and inward pain. And don't live as a *Maybelline* girl, as in *'maybe'* I will do this, or *'maybe'* I will do that. Be intentional and deliberate about your walk with God and your heart transformation. *"People who cover over their sins will not prosper. But if they confess and forsake them, they will receive mercy."* Proverbs 28:13

"A double minded man is unstable in all his ways." James 1:8 KJV

Purpose Point: "You can't heal what you won't reveal." For example, if you go to the doctor to get a wound treated, the doctor will have to see the wound first to determine the best course of action. In the same way, you must reveal your inner flaws, who you really are and what is really wrong to receive proper treatment to foster healing. But remember, you cannot be vulnerable with everyone, and you cannot be fearful, shameful, or intimidated either. Talk to someone you can trust or seek therapy (professional counseling) to uproot anything that may be hindering your heart transformation. *"The purpose in a man's heart is like deep water, but a man of understanding will draw it out."* Proverbs 20:5 ESV Covering up or concealing is never good when you are trying to build your life on a flawless foundation – the Word of God. Anytime you try to save face by any means necessary, often by covering up and lying to protect yourself (or others), you lose the freedom God wants to provide. The more you release what is inside, the more God can release to you.

Purpose Point: Once you accept Jesus Christ as your Lord and Savior, God will begin to change you from within. You will not have to do it alone. How will God do it? He will begin to change the way you think. But you must also do your part and refuse to behave like the world. Do away with the old sinful person and ugly heart and allow God to birth a new person in you whose heart is beautiful.

"Don't copy the behavior and customs of this world, but let God transform you into a new person by changing the way you think. Then you will know what God wants you to do, and you will know how good and pleasing and perfect his will really is." Romans 12:2

Guard your Gates

Purpose Point: When you protect the gateway, you secure the pathway.

"It's all about MEE!" (Mouth, Eye and Ear gates)

Your heart becomes ugly, unattractive and filthy through three (3) important gateways:

- ♥ **(1) Mind/Mouth gate (thoughts and words)** – What you think or believe, will determine your actions and who you will become. This fundamental statement is supported by a fundamental scripture, *As a man thinketh in his heart, so is he* (Proverbs 23:7 KJV). For example, if a girl thinks that cheating on tests and skipping school are okay and subsequently practices this behavior, she becomes a cheater.

  In some cases, however, one bad thought could override one good thought. For example, this girl may not believe that cheating and skipping class are right to do; she thinks it is wrong (good thought) but believes that this is the only way she could pass a test (bad thought). As a result, she cheats and lies because she does not believe she can do any better. In this case, the one bad thought of believing that she is not smart enough supersedes or replaces the thought of believing that cheating is wrong. If this girl wanted to change for the better, she would first have to change her thinking (believe she is smart enough) and change or ignore the negative environment (i.e. the inner circle of friends who also cheat, family/friends who call her stupid, etc.).

  How does someone come to think that something is bad or good? A person's thoughts are born from what is allowed to enter their eye and ear gates. People are taught through various means (TV, music, social media, family, and friends) what to think. *Osmosis*, a subtle or subliminal assimilation of information, through the eye and ear gateways contribute significantly to your thinking patterns.

  To overcome a negative mind set or thought, one must renew their mind with the Word of God to get rid of bad thoughts. Our thoughts have power. Thoughts can create things into existence. Bad thoughts create bad things and good thoughts create good things. This is why God wants us to think on things that are good, so that we can create good in our life. *"...Fix your thoughts on what is true and honorable and right. Think about things that are pure and lovely and admirable. Think about things that are excellent and worthy of praise."* Philippians 4:8

Secondly, we must change our environment; and stop watching, listening to, or hanging around negative influences and osmotic pressures.

Watch your Words, Steer your Speech, Master your Mouth, Tame your Tongue and Limit your Language

Our thoughts not only dictate what we do or what comes to be in our life, but they also dictate what we say. One reason why our thoughts are so powerful is because of their strong ability to produce the words that we say. Words are so powerful and can also create things into existence.

For instance, God created the world by the words He spoke. God said, *"Let there be light"* and there was light...; God said, *"Let there be space between the waters, to separate water from water..."* And it was so. God said, *"Let the waters beneath the sky be gathered into one place so dry ground may appear..."* And it was so. God said, *"Let the land burst forth with every sort of grass and seed-bearing plant... And let there be trees that grow seed-bearing fruit..."* And it was so. God said, *"Let bright lights appear in the sky to separate day from night..."* And it was so. God said, *"Let the waters swarm with fish and other life... Let the skies be filled with birds of every kind..."* And it was so. God said, *"Let the earth bring forth every kind of animal..."* And it was so. God said, *"Let us make people in our image...they will be masters over all life... "And it was so. Genesis 1:3-26

So, you see, God did not create the world with His hands, He created the world with His words. God said, He would make people like Him – in His image, so that means if God's words have power then our words have power too. For instance, if you say you are sick, then you will be sick. If you say you are stupid, then that is what you will be.

Sometimes, we say stuff just to be saying it without really knowing what we are speaking into our lives. For example, most people say when they have a really bad headache that their head is killing them. They really do not believe their head is killing them, but the pain they experience could be so unbearable and excruciating that they say, *"My head is killing me."* Those words have power and could create an incident where their head could kill them one day, whether it be through a brain injury, tumor, or an aneurism. You should not speak bad or negative things over your life or anyone else's. Be careful about what you say.

Moreover, you must control your thoughts so that you can control your tongue and mouth, and essentially your life. I am sure you have heard the popular saying, *"If you don't have anything good to say, don't say anything at all."* Although difficult at times, this is so true. If you don't have anything good to say about yourself or someone else, then it is best not to say anything at all. It is better to be silent.

Another saying also proves true – *"Think before you speak."* Not thinking before speaking could result in saying things that could hurt others or get you in trouble. We should speak in love, truth, and positivity. Cursing, gossiping, lying, libel/slander, verbal threats, and foul language are some things that could get you in trouble and create bad things in your life.

Supporting Scriptures:

"We all make many mistakes, but those who control their tongues can also control themselves in every other way...The tongue is a small thing, but what enormous damage it can do. A tiny spark can set a great forest on fire. And the tongue is a flame of fire. It is full of wickedness that can ruin your whole life. It can turn the entire course of your life into a blazing flame of destruction, for it is set on fire by hell itself. People can tame all kinds of animals and birds and reptiles and fish, but no one can tame the tongue. It is an uncontrollable evil, full of deadly poison. Sometimes it praises our Lord and Father, and sometimes it breaks out into curses against those who have been made in the image of God. And so blessing and cursing come pouring out of the same mouth. Surely my brothers and sisters, this is not right!" James 3:2, 5-10

"The mouths of fools are their ruin; their lips get them into trouble." Proverbs 18:7

"Those who love to talk will experience the consequences, for the tongue can kill or nourish life." Proverbs 18:21

"Avoid all perverse talk; stay far from corrupt speech." Proverbs 4:24

"Avoid godless, foolish discussions that lead to more and more ungodliness. This kind of talk spreads like cancer." 2 Timothy 2:16

"keep your tongue from evil and your lips from telling lies." Psalm 34:13 NIV

"So whenever you speak, or whatever you do, remember that you will be judged by the law of love, the law that set you free." James 2:12

> ♥ **(2) Eye gate** – Our thoughts are usually triggered by what we allow to enter through our eye and ear gates. What you watch on TV, the internet and what you see in your inner circle of family and friends, or behaviors you observe publicly, are some things that influence your thoughts by what you see. For example, watching pornography promotes lust and sexual immorality. It gives the illusion that premarital, unprotected and promiscuous sex are all okay. It portrays false and perverted images of how love making should be. Many marriages have ended in divorce due to pornography because the husband (or wife) would be so addicted to watching porn that he no longer engages in intimacy with his wife, or he may overly suggest that his wife perform the same sexual acts the other women perform in the videos – which ultimately makes her feel devalued and degraded.
>
> Some husbands even believe that they are missing out on something because they feel that their wife does not measure up to the other women in the video. With porn, passionate intimacy is perverted and converted to wild, illicit and hard-core sex. Lust, lack of love and self-seeking pleasure defiles the person's heart. This works the same with the movies and TV shows you watch. The TV (television or 'tell' a vision) gives the illusion that murder, sex, drugs, adultery, violence, theft, rebellion, and foul language are all okay when in fact they are not. Additionally, the friends that you hang around with that argue, fight, curse, drink, smoke and have premarital sex give you the

illusion that it is all okay when in fact it is not. These illusions are all lies and affect your way of thinking! They have no truth in them. These things are not okay and could ruin your life by defiling your heart. You could fool yourself into thinking that if you watch these things or hang around people who do these things that it will not affect you, but it can, and it will.

Minute Memoir: For instance, my desire for sex did not come until I saw a sex scene on TV. I did not start having sex until I started hanging around people who were…they talked about it all the time. Not to mention the music and videos that I listened to and watched, which all promoted sexual encounters. I allowed my eye and ear gates to be flooded with sexual scenes, situations and scenarios, and lust entered my heart. Today, reality shows are another issue…replete with women who go from one man to another for fortune and fame while degrading themselves just to be seen. Repeating these same behaviors could ruin your reality.

Additionally, watching music videos of women gyrating or dancing wildly on men affected my thinking as well. Lust filled songs can bring painful tunes into your life if you allow the music to negatively change your behavior. The wrong type of music also encouraged me to seek inappropriate affection from boys and inspired me to have sex at an early age.

♥ **(3) Ear gate** – Hence, what you listen to is so important. If you listen to someone who tells you that you are ugly and will never amount to anything, then those words will get in your heart and generate your thinking. Soon you will start to think, believe, and maybe even say that you are ugly and will never be anything. Furthermore, if you listen to music with lyrics like, *"shake your booty, party wild, do what pleases you"*, then soon you will think it is okay to shake your booty and party wild. Or, if you listen to music that encourages promiscuous activity and bad attitudes, then these negative messages are getting into your ear gate and molding the way you think. You might think that it has no effect on you, but it does.

Moreover, listening to foul conversations and dirty jokes could also affect you. For example, if you have a friend who always talks about the guys she has had sex with, how much alcohol she drinks and what other people do when they get drunk at wild parties (i.e. cruel pranks, dirty jokes, drugs, etc.), then soon these conversations can affect your way of thinking. When you are bored, you may consider partying and drinking too, or consider engaging in unhealthy relationships. It is best to avoid listening to anything that could change your thinking in a negative way. If you are ever in a situation where you have no choice but to listen, like a parent or teacher telling you that you are nothing and stupid, then drown those words out as much as possible by thinking about something positive in your mind. When you are concentrated or thinking of something else in your head, you really are not paying attention to what someone is telling you and cannot absorb or take in those negative words into your thoughts. Or, if someone is telling you something bad about yourself with ill intent to put you down, then just think the opposite.

For example, if someone says you are stupid, think that you are smart. If they say you are ugly, know that you are beautiful. Speak and declare the opposite of what they say to cancel out all negative words spoken, (i.e. I am smart, I am beautiful, I am somebody, I will survive, etc.). Do not tune your ears to negativity, gossip, arguments, cursing, fussing, unhealthy music, and TV, but tune your ears to God's Word and wisdom.

"Obscene stories, foolish talk, and coarse jokes—these are not for you. Instead, let there be thankfulness to God." Ephesians 5:4

Purpose Point: Be selective about what you watch and the music you choose to listen to. You must have this attitude towards toxic voices and music... *"Away with the noise of your songs! I will not listen to the music of your harps."* Amos 5:23 NIV

Powerful Proverb: *"**Tune your ears to wisdom**...Then you will understand what is right, just and fair, and you will know how to find the right course of every action every time. **For wisdom will enter your heart** and knowledge will fill you with joy...understanding will keep you safe."* Proverbs 2:2-11

Things that you allow to enter your *"ear"* and *"eye"* gates get into your *"mind and thoughts (heart)"*. Your *"mind and thoughts (heart)"* then produce spoken words and actions. To reverse the process, you must change your thoughts which will in turn change what you say (words) and do (actions).

For example, a girl named Stacy had friends that did drugs and always talked about how good the drugs made them feel. After a few months, Stacy started doing drugs and talking about how good the drugs made her feel. But one day, Stacy decided it was not cool to do drugs anymore because she got arrested and kicked out of school. As a result, she stopped doing drugs and hanging around her friends, and ceased from talking about how the drugs made her feel. She thinks differently and believes doing drugs is wrong.

In this example, Stacy allowed her friends to enter her *"eye"* gate by watching them do drugs and *"ear"* gate by listening to her friends talk about drugs. Seeing and hearing these things made Stacy want to do drugs too because she started thinking in her *mind and heart* that it was okay to do. But something happened that made Stacy want to change, so she changed her actions by not doing drugs and stopped hanging out with her friends (actions). She also stopped saying how good the drugs made her feel (words).

Purpose Point: You have the potential to dwell on anything that enters your gateways. When you constantly think, ponder, and ruminate about something, this is referred to as meditation. Whatever you meditate on, will eventually get in your heart; therefore, you must meditate on the right things – which is why God tells us to meditate on His Word (the Bible).

"Study this Book of Instruction continually. Meditate on it day and night so you will be sure to obey everything written in it. Only then will you prosper and succeed in all you do."
Joshua 1:8

Action Activity: Pray this: *"Let the words of my mouth and the meditation of my heart be acceptable in your sight, O LORD, my rock and my redeemer."* Psalm 19:14 ESV

Purpose Point: Have you ever noticed that when you are around someone all the time you begin to say some of the things they say and do some of the things they do? This is because you have allowed them to enter your gates – mind, eye, and ear. You must guard your gates with all diligence to create and maintain a beautiful heart. If you feel that your heart is already ugly, filthy and wicked, repent and ask God to come into your heart and take away anything that is not of Him. Remember, God is faithful and will forgive and cleanse you from all unrighteousness, if you are honest with Him. Trust Him to transform your heart to beauty and do your part by getting rid of anything in your life that is not of Him, such as bad friends/associations, bad habits, negative music and TV, porn, drugs and alcohol.

- *"So get rid of all the filth and evil in your lives, and humbly accept the message God has planted in your **hearts**, for it is strong enough to save your souls."* James 1:21

- *"Don't copy the behavior and customs of this world, but **let God transform you into a new person by changing the way you think.** Then you will know what God wants you to do, and will know how good and pleasing and perfect His will really is."* Romans 12:2

You must evaluate and change what you think, what you see and who/what you listen to. If you will do your part, God will do His part; but it is important to know that you cannot do it in your own strength. You must depend on God to help you. If you want your life to be better, your mind (thinking) and heart MUST change.

Purpose Point: Remember, God created you and gave you the gift to see and hear; therefore, you should use your eyes and ears to bring positive/godly messages into your heart and to do good in your life and in the lives of others.

"Ears to hear and eyes to see – both are gifts from the Lord." Proverbs 20:12

Purpose Point: Your thoughts and beliefs determine your actions and reflect your heart.
"As a face is reflected in water, so the heart reflects the real person." Proverbs 27:19

What is the reflection of your heart? What do people see when they look at you?

Purpose Point: It is through your heart that your personality and character are formed. A person's character consists of the attributes that make them who they are. For example, a person who kills and steals has a horrible character with poor attributes of evil, hate and wickedness. This is because the person's heart is ugly and defiled. On the other hand, a person who is kind and helps the poor exemplifies a good character with positive attributes of kindness, love, and generosity. However, it is important to understand the fundamental essence of a good heart. It is not derived from charity but from Christ. You can give away all your money, but if you do not have Christ, your charitable contributions will not get you into heaven.

A person's reputation is what others know or assume to know about a person's character which could be based on fact or fiction (i.e., false rumors, pre-judgments, opinions, etc.). For example, if a girl at your school actually slept around with multiple boys in your class, she would have poor character precipitated by promiscuity and uncleanliness. She would also probably have a bad reputation at school; people may talk and think of her as being loose or a "slut". It is important to build a good reputation for yourself. You do this by beautifying your heart to exemplify exceptional character and integrity, thus establishing a good reputation. Note: Pray for those who make poor life choices because their actions may stem from a place of trauma and pain. Furthermore, never give up on yourself because of a negative label someone has placed on you. You are <u>not</u> who people say you are, you are who you choose to be and who God says you are.

*"My child, never forget the things I have taught you. Store my commands in your **heart**, for they will give you a long and satisfying life. Never let **loyalty** and **kindness** get away from you! Wear them like a necklace; write them deep within your **heart**. Then you will find favor with both God and people, and you will gain a **good reputation**. Trust in the Lord with all your heart; do not depend on your own understanding. Seek his will in all you do, and he will direct your paths."* Proverbs 3:1-6

*"A **good reputation** is more valuable than the most expensive perfume."* Ecclesiastes 7:1

Purpose Point: Many people give the appearance of godliness and/or good, but inwardly they are wicked and wounded. They pretend to be someone they are not and may operate under the guise of a good reputation but will soon be exposed (Proverbs 26:24-26).
"...having the appearance of godliness, but denying its power." 2 Timothy 3:5 ESV

Purpose Point: What you allow to come in will determine what will come out. If you allow junk into your heart, junk will come out – garbage in, garbage out! Conversely, if you allow wisdom and truth into your heart, wisdom and truth will prevail. Do not allow junk to enter your heart – guard your gateways! Know that your mind, eyes, and ears are not a garbage disposal where people can freely dump their mess. *"Above all else, guard your heart, for it affects everything you do."* Proverbs 4:23

Purpose Point: Allowing things to enter and settle within your gates, permits things to take up residence in your heart. For instance, letting something positive or good enter your gates such as God's Word (Bible and church) or positive role models and friends will bring goodness and beauty into your heart. But letting something negative or bad enter your gates such as bad associations, obscene music/TV, gossip, etc. could bring evil and wickedness into your heart.

Purpose Point: God instructs you to guard two important things: your heart and His instructions – the Word of God.

1. *"...**guard your heart**..."* Proverbs 4:23
2. *"Carry out my instructions; don't forsake them. **Guard them**, for they will lead you to a fulfilled life."* Proverbs 4:13

When you guard what is important to God, God will guard you on your path's journey.
*"He grants a treasure of common sense to the honest. He is a shield to those who walk with integrity. **He guards the paths of the just** and protects those who are faithful to him."*
Proverbs 2:7-8

Accepting and applying God's wisdom and knowledge will help you to guard your gates and heart.

"Don't turn your back on wisdom, for she will protect you. Love her, and she will guard you." Proverbs 4:6

"My people are destroyed for lack of knowledge." Hosea 4:6 ESV

Purpose Point: People tend to try to make their outward appearance beautiful with makeup, jewelry, and fancy clothes. God wants you to be different. He wants you to clothe your inside more than your outside. He wants you to decorate your heart with mercy, kindness, humility, gentleness, patience, obedience, and forgiveness. Remember, God has forgiven you for your sins so you must forgive others. The most important piece of clothing you must wear is LOVE (Colossians 3:12-14). You must love God, yourself, and others to establish and exemplify a beautiful heart which will also clothe you with strength and dignity.

"She is clothed with strength and dignity..." Proverbs 31:25

Candid Clarification: There is nothing wrong with wanting your outward appearance to look pretty by wearing nice clothing, shoes, jewelry, and makeup. You are a princess; therefore, you should look the part modestly and conservatively in your attire, presentation, and dress. Your focus, however, should be more on your inward appearance. Your inward appearance 'your heart' should be more important to you than your outward appearance. Remember, God is more concerned with your heart.

Purpose Point: Freedom of expression does not always equate to inward freedom. In fact, oftentimes, it is quite the opposite. When you are broken, wounded or feel trapped inwardly, the impulsive, erratic, and casual behaviors are mere manifestations stemmed from the bondage within.

Minute Memoir: I remember in my teen years I always tried to make my outward appearance look better, only making myself look older, classless, and unattractive. I tried to cover the low self-esteem, pain, and hurt that I had inside by wearing an excessive amount of make-up comprised of liquid foundation, face powder, eyeliner, mascara, and lipstick. I also wore outlandish hairstyles, large earrings, and multiple piercings. There was a battle going on inside of me that I tried to win outwardly. My freedom to express myself was really me trying to break free. It is important to remember that we cannot improve our inward being by enhancing our outward appearance. We must improve ourselves from the inside out by allowing God to come into our heart and renew our hearts and minds with the Word of God. God's Word will heal your hurts, lift you from low self-esteem, stimulate your true natural beauty, and radiate your spirit giving you a lasting glow.

Purpose Point: Applying God's Word to your heart will also make you wise and help you to make right decisions. To maximize your heart's beauty, you must gain wisdom and apply it.

"A woman who is beautiful but lacks discretion is like a gold ring in a pig's snout."
Proverbs 11:22

To treat an ugly (ill) heart, transform your inner man, and make your heart beautiful, you must humble yourself, pray, repent, read, renew, and obey. Here is how:

- ♥ **Step 1. Judge (self-examine/evaluate) and Humble yourself - thoughts and actions**
    - Judge yourself by heeding to your conscience and inner convictions; recognize and admit your wrong actions/attitudes and surrender or sentence yourself to positive life change (choices) and God's authority.
        - *"But if we examine ourselves, we will not be examined by God and judged..."* 1 Corinthians 11:31
        - *"Now, therefore, thus says the Lord of hosts: Consider your ways."* Haggai 1:5 ESV
    - Lean and let go—lean on God, let go of pride and selfish desires.

Humility is essential to true beauty.
Arrogance, vanity, haughtiness, and pride do not represent a beautiful person.

"But those who exalt themselves will be humbled, and those who humble themselves will be exalted." Matthew 23:12

Many years ago, God used a prophet to warn the women of Jerusalem who were full of pride and vanity. Although our God is a loving God who does not seek or sit around waiting to punish us, we can learn from the scriptures and understand from reading the following passage that these women were more concerned with their outward appearance than they were concerned about their heart and God.

"...the Lord will judge the women of Jerusalem who walk around with their noses in the air, with tinkling ornaments on their ankles. Their eyes rove among the crowds, flirting with the men...The Lord will strip away their artful beauty – their ornaments, headbands, and crescent necklaces; their earrings, bracelets, and veils of shimmering gauze. Gone will be their scarves, ankle chains, sashes, perfumes and charms; their rings, jewels, party clothes, gowns, capes, and purses; their mirrors, linen, garments, head ornaments, and shawls. Instead of smelling of sweet perfume, they will stink...their beauty will be gone. Only shame will be left to them" Isaiah 3:16-24

Purpose Point: Many people would rather look good than be good, putting too much emphasis on their outward appearance (clothing, jewelry, purses, etc.). The Bible refers to this as *"artful beauty"*. This kind of beauty can soon diminish and rust away – it is trifling and temporary. True beauty cannot be bought – you cannot find it on the internet, on an app, in the store, or at the cosmetic surgeon's office. Authentic beauty, a godly heart, comes from within – this is what pleases God and lasts forever.

- ♥ **Step 2. Pray/Acknowledge/Confess**
  Acknowledge God by going to Him in prayer; confess your sins and ask for forgiveness (1 John 1:9).

- ♥ **Step 3. Repent/Eliminate**
  - Turn away from sin, bad deeds, and bad habits such as drinking, promiscuous sex, drugs, cursing, disobedient to parents, strife, rebellion, etc. (2 Chronicles 7:14).
  - Clean out your mouth, ear, and eye gates. Eliminate bad relationships, bad music, movies/programs, negative speech/gossip; break free from wrong thinking and behaviors (James 1:21).
  - Clean out your room, personal surroundings, and devices as well. Get rid of anything that would encourage or entice negative thinking and wrong behaviors.

*"Repent and turn from your sins. Don't let them destroy you. Put all your rebellion behind you and **find yourselves a new heart and a new spirit**...turn back and live!"* Ezekiel 18:30-32

"Nevertheless, God's solid foundation stands firm, sealed with this inscription: "The Lord knows those who are his," and, everyone who confesses the name of the Lord must turn away from wickedness." 2 Timothy 2:19 NIV

- ♥ **Step 4. Read/Study (Gain Wisdom)**
  - Read and study God's Word to carry out the transformation of your heart. Allowing God's Word to enter your heart through your three gateways will begin your inner heart makeover by cutting deep into your innermost being and detoxifying your heart from spiritual dirt, toxins, and filth. Soon, bad things you once did, you will not want to do anymore.

  Note: Attending a Bible-based church is also essential to your spiritual makeover.

  *"My child listen to me and treasure my instructions. **Tune your ears to wisdom**...Then you will understand what is right, just and fair, and you will know how to find the right course of every action every time. **For wisdom will enter your heart** and knowledge will fill you with joy..."* Proverbs 2:1-2, 9-10

- ♥ **Step 5. Renew**
  - Renew your mind with the Word of God by becoming one mind with God – believing what He says in His Word and seeing yourself the way He sees you. Allow God's Word to change the way you think. *"Don't copy the behavior and customs of this world, but let God transform you into a new person by changing the way you think. Then you will know what God wants you to do, and you will know how good and pleasing and perfect his will really is."* Romans 12:2

  Purpose Point: When you allow God to reign from within, He will enhance your inner and outer beauty. His Greatness and Holiness will emit a natural glow.

- **Step 6. Obey**
    - Obey God's Word by obeying His commandments. Obedience is the key to true heart transformation and essentially begins with Step 1…humbling and submitting yourself to the authority of God.

    Jesus said, *"The most important commandment is this:…The Lord our God is the one and only Lord. And you must love the Lord your God with all your heart, all your soul, all your mind and all your strength. The second is equally important: Love your neighbor as yourself. No other commandment is greater than these."* Mark 12:29-31

    "If you love me, obey my commandments." John 14:15

    "Obviously, I'm not trying to win the approval of people, but of God. If pleasing people were my goal, I would not be Christ's servant." Galatians 1:10

Minute Memoir: My heart growing up
When I was growing up my heart was not that beautiful. I smoked, had sex, cursed, fought, went to clubs, skipped class, disobeyed my parents and so much more. But as I became older, I began to learn and do better as a person, or what some call to 'mature'. As I began to learn and read God's Word, it transformed my heart, but only until I eliminated some things from my life. At that point, I had no desire to do the things I once did. I behaved differently and even looked different because a transformation occurred within me. God is still to this day working on perfecting my heart, as it is not instantaneous; it is a process, a long-lived perpetual process.

Therefore, do not ever get discouraged if things are not happening as fast as you would like them to. It takes a while to dig up all the dirt before buried treasure is discovered. In this instance, the dirt would be the filth (sin) that surrounds an ugly heart – the pride, anger, deceit, lust, perversion, strife, jealousy, hate, rebellion, etc. that have been allowed to enter the gateways and take root in your heart over the years. It will take both you and God time to dig up all the dirt to uncover a beautiful heart, thus a beautiful person which is the buried treasure.

I think about my oldest niece who is five years younger than me. When we were growing up, I was so mean to her and put her in situations that she had no business being in. A few years ago, I called her and apologized for being such a terrible person when we were younger. She humbly accepted my apology and said, *"I really think you turned out to be a beautiful person."* Tears ran down my face because I knew she was not talking about outer beauty but inner beauty, and even more importantly, she had seen the change that occurred in me.

Purpose Point: When we are young, we really do not think about being a good person or having a good heart. We think more about getting our hair and nails done…we are more interested in the internet than our integrity, our clothes more than our character, our friends more than our faith. We focus more on our image, social media, TV/music, parties, and fitting in with everyone else. It is important, however, to work on your heart early in life to prevent bad things from happening that could affect or ruin your future, or someone else's. There have been many people who committed crimes or got caught up in some unfortunate situation at a young age and were later arrested and convicted to several years in jail or life in prison, or their life was drastically impacted in some way. It only takes one bad mistake to ruin your future; it does not matter how young you are. People die, get sick, and go to jail from all ages – young and old.

*"My child, if sinners entice you, turn your back on them! They may say, "Come and join us. Let's hide and kill someone! Let's ambush the innocent!...**Though they are in the prime of life, they will go down into the pit of death**...Don't go along with them, my child! Stay far away from their paths. They rush to commit crimes. They hurry to commit murder..."*
Proverbs 1:10-16

Have you ever had your heart broken? It hurts; it crushes you to the core. Breakups, disappointments, betrayals, rejection and let downs are all a part of life. Nevertheless, God cares about your heart; give it to Him. *"The Lord is close to the brokenhearted; he rescues those whose spirits are crushed."* Psalm 34:18 *"Give your burdens to the LORD, and he will take care of you..."* Psalm 55:22 **Allow God to hold the key to your heart; allow Him to unlock it to heal the pain, soften the inner self, and strengthen the soul.** *"Anxiety in the heart of man causes depression, but a good word makes it glad."* Proverbs 12:25 NKJV

Conclusion

By now you should have a thorough understanding about the difference between inner and outer beauty and how to make yourself innately beautiful. If you think you are ugly on the inside, then do the steps outlined in this chapter to make over your heart. But if you think you are ugly on the outside, then you need to switch mirrors and believe what God says about you. Remember, God says that you are fearfully and wonderfully made (Psalm 139:14). If you do not believe this, then you are looking in the wrong mirror – one that is broken and shattered.

"...Now we see things imperfectly as in a poor mirror, but then we will see everything with perfect clarity. All that I know now is partial and incomplete, but then I will know everything completely, just as God knows me now." 1 Corinthians 13:12

Start looking in God's mirror (the Bible) – allow Him to transform you inwardly, and thus outwardly. Again, it does not matter how you look physically on the outside, but how you look on the inside is what truly matters. True beauty comes from within – the heart.

Besides taking mirror selfies (photos of self), usually when someone constantly looks in the mirror it is because of three (3) reasons:
1. The person is so vain and conceited that they must continue to look at themselves just to see how beautiful they really are.
2. The person is so self-conscious or possess such a low self-image that he or she is always worried about the way they look.
3. The person wants to make sure there are no imperfections, or something is not intruding on their appearance such as food in teeth, oily face, smeared or diminished makeup, out of place hair, something in or on the nose/face, etc.

Purpose Point: God wants us to do a little bit of all three things mentioned above. He wants us to continually and faithfully look in His mirror, the Word of God, so that we can: (1) be reminded of how beautiful and valuable we really are; (2) grow in Him and become better and better, thus improving our self-image – the way we see our self and others; (3) and ensure that sinful imperfections are not intruding on our Christian appearance or dimming our Christian light. Remember, the Word of God shows us how we should look, think, and behave; it is our spiritual mirror. Use God's Word daily to freshen up your inward appearance. *Wake up to make up with God's Word – the Bible.* Allow it to give you a total makeover from head to toe – transforming you from the inside out.

Purpose Point: What is on the inside will manifest itself on the outside.

Purpose Point: Some people would rather be pretty outwardly than to be healthy inwardly and have a healthy heart. Nevertheless, choose to be a person who makes their inward beauty and heart health priority.

Purpose Point…Blind Spots
Watch out for the blind spots. Sometimes when we look in the mirror, we cannot see the things that are actually there…similarly to looking in a car's side mirror and not seeing that big red car on the side of you. Oftentimes, we see problems in others but cannot see them in ourselves, which is why I often say, *we are ALL hypocrites in our own right* (it is only through the righteousness and grace of God that we are made pure). In other words, there will be times when you cannot see your faults and imperfections, but you will be quick to judge or criticize others and see their faults and imperfections. It works both ways, hence double standards. Failing to see blind spots can cause you to crash in life. Pray and ask the Lord to reveal the blind spots – the hidden faults of your heart.

"How can I know all the sins lurking in my heart? Cleanse me from these hidden faults. Keep your servant from deliberate sins! Don't let them control me. Then I will be free of guilt and innocent of great sin. May the words of my mouth, and the meditation of my heart be pleasing to you, O Lord, my rock and my redeemer." Psalm 19:12-14

Jesus said, *"And why worry about a speck in your friend's eye when you have a log in your own? How can you think of saying to your friend, 'Let me help you get rid of that speck in your eye,' when you can't see past the log in your own eye? Hypocrite! First get rid of the log in your own eye; then you will see well enough to deal with the speck in your friend's eye."* Matthew 7:3-5

Minute Memoir: One night, God spoke to me while sleeping. He said, *"I am perfecting you; I am mirroring you unto myself."* God wants our hearts to reflect His heart – full of love, godliness, compassion, patience, and kindness. He wants our will to reflect His will; our desires to reflect His desires, and our behaviors to reflect His behaviors. Essentially, He wants us to be holy – one mind with Him. **When people see you, they should also see the God in you.** Our ways and actions should mimic God's ways and wisdom.

*"**And all of us have had that veil removed so that we can be mirrors that brightly reflect the glory of the Lord**. And as the Spirit of the Lord works within us, we become more and more like him and reflect his glory even more."* 2 Corinthians 3:18

Purpose Point: Do not live your life in someone else's shadow or reflection. Don't allow peer pressure and negative influences to change who you were created to be. Don't allow it to distort your inner beauty. Mirror yourself in the image of God by being who He created you to be. Open your heart to His wisdom and His ways. *"O my son [daughter], give me your **heart**. May your eyes delight in my ways of wisdom."* Proverbs 23:26

Flawless Foundation

Supporting Scriptures:

*"The human **heart** is most deceitful and desperately wicked. Who really knows how bad it is? But I know! I, the Lord, search all hearts and examine secret motives. I give all people their due rewards, according to what their **actions** deserve."* Jeremiah 17: 9

*"I know, my God, that you examine our **hearts** and rejoice when you find integrity there..."* I Chronicles 29:17

*"The Lord's searchlight penetrates the human spirit, exposing every **hidden motive**."* Proverbs 20:27

*"My child, listen and be wise. Keep your **heart** on the right course."* Proverbs 23:19

Jesus said, *"...But evil words come from an **evil heart** and defile the person who says them. For from the **heart** come evil thoughts, murder, adultery, all other sexual immorality, theft, lying, and slander. These are what defile you..."* Matthew 15:18-20

*"Anyone who loves a pure **heart** and gracious speech is the king's friend."* Proverbs 22:11

*"Haughty eyes, a proud **heart**, and evil actions are all sin."* Proverbs 21:4

*"People may think they are doing what is right, but the Lord examines the **heart**."* Proverbs 21:2

*"Everything is pure to those whose **hearts** are pure. But nothing is pure to those who are corrupt and unbelieving, because their minds and consciences are defiled. Such people claim they know God, but they deny him by the way they live. They are despicable and disobedient, worthless for doing anything good."* Titus 1:15-16

*"A youngster's **heart** is filled with foolishness, but discipline will drive it away."* Proverbs 22:15

*"How can a young person **stay on the path of purity**? By living according to your word."* Psalm 119:9 NIV

*"Run from anything that stimulates youthful lust. Instead, pursue righteous living, faithfulness, love, and peace. **Enjoy the companionship of those who call on the Lord with pure hearts**."* 2 Timothy 2:22

Wherever you go, let your actions reflect a beautiful heart and your life exude as a sweet perfume. On your life's journey, beautify every place that you go – every room you enter. *"Our lives are a fragrance presented by Christ to God. But this fragrance is perceived differently by those being saved and by those perishing. To those who are perishing we are a fearful smell of death and doom. But to those who are being saved we are a life-giving perfume..."* 2 Corinthians 2:15-16

"May our sons flourish in their youth like well-nurtured plants. May our daughters be like graceful pillars, carved to beautify a palace." Psalm 144:12

Purpose Point: The Lord *"placed the world on its foundation so it would never be moved."* Psalm 104:5

In the same way, you must also place your world on the firm and flawless foundation of God's Word so you will not be moved by negative peer pressure and worldly influences. You must stand firm and allow your true beauty to radiate for all to see.

Purpose Point: First impressions are important. Researchers show that people form an impression or opinion of you within the first 30 seconds of meeting you…judging you by your interior and exterior – your personality, abilities, hair, dress, smile, visual hygiene, speech and nonverbal communications. Appearances do matter, but people will essentially remember you by your interior and not necessarily your exterior. The person you are and the way you treat others will be captured in the memory of those whose path you cross. You may forget how a person looks, but you will never forget how that person made you feel.

Carl W. Buehner and Maya Angelou described it a little differently, *"People will forget what you said, people will forget what you did, but people will never forget how you made them feel."*

To sum it all up, God will judge you by your words and actions (including motives and intent) towards Him, yourself, and others. He will give no thought to your exterior (the way you look) but will judge you by your interior – your heart. **A change of heart means a change in direction.**

God desires a heart of love, a heart of compassion, a heart of right living, a heart of giving, a heart of forgiving, a heart of sacrifice, a heart of obedience, a heart of faith and trust in Him, and a heart of wisdom.

> Lord, *"Teach us to number our days, that we may gain a heart of wisdom."*
> Psalm 90:12 NIV

> *"And it is impossible to please God without faith. Anyone who wants to come to him must believe that God exists and that he rewards those who sincerely seek him."*
> Hebrews 11:6

> *"The LORD is my strength and my shield; my heart trusts in him, and he helps me. My heart leaps for joy, and with my song I praise him."* Psalm 28:7 NIV

**Allow God's Word to give you a spiritual makeover –
a heart transformation that will *revolutionize* your entire being.**

His Word and supernatural touch will *rejuvenate* your true beauty, *renew* your mind, *restore* your health, *resuscitate* your heart, *reinvigorate* your youth, *release* a sweet fragrance of love, *revive* your spirit, *regenerate* your soul and *reflect* in your outward being…. True beauty is formed from the inside out.

> ***"God has made everything beautiful for its own time.
> He has planted eternity in the human heart…"*** Ecclesiastes 3:11

---

*Give your heart to Jesus by accepting Him as your Lord and Savior.
May the Lord satisfy the longing of your heart.
May "the Lord bless you and keep you."
May "the Lord make his face shine on you and be gracious to you."
May "the Lord turn his face toward you and give you peace."* Number 6:24-26

Chapter 4
Validated Value

Stand to be validated!
God is your judge, and He approves you.
You are fearfully and wonderfully made (Psalm 139:14).

"...She is worth more than precious rubies." Proverbs 31:10

Let's start by defining value. What is value? Value is worth measured in usefulness or importance. In other words, if something is significantly useful or important it is considered highly valued. Take a $150,000 Mercedes, for example, with a V12 engine and 510 horsepower. This car is of course highly valued because of its usefulness, importance, and perceived brand of quality. The company that built the Mercedes knows its value because they know what it is capable of, what it is made of and the parts that have been put inside it; therefore, they can price their creation at $150,000.

Know who you are
Understand your value, capability and purpose

Establish & cultivate positive relationships
Love, respect and forgive others, including self

What would you say to someone who had a $150,000 Mercedes and did not clean it, allowed anybody to drive it, left the doors unlocked so anyone can have access to it and neglected regular car maintenance? Many people would probably say, *"Are you crazy, don't you know how much this car costs; don't you recognize its value?"*

In a similar manner, don't you realize that you are worth more than a $150,000 Mercedes? That is right; the one that created you put so many valuable parts inside of you and declared that your price is far above rubies (Proverbs 10:31). So don't let anybody drive you, don't neglect regular maintenance (i.e. doctor check- ups, nutritious foods, basic hygiene, exercise), and most importantly don't leave your valuables unlocked for anyone to enter in. You are valuable, and like the company that built the Mercedes, your creator knows what you are capable of, what you are made of and what He has put inside of you – your talents, gifts, capabilities.

As you have learned, what makes you beautiful and valuable is not what is on the outside but what is in the inside. If a $150,000 Mercedes only had the exterior parts, such as the 18-inch alloy wheels, tires, power locked doors and automatic windows, but did not have the most important parts inside, such as the V12 engine and transmission, the car's value would greatly diminish and be nearly worthless. Why? Because the most important parts that enable the car to drive are missing, hence, the car would be virtually useless.

It is the exact same way with you. You may look good on the outside but be empty on the inside. Your value is not validated or confirmed until you get the most important part inside of you. This special part will greatly shape you into the person you were created to be; it will heal you, deliver you, restore you, dwell in you, guide you, direct you, comfort you, speak to you and most of all, love you. It will allow you to drive full force, giving you a smooth safe ride in life as you travel down the Princess's Pathway. There may be some bumps in the road along the way, nevertheless, this special part will help you get to your destination safely. You may ask what part can do all these things. I am glad you asked, but first you should know that it is not a part, but a person, and his name is Jesus.

"For we are his workmanship, created in Christ Jesus for good works, which God prepared beforehand, that we should walk in them." Ephesians 2:10 ESV

Just like the Mercedes-Benz manufacturer created the Mercedes-Benz vehicle to perform good works, you are God's workmanship, created in Jesus Christ for good works.

Purpose Point: In worldly terms "value-added" means the enhancement added to a product or raw material before the product is sold to the customer. However, this does not prove true with the children of God because we were already made valuable in our mother's womb. God engineered you with priceless value before you were born into the world; however, in order for that value to be validated, confirmed or realized you must accept Jesus as your Lord and Savior. Jesus wants you to come to him just as you are, as mere raw materials so that he can validate you and mold you into the person He created you to be.

Text Term: Validated means to confirm or approve.

Purpose Point: You were born valuable; it cannot be added… it simply must be validated!

Purpose Point: Simply put, your value is not determined by *addition*; it is determined by *acceptance*.

Therefore, your value is not determined by where you live, performance or popularity, position/title, affiliations, associations, material possessions, how much money you (or your family) have, education level, relationship status (single/married) or skills/talents. Again, it cannot be added.

Your value is determined by your <u>acceptance</u> of the Lord Jesus Christ. Apart from Him you can do nothing. Jesus said, *"I am the vine; you are the branches. If you remain in me and I in you, you will bear much fruit;* ***apart from me you can do nothing****."* John 15:5 NIV

Purpose Point: You can become a person *of* value by the services you offer via your skills, talents and expertise (legally and with a positive attitude), but you cannot make yourself inherently valuable without Jesus.

You are a child of God if you accept Jesus and obey him. And since Jesus is also a child of God, then that means Jesus is not only your Savior, but he is also your brother, and you are his sister.

"There was a crowd around Jesus, and someone said, "Your mother and your brothers and your sisters are outside, asking for you." Jesus replied, "Who is my mother? Who are my brothers? Then he looked at those around him and said, "These are my mother and brothers. Anyone who does God's will is my brother and sister and mother." Mark 3:32-35

"For God knew his people in advance, and he chose them to become like his Son, so that his Son would be the firstborn among many brothers and sisters." Romans 8:29

Big brothers are often protective of their little sisters. They do not want their beloved sisters dating the wrong guy or anyone who will take advantage of them. Jesus is also protective of his little sisters. He watches over you and will protect you from any harm or danger. You are valuable to him, and God loves you just as much as He loves Jesus (John 17:23).

Candid Clarification: Jesus is first and foremost your Savior and Lord because he died for you. It is only through this occurrence that we could become sisters and daughters in Christ…. that we could become adopted into His royal family. If you currently have a big brother in life, you may not feel obligated to obey him. But Jesus is different; he desires and deserves our complete obedience. Obeying him is the same as obeying the Father.

Supporting Scriptures:

God said, *"...This is my Son, my Chosen One; listen to him!"* Luke 9:35 ESV

Jesus said, *"Anyone who loves me will obey my teaching. My Father will love them, and we will come to them and make our home with them. Anyone who does not love me will not obey my teaching. These words you hear are not my own; they belong to the Father who sent me."* John 14:23-24 NIV

Jesus said, *"The Father and I are one."* John 10:30

He also said, *"Have I been with you all this time… and yet you still don't know who I am? Anyone who has seen me has seen the Father! So why are you asking me to show him to you?"* John 14:9

"So now Jesus and the ones he makes holy have the same Father. That is why Jesus is not ashamed to call them his brothers and sisters. For he said to God, "I will declare the wonder of your name to my brothers and sisters. I will praise you among all your people."
Hebrews 2:11-12

Purpose Point: Your value is not validated until you accept Jesus Christ as your Lord and Savior. Once you do that, you allow the King of kings and Lord of lords to come and live in you (the most important part) – adopting you into His royal family and transforming you into His image comprised of His likeness, ways, and wisdom. You learn firsthand from the King himself how to conduct and value yourself as a princess…as a lady. If you have a negative self-image and low self-esteem, you <u>must</u> change your thinking about yourself. You must know that you are special, valuable and deserve the best – nothing less.

Jesus Christ gave his life especially for you. This proves that you MUST be exceedingly valuable for someone to have died for you. When you feel as though no one loves you or sees your value, remember that Jesus died and suffered because he saw how valuable you are. In fact, <u>your value is so great that it could be seen before you were ever born.</u>

"…before you were born I set you apart and appointed you as my spokesman to the world." Jeremiah 1:5

Fools and Faulty View of Value

Purpose Point: Feelings of rejection are experienced when one is seeking their self-worth and significance from someone else, and this person fails to deliver. If you do not believe that you are already valuable through Christ, you will forever experience rejection and disappointment because people will always fail to deliver and fulfill your expectations.

A fool will not see value and will cast you away. Don't be fooled into believing that this is a reflection of you. A fool cannot even see the value of God, and sadly believes that there is no God. Do you really think that this absurd belief makes God non-existent or not highly valued? Of course not! Regardless of what a fool believes, God is still all powerful, all knowing and the supreme Creator of the universe; and you are still a person of value.

"Only fools say in their hearts, "There is no God." Psalm 14:1

Purpose Point: Ignorance does not change your value; it only shows how stupid a fool really is.

The people who orchestrated the death of Jesus valued him as being worth only 30 pieces of silver. Surely, a person who is the Son of the living God, born of a virgin, turned water into wine, healed the sick, raised the dead, fed a crowd of 5,000 people with five loaves of bread and two fish, and walked on water was worth more than just 30 pieces of silver. What fool could ever put such a meager price on Jesus? So, you see, you cannot allow people to dictate or determine your value. You are worth more than all the riches in the world – a fool will not see this.

"They took the thirty pieces of silver – the price at which he was valued..." Matthew 27:9

Purpose Point: Therefore, if you cannot see your value then you are walking a thin line of being a fool too. Failing to see your value will make you feel invisible; however, understanding your value will improve your perceived visibility and make you feel as though you really exist and matter.

Purpose Point: You are not *invisible* – God sees you! No matter who walks away from you, God will always remain by your side. And because He is always there, that makes you *invincible*...forever victorious and valuable!

Purpose Point: Fools will be blind to your value. Don't allow this blindness to contaminate your thinking and deteriorate your perceived God-given value.

A fool's perception is out of touch with reality. It cannot be impacted by truth without a change of heart. If a fool does not wake up now, he or she will forever live their life with the terrible reality of regret (i.e. I wish I would have; I wish I could have; I wish I did this; I wish I did that...).

Purpose Point: What makes a person a fool is not necessarily what they do not know, it is what they cannot see.

Purpose Point: If you allow people to determine and dictate your value, your self-value and concept will decrease, deteriorate, and diminish.

Purpose Point: When someone devalues you, it is usually to make themselves feel better or more valuable.

Purpose Point: Whether you were adopted, abandoned, or abused YOU ARE valuable!
Do not allow the foolish acts afflicted on you by someone else to dictate your value.

Created with Purpose

It is important to know that the creator is more important than the creation. Without the creator, there would be no creation. You are reading this book right now only because of the one who created you. Your mother and father may have brought you into this world, but God was the one who breathed life into you. It was God who made the earth and everything in it, including you.

"The Lord, your Redeemer and Creator, says: "I am the Lord, who made all things. I alone stretched out the heavens. By myself I made the earth and everything in it." Isaiah 44:24

"For we are God's masterpiece. He has created us anew in Christ Jesus, so that we can do the good things he planned for us long ago." Ephesians 2:10

Every creator(s) makes a creation so that its creation will serve them. For example, the corporation that created the Mercedes created it to serve them by generating profits. Another example, although fiction, would be a mother baking a cake. If a mother baked a cake, most likely she created the cake so it could satisfy the taste buds and stomach of her family – so it could be eaten. What if, when the cake was done and removed from the oven, it looked up at the mom and said, *"Why did you create me this way? You can't eat me."* After the mom thinks that she has totally lost her mind, she would probably say, *"What right do you have to speak to me that way; I created you. If you do not want to be eaten, then I'll just throw you away."* Likewise, God created us to be used for His glory and purpose, and we have no right to question, argue or go against His purpose and plans for our lives.

"Destruction is certain for those who argue with their Creator. Does a clay pot ever argue with its maker? Does the clay dispute with the one who shapes it, saying, 'Stop, you are doing it wrong!' Does the pot exclaim, 'How clumsy can you be!' How terrible it would be if a newborn baby said to its father and mother, 'Why was I born? Why did you make me this way?' This is what the Lord, the Creator and Holy One of Israel says, 'Do you question what I do? Do you give me orders about the work of my hands? I am the one who made the earth and created people to live on it. With my hands I stretched out the heavens. All the millions of stars are at my command.'" Isaiah 45:9-12

God created you to serve Him. Once you recognize your value in God, you can effectively serve Him in two important ways:

1. Love God with all your heart, all your mind and all your soul. You do this by keeping His commandments, worshiping Him, and yielding to His purpose for your life.
2. Love your neighbor as you love yourself. Help others to experience love by experiencing God, for God is Love (Luke 10:17; 1 John 4:8).

God wants you to serve Him all the days of your life, especially while you are young. He wants the best years of your life, your youth. God has given you His best; therefore, you should also give Him your best while you are young.

"Don't let the excitement of youth cause you to forget your Creator. Honor him in your youth before you grow old and no longer enjoy living. *It will be too late then to remember him, when the light of the sun and moon and stars is dim to your old eyes, and there is no silver lining left among the clouds. Your limbs will tremble with age, and your strong legs will grow weak. Your teeth will be too few to do their work..."* Ecclesiastes 12:1-3

"Yes, remember your Creator now while you are young..." Ecclesiastes 12:6

Know that you are worth more than a $150,000 Mercedes, so don't allow any and everybody to stick their nozzle in your tank or you will surely run empty and break down along the way.

Do not park yourself in everybody's garage. You are a princess, royalty and highly valued. Your tank is sacred and intended for your king (husband) – lock it up! No test drives are allowed! If any man wants a ride, he will have to purchase you with a wedding ring and sacred vows. When you hear your alarm go off, do not deactivate…do not ignore. This is your conscience and Creator, God, warning you: *'Don't do it'*, *'He is not the one'*, *'You are worth more than this'*, *'He is not worth it'*, *'Stay away'*, *'Don't give him the time of day'*, *'Run!'*.

"Run from anything that stimulates youthful lusts. Instead, pursue righteous living, faithfulness, love, and peace. Enjoy the companionship of those who call on the Lord with pure hearts." 2 Timothy 2:22

If you lease or loan yourself to many hoping that one day someone will finally do right by you and take you as their very own, you will run yourself down, break down, and open yourself up for misuse and abuse.

Purpose Point: God is like an OnStar and GPS system in a car. He knows where you are, your trajectory in life and what you are doing at all times. He is trying to get you to go in the right direction, but you must follow His instructions. Denying His instructions and rejecting His guidance and navigational nuggets will get you lost down a sure path to a "dead end" — a crooked cul-de-sac.

God knows how valuable you are because He created you. However, when you were born into the world, sin also saw your value and purchased you as its slave, so God had to buy you back through the death and blood of Jesus. Therefore, your body belongs to God. He is your rightful owner – you are not your own. Take care of your body and use it to honor and glorify God.

"Don't you realize that your body is the temple of the Holy Spirit, who lives in you and was given to you by God? ***You do not belong to yourself, for God bought you with a high price****. So you must honor God with your body."* 1 Corinthians 6:19-20

Purpose Point: Usually, things that are highly valuable are used less often and for a special purpose. For example, a woman would not wear an elegant expensive diamond necklace every day; instead, she would wear it only during special occasions. Like so, do not make yourself cheap by abusing your body with drugs, alcohol, promiscuous sex, etc. Your body should be treasured and used for special occasions, like marriage and ministry. If you treasure yourself and keep your heart pure as gold, your life will be better and God will show you off as His special treasure, using you for every good work. But again, even if we mess up or get messy, God can clean us up and still use us when we go to Him with a contrite heart.

"In a wealthy home some utensils are made of gold and silver, and some are made of wood and clay. The expensive utensils are used for special occasions, and the cheap ones are for everyday use. If you keep yourself pure, you will be a utensil God can use for his purpose. Your life will be clean, and you will be ready for the Master to use you for every good work."
2 Timothy 2:20-21

God has validated your value, but you are responsible for walking in that value. If you are to walk in God's validated value, you must see yourself through the eyes of your Creator. God says your price is far above rubies, but if you see yourself as a fake cubic zirconia, worthless and unimportant, then the value that God has validated is meaningless.

Likewise, if you think of yourself as a rundown station wagon full of dents and dings, instead of a brand new Mercedes-Benz, Bentley or Ferrari, then you must reprogram your mind to line up with what God says about you – *"your price is far above rubies"*. You must see yourself as valuable and not cheap or subpar, or you will not be able to fulfill your God-given destiny. **With a perceived sense of value comes confidence, boldness, assured identity, self-respect, self-love, and victory. Accept and love yourself because God has accepted and loves you!**

No matter what you have done or what has been done to you, God has validated your value and loves you beyond measure. It does not matter what anyone else thinks, says or does, the Creator of the universe has validated you!! He has given you His stamp of approval!! No one else matters. If God is for you, who can be against you?

*"...**If God is for us, who can ever be against us?** Since God did not spare even his own Son but gave him up for us all, won't God, who gave us Christ, also give us everything else?"* Romans 8:31-32

*"Not even a sparrow, worth only half a penny, can fall to the ground without your Father knowing it. And the very hairs on your head are all numbered. So don't be afraid; you are more **valuable** to him than a whole flock of sparrows."* Matthew 10:29-31

*"**And I am convinced that nothing can ever separate us from God's love**. Neither death nor life, neither angels nor demons, neither our fears for today nor our worries about tomorrow—not even the powers of hell can separate us from God's love. No power in the sky above or in the earth below—indeed, nothing in all creation will ever be able to separate us from the love of God that is revealed in Christ Jesus our Lord."* Romans 8:38

Purpose Point: God has already approved and validated your value; you do not have to go desperately searching for someone, something, or social media to approve and validate you. God has given you all the "likes" you will ever need through his infinite love; in other words, He doesn't just like you, He LOVES you. He offers so much more than anyone ever could. You are never an afterthought because you are always on His mind. When you are secure in God, secure in His love, nothing else really matters. Your insecurities will dissipate as you anchor yourself in His love.

Purpose Point: Many people look to social media for validation. They base their value on their popularity, how many friends or followers they have, who liked or commented on their post or picture, how many friend requests they received, and/or who requested to be their friend. Be honest with yourself, are you seeking validation from other means or media? Remember, it is not about how many friends you have accepted, but WHO you have accepted. Jesus is the only person who can truly validate you. It is not about who follows you; it is about WHO you choose to follow. When you follow Jesus, you will not be turned around by people.

Purpose Point: Most importantly, DON'T LOOK FOR A MAN TO VALIDATE WHO YOU ARE! Do not degrade yourself to get a boyfriend, and don't destroy yourself to get back at him. Don't *reduce* yourself to *revenge*. Don't *error* to get *even*.

Purpose Point: Your self-worth and concept are how you view yourself as it relates to your value and importance. Some factors that can either increase or decrease your self-worth include your self-esteem (how you feel or think about yourself) and your self-confidence or efficacy (believing that you can achieve a desired result). Your instruction manual (the Bible) teaches you who you are in Christ so you can know what to think about yourself and reveals to you what you are capable of to improve self-confidence. For example, the Bible says that you can do all things with the help of Jesus (Philippians 4:13). Therefore, read your instruction manual to renew your mind about yourself and ask Jesus to help you improve your self-esteem and confidence. In this way, you can start seeing yourself as the priceless ruby you are, and not the cheap cubic zirconia. Once you improve your self-worth/concept and realize your value, you will not accept just anything. You will not allow people to treat you any kind of way or drive you crazy in the process.

Fast Fact: Studies show that children with a high self-efficacy level perform better in school.

Purpose Point: It is important to recognize your value, so you won't mistreat yourself and/or allow others to mistreat or take advantage of you. When a person does not know the purpose or value of something, they will be quick to abuse and misuse it. *One way that people misuse and abuse themselves and others is with sin – becoming a slave to sin and enjoying its pleasures. Remember, God's validation of your value through His wonderful grace is not a debt-free offer or pre-approval to drive haphazardly through life doing what you want to do. Sin always has a cost – a consequence and its interest rate is astronomical – extremely high. Sin destroys and depreciates your God-given asset — you.*

Purpose Point: *If you don't value yourself, no one will.*

What if someone with a $150,000 Mercedes came and picked you up for a ride. When you got in the car, it was trashy with paper and empty drink cans everywhere. You all decide to stop by the drive-thru at McDonald's to get something to eat. After you all are done eating and drinking soda, the driver of the Mercedes just throws the empty McDonald's bag and drink cup on the floor and places used ketchup packages on the dashboard. It is evident that this person does not value their $150,000 Mercedes. As a result, you would most likely throw your empty McDonald's trash bag and drink cup on the floor too. Your thinking would probably be, 'if they don't value their car why should I.' The same works with you. You are worth more than a $150,000 Mercedes, but if you are trashy, filthy, and let anybody drive you any kind of way, no one will value you because you do not value yourself.

Purpose Point: You are not trash, so don't accept junk. A princess deserves a prince as a queen deserves a king at the appropriate God-given time. **You are worth waiting for.**

Purpose Point: Anything worth having is worth waiting for and worth working for.

"That Which We Obtain Too Easily, We Esteem Too Lightly." – Thomas Paine

Purpose Point: A car's mileage is often linked to its value. Typically, the more miles a car has, the less its value. Many people do not like to buy used or high mileage cars with multiple owners, numerous accidents, and severe damage because they think the car is not worth the investment and will eventually break down along the way – requiring a lot of maintenance, care, and attention.

Refuse to allow boyfriends and unhealthy relationships to make you a high mileage/multiple driver person – full of dents, dings, depression, disease, and a whole lot of baggage. However, if you are already in a high mileage state, God's grace is sufficient for you! Only He has the power to wash you clean, wax away the debris, and reset your odometer back to 0 (like brand new) … restoring your full value and worth. If any man (woman) be in Christ, he/she is a new person.

"This means that anyone who belongs to Christ has become a new person. The old life is gone; a new life has begun!" 2 Corinthians 5:17

Purpose Point: Figuratively speaking, why are you trying to put all those miles on you? You are already valuable as you are, so do not go looking for validation. Wait for a serious buyer, one who is willing to sign on the dotted line at the appropriate time and take you home as his own valuable possession – his wife. Put yourself in park and wait for your king…wait for your husband!

Purpose Point: ***Don't allow a relationship or breakup to dictate your value.*** If someone can walk away from you (the relationship) let them walk.

God was and is still today in a covenant relationship with a chosen group of people, Israel, who He loves very dearly. God loved Israel so much that He would do anything for them. In fact, many, many years ago He did. Some of His most famous wonders were performed to rescue Israel such as turning water into blood, parting the Red Sea, sending plagues to their enemies, etc. God loved Israel unconditionally and met their every need. When they were hungry, He gave them food; when they were thirsty, He provided water. But no matter what God did for them, they were ungrateful, disrespectful, and complained all the time; they were just not happy regardless of what God did. They betrayed and rejected God by loving something or someone else. They cheated on God with idols, one of which was a figure of a calf made from gold. The more God revealed and proved Himself to them, the more they rejected Him and denied His love.

God said, *"I thought to myself, 'I would love to treat you as my own children! I wanted nothing more than to give you this beautiful land – the finest inheritance in the world. I looked forward to you calling me 'Father', and I thought you would never turn away from me again. But you have betrayed me, you people of Israel! You have been like a faithless wife who leaves her husband,' says the Lord."* Jeremiah 3:19-20

Have you ever thought to yourself that you would have loved to make your father, boyfriend or husband happy, and that you wanted nothing more than to give them love, the finest in the world? You looked forward to them calling you daughter, girlfriend, or wife, but suddenly they betrayed you and left you for something or someone else. God, your Creator, can absolutely relate to how you feel and understands your pain. People rejected Him in the past and will continue to reject Him in the present and future – every single day.

Most of us have been rejected, cheated on, mistreated, or betrayed in some way. But you must know that no matter what someone did to you, a relationship does not dictate your value. Do you believe that just because Israel rejected God that it made Him less of a God? Absolutely not! God was still powerful, mighty, magnificent, sovereign, and awesome, regardless of how foolish Israel behaved. His value did not diminish because of the ignorance of fools. Someone may have cheated on you, and when you saw the female that he cheated on you with, maybe you thought she looked like a calf (similarly to the idol Israel created) – just kidding. The truth is, if someone does not see your value, then they are a fool. And if you cannot see your value, then you are a fool too! Remember, fools will not see value and will cast it away because they are blinded by selfishness and fear. Take Israel for example, they were selfish in wanting their own plans and pleasures, fearing that God would not do what He promised.

Purpose Point: Perfect love casts out fear. *"Such love has no fear because perfect love expels all fear."* 1 John 4:18   God loves you perfectly! **You may have been rejected by some, but you are CHOSEN by God.**

Moreover, if someone really loves you, they will not allow fear or selfishness to prevent them from loving and respecting you. Selfishness is nothing but groundless fear – fear of losing, fear of not getting desires fulfilled, fear of commitment, fear of being hurt, fear of being rejected, fear of being teased, taunted or made fun of, fear of not fitting in, fear of not having enough, etc.

Jesus' act of dying for you on the cross exemplified perfect love. He did not follow his own desires of selfishness or allow fear to distract him from being beaten, whipped, and crucified for you. There is no greater love than this!

"But he was wounded and crushed for our sins. He was beaten that we might have peace. He was whipped, and we were healed! All of us have strayed away like sheep. We have left God's paths to follow our own. Yet the Lord laid on him the guilt and sins of us all." Isaiah 53:5-6

"We know how much God loves us...God is love, and all who live in love live in God, and God lives in them. And as we live in God, our love grows more perfect..." 1 John 4:16-17

Purpose Point - "Love vs. Lust": A person who genuinely loves you will see your value and treat you as the valuable person you are. But a person who lusts after you may not be able to see your value and will probably mistreat you. How can you tell the difference between love and lust? I heard someone say once, *"Love is what you can do for that person; lust is what that person can do for you."* For example, a person who loves you will do nice and thoughtful things for you, stick with you through the difficult times, and give and seldom take. On the other hand, a person who is in lust might always want you to do things for them, and often takes but hardly gives. Remember, you are more than just your body and physicality. If a person really loves you, they will see beyond your physical characteristics and focus on what they can do for you, and not on what you can do for them. However, be not deceived. Pretenders always give a little in the beginning to lure you into their lustful trap.

Purpose Point: Making more withdrawals than deposits (if any) will put a relationship in a negative state.

The Bible defines love as follows:

"Love is patient and kind. Love is not jealous or boastful or proud or rude. Love does not demand its own way. Love is not irritable, and it keeps no record of when it has been wronged. It is never glad about injustice but rejoices whenever the truth wins out. Love never gives up, never loses faith, is always hopeful, and endures through every circumstance. Love will last forever..." 1 Corinthians 13:4-8

Minute Memoir: The reason that I accepted abuse and allowed my boyfriend to treat me any kind of way was because I did not know my value. My father had never affirmed me or told me that I was special. So, like many of us I went looking for love in all the wrong places.

I often wondered why I was born and what my purpose was in life. Have you ever wondered this? If so, then keep reading and you will receive the answers you have been looking for. The moment you believe and know why you were created, who you are, whose you are and your value as a person, things will change. You will begin to see yourself in a different way and take less from people who do not see you in the way that they should.

Victory in Validated Value
Someone may have abused, raped, or molested you, your father may have abandoned you, someone may have told you that you are worthless, ugly and unpopular, your boyfriend may have cheated on you, your friend may have betrayed you, regardless of what has happened to you it doesn't dictate your value. If someone has done you wrong, it's that person's loss, not yours. Therefore, walk away from anyone who treats you like you are worthless because their eyes are blind to seeing how valuable you are. Your Creator sees your value and understands your pain because He has been through it too.

You must remember that the Creator of the universe dictates your value, and He says you are precious, valuable, and victorious. He says you are a princess...His daughter and His love. Jesus said, I have come that you might have life and have it more abundantly (John 10:10), so forget about everyone else and fix your eyes on your Creator. Who better knows the Mercedes than the one who created it? Who better knows you than the one who created you? God knows your hurts, pains, sorrows and troubles. His love is unconditional. He will never leave you or forsake you.

"Even if my father and mother abandon me, the Lord will hold me close." Psalm 27:10

Purpose Point: ***Don't allow your family upbringing or childhood traumas to dictate your value.*** When you go through experiences that are traumatic and painful, you must yield yourself to God to foster healing and lean on those you trust for support and guidance. And throughout this process, you must know that you are highly valued.

"...Do not be afraid, for I have ransomed you. I have called you by name; you are mine. When you go through deep waters, I will be with you. When you go through rivers of difficulty, you will not drown. When you walk through the fire of oppression, you will not be burned up; the flames will not consume you. For I am the LORD, your God, the Holy One of Israel, your Savior..." Isaiah 43:1-3

Despite what you may feel, avoid allowing the wrong things and thinking to Define, Describe, Determine, and Dictate your Value.

Purpose Point: *Don't allow your sexual status (virgin or non-virgin), sexual history or sexual encounters to dictate your value; however, be pure in heart.*

Regardless of your past, when you beautify your heart and seek to please God, your purity is restored. *"God blesses those whose hearts are pure, for they will see God."* Matthew 5:8

In biblical days and sometimes still practiced today, when a virgin had sex with a man for the first time, he was required to pay for her and marry her. This custom is a testament to the significance and value of women. In today's times, however, the world often devalues virginity and women; therefore, this custom is seldom the norm today.

"If a man seduces a virgin who is not engaged to anyone and has sex with her, he must pay the customary bride price and marry her." Exodus 22:16

Sex, money, position, and power are commonly associated with determining a person's value. The greatest temptation that people fall prey to is sex. Pre-marital sex, promiscuous sex, perverse sex, and sexual assault (molestation, rape, and incest) are the primary experiences that bring a sense of devaluation to a person, or a feeling of reduction in value and worth.

However, oftentimes it is a matter of perception – how a person sees things and people. For example, a prostitute may believe that having promiscuous sex makes her more valuable because she gets paid for it. But another person may see a prostitute as worthless because she devalues her body. Additionally, a person may view a virgin as more valuable than a single person who is not.

Purpose Point: Regardless, if you are a virgin, vixen or victim, past sexual experiences and encounters do not dictate your value. *Break free* from any negative mindsets and *walk in your worth.*

Purpose Point: Do not be willing to have sex with someone just to be able to say that you got a man, or to fit in with friends or worldly culture. A guy does not dictate your value, but he can make you feel less than who you are.

Purpose Point: *Don't allow worldly associations (i.e., people, groups, clubs, sororities, etc.) to dictate your value.*

A person with perceived or acclaimed high value can make others feel highly valued simply by association. For example, if you as a normal person (without fame) knew a celebrity personally and shared their company frequently you would probably feel important or valued simply by associating with her or him.

Like so, when you know your Father God and the fact that He possesses and made the entire riches of the world, your value is validated through your association with Him and not by people who consider themselves valuable or important. So what, if a person is well known and connected. So what, if they have a nice car, a lot of money, a big house, or a bigwig job…none of that compares to what your Heavenly Father has. Therefore, you should not be impressed, intimidated, or seduced by other peoples' possessions and position. They may have some things that the world deems as valuable, but your Daddy God has it all, and He desires to give it all to you.

"Now to Him who is able to do exceedingly abundantly above all that we ask or think, according to the power that works in us…" Ephesians 3:20 NKJV

Purpose Point: Never feel inferior because of who you don't know, and never feel superior because of who you do know. Always remain humble, yet confident, never thinking of yourself as less, but thinking of yourself less often - doing for others, treating others with respect and dignity, and gaining your spiritual superiority from God.

Purpose Point: You are neither superior nor inferior, you are invaluably you!

Purpose Point: You are not somebody because of who you know, you are somebody because of who you are – a princess, a child of the Most High God. Never look to any association to validate your value; your Heavenly Father has already done so.

In addition to personal associations, associations can also include sororities, societies/clubs, cliques/groups, teams, social media connections, religious denominations, political party affiliations, etc. These too have no bearing on your value. Jesus Christ is your greatest and most valuable connection. When you are *"linked in"* to Him you can never be denied, diminished, demeaned, devalued, demoted, or depreciated. In Him, you are the head and not the tail, above and not below (Deuteronomy 28:13).

Purpose Point: *Don't allow your looks to dictate your value.*

Many people believe that if they have 'so-called' ugly or unattractive features, or are obese or overweight, then that means they are less valuable. *No matter your size, skin color, hair type/texture, facial features, body shape, height, weight, disability, disorder, or deformity, you are valuable and beautiful.* Remember, God says that you are fearfully and wonderfully (beautifully) made (Psalm 139:14), and if you cannot see that then you are looking in the wrong mirror. It does not matter how ugly you *think* you are, or how fat or skinny you *think* you may be; your value is not based on your looks or figure. God made us all uniquely different. Change your thinking!

Have you ever seen a good-looking man with a girl who you thought was unattractive, or vice versa? Usually, when a person dates someone less attractive it is either because that person has something that they want such as money, or the person sees something special inside of them.

Now that you have beautified your heart, people will be more attracted to your inside appearance. They will see something special inside of you. You will have this radiant glow that will draw the right people close. Just smile on the outside and let God work in the inside, which will extend to the outside as He works to draw the right person near at the proper time.

Purpose Point: *Don't allow your overall outward appearance - clothes, shoes, purse, makeup or hair to dictate your value.* Oftentimes, if a woman does not feel beautiful or attractive on the outside, she devalues herself and other people who appear not to measure up. Many women long for attention, compliments, and affirmation, so they dress provocatively and raunchy, wear revealing and tight-fitting clothing, sport the latest fashions, and may go over the top with hair and makeup. They think if people notice me, then I will be special. **Remember, making yourself more visible, will not make you more valuable**. You can look cute and classy in Christ without advertising your goods and living ostentatiously or living to impress others.

Purpose Point: *Don't allow a job to dictate your value.*
A job does not dictate how much you are worth. You may be working somewhere earning the minimum wage but that is absolutely not how much you are worth. The world often defines a person's value by their assets or how much money a person has (net worth), but God dictates a person's value by their heart. It is, however, important that you go to school and college to try to get a better job and increase your income, but your worth is not based on how much money you have, where you work or the job you perform. You could be the most valuable person as a waitress making $5.00 an hour plus tips, or approximately $15,000 a year, if you believe and trust in God, as compared to someone who makes $300,000 a year and does not believe in God. Remember, you are God's MVP – **Most Valuable Princess** with a net worth of PRICELESS. *"It is better to be a poor but wise youth than an old and foolish king who refuses all advice. Such a youth could rise from poverty and succeed."* Ecclesiastes 4:13-14

Purpose Point: Your self-worth is more important than your net worth.

Purpose Point: Some things are worth more than dollars.

Purpose Point: *Don't allow your financial situation to dictate your value.*
It is easy for you to feel down and worthless when you have little to no money, mountains of debt, or when you are just working to pay bills with no extra cash to enjoy life. But remember, this too is subject to change. God can open new doors of opportunity and bring increase in your life if you trust, obey, and depend on Him. I remember working as a single mother earning a low salary, but I continued to tithe and trust God for promotion and He promoted me within 15 months on my job – doubling my salary. He can do the same for you and your family if you trust Him.

Purpose Point: The love, salvation, peace, joy, and favor of God are more valuable than money, or anything or anyone.

Purpose Point: *Don't allow a sickness or disease to dictate your value.*
All of us will face some kind of sickness or disease in life. And when this happens, we cannot allow it to make us feel less than who we are. I remember watching this real-life special or documentary on TV one day. It was about this Christian girl who had HIV (Human Immunodeficiency Virus). She did not allow this disease to stop her from living her life. She taught others about HIV/AIDS (Acquired Immunodeficiency Syndrome) in schools and health centers. One day, when she was walking home, she met a guy. This guy saw something special inside of her and later married her even though she had HIV and despite him not having the disease. This girl did not allow the disease to take away her value. She went on with her life

with her head up high showing off her beautiful heart; and because of this she met her husband who was able to see her value as well.

Purpose Point: *Don't allow a degree or your educational level to dictate your value*

Don't let a degree guide you; guide the degree. Don't let a degree make you; make the degree. Your destiny is not dictated by your degree or the lack thereof. The Bible talks about women who are always learning but denying the power and plans of God. He refers to these women as 'silly women' – weak and gullible. Hence, you can be *smart* and *silly* at the same time when you focus only on the degree(s) and worldly knowledge but deny the ways of God. God wants you to not only be *smart* but possess *spiritual maturity* and acquire/apply fundamental and long-lasting *'truth'*, wisdom and understanding established by His Word.

"...having the appearance of godliness, but denying its power. For among them are those who creep into households and capture weak [silly]* women, burdened with sins and led astray by various passions, always learning and never able to arrive at a knowledge of the truth."
2 Timothy 3:5-7 ESV   * [silly] – KJV

The world uses degrees, among other things, to dictate or determine your future, salary, and lifestyle. With God, however, your future is dictated by your obedience, faithfulness, and love for Him. God can take you where a degree will not. He can give you favor and innovative ideas to create your own wealth (Deuteronomy 8:18). And even when you seek to get hired for a position, God has the power to influence the hiring manager(s) to lean towards hiring you despite your shortcomings and lack of qualifications. *"The king's heart is like a stream of water directed by the Lord; he turns it wherever he pleases."* Proverbs 21:1

"We can gather our thoughts, but the Lord gives the right answer." Proverbs 16:1

Candid Clarification: Please do not misunderstand. Secondary and advanced education can boost your earning and intellectual potential. Education has significant value, but do not allow it to dictate your value.

Many people allow their degree to dictate their future instead of God. For example, a person may receive a bachelor's degree as an engineer, but instead of designing and building things, God may want the person to build a church as a pastor. If a person is dedicated to their degree, they cannot be devoted to their destiny – the plan that God has predestined for them. God's desire and your desire to please Him should override any degree.

"When the ways of people please the Lord, he makes even their enemies live at peace with them." Proverbs 16:7

Purpose Point: Make plans after seeking God in prayer; allow God to be the ultimate decision maker. *"We can make plans, but the Lord determines our steps."* Proverbs 16:9

Purpose Point: *Acceptance* and *acknowledgement* with the right *attitude* can take you to a higher altitude both professionally and personally.

"In all your ways acknowledge Him, and He shall direct your paths." Proverb 3:6 NKJV

Purpose Point: A degree may make you more valuable in the eyes of men, but not in the eyes of God. God loves you with or without a degree; He can teach you things that can take you higher in this world and the next.

Purpose Point: Your *profession* should not be confused with your *purpose*. Many people are blessed to live out their purpose in their current profession such as a person who is called to be a pastor working as a pastor, or a person who is called to foster healing working as a doctor. But oftentimes a person's career has little or nothing to do with what they were called to do; therefore, sometimes you may have to juggle your profession, purpose, and assignment to arrive at your destiny.

Fast Fact: Bi-vocational ministry is when a person works any job outside the church and pastors a church as well.

Candid Clarification: A college education is important and should be pursued; however, your value, identity and destiny should not be based on your college attendance, attainment, achievement, accomplishment, or association.

Purpose Point: Knowing the Bible is an important part of essential education and the foundation of wisdom.

Purpose Point: *Don't allow the mistakes of the past to dictate your value.*

Regret, guilt, and shame have no place in you. Learn from the past; don't continue to live in it. As it has been often stated, "do not allow the past to define you"; instead, allow your past experiences to refine you into a better version of you.

"But if we confess our sins to him, he is faithful and just to forgive us our sins and to cleanse us from all wickedness." 1 John 1:9

"So now there is no condemnation for those who belong to Christ Jesus." Romans 8:1

Summary: When you allow people, things, titles, and situations to dictate your value you lose your sense of value when they are taken away, when they walk away or when they do or do not stay. You are not these things – you are not a mistake, you are not material possessions, you are not a disease, you are not alone, you are not abandoned, you are not your looks, you are not a position/title, you are not a degree, you are not a grade or score, you are not your salary, you are not worthless – you are a child of God.

<u>**Now let's learn about you, the valuable princess who God created…**</u>

Let's learn *why you were created or born*, also known as <u>*your purpose*</u>:

- ♥ You were created to worship and serve God (your spiritual King) and to have an intimate relationship with Him. You were created for God's pleasure! (Ephesians 1:14)
    - o You worship and serve God by loving and obeying Him. Worshiping God also includes singing to Him, praising His name, telling Him how good and awesome He is, etc. – see Powerful Prayers for prayers of worship

"You are worthy, O Lord our God, to receive glory and honor and power. For you created everything and it is for your pleasure that they exist and were created." Revelations 4:11

"And so, dear brothers and sisters, I plead with you to give your bodies to God because of all he has done for you. Let them be a living and holy sacrifice—the kind he will find acceptable. **This is truly the way to worship him***."* Romans 12:1

- ♥ You were created to LOVE and be loved
  - ♥ Created to Love:

Jesus said, *"You must love the Lord your God with all your heart, all your soul, and all your mind. This is the first and greatest commandment. A second is equally important: 'Love your neighbor as yourself.' All the other commandments and all the demands of the prophets are based on these two commandments."* Matthew 22:37-40

Purpose Point: If a person does not love God, they cannot fully love themselves; and if they cannot fully love themselves, they cannot effectively love others. If a person does not love, he or she has no value. Therefore, it is required that you have God to become valuable because God is Love.

"If I gave everything I have to the poor and even sacrificed my body, I could boast about it; but ***if I didn't love others, I would be of no value whatsoever.****"*
1 Corinthians 13:3

"...God is love, and all who live in love live in God, and God lives in them."
1 John 4:16

Purpose Point: Wickedness is what diminishes a person's value or makes them of no value at all. Wickedness leads to worthlessness.

"Here is a description of worthless and wicked people: They are constant liars...Their perverted hearts plot evil. They stir up trouble constantly." Proverbs 6:12

"The tongue of the righteous is choice silver, but the heart of the wicked is of little value." Proverbs 10:20 NIV

Purpose Point: God always restores a person's value when they have a contrite heart…when the person repents and decides to live for Him. With reconciliation comes restoration.

- ♥ Created to be Loved

"...Others died that you might live. I traded their lives for yours because you are precious to me. You are honored, and I love you." Isaiah 43:4

"For God so loved the world that he gave his only Son, so that everyone who believes in him will not perish but have eternal life." John 3:16

"...nothing can ever separate us from God's love. Neither death nor life, neither angels nor demons, neither our fears for today nor our worries about tomorrow—not even the powers of hell can separate us from God's love. No power in the sky above or in the earth below—indeed, nothing in all creation will ever be able to separate us from the love of God that is revealed in Christ Jesus our Lord."
Romans 8:38-39

- ♥ You were created to help and honor your husband (your natural king).

"Then the LORD God said, 'It is not good for the man to be alone. I will make a helper who is just right for him.'" Genesis 2:18

- ♥ You were created to procreate life through divine order.
    - o Procreate means to produce children. Divine order is the way in which God wants you to produce children which is in a healthy marriage relationship. God wants parents to raise godly children using His Word.

"Then God blessed them and said, 'Be fruitful and multiply. Fill the earth and govern it. Reign over the fish in the sea, the birds in the sky, and all the animals that scurry along the ground.'" Genesis 1:28

"Didn't the LORD make you one with your wife? In body and spirit you are his. And what does he want? Godly children from your union. So guard your heart; remain loyal to the wife of your youth." Malachi 2:15

Purpose Point: If you never marry or have children, your value still stands as a child of God. Paul (a servant of God) said, *"I wish everyone could get along without marrying, just as I do. But we are all not the same. God gives some the gift of marriage, and to others he gives the gift of singleness."* * 1 Corinthians 7:7
Note: * Singleness in this context refers to celibacy or abstinence—refraining from sexual encounters.

- ♥ You were created to use your God-given gifts and to tell others about Jesus (be a witness for Jesus—Acts 1:8) so they can worship and serve God too. God may have called you to do this as an apostle, prophet, evangelist, pastor, minister, teacher, friend, counselor, helper, or mentor. Pray and seek God for guidance to determine what capacity He will have you to serve. All gifts are invaluable to the kingdom of God, and we are all ministers of reconciliation (2 Corinthians 5:11-21).

Jesus "is the one who gave these gifts to the church; the apostles, the prophets, the evangelists, and the pastors and teachers. Their responsibility is to equip God's people to do his work and build up the church, the body of Christ, until we come to such unity in our faith and knowledge of God's Son that we will be mature and full grown in the Lord, measuring up to the full stature of Christ." Ephesians 4:11-13

"In his grace, God has given us different gifts for doing certain things well. So if God has given you the ability to prophesy, speak out with as much faith as God has given you. If your gift is serving others, serve them well. If you are a teacher, teach well. If your gift is to encourage others, be encouraging. If it is giving, give generously. If God has given you leadership ability, take the responsibility seriously. And if you have a gift for showing kindness to others, do it gladly." Romans 12:6-8

"...And God has given us the task of reconciling people to him." 2 Corinthians 5:18

Purpose Point: It is important to know that **you were born for others, and not for yourself.** Selflessness without selfishness is an important component of authentic value. When you lend yourself to love…when you give, advocate, and help others, you walk in your God-given value. But **when you live a life to please only yourself your value lies dormant.** Remember, God has tasked us all to draw others to Him.

How you were created:

- ♥ You were made in God's image – Genesis 1:26
- ♥ God made all the delicate, inner parts of your body and knit you together in your mother's womb – Psalm 139:13
- ♥ You were fearfully and wonderfully made – Psalm 139:14

Purpose Point: *"...Trust yourself to the God who made you, for he will never fail you."* 1 Peter 4:19

Purpose Point: I cannot say it enough; your value is not validated until you accept Jesus Christ as your Lord and Savior. Who you are, your value, whose you are and where you are going, are based solely on this vital relationship. When you accept and obey Jesus, the following relates to you:

Who you are:

- ♥ You are God's workmanship, masterpiece, and how marvelous you are – Psalm 139:14
- ♥ You are an heiress to the throne. You are a temple of God – Romans 8:17; 1 Corinth. 6:19
- ♥ You are a daughter of God, a child of the King – 2 Corinthians 6:18
- ♥ You are in the bloodline of Jesus; he is your Savior and Lord – Romans 8:29
- ♥ You are a princess, designed to mature into a queen – Ephesians 4:13
- ♥ You are loved, chosen, saved/sealed, and a new person in Christ – Ephesians 1-2;1 Peter 2:9

Purpose Point: Live your life in a way that reflects who you are, a child of God.

Your value:

- ♥ Your price is far above rubies - Proverbs 10:31
- ♥ God bought you with a high price - 1 Corinthians 6:20
- ♥ God purchased your freedom with the blood of His Son, rescuing you from sin and death - Ephesians 1:7
- ♥ Your present value (PV) is priceless; your future value (FV) is priceless.
- ♥ Your face value is priceless. Never inflated, always infinite = forever priceless. Remember, you are so valuable that a price cannot be applied to you!

Purpose Point: Your value cannot be measured to a dollar amount. Know that you have a high value far above rubies or any expensive luxurious car.

Moreover, let's look at this from a deeper perspective. Would you sell your legs for $1 million dollars, or your arms for $2 million? Would you sell your eyes and ears for $5 million? One secret to realizing value is to take inventory of what is valuable – and thank God for it. When you look at it from this perspective, it confirms that you are more valuable than you know. Being grateful and valuing yourself leads to a better quality of life. The most expensive car, house or diamond cannot be compared to your true worth. **Never sell yourself short or settle for less than you deserve.**

Purpose Point: True value comes from God. Anything that God validates as valuable will last forever; it will never depreciate or perish such as salvation, a new spirit, wisdom, and eternal life.

Material things that people consider valuable such as houses, clothes, jewelry, and cars will depreciate or perish sooner or later.

Purpose Point: If you have received Jesus as your Lord and Savior, you have received a new spirit – this is what makes you valuable, not your works, possessions or looks. Your new spirit will experience eternal life if you remain in God. The common saying 'nothing lasts forever' is untrue to a certain extent. Your new spirit will live forever in heaven with God.

<u>**Whose you are:**</u>
- ♥ You are a child of the King, the Most High God, the Creator of the universe – (Galatians 3:26; Romans 8:19). You've been adopted into His family – Ephesians 1:5
- ♥ God is both your Creator and Heavenly Father – you belong to Him (Genesis 1:37; Galatians 4:6)

You may have come from a poor or dysfunctional family, or maybe you had no family at all, but when you accept Jesus you become adopted into a new family, a royal family with royal blood. All things become new. **Jesus is the King of all kings, Lord of all lords and the Prince of Peace. And since you have been adopted into his royal family that makes you a princess designed to mature into a queen.**

Purpose Point: Value yourself, value your God, value your privacy, and value others.

<u>**Where you are going and what you have to look forward to (what belongs to you):**</u>
- ♥ You have a wonderful future (Jeremiah 29:11) on the path to greatness – a path paved with God's promises (e.g. provision, protection, favor, healing, peace, joy, prosperity, deliverance, hope, eternal life/heaven, and rewards for carrying out your calling). You have an inheritance (Ephesians 1:11).

Purpose Point: Jesus knew who he was (John 14:6), his purpose, where he came from and where he was going, and so should you. Jesus said, *"I came from the Father and entered the world; now I am leaving the world and going back to the Father."* John 16:28 NIV

Now that you know why you were created, who you are, whose you are, how valuable you are and where you are going, your way of thinking must change. Refuse to believe negative words spoken to you or about you. If you are hurt, depressed or have a low self-esteem, you must change your view about yourself to realize your intrinsic value. The only way to do this is for you to renew your mind with the Word of God and see yourself through the eyes of the one who created you. Read your Bible to learn just how valuable you are and discover all your priceless features and capabilities. You can do all things through Christ who strengthens you.

Purpose Point: Change the way you think about yourself by improving your perception – your reality of you. <u>No need to *verify*</u> what has already been *validated*. <u>No need to *reason*</u> with what has already been deemed *royalty*. **You must change the 'current' you by changing the way you think to manifest who you are (the person you were created to be).**

*"Don't copy the behavior and customs of this world, but **let God transform you into a new person by changing the way you think.** Then you will learn to know God's will for you, which is good and pleasing and perfect."* Romans 12:2

You are God's prized possession; He will not reject or abandon you. You are wanted, you are loved, and you are valued. Say it with me, *'I am wanted, I am loved, I am valued, I am significant, I am special, I have purpose...'*

"...We, out of all creation, became his prized possession." James 1:18

"The Lord will not reject his people, he will not abandon his own special possession."
Psalm 94:14

Whenever you feel less than, unworthy, insignificant, invisible, insufficient, or unwanted, speak and declare what God says about you and the situation. For instance, say, *"I am beautiful, I am valuable, I am a child of God, God loves me, I can do all things through Christ, I am victorious, I am special."* Remember, the Word of God is truth, there is none other. Hence, anyone who speaks contrary to what God says about you is a liar. Do not make yourself out to be a liar by speaking or believing negative things about yourself.
You have built-in meaning – you matter.
So you do not have to look for value or long for it,
simply live what is already in you. You have a purpose on your life!

There is Only one God, Only one Truth, and Only one VALUABLE you!
No matter what you have done, or what someone did to you,
You are highly valued – a Princess, beautiful and amazing.
God has validated your value and created you to be His royal princess…

"Arise, shine, for your light has come, and the glory of the LORD rises upon you."
Isaiah 60:1 NIV

STAND "Your royal <u>Highness</u>" …
You are a child of the King and your value is infinitely High!
Therefore, hold your head up high and *Walk in your Woman's Worth!*
Release the Princess within you!

"...walk in a manner worthy of the calling to which you have been called,"
Ephesians 4:1 ESV

*"And now, my daughter, do not fear. I will do for you all that you ask, for all my fellow townsmen know that **you are a worthy woman**."* Ruth 3:11 ESV

God's love is the true love you have been longing for; only He can fill this void.
Your value and identity are found in God…know who you are!

"...Once you had no identity as a people; now you are God's people. Once you received no mercy; now you have received God's mercy." 1 Peter 2:10

"Victory in Value" Prayer: *"I pray that from his glorious, unlimited resources he will empower you with inner strength through his Spirit. Then Christ will make his home in your hearts as you trust in him. Your roots will grow down into God's love and keep you strong. And may you have the power to understand, as all God's people should, how wide, how long, how high, and how deep his love is. May you experience the love of Christ, though it is too great to understand fully. Then you will be made complete with all the fullness of life and power that comes from God. Now all glory to God, who is able, through his mighty power at work within us, to accomplish infinitely more than we might ask or think. Glory to him in the church and in Christ Jesus through all generations forever and ever! Amen."*
Ephesians 3:16-21

Chapter 5
Predestined Princess

*"In him we have obtained an inheritance, having been **predestined** according to the purpose of him who works all things according to the counsel of his will..."* Ephesians 1:11 ESV

Text Term: Pre·[des·tine] - to destine, decree, determine, appoint, or settle beforehand; to designate, assign, or dedicate in advance (Source: Meriam-Webster); to destine in advance; foreordain; predetermine; to set apart for a particular use, purpose or design (dictionary.com).

Did you know that you existed as God's special princess before you were born? That's right, God took you out of eternity and placed you on earth for such a time as this. Before the foundations of the world, God knew you. He set your end before the beginning. God said, *"I make known the end from the beginning...My purpose will stand..."* Isaiah 46:10 NIV

"He has made everything beautiful in its time. He has also set eternity in the human heart; yet no one can fathom what God has done from beginning to end." Ecclesiastes 3:11 NIV

God said, *"**I knew you before I formed you** in your mother's womb. **Before you were born I set you** apart and appointed you as my prophet to the nations."* Jeremiah 1:5

*"Even **before he made the world, God loved us and chose us in Christ** to be holy and without fault in his eyes. **God decided in advance to adopt us into his own family by bringing us to himself through Jesus Christ.** This is what he wanted to do, and it gave him great pleasure."* Ephesians 1:4-5

So, you see, you do not have to dream about being a princess, you were born that way. Now that you know your value, God is saying, *'Will my Princesses please STAND and prepare for purpose!'* He wants you, the beautiful woman that He created before time, to stop wandering around trying to be like everyone else. He wants you to stop wondering about your self-worth and wallowing in low self-esteem, self-pity, and wrong thinking. Instead, He wants you to beautify your heart, know your identity and value, and STAND like the Princess you are!!!

Know who you are
Understand your value, capability and purpose

Make life-long positive choices
Choose to do what is right...apply godly principles

He is ever ready and waiting to cause something new and exciting to happen in your life, so STAND and grab hold to your crown!

*"...**he will give a crown of beauty** for ashes, a joyous blessing instead of mourning, festive praise instead of despair. In their righteousness, they will be like great oaks that the LORD has planted for his own glory."* Isaiah 61:3

"How long will you wander, my wayward daughter? For the Lord will cause something new and different to happen..." Jeremiah 31:22

*"I am writing to the **chosen lady** and to her children, whom I love in the truth — as does everyone else who knows the truth — because the truth lives in us and will be with us forever."* 2 John 1:1-2

*"...**And those he predestined, he also called**; those he called, he also justified; those he justified, he also glorified."* Romans 8:30 NIV

God says, "You are a Predestined Priceless Precious Princess Possessing Powerful Purpose...S.T.A.N.D.!!!"
Set yourself apart
Take your place
Affirm your identity
Nullify your past
Demonstrate your purpose

"Listen to me, O royal daughter, take to heart what I say." Psalm 45:10

Set yourself apart

Before time, when God predestined you to be a princess, He did so by setting you apart and choosing you as His very own.

*"**But you are a chosen people, a royal priesthood**, a holy nation, God's special possession, that you may declare the praises of him who called you out of darkness into his wonderful light."* 1 Peter 2:9 NIV

*"For God knew his people in advance, and **he chose them** to become like his Son..."* Romans 8:29

*"**You didn't choose me. I chose you. I appointed you to go and produce lasting fruit** [results], so that the Father will give you whatever you ask for, using my name."* John 15:16

Setting someone apart means to separate and make different from everyone else, to make available for a specific purpose. God is all knowing; He knows the end from the beginning. He knows what will happen before it actually does. He finishes before He starts. God knew His plans and purposes for you before your mother and father conceived you. These plans are good plans and will lead you to a good life via the Princess's Pathway. But these plans can only come to pass when you accept Jesus and surrender your life to Him.

Remember, *"The Lord...said, I knew you before I formed you in your mother's womb. Before you were born **I set you apart**..."* Jeremiah 1:5

"For I know the plans I have for you, says the Lord. They are plans for good and not for disaster, to give you a future and a hope." Jeremiah 29:11

When you surrender your life to God, you now stand on common ground with Him. Just as He has set you apart in the spiritual, you should begin to set yourself apart physically and mentally by making the right decisions in the natural. One important aspect of standing is to not only realize your value, but to implement godly values and standards as well.

Purpose Point: Before you walk with God, you must first stand for God. Stand and walk in God's ways! Stand on the Word of God...Stand for the Word of God...Stand boldly in life so you can stand confidently before God after death. Stand firm in the faith!

The Lord says, *"...Unless your faith is firm, I cannot make you **stand firm**."* Isaiah 7:9

*"It is by our actions that we know we are living in the truth, so we will be confident when we **stand** before the Lord..."* 1 John 3:19

*"The grass withers, and the flowers fade, but **the word of our God will stand forever**."* Isaiah 40:8

Purpose Point: A common saying is, *"If you don't stand for something, you'll fall for anything."* In other words, if you do not strongly believe in something and support what you believe in, then you will have no limitations and will do or accept anything that comes your way. Taking a stand also means to consciously decide to do or not to do something.

For example, if a person took a stand against drugs by deciding not to do drugs, then when someone offered him drugs, he would most likely reject it. Whereas a person who has not yet made the decision to not do drugs would probably think about it when someone offered. Therefore, it is so important to decide early in life what you will and will not stand for. Deciding early will help you to make the right decisions when things come your way (i.e. peer pressure, temptation, new doctrines, unhealthy associations, etc.)

Dr. Martin Luther King, Jr. once said, *"If you cannot find something in life to die for, then life is not worth living."* In other words, you should find something in life to stand for and act on what you believe; if you do not, then your life is really not fit to live. You should live your life in a way to make it count for something and to make a difference in the world. Dr. Martin Luther King, Jr. stood for civil rights and racial equality and was willing to die for it. If he and others did not take this stand, racial injustice and inequality would have stood unhindered.

God wants you to stand for Him, believe in Him and do what you believe by obeying His commands. He is not asking you to die for Him physically, although some people did and still do today, but He is asking you to die to sin and self by refusing to do the wrong things. He wants you to be loyal and faithful to what you stand for and not engage in behaviors that contradict His Word. When you engage in activities that are different from what you believe and profess, we call this hypocrisy or a double standard – *"The Lord despises double standards of every kind."* Proverbs 20:10

Purpose Point: Accepting Jesus, standing for good things and not standing for bad means standing for God – when you stand for something you make your life count for something.

Purpose Point: One important principle to standing and setting yourself apart is to set standards for yourself. **Setting standards means establishing rules for yourself or moral principles that guide your conduct and behavior**. The foundation of these rules and principles should be based on God's Word – the Bible. For example, in the Bible God says, "Do not steal" (Exodus 20:15); therefore, one standard you should set for yourself is not to steal.

Standards without Christianity and Christianity without standards leads to failure and destruction.

Purpose Point: Your belief and trust in God should define who you really are. The Christian principles and standards that you stand on should guide you in your decision making. **Without standards you will fall for anything, and without Christianity (Jesus) you could fall to ruin despite your standards.**

"Stop fooling yourselves, if you think you are wise by this world's standards, you will have to become a fool so you can become wise by God's standards. For the wisdom of this world is foolishness to God." 1 Corinthians 3:18-19

God says, when the devil comes in like a flood by attacking you from every angle – problem after problem, God will lift up a standard against him. In the same way, when gangs, no good guys, so-called friends, perpetuators, and negative peer pressure (your enemies) come in like a flood to try to get you to do wrong, you should lift up the ***standards*** you have set against them. Say "No" and mean it, walk away…STAND your ground!

"When the enemy comes in like a flood, The Spirit of the LORD will lift up a standard against him." Isaiah 59:19 NKJV

Purpose Point: Not setting standards for yourself empowers and encourages your enemies.

Some additional standards or rules you should set for yourself that are based on the Word of God, include, but are not limited to:

1. Do not kill (Exodus 20)
2. Do not envy or covet (Exodus 20)
3. Do not lie or take the Lord's name in vain (Exodus 20)
4. Do not engage in sexual immorality (Romans 1:26-28, 1 Corinthians 6:18)
5. Do not disobey your parents (Exodus 20; Ephesians 6:1)
6. Do not worship other gods/idols (Exodus 20; Exodus 34:14)

7. Do not disrespect authority (Romans 13:1)
8. Do not hate others (Mark 12:31)
9. Do not hold unforgiveness against someone (Matthew 6:14-15)
10. Do not curse or speak evil (Exodus 22:28; Psalm 59:12)

"Your laws are always right; help me to understand them so I may live." Psalm 119:144

S.T.A.N.D. AND LIFT UP YOUR STANDARD!! Reign in life by the rules, restrictions, and restraints that both you and God have set to be successful. You exemplify your value when you exhibit godly values. *"The godly walk with integrity; blessed are their children who follow them."* Proverbs 20:7

"For God knew his people in advance, and he chose them to become like his Son, so that his Son would be the firstborn, with many brothers and sisters." Romans 8:29

Before you were born, God predestined you to be a princess. It has always been God's plan for you to accept and confess Jesus as your Savior and to become adopted into His royal family. Jesus reigns; he is the King of kings and the Lord of lords. He is seated on a throne in heaven at the right hand of God.

You are now a part of His royal family, if you have confessed and believed, and you too will reign, as a princess and queen, but you <u>must</u> act as such. Remember, it is not enough for you to just say you believe in God, you must also obey Him; and it is not enough to say that you are a princess, you must act the part.

Here is how: God is a gentleman. He will not force his plans and purposes on you. He allows you to make your own decisions about your life. He will tell you what you should do, but He will not force you to do it. Although God has already set you apart, you must agree with this divine separation and <u>make a conscious decision to be different from everyone else</u>. If you want God's plans and purposes to work in your life, you must surrender by agreeing and accepting God's plans for you and be different. Remember, you cannot be a daughter, princess, or friend of God, if you live like the world. Therefore, it is so important that you set yourself apart from the world to be like your Father God and become His daughter, a princess.

"We know that God loves you…and that he chose you to be his own people."
  1 Thessalonians 1:4

"Don't you realize that friendship with this world makes you an enemy of God? I say it again, that if your aim is to enjoy the world, you can't be a friend of God…So humble yourselves before God. Resist the Devil, and he will flee from you. Draw close to God, and God will draw close to you…" James 4:4; James 4:7

"Do not join a crowd that intends to do evil…" Exodus 23:2

Moreover, God wants you to be holy, just as He is holy. It is important to understand that holiness is not living like a nun in a church or wearing long dresses and no makeup. <u>Simply put, holiness is one mind with God</u> – believing what God believes and doing what He says to do. You are God's special princess, His daughter; therefore, you should possess your Father's characteristics by thinking like Him and acting like Him. In order to possess your Father's characteristics and act like Him, you must set yourself apart from everyone else. You must be different from the world; you must follow God's ways and not the world's ways. *"...You should behave instead like God's very own children, adopted into his family – calling him Father."* Romans 8:15

Setting yourself apart also means <u>sanctification</u>. When you sanctify yourself, you are taking yourself out of the world's way of doing things to be used for God's special purpose. Sanctification does not mean you are a religious fanatic; it only means that you are preparing yourself to be used by God in a mighty way. This is not a bad thing as the world makes it out to be. The world makes fun of things it does not understand.

Purpose Point: The sanctification *process* is a team effort, where you *choose* to live a life according to God's commands and He empowers you to do so by the power of His Holy Spirit. *A process takes time; it is not instantaneous. God is with you throughout the sanctification process. He is working with you and in you* (Philippians 2:13).

Setting yourself apart for God allows you to be everything that God created you to be. Separating yourself will assist you in fulfilling your purpose and destiny. Everybody was created for a purpose, and for us to discover and fulfill that purpose we must separate ourselves from the world to break free from all the distractions, hindrances, temptations, and negative influences. God wants His daughters, His princesses, to separate themselves from sinful behaviors and those who live a life full of disobedience and wickedness.

Purpose Point:

- Setting yourself apart simply means <u>not</u> doing what the world does, such as drugs, violence, sexual immorality, lying, stealing, fighting, gossiping, cheating, murdering, being disobedient to parents, disrespecting authority, being selfish, prideful, rude and malicious, engaging in criminal activities, etc.
- The secret to setting yourself apart is to set your mind or make a conscious decision to be set apart for God and His purpose for your life. Colossians 3:2 NIV states: *"Set your minds on things above, not on earthly things."*
- Setting yourself apart means to live for God and possess His characteristics such as love, kindness, honesty, loyalty, respect, integrity, wise speech, humility, purity, forgiveness, mercy, grace, marriage, etc. This is true kingdom living!

"...For we are the temple of the living God...As God said: I will live in them and walk among them. I will be their God, and they will be my people. Therefore, come out from them and <u>**separate yourselves**</u> *from them, says the Lord. Don't touch filthy things, and I will welcome you. And I will be your Father, and you will be my sons and* **daughters***, says the Lord Almighty."* 2 Corinthians 6:16-18

When you accept Jesus as your Lord and Savior, turn away from your sins (repent) and refuse to act like the world, you have set yourself apart – you have separated yourself from foolish living.

"There was a time when some of you were just like that, but now your sins have been washed away, and you have been **set apart** *for God. You have been made right with God because of what the Lord Jesus Christ and the Spirit of our God have done for you."* 1 Corinthians 6:11

Purpose Point:
- Don't be similar, be different
- Don't be normal, be abnormal
- Don't be common, be uncommon
- Don't be usual, be unusual
- Don't be ordinary, be extraordinary
- Don't be average, be excellent
- Don't be everywhere, be rare
- Don't be unholy, be holy
- Don't be ungodly, be godly
- Don't be natural, be supernatural
- Don't be "one size fits all", XL (eXceL)

Purpose Point: Which would you rather be – a blender or a coffee maker?

A blender mixes ingredients and a coffee maker produces one particular ingredient. Don't be a blender and try to blend in with everyone else. If you do, you will surely get mixed up and messed up in the process. Be a coffee maker; produce one exceptional ingredient that will energize and maximize your purpose.

Purpose Point: When you set yourself apart, people may talk about you. But be confident and stand firm. Don't be afraid. God saved you to sanctify you for His purpose and glory.

"Of course, your former friends are very surprised when you no longer join them in the wicked things they do, and they say evil things about you. But just remember that they will have to face God, who will judge everyone, both the living and the dead." 1 Peter 4:4-5

Jesus said, God redeems people *"...to open their eyes, so that they may turn from darkness to light and from the power of Satan to God, **that they may receive forgiveness of sins and a place among those who are sanctified by faith in me**."* Acts 26:18 ESV

Purpose Point: Being different does not block your success, it creates it.

God set people apart all throughout the Bible...

*"...Aaron and his sons...will be **set apart** from the common people. They will be my priests and will minister to me. Make special clothing for Aaron to show **his separation to God** – beautiful garments that will lead dignity to his work."* Exodus 28:1-2

Some people of the Bible proudly displayed how they were set apart for God by wearing medallions – they were not afraid or ashamed of their commitment to God...

*"...They made the sacred medallion of pure gold to be worn on the front... they inscribed it with these words: **"SET APART AS HOLY TO THE LORD."*** Exodus 39:30 (Exodus 28:36-37)

Don't be ashamed to profess or exhibit your devotion to God.

Purpose Point: A princess is not ashamed of her king. She stands by him confidently for everyone to see. Like so, as a true princess, you cannot be ashamed of your King, Jesus. It is because of him that you are a princess in the first place. God adopted you into His royal family because of what Jesus did. He has given you so much, from salvation to eternal life; therefore, separate yourself from the world and prepare yourself for your King! Stand by him confidently and boldly! Don't be ashamed to tell people that you have set yourself apart for God.

Jesus said, if anyone is ashamed of him and his message, he will also be ashamed of that person.

"If anyone is ashamed of me and my message, the Son of Man will be ashamed of that person when he returns in his glory and in the glory of the Father and the holy angels." Luke 9:26

God separated Jesus from the world...

*"...He has been **set apart from sinners** and has been given the highest place of honor in heaven."* Hebrews 7:26

Jesus was divinely separated and given the highest place of honor in heaven – seated at the right hand of God. Like so, when God separated you as His princess, He gave you the highest place of honor on earth. Therefore, you must stand and take your rightful place in the world.

<u>T</u>ake your place

Have you ever been told to get in line in an assigned order or position? For instance, may be when you were younger in school you were required to get in a straight line by last name – or maybe when you were involved in a ceremony like a wedding or graduation you were asked to get in a particular order. But before you were able to take your place in line and get to the right position, you first had to stand and walk (maneuver) to get there, right? Like so, as God's predestined princess, He has assigned you to a certain position on earth. I am not talking about getting in a physical line, but in a spiritual position. However, you must first S.T.A.N.D. and walk in your God-given purpose to get there. As a special princess, you have a special role to play in your life and in the lives of others. This position or role is the place where you carry out your purpose in life. Remember, your purpose is the reason why God created you and permitted you to be born.

Purpose Point: God is calling you to a higher place. *STAND* behind Jesus and *follow* Him.

What is your position? How do you get to your place of position?

When we talk about your position or place, we are talking about your title, duties, responsibilities and/or authority. For instance, a person who works for a company may have the position as a Customer Service Representative (CSR). Hence, their title would be a CSR, and their duties and responsibilities may be to assist customers, resolve customer issues and increase sales. Their authority would be in the scope of talking to customers and resolving issues.

Likewise, you serve or work for the Kingdom of God. Your position is a woman of God, a princess. Your duties and responsibilities include loving your spiritual King (God/Jesus) by obeying His commands, worshiping, praising, and ministering to Him, loving and serving others, loving your natural king (husband) and family, telling others about Jesus and discipling or mentoring them. You specialize in human resources, hospitality, operations management, and engineering by helping to fulfill the needs of others and build the kingdom of God.

God has given you the authority to change your life and the lives of others. He has also given you authority over anything that gets in your way such as your enemies – obstacles, oppositions, the devil, and demons, which we will talk about later. Therefore, take your rightful place and stand in your delegated authority! Jesus said, *"With my authority, take this message of repentance to all the nations...There is forgiveness of sins for all who turn to me. You are witnesses of all these things."* Luke 24:47-48

Purpose Point: Have you ever heard an adult say, *"You need to stay in a child's place?"* In other words, a child's place is just that, that of a child. And the child's duties and responsibilities include respecting parents and adults/authority, attending school and performing well academically. A child does not have any authority to make decisions over an adult. Hence, if you are a child/teen, your duties and responsibilities are to respect your parents, go to school, make good grades, and stay out of trouble. Just like your parents' duties and responsibilities are to protect, feed, shelter and clothe you. **Respect authority.** Remember, obeying your parents is God's first commandment with a promise. **And this is the promise – if you obey and honor your parents, then you will live a long life, full of blessing** (Ephesians 6:1-3).

To sum it up, to get to your place, your God-given position in life...
- First, you must believe, confess, and obey Jesus
- Secondly, you must beautify your heart by looking in the mirror (the Bible), guarding your gateways and eliminating ungodly things and people from your life
- Thirdly, you must realize your value and renew your mind with the Word of God
- Lastly, you must set yourself apart from the world.

Purpose Point: When you take your proper place and position in life, you will not have to struggle or fight through life's obstacles on your own. You can walk in victory on the Princess's Pathway. God declares in 2 Chronicles 20:17, *"But you will not even need to fight.* ***Take your positions; then stand*** *still and watch the LORD's victory. He is with you..."*

God will help you to get to your proper place. As I said earlier, God is like a navigation system (GPS). He will give you clear instructions on how to get to your destination safely, but you must follow them. He will help you to avoid the danger zones, dead ends, roadblocks, and rough roads, if you listen and obey. Only by listening and obeying was Jesus able to get to his highest place of honor in heaven – right next to God. *The LORD says, "I will guide you along the best pathway for your life. I will advise you and watch over you."* Psalm 32:8

Pray to God: *"Guide my steps by your word, so I will not be overcome by evil."* Psalm 119:133 *Let the morning bring me word of your unfailing love, for I have put my trust in you. Show me the way I should go, for to you I entrust my life. Rescue me from my enemies, Lord, for I hide myself in you. Teach me to do your will, for you are my God; may your good Spirit lead me on level ground. For your name's sake, Lord, preserve my life..."* Psalm 143:8-11 NIV

Purpose Point: Only by obeying God and setting yourself apart are you able to get to your highest place of honor.

Purpose Point: When you are in God's will and purpose you are in the right place. His favor, doors of opportunity, big breaks and bountiful blessings will follow and precede you. He alone will help you to be in the right place at the right time. *"The LORD directs the steps of the godly. He delights in every detail of their lives. Though they stumble, they will never fall, for the LORD holds them by the hand."* Psalm 37:23-24

Purpose Point: Lead others and do not follow those who live or lead in error. If you follow, you could get lost and arrive at a dead end. Know where you are going, and let others follow you. It is okay, however, to follow godly leaders who will help you to get to your place of purpose (Hebrews 6:12; 1 Corinthians 11:1). It is only through following a true leader that we become leaders within ourselves. Jesus is the great Leader and possesses all the qualities of impeccable leadership. He goes before you paving, preparing, and protecting the pathway... Follow Jesus! Jesus said, *"If anyone wants to come after Me, he must deny himself and take up his cross and follow Me."* Matthew 16:24 BSB

Purpose Point: Leaders stand and mark their own path of success. Followers can sometimes be weak; it is only through following a leader that they are made strong. Be that leader and stand firm! Be a good influence on others and impact lives in a positive way.

*"So take a new grip with your tired hands and **stand firm on your shaky legs.** Mark out a straight path for your feet. Then those who follow you, though they are weak and lame, will not stumble and fall but will become strong."* Hebrews 12:12

Purpose Point: If you are not in the right place, you are out of order and cannot fulfill your definite divine purpose. If you fall out of line, get up and get back in line in the correct position.

"Notice the way God does things; then fall into line. Don't fight the ways of God, for who can straighten out what he has made crooked?" Ecclesiastes 7:13

Purpose Point: God is a God of order so you must get in order by getting in the proper position or place that God has predestined for you to be. Pray and ask God to put you in the proper position. When you follow God, you become positioned for success – a place of prosperity.

Purpose Point: Everyone's position or place is different because everyone has a different purpose and serves a different role. Some may be first, second or last in a worldly or spiritual gift sense (later discussed), but all God's children are first in His heart. He loves us all the same.

For example, from a worldly or workplace perspective, a CEO of a company would come first in terms of his authority, secondly an Executive Director, then a Manager and so on. Although the CEO may be perceived as first, God loves them all equally. And from a spiritual gift standpoint, the Bible says: *"Now all of you together are Christ's body, and each one of you is a separate and necessary part of it. Here is a list of some of the members that **God has placed** in the body of Christ: "First are apostles, second are prophets, third are teachers, then those who do miracles, those who have the gift of healing, those who can help others, those who can get others to work together, those who speak in unknown languages."*
1 Corinthians 12:27-28   In the same manner, God loves them all the same.

Take your place as a woman and daughter of God, as a minister of God, as a believer of God. Take your place in purity, obedience, love, value, kindness, humility, wisdom, faith, and peace.

Affirm your Identity

Text Term: Affirm means to confirm what is true; an affirmation is a confident assurance or valid statement of positive declaration. Affirmations include praise, positive reinforcement, and words of encouragement from others or self, which help form who you become and thus who you are.

Our parents or guardians should affirm us early in life and guide, teach and tell us who we are as a woman. They should affirm our value by making us feel important and loved, and direct us to successful womanhood. They should teach us about boys, sex, dating, marriage, and other important matters so we know what to expect and how to respond. When our parents do not tell us who we are early in life, we become curious and start searching on our own. We begin to get involved in unhealthy relationships while subconsciously hoping that someone will tell us who we are and give us the attention and affirmation we desperately seek and long for.

The bad and unhealthy relationships that people fall prey to will most likely involve pre-marital sex, drugs, alcohol, gangs, criminal activities, or other negative behaviors—which could all bring an enormous amount of heartache, pain, and emotional turmoil. These relationships damage our self-esteem, fill us with rejection and take the little dignity and identity we once had. We are then left worse off than before. But even if your parents didn't affirm your value or explain your significance as a woman, and even if someone has hurt you and damaged your self-esteem, you must affirm your identity (who you are in Christ) to get where God wants you to be. Your identity is who you are; and as you've learned you are a child of the Most High God. You are highly valued, a royal princess.

STAND with your head up high, shoulders straight and affirm your identity by saying,

"I am who God says I am; I am a daughter of God; I am valuable and precious; I am beautiful; I am an overcomer; I am victorious; I am healed; I am loved; I am a royal princess awaiting my king and I am fulfilling my destiny."

This is your validated identity and you have just affirmed it; now believe it and see yourself as the valuable princess you are! Stand and walk in your worth!

Purpose Point: Self-talk affirmations are positive and in the now. For example, 'I am amazing' and not 'I will be amazing' or 'I was amazing'. For best results, repeat affirmations in the mirror.

Purpose Point: Say affirmations daily to allow it to sink deep into your heart. Most importantly, meditate on God's Word – His promises, plans and declarations concerning you and affirm what His Word says about you.

Nullify your past

Text Term: Nullify means to void or make inoperative.

Purpose Point: No matter how dark your past, Jesus is the light.

Nullifying your past is such an important topic; it means to not allow the bad things that have happened to you prevent you from enjoying your present and future. Many people allow their past to hold them back in life. They regret something that they did or did not do or regret something that happened to them. They wish they could go back in time and change what happened. They have a hard time forgiving themselves and others for a wrong that was done.

Minute Memoir: Nullifying my past was a big problem for me…forgetting my past and not allowing it to affect me. At one point, I always thought about my past – wondering why this happened and why that happened, and why God allowed it to happen. I hated myself constantly for degrading and debasing myself as a teen and letting a boy treat me any kind of way. But I soon discovered by renewing my mind with the Word of God that what happened is done; I cannot change it, but I can find some purpose in it. I thought to myself and concluded that everything that happened in my life does not have to be in vain; it could be used to help someone else. This very thinking inspired me to write this book.

While constantly looking back in my past, I felt the anger and resentment for myself and my ex-boyfriend get stronger and stronger. It was like I was paralyzed to live; my mind constantly screamed "why, why, why". I could not think about anything else. I constantly compared myself with others thinking how much better, prettier, and happier they are and wished I could be in their place. I could not enjoy my present life and could not see a future for me. I thought that everything was hopeless and that I really screwed up. I soon found hope in God, and He gradually changed my view about myself. *I grew from pitiful to powerful, from a victim to a victor and from a pessimist to a princess. A purpose was born from a thorn – an annoying, relentless pain that just did not seem to go away. God stepped in, helped me out and pulled me through — and I followed His lead.* You must let the bad things from your past go, if you want to get to the place God has for you.

Purpose Point: When it comes to a painful past, *learn from it, and let it go!* Do not allow the past to determine who you are, instead allow it to fine-tune and refine you…making you stronger, wiser, and better. Do not allow the past to take you under, allow it to bring you over into something greater.

Purpose Point: We cannot change our past, but we can change our present and future – focus on what you can change!

One of my favorite prayers is the Serenity Prayer:

"God grant me the serenity
To accept the things I cannot change;
Courage to change the things I can;
And wisdom to know the difference.
Living one day at a time; Enjoying one moment at a time;
Accepting hardships as the pathway to peace; Taking, as He did, this sinful world
As it is, not as I would have it; Trusting that He will make all things right
If I surrender to His Will; So that I may be reasonably happy in this life
And supremely happy with Him
Forever and ever in the next.
Amen." – Attributed to Reinhold Niebuhr

Minute Memoir: For many years I hated myself for the mistakes I made in my past as a teen. It was extremely difficult for me to forgive myself for the wrong choices I made, particularly the decision to have sex at such an early age. But I knew that in order to move forward in life, I had to forgive myself. I thought to myself, *'Yes, I made a mistake. Yes, I caused myself unnecessary pain and turmoil'* but making the decision to believe and accept Christ far outweighs and supersedes all the wrong decisions that I ever made in the past and will ever make in the future.

God did not force me to believe in Him or accept Jesus, that was a decision that I made on my own. And once I believed and accepted Jesus, I was saved by God's special favor. I cannot take credit for salvation because salvation is a gift that cannot be bought or earned. But I can take credit for making the most important decision that I would ever make in my life – and that is choosing to accept Jesus as my Lord and Savior. **Therefore, give yourself some credit and don't be too hard on yourself.** Regardless of your past, God can restore what is broken and bruised and give you a new life free from the past and pain, if you believe and surrender it to Him.

*"...**he will give a crown of beauty** for ashes, a joyous blessing instead of mourning, festive praise instead of despair. In their righteousness, they will be like great oaks that the LORD has planted for his own glory."* Isaiah 61:3

"God saved you by his special favor when you believed. And you can't take credit for this; it is a gift from God." Ephesians 2:8

Purpose Point: Constantly talking about the past is reliving the past; talk positively about your present and future and live there instead. However, if you do constantly talk about the past, let it be for the purpose of informing and transforming the lives of others. *Information coupled with experience results in transformation.* You can know something, but if you never experienced it, your knowledge is minimum; but if you know something and experienced that very thing, your knowledge is maximized and transformational. **You can change what the enemy meant for your bad by packaging your past differently, and delivering it with authenticity, humility, grace, courage, and lessons learned.** Another instance where you may talk about your past is when you are seeking help to transform and heal self through counseling or therapy – this too can prove to be beneficial.

Purpose Point: If what was behind you was really important, don't you think God would have given you eyes in the back of your head? God gave us eyes in the front so that we can see up close in our present, and vision to see far away into our future. The only way we can see what is behind us is if we look back; another possible way would be through a mirror. Mirrors reflect anything in its path, including everything behind you if you are looking ahead in front of it. To help you get over your past, you may need to remove some mirrors. These mirrors may include bad relationships, mementos (cards, letters, gifts, pictures, videos, keepsakes, etc.) and familiar places. You might be trying to look ahead, but these mirrors are reflecting your past, the things that are behind you. Remove these mirrors and emotional strongholds, and do not look back.

Sodom and Gomorrah
Many years ago, God destroyed two cities, Sodom and Gomorrah, because the people who lived there were wicked. The men had sex with other men, and they even tried to have sex with God's male angels which at the time were in human form. The people were hateful, cruel and evil, and participated in every kind of wicked act. As a result, God decided to destroy them by raining fire from the sky, but He allowed those who were godly to escape the fiery destruction. His angels directed all the godly people out of the city before it was destroyed; however, the angels told them while they were leaving that they could not look back or they would die too. One lady did not listen, and she looked back. She was immediately destroyed and turned into a pillar of salt. The reason that I mentioned this story was to stress the importance of not looking back when it can negatively impact your life.

Purpose Point: God is trying to destroy your painful past and take you to a new life...but are you still looking back? Do not allow your past to turn you into a pile of pain with grains of depression, regret, guilt, and low self-esteem. Keep looking ahead so you can live. Trust in God to lead you through all the difficulties of your past.

Purpose Point: If you live in the past, you cannot live in the present or grow in the future. And if you don't grow, you cannot truly live and fulfill your purpose. We must get pass the past, embrace the present, envision and prepare for the future.

Four (4) other stories that come to mind from the Bible are:

1. King David
King David was highly favored by God. He loved him dearly. God gave David all the riches in the world and set him above all his enemies. But one day David began to do evil things in the sight of the Lord. As David was looking out over his city from a roof, he saw this beautiful woman from afar. He was instantly captivated by her beauty and wanted to sleep with her. He sent his servant to find out who she was and soon discovered that she was married. He later ordered his servants to summon her to his room. She came as requested; he slept with her and she became pregnant. He later ordered her husband into battle and put him on the front line so that he could be killed. Her husband died and David then took her as his wife; hence, David was both a murderer and an adulterer. God sent one of his prophets to convict David of his sins. David then confessed his sins against God (2 Samuel 11-12). The prophet then told David, *"...the Lord has forgiven you, and you won't die for this sin..."* 2 Samuel 12:13 God did, however, chastise David for his mistakes, but He did not deny him. God continued to love David, despite his many transgressions. What made David so different from other transgressors was that he had a heart for God. For God said, *"David son of Jesse is a man after my own heart, for he will do everything I want him to."* Acts 13:22

Purpose Point: You know you have a heart for God when your main aim and purpose is to please Him. And when you have a heart for God, God grants you a fresh start with fresh favor despite your past and present mistakes.

2. Saul, also known as Paul

Saul was also a murderer. He persecuted Christians. He was eager to destroy all the people who followed Jesus. But Jesus appeared to him one day and asked, *"Saul! Saul! why are you persecuting me?"*; he also made Saul blind (Acts 9:3-16). This one incident changed Saul's life and motivated him to believe and serve God. God later restored Saul's vision and changed his name from Saul to Paul. Despite what Saul did, God still chose him to preach his message and write nearly half of the New Testament in the Bible.

The Lord said, *"...for Saul is my chosen instrument to take my message to the Gentiles and to kings, as well as to the people of Israel."* Acts 9:15

3. Joseph

A young man named Joseph had several brothers who were very jealous of him. They were jealous because God had revealed to Joseph many great dreams. They were also jealous because they felt their father loved Joseph more than he loved them. One day they saw Joseph walking towards them, and they all decided to kill him. But one of Joseph's brothers spoke up and said, *"Let's not kill him...throw him alive into this pit...that way he will die without our having to touch him."* Genesis 37:21-22   So they threw him into a pit, but they later saw some people coming who purchased slaves, so they took Joseph out of the pit and sold him into slavery. Afterwards, they took Joseph's coat and dipped it in camel's blood. They then took his coat to their father and told him that Joseph was attacked and eaten by a wild animal. His father was devastated and mourned the concocted death of his son.

The people who purchased Joseph as a slave took him to Egypt. God gave Joseph favor with the king of Egypt and Joseph was later appointed as governor of Egypt. Joseph lived lavishly in a palace with abundant riches, while back at home Joseph's brothers and father ran out of food and were on the verge of starving to death. His brothers then went to Egypt to buy food unaware that Joseph was there and not knowing that Joseph was the governor. When they saw Joseph, they did not recognize him, but Joseph recognized them. Joseph later revealed himself to his brothers and they were speechless (Genesis 37-45). Joseph said, *"But **don't be angry with yourselves** that you did this to me, for God did it. He sent me here ahead of you to preserve your lives."* Genesis 45:5

Purpose Point: Don't be angry with yourself. You may not always understand the pit, but sometimes it is used to get you to your palace.

Purpose Point: Some things that happen in our past happen for a reason. When these things are happening, it may seem bad at the time, but later we could discover the real reason for it. God uses people and situations (good or bad) to take us to our destiny. He does not waste anything. Although it may seem that people are working against us, God could be using them to bring us to our place of purpose. The unfortunate events that happened in my teen years were the very circumstances that led me to an intimate relationship with God.

"...God causes everything to work together for the good of those who love God and are called according to his purpose for them. For God knew his people in advance, and he chose them to become like his Son [Jesus], so that his Son would be the firstborn, with many brothers and sisters." Romans 8:28-29

"For God can use sorrow in our lives to help us turn away from sin and seek salvation. We will never regret that kind of sorrow. But sorrow without repentance is the kind that results in death." 2 Corinthians 7:10

Purpose Point: Our past can be used to produce good in our lives and in the lives of others. Through our past comes experience. We can use our past experiences to help others and help ourselves to grow and become better.

4. Jesus

As you know, Jesus was killed for your sins. He was bruised, wounded, beaten, whipped and then nailed to the cross through the piercing of his hands and feet. He was the ultimate sacrifice submitted to God for the forgiveness of your sins and the assurance of eternal life. But before Jesus died, he said, *"Father, forgive these people, because they don't know what they are doing."* Luke 23:34

People also killed the disciples of Jesus. One disciple, Stephen, was viciously murdered. They threw stones at Stephen and killed him because he told people about Jesus. But before Stephen died, he said, *"'Lord, don't charge them with this sin.' And with that, he died."* Acts 7:60   Saul (later known as Paul) helped to kill Stephen.

Purpose Point: The first two stories of David and Saul dealt with mistakes that they made on their own and later regretted to the extent of them having to forgive themselves. The last two stories of Joseph and Jesus dealt with things that were done to them by other people to the extent of them *choosing* to forgive others. The point is that you must find it within yourself the courage to forgive yourself and others. If you have confessed and repented to God, God has forgiven you for all your sins, and has also forgotten them.

So again, regardless of what you have done, if you have confessed and repented, God has forgiven you. If David and Saul (Paul) did not forgive themselves, they could have not fulfilled their purpose or been used by God. There may be some consequences that you must face as a result of your mistakes, but the fact is that God has forgiven you, doesn't remember your sins (Hebrews 8:12), and will help you through all the difficulties of your past, if you trust Him.

Jesus said, *"I assure you that any sin can be forgiven, including blasphemy; but anyone who blasphemes against the Holy Spirit will never be forgiven."* Mark 3:28-29

The Lord said, *"...And I will forgive their wickedness, and I will never again remember their sins."* Jeremiah 31:34

Purpose Point: If God can forgive and forget, so can you. God wants to do something new in your life. He says: *"But forget all that—it is nothing compared to what I am going to do. For I am about to do something new. See, I have already begun! Do you not see it? **I will make a pathway through the wilderness**. I will create rivers in the dry wasteland."* Isaiah 43:18-19
When you forgive yourself and others, you position yourself to be used by God. God cannot use you if you are sad, angry, bitter, guilt-stricken and depressed all the time. Forgiving yourself and others releases you from the stress, sadness and depression that holds you down and holds you bound. Saul killed many Christians, and later became a Christian himself. Think about how hard it was for him to forgive himself, but he did. It was only until Saul forgave himself and put his past behind him that he was able to be used by God. Saul, later named Paul, asserted the following:

"...those who become Christians become new persons. They are not the same anymore, for the old life is gone. A new life has begun! All this newness of life is from God, who brought us back to himself through what Christ did..." 2 Corinthians 5:17-18

"So now there is no condemnation for those who belong to Christ Jesus." Romans 8:1

"...I keep working toward that day when I will finally be all that Christ Jesus saved me for and wants me to be. No, dear friends, I am still not all I should be, but I am focusing all my energies on this one thing: **_Forgetting the past and looking forward to what lies ahead, I strain to reach the end of the race and receive the prize for which God, through Christ Jesus, is calling us up to heaven._** *I hope all of you who are mature Christians will agree on these things. If you disagree on some point, I believe God will make it plain for you. But we must be sure to obey the truth we have learned already. Dear friends, pattern your lives after mine, and learn from those who follow our example. For I have told you often before...there are many whose conduct shows they are really enemies of the cross of Christ. Their future is eternal destruction. Their god is their appetite, they brag about shameful things, and all they think about is this life here on earth"* Philippians 3:12-19

"Dear brothers and sisters, I love you and long to see you, for you are my joy and reward for my work. So please stay true to the Lord, my dear friends." Philippians 4:1

"...Fix your thoughts on what is true and honorable and right. Think about things that are pure and lovely and admirable. Think about things that are excellent and worthy of praise." Philippians 4:8-9

What Paul is saying in the above scriptures is that when we become adopted into God's royal family, we become a new person spiritually. We are no longer the same old person we use to be. All things become new, so this means the old is no more – it is gone, including your past. Therefore, we no longer have to feel guilty or condemned for what we did or did not do in our past. We should instead work to be all that God created us to be by giving up that old sinful nature – and be all that Jesus died for us to be by forgetting our past and looking forward to what lies ahead. Rather than thinking of bad things from your past, you should think about good things in your present and future and have faith for it (i.e. things that are lovely, excellent, admirable and honorable). Think of the new person you have become – a princess, who is lovely, pure, valuable, and worthy of praise.

And if your past or heart condemns you and declares you to be guilty and unworthy because of the things from your past, remember God is greater than your heart and knows everything about you. If we obey God by loving him and each other, we are no longer guilty even if our thoughts and heart say we are. Your thoughts may say things like: 'You are a nobody; Remember what you did; You're not worthy; You don't deserve to be forgiven; No one loves you; No one wants you.' These are all bad thoughts that try to make you feel bad about yourself, prevent you from forgiving yourself and becoming all that God created you to be. Take Paul's advice; think about good things and believe that you are somebody; believe you are a new person – a princess; believe your past is behind you and good things are ahead of you; believe you are worthy; believe that God has forgiven you; and believe that God will deliver you from all the difficulties of your past.

"Dear children, let us stop just saying we love each other; let us really show it by our actions. It is by our actions that we know we are living in the truth, so we will be confident when we stand before the Lord, even if our hearts condemn us. For God is greater than our hearts, and he knows everything." 1 John 3:18-20

Purpose Point: When we forgive and pray for others it helps God to work in our life and the lives of those who may have hurt us. Saul helped to kill many of Jesus' followers, including Stephen. But before Stephen died, he said, *"Lord don't charge them with this sin."* It could have been this very prayer that encouraged God to work in Saul's life and change him for the better. Maybe you hate those who have hurt you and do not want God to work in their lives for the better. Maybe you wish that something bad will happen to them; but who are you? What makes you so special that you cannot forgive? If Jesus can forgive, if God can forgive, then you can forgive too. Remember, if you do not forgive others, God will not forgive you (Mark 11:26). Not forgiving someone is not worth losing your peace, mind, and soul over. Forgive and pray for those who have hurt you and ask God to help you!

"Make allowance for each other's faults, and forgive anyone who offends you. Remember, the Lord forgave you, so you must forgive others." Colossians 3:13

Minute Memoir: It was extremely difficult for me to forgive my ex-boyfriend, but I did. At one point, I disliked him so much that I did not even want to hear his name, let alone pray for him. But God gave me the strength to do it and gave me empathy for him. He helped me to see *why* he behaved the way he did, instead of concentrating on *what* he did. When growing up my ex-boyfriend saw his stepfather abuse his mother repeatedly, so he only did what he saw. Seeing his mother being abused entered his eye gate and affected his heart in the worst way. His actions were a direct result of what had entered his heart.

Consequences of the Past

Sometimes when you make mistakes and/or when people do you harm, you suffer the consequences for it. These consequences may make it hard for you to forgive yourself and others and can turn into your enemies by holding you back from moving forward. It is important to know that regardless, if your enemies were a direct result of a mistake that you made or a direct result of what someone did to you, God can and will deliver you from <u>all</u> your enemies. Enemies can include a sickness, disease, disorder, a relationship gone wrong, poverty, lack, low self-esteem, guilt, shame, rejection, bad record (i.e. academic transcript, driving record, criminal or credit records), lack of education, etc. All these things can severely put you in a state of depression and hold you back which makes them all an enemy – but God can deliver you from your enemies and restore you with so much more. Our God is full of loving-kindness and tender mercies.

Supporting Scriptures:

"I will rebuild you...you will again be happy and dance merrily..." Jeremiah 31:4

"But in that coming day, all who destroy you will be destroyed, and all your enemies will be sent into exile. Those who plunder you will be plundered, and those who attack you will be attacked. <u>I will give you back your health and heal your wounds, says the Lord.</u>"
Jeremiah 30:16-17

"...I was like a calf that needed training for the yoke and plow. Turn me again to you and restore me, for you alone are the Lord my God. I turned away from God, but then I was sorry. I kicked myself for my stupidity! I was thoroughly ashamed for all I did in my younger days.' Is not Israel still my son, my darling child?", asks the Lord ... I still love him. I long for him and surely will have mercy on him." Jeremiah 31:18-20

"...I have abandoned them because of all their wickedness. Nevertheless, the time will come when <u>I will heal...and give her prosperity and peace. I will restore the fortunes...and rebuild. I will cleanse</u> away their sins against me, and I will forgive all their sins of rebellion. Then this city will bring me joy, glory and honor before all the nations of the earth! The people of the world will see the good I do for my people, and they will tremble with awe at the peace and prosperity I provide for them." Jeremiah 33:5-9

Purpose Point: You can also bring God joy, glory, and honor by doing good and bringing joy to others. God will then manifest good in your life for all to see.

Purpose Point: When you trust God, He can deliver you from the enemies of your past, even if you were wrong or brought it upon yourself.

Purpose Point: Sometimes a person's past does not always equate to bad memories. Their past may have been fun and exciting amid a sinful and selfish lifestyle or living the world's way. This can also become an enemy by tempting someone to go back to living that way after knowing God and accepting Jesus. This temptation can be referred to as a 'nostalgic urge'. When a person gives in to this urge and returns to their past life they are in a backslidden state. The Bible says, *"Don't long for 'the good old days', for you don't know whether they were any better than today. Being wise is as good as being rich; in fact, it is better. Wisdom or money can get you almost anything, but it is important to know that only wisdom can save your life."* Ecclesiastes 7:10-12 In other words, do not look back; be wise and walk into your future!

Moreover, if you have truly beautified your heart, you should not have a desire to live a life contrary to God's Word. You may mess up, but you should not want to remain in the mess. After Paul's conversion and when he truly changed his heart, he said, *"I have been crucified with Christ. It is no longer I who live, but Christ who lives in me. And the life I now live in the flesh I live by faith in the Son of God, who loved me and gave himself for me. I do not nullify the grace of God..."* Galatians 2:20 ESV

"Since Christ has suffered physically, take the same attitude that he had. (A person who has suffered physically no longer sins.) That way you won't be guided by sinful human desires as you live the rest of your lives on earth. Instead, you will be guided by what God wants you to do. You spent enough time in the past doing what unbelievers like to do. You were promiscuous, had sinful desires, got drunk, went to wild parties..." 1 Peter 4:1-3 GW

There are two things that I believe we must do to nullify our past and move forward – (1) Forgive and (2) Trust:

1. Forgive

Forgive yourself

Purpose Point: When you do not forgive yourself, you fight against yourself. And if you fight against yourself, you are doomed and will collapse – you cannot stand.

Jesus said, *"A kingdom at war with itself will collapse. A home divided by itself is doomed. And if Satan is fighting against himself, how can he stand? He would never survive."*
Mark 3:24-26

Purpose Point: Sometimes, it may be hard to forgive yourself because someone is holding unforgiveness against you; and sometimes you have terrible regret and enormous guilt about something you have done. You cannot let this hold you back from forgiving and loving yourself. Do your part by confessing and repenting to God, and let that person know that you made a mistake and sincerely apologize for it. Some situations may be more difficult than others, but that is all you can do. You cannot go back and change the past. I am sure you would, if you could, but you cannot. If that person cannot forgive you, then that is something they will have to deal with on their own. Pray and ask God to help that person to forgive you and help you to forgive yourself.

Forgive others

Purpose Point: If you do not forgive others, including yourself, God will not forgive you (Mark 11:25-26).

Purpose Point: When you genuinely pray for others who have hurt you, it shows that you have forgiven them; this helps to heal the hurt.

Purpose Point: The moment you forgive someone who has hurt you and you convey that forgiveness, it helps the person to begin to forgive themselves.

Purpose Point: When you forgive others, you do it for your benefit, and not necessarily for them. Forgiving others does not mean that you are letting them off the hook, it simply means that you are determined to maintain your hook up with God and the peace that He provides. Forgiving someone releases you from anger, hate, bitterness, resentment, misery, and potential sicknesses and diseases caused by the stress of carrying unforgiveness. Conversely, when you hold unforgiveness against someone these same negative effects could manifest as a result. Remember, if you do not forgive others for their wrongs, God will not forgive you for your wrongs. Therefore, when you forgive others, it benefits you more than it benefits them because God forgives you – which will birth positive things into your life such as inner peace, health, favor, prosperity and the gift of eternal life. Holding unforgiveness against someone is a huge burden that God never intended for us to carry – it is the type of burden that keeps you up at night.

Purpose Point: When you truly forgive others, you do not keep talking about what they did and throwing it up in their face. If you do this, it shows that you have not really forgiven them.

Purpose Point: *What does it mean to forgive and forget?* Forgiving means to release and dismiss a person's offense against you. Forgetting means to not allow what a person did to you to dominate your thinking and behavior. Due to your natural memory function, it is extremely difficult to self- activate amnesia and completely forget a particular occurrence or offense. But you can control what you think, and who you allow to control and affect you negatively. When you constantly rehearse an offense in your mind, you glue it to your heart, and cement the hurt. When you truly forgive, you can truly forget. Releasing the offense through sincere forgiveness removes it from your working (active) memory.

Forgive God

Minute Memoir: Oftentimes, we blame God for all the bad things that has happened in our lives. There were many times that I wondered why God allowed bad things from my past to occur. I looked at other peoples' lives who appeared to be so happy and sure of themselves, and asked God, 'Why me?'. I drove myself crazy trying to figure things out. I finally gave up realizing that I may never figure out the 'why', but I needed to start seeking the 'Who' and discovering the 'What'. I had to start seeking God, the one who created me and knows all things. I had to discover what He wanted me to do with the rest of my life. I realized that there was nothing I could do about my past. I can't change it…and blaming God would get me nowhere. I knew if I had continued to blame myself and God I would forever be unhappy, depressed and oppressed. I knew that I could never benefit or enrich anyone, including myself, living an unhappy and stressed out life playing the victim.

There will be many things to happen in our lives that we will not fully understand. And when these things happen, we will be tempted to blame God for all the bad occurrences. When good things happen, we don't try to figure out why it happened, and seldom do we thank God. But when bad things happen, we try to figure out why it happened and quickly blame God. Maybe you did something wrong for the bad to happen, or maybe you did nothing wrong and bad still happened; regardless, we may never know the real reason for why it happened. And if you blame God, you will stay stuck in a bitter position until you choose to move on.

Purpose Point: God does the impossible in our lives every day. The loss, sorrow, disability, hardship or sickness you face temporarily is a grim reminder of the world we live in. Jesus too suffered in this world, and unfortunately, we are not exempt. Oftentimes, God uses difficult situations to propel you or someone else to a higher place in Him. You may think that you have been dealt a bad deck in life, but with God you will never lose. He knows how to reshuffle the deck – restore, renew, rebuild, and reconcile.

When negative situations come our way, it is difficult to try to make sense of things we do not understand. We sometimes wonder how a loving God could allow something so cruel and terrible to happen. We wonder how a loving God could allow people to suffer and die senselessly. There are many things we will never understand but what I do know is that God is good and He loves us. He does not send sickness or suffering. He is a God of LIFE. God created everything that exists, knows all things and is everywhere. He is sovereign. And if He allows something to happen, then it is for a reason, and we are not in a position to question or argue with Him.

Candid Clarification: Everything that happens does not come from God. We all have an evil enemy in the world who seeks to kill and destroy us. I know it can be hard sometimes, but we must trust God when bad things happen and seek Him to move forward in the process. If we try to figure out God and our circumstances, our mind will become confused and dark towards Him.

"Yes, they knew God, but they wouldn't worship him as God or even give him thanks. ***And they began to think up foolish ideas of what God was like.*** <u>**The result was that their minds became dark and confused.**</u> *Claiming to be wise, they became utter fools instead."*
Romans 1:21-22

A lot of people tend to blame God when a close loved one dies, especially a child or parent. I cannot really speak to this because I have not lost someone who I was extremely close to. I lost my father, but the relationship was very turbulent; nevertheless, I still loved him dearly.

Through it all, we must remember that it was God who created heaven and gave the gift of eternal life. If it were not for this, we would never get the opportunity to see our loved ones again after death. We cannot blame God and appreciate Him at the same time. Appreciate God for who He is first, and then for what He has done. He alone has provided a joyous and peaceful haven for you and your loved ones to reside after death. Thank Him for the wondrous gift of eternal life, a place where you will live with your loved ones again for eternity.

Purpose Point: Pain and suffering are temporary, but heaven and the gift of eternal life are forever. There is no pain or suffering in heaven. Think about Jesus, he never once blamed God for allowing him to suffer and die; he knew that there was something much greater in store for him on the other side.

Purpose Point:
- We get nowhere by blaming God; we get exceedingly far by trusting Him.
- Blaming God keeps us in our current position; trusting God promotes us to a new position with greater power and authority.
- Blaming God will keep you living in the past; trusting God will allow you to live in the present and expect greater for the future.

Purpose Point: God can use what appears to be bad for our good and for the good of others. Recall the story of Joseph and our Savior Jesus mentioned earlier.

Another example is a true story about a famous female actress. In 2009, this actress died tragically from a skiing accident. She suffered a severe internal head injury, Epidural Hematoma, but she was not aware of this injury (no external signs) so she refused medical attention. She later started having symptoms of severe head pain and went to the hospital where she died. About two weeks later, I saw a story about this little girl who got hit in the head with a baseball and later started having the same symptoms as the actress. The little girl's parents took her to the doctor immediately and it was discovered that she had the same injury as the actress. Her parents said that if it were not for the death of the actress and the subsequent widespread media coverage concerning her injury, they would have never known the symptoms to look for and probably would have never taken their little girl to the doctor. If they did not, the little girl would have died; hence, the little girl is alive today because of God's grace to the extent of her parents being aware of what happened to the actress.

Sometimes when bad things happen in our lives, it is to achieve a greater purpose in our life and/or in the lives of others. **Miracles are sometimes a mystery. An unfortunate event for one could be a miracle for another.**

"And we know that God causes everything to work together for the good of those who love God and are called according to his purpose for them." Romans 8:28

Purpose Point: Remember, everything bad that happens does not come from God (see Evil Enemy for more information), but God can cause *everything* to work together for your good and the good of others. *Everything* includes the good and bad – mistakes, misfortunes, mishaps, missteps, misdeeds, and misunderstandings. Trust God and know that, *"The Lord is righteous in everything he does; he is filled with kindness."* Psalm 145:17

Purpose Point: The Bible says that godly (just) people will have many afflictions and trials, and so will the ungodly. However, the difference is when the people of God have trials, they can experience hope and the peace of God. God will rescue them from their troubles. It is often difficult to figure out why bad things happen because bad things happen to everyone – good and bad people. As stated in the scripture below, it rains on the just and unjust. However, the good thing about the just (righteous people) is that they have an umbrella of protection, peace, joy, and divine favor—and a Savior who calms and stops the storms of life.

"In that way, you will be acting as true children of your Father in heaven. For he gives his sunlight to both the evil and the good, and he sends rain on the just and the unjust alike." Matthew 5:45

"The righteous person faces many troubles, but the Lord comes to the rescue each time." Psalm 34:19

"When you go through deep waters, I will be with you. When you go through rivers of difficulty, you will not drown. When you walk through the fire of oppression, you will not be burned up; the flames will not consume you." Isaiah 43:2

"The eyes of the Lord watch over those who do right; his ears are open to their cries for help." Psalm 34:15

"The Lord hears his people when they call to him for help. He rescues them from all their troubles." Psalm 34:17

"...if you are suffering according to God's will, keep on doing what is right, and trust yourself to the God who made you, for he will never fail you." 1 Peter 4:19

"Calamity will surely overtake the wicked, and those who hate the righteous will be punished. But the Lord will redeem those who serve him. Everyone who trusts in him will be freely pardoned." Psalm 34:21-22

2. **Tr<u>us</u>t**

   One word found within the word trust is "us" which means trust always involves two or more people. I believe that there are two types of trust and these types serve as the foundation of faith. *"Now faith is the substance of things hoped for, the evidence of things not seen."* Hebrews 11:1 KJV

1. **Trust to believe (independent)**
   This type of trust involves choosing to believe someone. It involves questioning a person's character, intent, and motives independently to determine if the truth is really being told. It may cause a person to be either suspicious or confident in another person. When we first hear about God, we are in this stage. We are contemplating whether to believe what we are hearing is really the truth. But hopefully, you have already established that God's Word is true, and that Jesus is real.

   Have you ever allowed someone to borrow money and he/she did not pay you back? Usually, when you let someone borrow something you first start to think about this person's character and go on to wonder if you can really believe or trust what they are telling you. If you choose to believe them and let them borrow the money and they did not pay you back, then you would probably be really disappointed and vow to never trust them again. You do not have to worry about this kind of behavior with God because the Bible assures you that if you believe in Him you will not be disappointed.

   "...anyone who believes in him will not be disappointed." Romans 10:11

   "There is no judgment awaiting those who trust him. But those who do not trust him have already been judged for not believing in the only Son of God." John 3:18

   Jesus said, *"The world's sin is unbelief in me."* John 16:9

2. **Trust to depend (dependent)**
   This type of trust involves fully believing someone and being confident in their character, capabilities, motives, and intent. A person has made the choice to believe the other person and has determined that he/she is trustworthy. As a result, the person has dependently formed an emotional connection with the other person and strongly depends on the person to do what they have said or conveyed. However, this type of trust can be extremely detrimental if certain expectations are not met due to the emotional attachment and involvement. When we truly believe in God and believe that Jesus died for our sins, we are now able to fully depend on God to perform His promises in our lives. These promises include salvation (eternal life), forgiveness, deliverance, favor, long life, healing/health, peace, joy, wisdom, protection, prosperity, provision, and restoration.

   *"When you bow down before the Lord and **admit your dependence on him**, he will lift you up and give you honor."* James 4:10

   Purpose Point: Only until you believe in God are you able to depend on God. When you depend on a person, you believe that they will alleviate inner worries and fears by solving your problems and staying committed to their word. You lean on them for support, and trust that they will follow through and deliver. God wants you to trust Him, believe in Him and depend on Him for help. He can help you to nullify your past and achieve success in life if you forgive and trust Him.

- Trust and believe that God's Word, the Bible, is 'the truth'
- Trust God to help you forgive and/or help others to forgive you
- Trust God to deliver and rescue you from every enemy of your past
- Trust God with everything that happens in your life whether good or bad; know that everything that happens is for a reason and that He will deliver you
- Depend on God, not yourself or others

"Trust in the Lord and do good. Then you will live safely in the land and prosper. Take delight in the Lord and he will give you your heart's desires. Commit everything you do to the Lord. Trust him, and he will help you. He will make your innocence as clear as the dawn, and the justice of your cause will shine like the noonday sun. Be still in the presence of the Lord, and wait patiently for him to act. Don't worry about evil people who prosper...Stop your anger! Turn from your rage. Do not envy others—it only leads to harm." Psalm 37:3-8

*"**Trust** in the Lord with all your heart; **do not depend on your own understanding.** Seek his will in all you do, and he will direct your paths."* Proverbs 3:5

"For you will rescue me from my troubles and help me to triumph over my enemies."
David – Psalm 54:7

Purpose Point: When you do not trust God (believe and depend) you are showing that your heart is full of pride. Pride is dangerously believing and trusting in self. A prideful person believes that they can do things on their own without any help. They also believe that their thinking or beliefs are primary or better than God's will, ways, and wisdom. God hates pride (Proverbs 16:5); therefore, do not operate from a prideful heart – believe God.

"My thoughts are nothing like your thoughts," says the LORD. "And my ways are far beyond anything you could imagine. For just as the heavens are higher than the earth, so my ways are higher than your ways and my thoughts higher than your thoughts." Isaiah 55:8-9

Purpose Point: No matter what you have done or what has been done to you, God has chosen you to be his instrument and take His message to others. You are not so screwed up that God can't use you. But in order for Him to use you and take you to your place of destiny, you must void out or nullify all the bad things from your past – don't allow it to hold you back.
Forgive, trust and FOCUS!!

F - Forget about your past and Fend off distractions
O - Obey God and Overcome obstacles
C - Cultivate God's promises, purposes, and plans for your life
U - Usher in the way of the Lord (live for Jesus and tell others about him)
S - Succeed in fulfilling your definite divine purpose

*"...I am still not all I should be, but I am **focusing** all my energies on this one thing: **Forgetting the past and looking forward to what lies ahead**..."* Paul – Philippians 3:13

Purpose Point: The past is gone; only resurrect it to learn from it, not to live in it. Allow, however, the beloved memories of loved ones and special life moments to live on (Philippians 4:8).

Demonstrate your purpose (Show up for duty)

*"**I, the Lord, have called you to demonstrate my righteousness**. I will guard and support you...you will be a light to guide all nations to me..."* Isaiah 42:6

"The Lord has made everything for his own purposes..." Proverbs 16:4

    The reason(s) why you were created or born is also known as your purpose. As stated earlier, these reasons are to love and worship God; to love and to be loved; to help your natural king (husband); and to procreate life through divine order. However, your ultimate (definite and divine) or highest purpose in life is to build God's kingdom by telling or teaching others about Jesus. God put a special gift inside of you to help you to do this. This gift (calling) may be the gift to prophesy (assert the future and speak through divine inspiration), to evangelize (travel the world to tell people about God), pastor (oversee a church), or minister/teach (reconcile people to Christ and teach others about the things of God inside and outside the church). There is also the gift of an apostle who initiates fresh understanding of God's Word and new vision for the people of God. Your highest purpose in life may be that of an apostle, prophet, evangelist, pastor, minister, teacher, helper, speaker, interpreter, counselor, adviser, etc. God will reveal your gift to you when the time is right, but you should pray and ask Him to do it.

    You do not have to wait until you know your gift to demonstrate your purpose. You can immediately demonstrate your essential purposes such as loving and worshiping God, loving and helping others, and telling others about Jesus. You can also serve in your church, as this is where a lot of kingdom business building is done. However, when God does reveal your specific purpose and gift, take a bold step...step out to demonstrate your purpose.
Be courageous and make it happen.

"God has given gifts to each of you from his great variety of spiritual gifts. Manage them well so that God's generosity can flow through you. Are you called to be a speaker? Then speak as though God himself were speaking through you. Are you called to help others? Do it with all the strength and energy that God supplies. Then God will be given glory in everything through Jesus Christ. All glory and power belong to him forever and ever. Amen." 1 Peter 4:10-11

"Now there are different kinds of spiritual gifts, but it is the same Holy Spirit who is the source of them all. There are different kinds of service in the church, but it is the same Lord we are serving. There are different ways God works in our lives, but it is the same God who does the work through all of us. A spiritual gift is given to each of us as a means of helping the entire church. To one person the Spirit gives the ability to give wise advice; to another he gives the gift of special knowledge. The Spirit gives special faith to another, and to someone else he gives the power to heal the sick. He gives one person the power to perform miracles, and to another the ability to prophesy. He gives someone else the ability to know whether it is really the Spirit of God or another spirit that is speaking. Still another person is given the ability to

speak in unknown languages, and another is given the ability to interpret what is being said. It is the one and only Holy Spirit who distributes these gifts. He alone decides which gift each person should have." 1 Corinthians 12:4-11

Minute Memoir: After developing a relationship with God, my greatest fear was dying without fulfilling my God-given purpose. I felt that if I died without achieving my purpose, my life was not worth living.

Kingdom Building – What is God's kingdom and where is it?

The kingdom of God is found in the people of God. It lives in us, as the same Spirit that raised Jesus from the dead lives in us (Romans 8:11). Jesus said, *"The kingdom of God does not come with observation; nor will they say, 'See here!' or 'See there!' For indeed, the kingdom of God is within you."* Luke 17:20-21 NKJV

When you utilize your God-given gifts and talents and tell others about Jesus you demonstrate your purpose by helping to build the kingdom. Figuratively speaking, each person who believes, confesses, and obeys God is a brick. When you help people to believe, confess and obey by telling them about Jesus, you help to add another brick to the kingdom of God. In other words, you help to save people from eternal death. So be about your Father's business, kingdom business – lead others to Jesus. He has already given you the authority and permission to take his message of forgiveness and repentance to the world. Take your place and demonstrate your purpose – tell your friends, family, and others about Jesus and his love for them.

"And you are living stones that God is building into his spiritual temple..." 1 Peter 2:5

Jesus said: *"With my authority, take this message of repentance to all the nations... 'There is forgiveness of sins for all who turn to me'. You are witnesses of all these things."* Luke 24:47-48

*"I, the Lord, have called you to **demonstrate** my righteousness. I will guard and support you, for I have given you to my people as the personal confirmation of my covenant with them. And you will be a light to guide all the nations to me. You will open the eyes of the blind and free the captives from prison. You will release those who sit in dark dungeons."* Isaiah 42:6-7
So many people need your help; they are waiting for you to remove the spiritual blindfolds of evil and deception from their eyes, to free them from the imprisonment of trauma, rejection and pain, and to release them from the dark dungeons of depression and despair.

"For the Kingdom of God is not a matter of what we should eat or drink, but of living a life of goodness and peace and joy in the Holy Spirit. If you serve Christ with this attitude, you will please God..." Romans 14:17-18

Everyone who believes and obeys God makes up the church – the kingdom of God and the body of Jesus Christ. I am not referring to the physical fleshly body of Jesus or a brick and mortar building, but rather a construct that is symbolic of Jesus living and working through us (our bodies) which become his body when we become Christians. Remember, when we accept Jesus and confess him as Lord, we become a new creature and receive a new spirit – the Spirit of God who lives and works through us. All of us make up the body of Jesus Christ and the church; therefore, the church is not a building, but the people of God. And as people of God we should all have one common goal, path, and purpose which is to build up the church and the kingdom – the body of Christ.

"We are all one body, we have the same Spirit, and we have all been called to the same glorious future. There is only one Lord, one faith, one baptism, and there is only one God and Father, who is over us all and in us all and living through us all. However, he has given each one of us a special gift according to the generosity of Christ...He is the one who gave these gifts to the church: the apostles, the prophets, the evangelists, and the pastors and teachers. Their responsibility is to equip God's people to do his work and build up the church, the body of Christ, until we come to such unity in our faith and knowledge of God's Son..."
Ephesians 4:4-13

"Don't you realize that all of you together are the temple of God and that the Spirit of God lives in you? God will bring ruin upon anyone who ruins this temple. For God's temple is holy, and you Christians are that temple." 1 Corinthians 3:16-17

Purpose Point: Building God's kingdom is essentially *saving souls* and includes encouraging and training other believers to live for God and fulfill their God-given purpose.

See the 'Powerful Prayer' chapter for a guide on how to win and save souls.

You save a soul from eternal death (eternal separation from God) when you help someone (an unbeliever) to believe and give their life to Jesus or when you encourage someone to remain in the faith. It is only by S.T.A.N.D.ing that you are able to do this.

Purpose Point: *"By standing firm, you will win your souls."* Luke 21:19

What happens when you build the kingdom?

When you tell others about Jesus and the ways of God you are planting a seed (God's Word) in their hearts. God will bring other people in their lives to water this seed and God himself will make it grow. When the seed grows, the person will believe in the ways of God, become a part of the kingdom and hopefully fulfill their purpose on earth. But remember, the only way to build the kingdom is with the Word of God (speaking what the Bible says - speaking truth with love). Jesus and his great love must be included in what you tell others, as he is the only way to salvation and eternal life. Paul was a kingdom builder and asserted to be an expert builder of Jesus Christ. He said:

"...we're only servants. Through us God caused you to believe. Each of us did the work the Lord gave us. My job was to plant the seed in your hearts, and Apollos watered it, but it was God, not we, who made it grow. The ones who do the planting and watering aren't important, but God is important because he is the one who makes the seed grow. The one who plants and the one who waters work as a team with the same purpose. Yet they will be rewarded individually, according to their own hard work. We work together as partners who belong to God. You are God's field, God's building...Because of God's special favor to me, I have laid the foundation like an expert builder. Now others are building on it. But whoever is building on this foundation must be very careful. For no one can lay any other foundation than the one we already have – Jesus Christ." 1 Corinthians 3:5-11

Purpose Point: When we help to build the kingdom of God, we will be rewarded for our work in heaven and on earth. These rewards will include treasures and mansions in heaven, and favor and blessings on earth.

Purpose Point: Everyone will have to answer to God and be judged for the work or building they have done. For instance, if you contributed to saving a soul(s) or helping someone to know Jesus and the ways of God, you will receive a reward for your work.

"But there is going to come a time of testing at the judgment day to see what kind of work each builder has done. Everyone's work will be put through the fire to see whether or not it keeps its value. If the work survives the fire, that builder will receive a reward. But if the work is burned up, the builder will suffer great loss. The builders themselves will be saved, but like someone escaping through a wall of flames." 1 Corinthians 3:13-15

"Store your treasures in heaven, where moths and rust cannot destroy, and thieves do not break in and steal." Matthew 6:20

Purpose Point: If we seek first to build the kingdom, then God will meet our needs, surround us with His blessings and give us our innermost desires (if aligned with His will).

"Your heavenly father already knows your needs, and he will give you all you need from day to day if you live for God and make the Kingdom your primary concern." Matthew 6:33 NLT

"But seek first his kingdom and his righteousness, and all these things will be given to you as well." Matthew 6:33 NIV

"Take delight in the Lord, and he will give you your heart's desires." Psalm 37:4

Purpose Point: Telling others about Jesus should never be done in an act of judging or condemning but should be done in *love*. Do not shove Jesus down people's throat by insisting that they believe or nagging them about the need to believe. Instead, look for the opportunity to tell others about Jesus. For example, if you see a girl who is sad and crying and she tells you that her boyfriend cheated on her and later broke it off, you could say: *"Don't worry, if he cheated on you, then he does not see your value and how special you are. Jesus sees your value and wants to be a part of your life. He loves you so much and will never leave you. God has someone special for you, someone who will treat you right when the time is right. Are you saved? Would you like for me to pray with you?"*

Purpose Point: When we separate ourselves (set a godly example) and live a godly life, we also help to draw others to God. You can inspire others by right living and making the right choices. Remember, if you lead, others will follow and become strong. Therefore, lead in your family; lead in your circle of friends and influence; lead on your social media platforms; and lead in your private time when no one is watching.

Purpose Point: Don't allow your youth to prevent you from building the kingdom and fulfilling your purpose. God wants you to serve Him now and build the kingdom while you are young. He does not want you to get old and gray before you choose to serve Him. Remember the reasons why you were born. You were not born just to have fun and do the things you want to do, but you were born for God and other people – His kingdom. One day when Jesus was a young boy (12 years old), he stayed behind in a city without his parents' knowledge after they had left the city of Jerusalem. When they discovered Jesus was missing, his parents were worried and desperately searched for him. When they found Jesus, Jesus said to them, *"Why did you seek Me? Did you not know that I must be about My Father's business?"* Luke 2:49 NKJV Therefore, **be about your Father God's business when you are young and old.**

"Don't let the excitement of youth cause you to forget your Creator. Honor him in your youth before you grow old and no longer enjoy living. It will be too late then to remember him, when the light of the sun and moon and stars is dim to your old eyes, and there is no silver lining left among the clouds. Your limbs will tremble with age, and your strong legs will grow weak. Your teeth will be too few to do their work..." Ecclesiastes 12:1-3

"Yes, remember your Creator now while you are young..." Ecclesiastes 12:6

Purpose Point: <u>Don't be afraid</u> to serve God or build the kingdom while you are young. You do not have to live long to make a monumental impact in the world.

Long ago, God chose a young man named Jeremiah to be His prophet. However, when God revealed this special gift to him, Jeremiah became afraid. He feared that he was too young to speak for God and nearly missed his purpose.

The Lord gave Jeremiah this message: *"He said, 'I knew you before I formed you in your mother's womb. Before you were born I set you apart and appointed you to be my spokesman to the world.' 'O sovereign Lord [said Jeremiah] I can't speak for you! I am too young!' 'Don't say that', the Lord replied, 'for **you must go wherever I send you and say whatever I tell you**. And **don't be afraid** of the people, for I will be with you and take care of you. I, the Lord, have spoken!' Then the Lord touched my mouth and said, 'See, I have put my words in your mouth! Today I appoint you to <u>stand up</u>... You are to <u>build others up</u> and plant them.'"*
Jeremiah 1:4-10

"This is why I remind you to fan into flames the spiritual gift God gave you...For God has not given us a spirit of fear and timidity, but of power, love, and self-discipline. So you must never be ashamed to tell others about our Lord..." 2 Timothy 1:6-8

Purpose Point: Fear is a spirit from the devil, and not from God. Therefore, it is the devil's plan to make you afraid so that you cannot build God's kingdom and speak for Him. Do not allow the devil to make you afraid, instead use the power and the gift(s) God gave you.

*"**For the Kingdom of God is not just a lot of talk; it is living by God's power.**"* 1 Corinth. 4:20

God has appointed you to speak for Him – do not be afraid because God is with you. You must do what God wants you to do – **STAND up, stand out, step out, be bold, and build others up!** God has supernaturally touched your mouth and will enable you to demonstrate your purpose. Your gift may not be a prophet like Jeremiah, but again we all have one common gift and that is to tell others about Jesus and help people to know Him.

"Arise, shine, for your light has come, and the glory of the LORD rises upon you."
Isaiah 60:1 NIV

Purpose Point: Don't allow people to think less of you because you are young.

"Teach these things and insist that everyone learn them. <u>Don't let anyone think less of you because you are young.</u> Be an example to all believers in what you teach, in the way you live, in your love, your faith, and your purity." 1 Timothy 4:11-12

Demonstrating your purpose is demonstrating character, integrity, godliness, and excellence.
Demonstrate who you are for the greater good and the Greater God.

Poetic Princess

SEIZE THE TIME
Seize the time, for it will soon fade away at the drop of a dime.
As I look at my hand, right now it looks young and brown.
But it will too fade away, buried in the ground someday.
Many times, we go through life, thinking there is never an end.
We focus on insignificant and material things.
Whether you are young, old, poor, rich, or middle class.
It really doesn't matter —it is all temporary; it won't last.
While we are young, we think we are guaranteed tomorrow.
When we are old, we think life is full of sorrow.
Everything that is and was created is for a purpose; and when that purpose is fulfilled or rejected, we soon expire — sometimes without warning.
'Life', what is it really all about?
It will certainly make you scream and shout!
Looking through a glass to an outside world,
One can see such pain and turmoil.
People are sick and poor, children are suffering, and national disasters are on the rise.
People are concerned only with themselves and would rather believe in lies.
'Life', so much can be said in that four-letter word.
Live like there is no tomorrow and trust in the Lord.

Fairytales
One day I received a text message from my youngest niece. The message informed me of her new cell number. At the end of her message it read, *"Live my life as if it was a fairy tale."* I thought to myself, she should not live her life as a fairy tale but needs to live it in reality. In fairy tales, there are no sexually transmitted diseases, murder, jail time, or sexual assaults. The world we live in is far from fantasy — one mistake could change your life forever. In the real world, it is not possible for you to go to your fairy god mother and ask her to change the past or erase a mistake; life is just not that simple. Fairytales are fantasy, not reality; however, God is so good and so great that He could saturate your life with abundant blessings wrapped in happiness, peace, and joy to the extent that your life seems like a fairytale…heaven on earth.

Jesus said, *"The thief comes to steal and kill and destroy. I came that they may have life, and have it abundantly."* John 10:10 ESV

The Glass Slipper – Does it fit?
Do you remember the story of Cinderella where the prince tried to find the woman whose foot could fit in the glass shoe? Imagine this cruel world around us as the glass shoe – transparent and hard to live in. The prince of this world, our evil enemy, (the devil – the thief) is trying to make you fit in this shoe, the world. He knows that you are special and wants to destroy you. As a princess, you must resist him and refuse to fit in with the world. You must live your life by doing all the things God created you to do.

It is true that we live in the world, but we should not be of the world. The Bible says that we are citizens of heaven and not citizens of the world which means we do not belong to this world – your eternal castle resides in heaven. We are destined to be a part of God's kingdom and must do things His way and not the world's way. The devil has already been judged and will spend eternity in the lake of fire (e.g. hell). He already knows that he is doomed and wants to take as many people as he can with him. Don't let him take you; don't fit in his shoe!

"For this world is not our home; we are looking forward to our city in heaven, which is yet to come." Hebrews 13:14

"But we are citizens of heaven, where the Lord Jesus Christ lives..." Philippians 3:20

Jesus said, *"The time of judgment for the world has come, when the prince of this world will be cast out."* John 12:31

"Judgment will come because the prince of this world has already been judged." John 16:11

Purpose Point: When we talk about the world, we are talking about the world of sin. Sin is simply doing what God told you not to do. Remember, some of the world's ways include hatred, idolatry, fighting, strife, pride, selfishness, lust, murder, stealing, jealousy, lying, deceit, sexual immorality/perversion, disobedience to parents and authority, unforgiveness, rebellion and unbelief in God/Jesus. These are common behaviors that many people of the world do. The world is the devil's domain; he walks along the earth seeking who he can devour and destroy. The devil is not in hell. He is in the world on earth encouraging people to live out his ways – the world's ways. If he can get you to live out his ways, he has the right to kill and destroy you. Don't live out his ways. Don't fit in with the world! Stand firm against him!

"Be careful! Watch out for attacks from the Devil, your great enemy. He prowls around like a roaring lion, looking for some victim to devour. **Take a firm <u>stand</u> against him**, *and be strong in your faith. Remember that Christians all over the world are going through the same kind of suffering you are."* 1 Peter 5:8-9

*"****<u>Resist</u>*** *the Devil, and he will flee from you. Draw close to God, and God will draw close to you."* James 4:7-8

Purpose Point: "Friendship with the world makes you an enemy of God."

"...Don't you realize that friendship with the world makes you an enemy of God? I say it again, that if your aim is to enjoy this world, you can't be a friend of God." James 4:4

Purpose Point: If you ever feel uncomfortable being around places and/or people who live the world's way, it is because you do not fit. If you wear a size 7 shoe, you cannot fit in a size 5 shoe, no matter how cute or appealing it is – it just won't work. Therefore, don't become a misfit...don't ever try to make yourself fit in with people or places where you feel uncomfortable, especially where people are engaging in wild and wicked living.

When you become saved and the Spirit of God comes to live in you, you will feel uncomfortable in places that are worldly and around people who do not honor God. This is a sign that you do not belong. So don't force it and straddle the fence – you are much bigger than that. If you try to make yourself fit, you will be negatively influenced and pressured to live the wrong way, and bunions of burdens will soon arise as you try to fit in the world's stinky shoe.

"...Bad company corrupts good character." 1 Corinthians 15:33

Remember, always guard your gates – mind, eye, and ear.

Mary – a True Princess

"Elizabeth gave a glad cry and exclaimed to Mary, "You are blessed by God above all other women, and your child is blessed." Luke 1:42

Mary, the mother of Jesus, was a princess and was blessed beyond all women. She had special favor from God. One day I asked God why He chose Mary and what made her so special. This is what the Lord revealed to me – God chose Mary because she was *popular* and possessed all the characteristics of a true princess. Not popular in a sense as known by people, but popular in a sense as known by God.

Mary was:
Pure
Obedient
Prayerful
United
Lowly
Attentive
Righteous

Pure

Text Term: Pure means free from dirt and defilement (clean and blameless) and has also been associated with a 'virgin'. Additionally, pure in heart means being sensitive to the Spirit of God, believing in God, being humble, obedient (aiming to please Him), and open to godly wisdom and change (the renewing of the mind). A pure heart is free from pride, ill intent, and deceit.

Mary was a virgin and maintained her sexual purity until marriage. She was engaged to be married before God made her pregnant with Jesus through His mighty power. But not only was Mary pure in body, she was also pure in heart. Mary had a beautiful heart full of love and kindness. She did not let the world around her affect who she was. She did not try to fit in with others or mimic negative behaviors.

"Now this is how Jesus the Messiah was born. His mother, Mary, was engaged to be married to Joseph. But while she was still a virgin, she became pregnant by the Holy Spirit."
Matthew 1:18

We take on our characteristics from our parents. If Jesus were to live a popular life of purity, his mother would also have to live a life of purity. Like his mother, Jesus was also a virgin and lived a pure life in body and heart. We too must strive to live a life of purity, just as Jesus did, if we believe in Him.

Candid Clarification: A common misconception is that a person is only pure if he or she is a virgin – never having sex. This is not true. Your heart, comprised of your will, thoughts, actions and beliefs dictate your level of purity. For instance, it is through the heart that a person chooses whether to have sex before marriage. The heart is what drives or propels action and proper conduct. *"Everything is pure to those whose hearts are pure. But nothing is pure to those who are corrupt and unbelieving, because their minds and consciences are defiled. Such **people claim they know God, but they deny him by the way they live**..."* Titus 1:15

The world's perception of pure is when a woman or man is a virgin. However, God's perspective of purity is when a woman or man believes in God, accepts Jesus as their Lord, repents, and aims to live a life that is pleasing to Him. A virgin could be a murderer at heart which negates any ounce of purity. And on the other hand, an unbelieving woman could have multiple sex partners, but the moment she has a change of heart and mind (repents or turn away from her sin) and chooses to accept Jesus, she becomes just as pure as a godly virgin because the blood of Jesus (his life sacrifice for her sins) makes her whiter than snow. Her past is behind her and her newness of life is active and alive. Remember, 2 Corinthians 5:17: *"anyone who belongs to Christ has become a new person. The old life is gone; a new life has begun!"*

Purity, like beauty, is permeated from the inside out.

"Purify me from my sins, and I will be clean; wash me, and I will be whiter than snow." Psalm 51:7 *Hide your face from my sins and blot out all my iniquity. **Create in me a pure heart, O God**, and renew a steadfast spirit within me."* Psalm 51:9-10 NIV

Purpose Point: Only the pure in heart will see God. In other words, only people with pure hearts will experience God's blessings, kingdom, favor and promises in their life. Remember, pure in heart means believing in God, obeying Him, being sensitive to the Spirit of God, and remaining humble – open and absorbent to godly wisdom and change. A hard heart that refuses to listen, obey, and accept godly wisdom and change opposes purity.

*"God blesses those whose **hearts are pure**, for they will see God."* Matthew 5:8

*"Even children are known by the way they act, whether their conduct is **pure** and right."* Proverbs 20:11

*"For I want you to understand what really matters, so that you may live **pure** and blameless lives until Christ returns."* Philippians 1:10

*"See how very much our heavenly Father loves us, for he allows us to be called his children, and we really are! But the people who belong to this world don't know God, so they don't understand that we are his children. Yes, dear friends, we are already God's children...And all who believe this will **keep themselves pure**, just as Christ is pure."* 1 John 3:1-3

Purpose Point: When you really understand how much your heavenly Father loves you and truly believe that you are a child of God – His princess, you will want to obey God and keep yourself pure, just like Jesus.

*"Because we have these promises, dear friends, let us cleanse ourselves from everything that can defile our body and spirit. And let us work toward **complete purity** because we fear God."* 2 Corinthians 7:1

Purpose Point: If you are or are not a virgin, try your best (with God's help) not to have sex until you are married, no matter what everyone else is doing or what anybody tells you. This will save you from a lot of heartache and pain. You are holy, precious, and highly valued. *"Don't waste what is holy on people who are unholy. Don't throw your pearls to pigs! They will trample the pearls, then turn and attack you."* Matthew 7:6

What happened to me is a prime example. I gave my pearls (sex) to my ex-boyfriend (pig) and sure enough he later turned and literally attacked me; he almost killed me. Sex without marriage could stir up negative activity in your life such as abuse, rejection, disappointment, discouragement, depression, soul ties, disease, pregnancy, hurt and pain. Your pearls are for your natural king, your husband. **Get your heart right so you can maintain or regain purity.**

If you are not a virgin, don't think for one second that you are not pure or valuable. If you have given your life to Jesus, you are not only saved, but you are also pure. Trust and depend on Him. Renew your mind and heart with the Word of God.

<u>O</u>bedient

Mary was obedient to the Lord. She accepted and did whatever God asked her to do. She believed God in all things.

Mary said, *"I am the Lord's servant, and I am willing to accept whatever he wants..."* Luke 1:38

"When Jesus' parents had fulfilled all the requirements of the law of the Lord, they returned home..." Luke 2:39

"Now that you have purified yourselves by obeying the truth..." 1 Peter 1:22 NIV

Purpose Point: The greatest expression of worship to God is obedience.

Purpose Point: When you obey God, you honor Him. When you disobey God, you dishonor Him – it is that simple. A princess is a woman of honor; she honors her King and Father, and in return she becomes honored by many.

"...Obedience is far better than sacrifice..." 1 Samuel 15:22

<u>P</u>rayerful

Mary talked to God; she prayed. Prayer is simply just that, talking to God. It also includes speaking or praying His Word, praising, and worshiping Him. Remember, communing with God (praying), praising, and worshiping Him are the primary reasons why you were created. Therefore, praying should not only include wants and needs (requests) but should also be used as an opportunity to thank God for all He has done and to magnify who He is.

As a true princess, we should seek the face of God in our prayers and not just His hand. In other words, we should first honor Him for the loving God He is, and not only seek to receive from Him. Doing this reflects a heart focus of giving and not just receiving.

Additionally, prayer helps us to fulfill our purpose, allows God to work in our lives, and gives Him the opportunity to speak to us quietly within our hearts. Praying connects us to God; therefore, be a praying and praising princess who is not afraid or ashamed to lift up her God.

Mary said, *"Oh, how I praise the Lord. How I rejoice in God my Savior!"* Luke 1:46

"They all met together continually for prayer, along with Mary the mother of Jesus, several other women, and the brothers of Jesus." Acts 1:14

Purpose Point: When we pray, we enter the supernatural realm of God's kingdom. We spiritually stand in front of His royal gate awaiting His presence. The Bible says, *"Enter his gates with thanksgiving; go into his courts with praise. Give thanks to him and bless his name. For the Lord is good..."* Psalm 100:4-5

Open your prayer by thanking, praising, and worshiping God because He is good! Mary understood this; she started off her prayer by saying, *"Oh, how I praise the Lord. How I rejoice in God my Savior!"* Mary was happy and joyful about praising and magnifying her God.

<u>United</u>

United means an act of coming together. Mary was united with God in spirit, mind (soul), and body. She was holy. Remember, to be holy is to be one mind with God – separated or set apart for His good use – believing what He says and doing what He commands. The Spirit of God was upon Mary which joined them together. As a princess, you should unite your mind with God's truth and believe, think and act like Him. The word "religion" comes from the root word religare*, meaning to rejoin or reunite (bind and connect). The Christian religion is simply reuniting with the source that keeps you alive, and this source is the one and only true and living God. But God wants us to go beyond *religion*; He wants us to have an intimate *relationship* with Him and connect our heart with His heart which is full of unconditional love. Investing time to develop a relationship with God will strengthen your union with Him.

Mary's relative Elizabeth said, *"You are blessed, because you believed that the Lord would do what he said."* Luke 1:45

*"For in Christ the fullness of God lives in the human body, and you are complete through your **union** with Christ."* Colossians 2:9-10

*"...Rather, be of one mind, **united** in thought and purpose."* 1 Corinthians 1:10

"Draw near to God, and he will draw near to you..." James 4:8 ESV

Purpose Point: Get united – get connected with your God. You do this by praying, reading His Word, and devoting time for Him (i.e. church, devotionals, quiet time, etc.)

*Source: Etymology Dictionary Online

Lowly

Mary was lowly, meaning she was humble and meek (lowliness of mind). She did not think haughtily or highly of herself and did not feel that she was better than everyone else. She feared and reverenced the Lord and exalted Him above all. She was not arrogant, prideful, vain, selfish, or conceited in any way. She did not fight, scheme, curse people out, or disrespect her parents and authority. She bragged about God and did not brag about herself. She did not need, nor desire, high status or abundant riches because she was rich at heart.

Mary was not lowly in a sense where she had a low self-esteem or a negative self-image about herself. She knew she was blessed and saw herself through the eyes of her Creator. Humility or lowliness is not thinking of yourself as less or being less but thinking of yourself less often and choosing to focus on the things of God and helping others.

Mary said, *"Oh, how I praise the Lord. How I rejoice in God my Savior! For he took notice of his **lowly servant girl**, and now generation after generation will call me blessed...He has taken princes from their thrones and **exalted the lowly**."* Luke 1:46-48, 52

"For the Lord delights in his people; he crowns the humble with victory." Psalm 149:4

This is what God requires of you…

*"No, O people, the LORD has told you what is good, and this is what he requires of you: <u>**to do what is right, to love mercy, and to walk humbly with your God.**</u>"* Micah 6:8

"So I,….appeal to you to live a life worthy of the calling to which you have been called [that is, to live a life that exhibits godly character, moral courage, personal integrity, and mature behavior—a life that expresses gratitude to God for your salvation], **with all humility [forsaking self-righteousness]**, *and gentleness [maintaining self-control], with patience, bearing with one another in [unselfish] love."* Ephesians 4:1-2 AMP

"Haughtiness goes before destruction; humility precedes honor." Proverbs 18:12

"Don't praise yourself; let others do it." Proverbs 27:2

The Lord says, *"…I will bless those who have **humble** and contrite hearts, who tremble at my word…"* Isaiah 66:2

*"As the scriptures say, God sets himself against the proud, but **he shows favor to the humble**. So **humble yourselves before God**."* James 4:6-7 *When you bow down before the Lord and admit your dependence on him, he will lift you up and give you honor."* James 4:10

*"Don't be jealous or proud, but **be humble** and consider others more important than yourselves."* Philippians 2:3 CEV

*"True **humility** and fear of the Lord lead to riches, honor, and long life."* Proverbs 22:4

*"Pride ends in humiliation, while **humility** brings honor."* Proverbs 29:23

Purpose Point: The Lord said in the above scripture that He will bless and honor those with humble hearts. This is one of the primary reasons why Mary was so blessed – because she had a humble and pure heart. **Remember, when your heart is right, everything else will fall into place.** Just like we need a heart to live in the natural, your heart is vital to becoming a true princess and living the blessed life God has planned for you. Everyone knew that Mary was abundantly blessed — even her relative's unborn baby knew it.

"...Mary hurried to the hill country of Judea, to the town where Zechariah lived. She entered the house and greeted Elizabeth. At the sound of Mary's greeting, Elizabeth's child leaped within her, and Elizabeth was filled with the Holy Spirit. Elizabeth gave a glad cry and exclaimed to Mary, "You are blessed by God above all other women, and your child is blessed. What an honor this is, that the mother of my Lord should visit me! When you came in and greeted me, my baby jumped for joy the instant I heard your voice! You are blessed, because you believed that the Lord would do what he said." Luke 1:39-45

Attentive

Mary was attentive. She was fully aware of the character of God – His ways, will and wisdom. She recognized God for who He was and what He did. She knew God to be holy, mighty, and faithful. Mary demonstrated her purpose by worshiping and praising God. She spoke good things and did not engage in foolish and perverted conversations. She spoke faith and not doubt. She was attentive to the needs of others, and the needs of her God.

Mary said, *"For he, the Mighty One, is holy, and he has done great things for me. His mercy goes on from generation to generation, to all who fear him. His mighty arm does tremendous things! How he scatters the proud and haughty ones! ...He has satisfied the hungry with good things and sent the rich away with empty hands. And now he has helped his servant Israel! He has not forgotten his promise to be merciful. For he promised our ancestors – Abraham and his children – to be merciful to them forever."* Luke 1:49-55

Through her attentiveness, Mary accepted, acknowledged, affirmed, and asserted God's truth.

Purpose Point: God honors those who give their full attention to Him; those who believe and trust in His Word.

Righteous

Mary had right standing with God; she was righteous. She believed in God and honored God by the way she lived – she obeyed Him.

*"**For it is believing in your heart that you are made right with God**, and it is by confessing with your mouth that you are saved."* Romans 10:10

*"Evil people are trapped by sin, but the **righteous** escape, shouting for joy."* Proverbs 29:6

*"Dear children, don't let anyone deceive you about this: When people do what is right, it is because they are **righteous, even as Christ is righteous.**"* 1 John 3:7

Purpose Point: God said this about His Son, Jesus: *"Your throne, O God, endures forever and ever. Your royal power is expressed in **righteousness**. You love what is right and hate what is wrong..."* Hebrews 1:8-9 In the same way, **your royal power is expressed in the righteousness that Christ provides.**

Purpose Point: Being righteous means having right standing with God. We cannot become righteous by our works alone or just by doing what is right. We become righteous when we accept Jesus as our Lord and Savior. He makes us righteous and enables us to do what is right.

'Therefore, since we have been made right in God's sight by faith, we have peace with God because of what Jesus Christ our Lord has done for us." Romans 5:1

"God made him who had no sin to be sin for us, so that in him we might become the righteousness of God." 2 Corinthians 5:21 NIV

**S.T.A.N.D. and strive to be popular with God and a true princess like Mary.
Do your best and trust God with the rest.**

Purpose Point: Remember, if something is popular with people and the world, more than likely it is not popular with God. Worldly popularity should never reign over God's purpose and principles. The only *"like"* you need is God's love; the only *"follower"* you need is the ONE you choose to follow – Christ.

13 Principles of a Princess when transposed and transformed makes a Proverbs 31 woman. When you transpose the number 13, for instance, it becomes the number 31. And when you transform the following 13 principles into action, you become a Proverbs 31 woman.

In the Bible, the book of Proverbs, Chapter 31, describes the type of woman God wants us to be. God has predestined His daughters, His princesses, to perform a specific role in life. The Proverbs 31 woman sets the precedent and gives the example of how a true godly woman, a princess and queen, should live.

1. <u>**A Princess obeys authority which includes God, parents, teachers, husband, boss, government, laws, etc.**</u> She is not disobedient, insubordinate, prideful, or disrespectful. She obeys and respects those who are in authority and due honor. She delights in obeying their commands – commands that are right, truthful, and godly. She does not obey unwillingly or dreadfully; she does it joyfully. She knows that it is through obeying God that she receives the favor of God. She shows respect to all people, regardless of their level of authority and beliefs. I recall a true story in the Bible about a queen named Vashti. She was so beautiful that her king wanted to show her off to everyone. One day her king ordered her to come to dinner wearing her crown so that he could show the dinner guests how beautiful she was. Vashti refused to come and did not obey authority. As a result, the king deposed her (took away her royal estate) and gave it to another woman named Esther.

Vashti was never allowed to enter the king's presence again (Esther 1-2).

Purpose Point: When you disobey authority, you always risk losing something.

- If you disobey God, you risk losing His promises and blessings.
- If you disobey the legal system, you risk losing money (fines, court costs, legal fees, bail bonds) and/or risk losing your freedom by going to jail.
- If you disobey your parents, you risk losing the long life that God promised as well as your freedom due to punishment or confiscation, and comfortable living because of spankings and physical punishment.
- If you disobey your teacher, you risk losing a good conduct and academic record due to the consequences of going to the principal's office, getting suspended, expelled, and punished at home.
- If you disobey your husband by not fulfilling your duties as a wife, you risk losing your marriage and your natural king (husband) to another woman, like Queen Vashti did. One truth about a man is that he likes and longs to feel respected. Disrespect drives him away (Ephesians 5:33).

Obey authority and stand to win!

Supporting Scriptures:

"He is especially hard on those who follow their own evil, lustful desires and who despise authority. These people are proud and arrogant, daring even to scoff at the glorious ones without so much as trembling." 2 Peter 2:10

"For the Lord's sake, accept all authority – the king as head of state, and the officials he has appointed. For the king has sent them to punish all who do wrong and to honor those who do right." 1 Peter 2:13-14

"Children, obey your parents because you belong to the Lord for this is the right thing to do. Honor your father and mother. This is the first of the Ten Commandments that ends with a promise. And this is the promise: If you honor your father and mother, 'you will live a good long life, full of blessing.'" Ephesians 6:1-3

"If you curse your father or mother, the lamp of your life will be snuffed out." Proverbs 20:20

"Show respect for everyone. Love your Christian brothers and sisters. Fear God. Show respect for the king." 1 Peter 2:17

"...You wives must accept the authority of your husbands... Your godly lives will speak to them better than any words. They will be won over by watching your pure, godly behavior." 1 Peter 3:1-2

"Young people who obey the law are wise; those with wild friends bring shame to their parents." Proverbs 28:7

"The prayers of a person who ignores the law are despised." Proverbs 28:9

"Remind your people to submit to the government and its officers. They should be obedient, always ready to do what is good." Titus 3:1

Purpose Point: Disobedience is an act of rebellion, and rebellion is as the sin of witchcraft.

"... Rebellion is as bad as the sin of witchcraft, and stubbornness is as bad as worshipping idols..." Samuel 15:23

Candid Clarification: Obey what is right. If someone who has authority is trying to get you to do something wrong, then of course obedience is not required. For example, if a teacher tells you to come over his house for personal pleasure in exchange for a good grade – this is absolutely wrong and should be reported to the authorities such as your parents, the principal or law enforcement. Some people abuse their authority and must answer for it. At some point they must face the consequences of their actions sooner or later.

Fast Fact: *Quid Pro Quo* (this for that) is a form of sexual harassment. It involves a person who abuses his or her authority to obtain favors (often sexual) and/or make unwelcomed advances to another individual in exchange for something else. An example of this is when a teacher asks a student if he could touch her private parts in exchange for a good grade, or a boss who asks an employee to date him in exchange for a promotion. This is totally unacceptable and is grounds for termination and prosecution in some cases. There is nothing worse than a person who abuses his or her authority to take advantage of others. People like this deserve to have their authority taken away – they are not worthy of it.

"When the godly are in authority, the people rejoice. But when the wicked are in power, they groan." Proverbs 29:2

2. **A Princess keeps herself pure and respects her body and Creator.** She is pure in body and heart – like Mary. She realizes that her body is the temple of God and doesn't engage in promiscuous sex by having sex with any and everybody. She does not have sex with every boy she calls her boyfriend or every boy who claims to like her. She realizes that her pearls (her body and the essence of her soul) are for her natural king, her husband. She knows that her spiritual King, her Creator (God) dwells in her; therefore, she doesn't abuse her body with immoral/illicit sex, drugs, smoking, alcohol, etc. She aims to honor her King and walk in her worth. Her heart is beautiful – transformed with the Word of God. She is holy–one mind with God. She aims to keep her body, soul, and mind sacred for the glory of God.

David, a servant of God, knew that purity was achieved with God – His Word. He asserted to God: *"How can a young person stay pure? By obeying your word and following its rules."* Psalm 119:9

*"And all who believe...will keep themselves pure, just as Christ is **pure**."* 1 John 3:3

3. **A Princess knows how and when to speak.** She does not curse, argue needlessly, or engage in inappropriate conversations. She speaks words of wisdom and not wickedness, faith and not doubt, blessings and not curses. She knows how to pray for others with her words and not persecute them with her mouth. She knows how to master her mouth and steer her speech in the right direction. She does not gossip or speak lies. She does not get involved in other peoples' business, unless she is asked or feels that it is appropriate and necessary. She is not compelled to put her two cents in a conversation and is able to "C" her way out by never interrupting in the first place when the conversation only included "A" and "B." She does not nag or constantly complain. She does not lie or go back on her word. She thinks before she speaks. She does not sow seeds of discord, dissention, division, or discouragement with her words.

Proverbs Chapter 31 verse 26:
"When she speaks, her words are wise...."

"Wise speech is rarer and more valuable than gold and rubies." Proverbs 20:15

"A person's words can be life-giving water; words of true wisdom are as refreshing as a bubbling brook." Proverbs 18:4

"There is more hope for a fool than for someone who speaks without thinking." Proverbs 29:20

"...they are likely to become lazy and spend their time gossiping from house to house, getting into other people's business and saying things they shouldn't." 1 Timothy 5:13

"No one who gossips can be trusted with a secret, but you can put confidence in someone who is trustworthy." Proverbs 11:13 GW

"In everything you do, stay away from complaining and arguing, so that no one can speak a word of blame against you..." Philippians 2:14

"A nagging wife is as annoying as the constant dripping on a rainy day. Trying to stop her complaints is like trying to stop the wind or hold something with greased hands." Proverbs 27:15

"The mouths of fools are their ruin; their lips get them into trouble." Proverbs 18:7

"Those who love to talk will experience the consequences, for the tongue can kill or nourish life." Proverbs 18:21

"It is better to say nothing than to promise something that you don't follow through on. In such cases, your mouth is making you sin. And don't defend yourself by telling the...messenger that the promise you made was a mistake..." Ecclesiastes 5:5-6

Purpose Point: God listens to your conversations. Everyone will have to stand before God one day and give an account for every harmful and idle word spoken.

*"This is what the Lord says...**I listen to their conversations and what do I hear?** Is anyone sorry for sin? Does anyone say, "What a terrible thing I have done?" No! All are running down the path of sin as swiftly as a horse rushing into battle!"* Jeremiah 8:4-6

Jesus said, *"...For whatever is in your heart determines what you say. A good person produces good words from the heart, and an evil person produces evil words from an evil heart. **And I tell you this, that you must give an account on judgment day of every idle word you speak.** The words you say now reflect your fate then; either you will be justified by them or you will be condemned."* Matthew 12:34-37

Purpose Point: You can hold bad words captive in your mind by refusing to open your mouth. Only by opening your mouth are words activated and born. You can also destroy bad thoughts and words by casting them down and changing your heart.

"Casting down imaginations, and every high thing that exalteth itself against the knowledge of God, and bringing into captivity every thought to the obedience of Christ;"
2 Corinthians 10:5 KJV

4. <u>**A Princess knows how to act and behave.**</u> She does not fight, act rudely or unbecomingly. She does not conduct herself foolishly or behave in a way that would harm her reputation or draw negative attention. She does not contradict what she believes in or stands for; she instead behaves like God's very own special child, full of love and compassion. She is classy and graceful – a lady. She possesses exceptional character and acts with integrity. She aims to do everything decently and in order.

    "But be sure that everything is done properly and in order." 1 Corinthians 14:40

    "...You should behave instead like God's very own children, adopted into his family – calling him "Father", dear Father." Romans 8:15

    "Avoiding a fight is a mark of honor; only fools insist on quarreling." Proverbs 20:3

    "Anyone who loves to quarrel loves sin; anyone who speaks boastfully invites disaster." Proverbs 17:19

    "A foolish child brings grief to a father and bitterness to a mother." Proverbs 17:25

    "The godly walk with integrity; blessed are their children after them." Proverbs 20:7

5. **A Princess is loyal.** She is loyal to her husband, family, friends, church, and commitments. People can trust and depend on her. She is persistent and faithful to God and the people around her. She is a woman of her word and does not lie. If she says it, she will do it. **Her loyalty enhances her royalty and makes her more attractive.**

   Purpose Point: When you are loyal, people will trust you. Disloyalty brings distrust.

   Proverbs 31 verse 11 - *"Her husband can trust her..."*

   "Loyalty makes a person attractive..." Proverbs 19:22

   *"...Never let **loyalty** and **kindness** get away from you! Wear them like a necklace; write them deep within your heart. Then you will find favor with both God and people, and you will gain a good reputation."* Proverbs 3:3-4

   Purpose Point: Being faithful is being loyal.

   Candid Clarification: It is important to choose the right relationships before dispensing loyalty – as it is difficult to be a powerful princess and hang around people who live the world's way and do not believe in or honor God. People who live worldly could influence you to live worldly; and therefore, are not worthy of loyalty. You must pick and choose your friends carefully. One way to choose your friends is to discern whether they fear or believe in God and obey His commands. If they do, then this could potentially be a friend for life who is worthy of your loyalty. You are wise if you choose the right friends, but if you choose wicked companions you bring shame to God, yourself, and your parents. The common ground of Christ is the start of a good and long-lasting friendship.

   Establish & cultivate positive relationships — Love, respect and forgive others, including self

   David said to God, *"Anyone who fears you is my friend – anyone who obeys your commandments."* Psalm 119:63

   "Young people who obey the law are wise; those who seek out worthless companions bring shame to their parents." Proverbs 28:7

   A gossip tells secrets, so don't hang around with someone who talks too much." Proverbs 20:19

   Purpose Point: If you have friends who live the world's ways and do not believe in or honor God, then these friends are an enemy of God. How can you claim to be a princess, confess God as your Lord and King, and hang around His enemies? This is not loyalty to God. Just think about it, how would you feel if your so-called friends hung around your enemies? You would probably feel betrayed and hurt.

   "...Don't you realize that friendship with this world makes you an enemy of God? I say it again, that if your aim is to enjoy this world, you can't be a friend of God." James 4:4

Purpose Point: A common saying is, *"Birds of feather flock together."* In other words, if you hang around people who are gossipers, evil and hateful then this indicates that you are also this way or possess a similar mindset. Your friends say a lot about who you are. Another popular truism is: *"If you ever want to truly know what a person is like, meet their friends."*

"Walk with the wise and become wise; associate with fools and get in trouble." Proverbs 13:20

"...Bad company corrupts good character." 1 Corinthians 15:33

Candid Clarification: Notice that the above scripture says that, "bad company corrupts good character", and not good character changes bad company. If God leads you to associate, witness, minister or pray for someone who lives a life contrary to God, by all means be led by His Spirit and attempt to redirect their soul to Christ. However, do not get caught up in their bad company (behaviors and thinking). Do not risk your salvation by trying to help someone find their own. Only God can change a person's heart; you can only sow the seeds and trust God to make them grow. But to do this effectively, you should be rooted and grounded in His Word.

"Blessed is the one who does not walk in step with the wicked or stand in the way that sinners take or sit in the company of mockers, but whose delight is in the law of the Lord, and who meditates on his law day and night. That person is like a tree planted by streams of water, which yields its fruit in season..." Psalm 1:1-3 NIV

Purpose Point: A loyal friend is extremely rare and hard to come by. Finding a friend who is going to be there for you no matter what is a gift from God. God wants you to be that gift; be loyal to your friends.

"Many will say they are loyal friends, but who can find one who is really faithful?" Proverbs 20:6

"A man who has friends must himself be friendly, but there is a friend who sticks closer than a brother." Proverbs 18:24 NJKV

"There are "friends" who destroy each other, but a real friend sticks closer than a brother." Proverbs 18:24 NLT

"A friend is always loyal, and a brother is born to help in a time of need." Proverbs 17:17

Purpose Point: If real friends stick closer than a brother, then we can conclude that a friend is also born to help in a time of need.

"Never abandon a friend – either yours or your father's. Then in your time of need, you won't have to ask your relatives for assistance..." Proverbs 27:10

Purpose Point: Some friends are better than relatives. They will be there for you like no kinship would, except maybe for close relatives like your parents. Remember, just because family are kin folk, does not make them kindred spirits. And just because someone claims to be your friend, does not mean they will always be by your side.

"The heartfelt counsel of a friend is as sweet as perfume and incense." Proverbs 27:9

"As iron sharpens iron, so a friend sharpens a friend." Proverbs 27:17

Purpose Point: It is important to exercise proper judgment when demonstrating loyalty and friendship.

"It's poor judgment to co-sign a friend's note, to become responsible for a neighbor's debt." Proverbs 17:18

6. <u>**A Princess is productive and has entrepreneurial abilities.**</u> A princess works hard! She is always busy providing for her family and helping others. She is energetic and refuses to give in to laziness. As an adult, she has her own money and does not depend on other people for it. She possesses entrepreneurial abilities – she makes and creates things and sells it. She uses her skills, talents, and earnings wisely by helping others and securing resources that can return a profit. She has muscle for hustle (gigs and business) and wit for wealth. She is creative, innovative, and strategic with her time and talents.

    Proverbs 31 verses 13 – 27
    *"She finds wool and flax and **busily** spins it. She is like a merchant ship; she brings her food from afar. She gets up before dawn to prepare breakfast for her household and **plan the day's work** for her servant girls. She goes out to inspect a field and **buys it; with her earnings** she plants a vineyard. **She is energetic and strong, a hard worker** … She extends a helping hand to the poor and opens her arms to the needy…She makes belt linen garments and sashes to sell to the merchants. She carefully watches all that goes on in her household and **does not have to bear the consequences of laziness**."*

7. <u>**A Princess loves and is kind.**</u> She has a good attitude and is not rude or arrogant. She possesses good manners and treats others respectfully in a way that shows they matter. She smiles and is courteous. People love to be around her. She does not act as though she is all that; she is humble. She does not look down on other people but is down-to-earth. She is caring, forgiving, helpful, encouraging, thoughtful and always ready to lift someone's spirit rather than tear them down.

    Proverbs Chapter 31 verse 26:
    "… kindness is the rule when she gives instructions."

8. <u>**A Princess prays.**</u> She knows that prayer is what connects her to her Creator and realizes that without this connection she could not sustain her position and fulfill her purpose. She engages in intercessory prayer by praying for others and is not concerned only with herself. She seeks the face of God (His will) and not just the hand of God (His blessings). She earnestly prays for her family (covering them in prayer every day) and prays that God's purpose will be done on earth. She is a prayer warrior, a praise giver, and a true worshiper.

9. <u>**A Princess is wise and is committed to becoming wiser.**</u> She loves to learn and understands that true wisdom comes from God. Her wisdom and intellect go hand and

hand making her glow inside out. She values knowledge and performs well in school. She participates in activities that will maximize knowledge and wisdom, such as reading her Bible, attending a word-based church, furthering her education, learning new skills, reading books, networking with others, mentorship, etc. She knows that it is through wisdom and knowledge that she will mature into a highly qualified queen.

Purpose Point: Wisdom brings you honor and the crown of life. Wisdom is your guide to a Princess's Pathway.

"Learn to be wise, and develop good judgment. Don't forget or turn away from my words. Don't turn your back on wisdom, for she will protect you. Love her, and she will guard you. Getting wisdom is the most important thing you can do! And whatever else you do, get good judgment. ***If you prize wisdom****, she will exalt you. Embrace her and she will honor you. She will place a lovely wreath on your head;* ***she will present you with a beautiful crown.****"* Proverbs 4:1-9

"A wise woman builds her home, but a foolish woman tears it down with her own hands." Proverbs 14:1

"It is better to be a poor but wise youth than to be an old and foolish king who refuses all advice." Ecclesiastes 4:13

"To acquire wisdom is to love oneself; *people who cherish understanding will prosper."* Proverbs 19:8

"Intelligent people are always open to new ideas. In fact, they look for them." Proverbs 18:15

"It is senseless to pay tuition to educate a fool who has no heart for wisdom." Proverbs 17:16

10. **A Princess serves and gives.** She gives whole-heartedly and not grudgingly. It makes her happy to help someone. She freely allows people to see the love of God inside her by helping others and making herself available to meet their needs.

    Proverbs 31 verse 20
    "She extends a helping hand to the poor and opens her arms to the needy."

11. **A Princess is modest.** She is not desperate for attention. She is humble and lowly, not conceited or arrogant. She does not think too highly of herself by looking down on others. She dresses decently and not degradingly. She is confident, not cocky. She does not advertise her body by wearing revealing clothing just to get attention or to feel better about herself. She behaves, walks, and conducts herself as a lady. She does not dress for the affirmation, acclamation, adulation, approval, or applause of others (the world), but for the glory of God. She is not primarily concerned with name brand clothing; she instead focuses on the name of Christ. Her *faith* outweighs fashion; her *sanctification* is more important than style. Her dress is aligned with her invaluable *dignity*; she covers up her cleavage to fully conceal her royal twins.

Proverbs 31 verse 22
"...She dresses like royalty in gowns of finest cloth."

Proverbs 31 verse 30
"Charm is deceptive, and beauty does not last; but a woman who fears the LORD will be greatly praised."

"...I want women to be modest in their appearance. They should wear decent and appropriate clothing and not draw attention to themselves...For women who claim to be devoted to God should make themselves attractive by the good things they do."
1 Timothy 2:9-10

"Women will be saved....by continuing to live in faith, love, holiness, and modesty."
1 Timothy 2:15

Purpose Point: Dress like royalty – decently, respectably, and classy. When it comes to human behavior, guys wonder; therefore, you should not provide them with a front row presentation of your body. Do not show off all your goods by packaging yourself in revealing, see-through and excessively short clothing. When a gift is packaged properly and sealed, people wonder what is inside, but when the package is open and placed in plain view, there is no wonder. You are that gift!!!

Do you recall what it is like to open wrapped presents on Christmas morning? No matter how old we get, receiving a wrapped gift makes you ecstatic. It is so exciting to open wrapped gifts because we do not know what is inside; we can only imagine. If the gifts were wrapped in see-through paper, they would not be as exciting or special. Therefore, as the old folks say…leave some things for the imagination; do not show off your goods and advertise yourself.

Purpose Point: Look classy! You are a princess, highly valued, growing into a mature queen. You represent the royal family. Remember this: *A lady with class does not show her ass.* This may sound harsh to some, but I must keep it real both directly and informally. In other words, a woman with class does not show every man her physical body by engaging in promiscuous sex and wearing revealing clothing, and she does not show out through obnoxious talking, profanity, gossiping (spreading rumors), fighting and arguing.

Purpose Point: Humility (lowliness) is a form of modesty. Not thinking too highly of yourself, and not thinking that you are better than others, reflects a humble heart.

"Don't be selfish; don't live to make a good impression on others. Be humble, thinking of others as better than yourself." Philippians 2:3

12. **<u>A Princess is confident; she knows who she is and is not jealous.</u>** A princess walks in her validated value, knowing that she is a priceless gift, worth more than anything in the world. She knows her value and what she is capable of; she knows her Creator and why she was created.

She is an overcomer; she does not allow depression, rejection, and low esteem to dominate her. She is optimistic about her future and the future of her family. She is not jealous of other women because she knows why God created her and that she is fearfully and wonderfully made – uniquely different. She does not engage in destructive, futile comparisons because she knows she is priceless and incomparable. She knows no one can beat her at her own game – becoming into the person she was created to be.

There are two kinds of jealousy:

- (1) Jealousy derived from indignation

Text Term: Indignation is justifiable or righteous anger such as being angry at someone or something when you have a right or just cause to be.

For example, if a husband sees his wife in a restaurant having dinner with another man (unbeknownst to him), he will most likely become very jealous; in this case, he has a right to be because she is his wife. In biblical days, when a husband became jealous due to suspicions of his wife cheating, it was required that he submit a jealousy offering or payment to the priest. The priests would then try to determine if she is guilty or not (Numbers 5:11-31). This indicates that jealousy derived from indignation is more accepted and understood by God when it is justified, rather than jealousy derived from inner self. There is no way God would allow a jealousy offering to be presented to His priests if God did not understand this kind of jealousy. Note: You can be angry, but do not sin (Ephesians 4:26).

Another example of this type of jealousy is God becoming jealous when we worship fake gods (idols) or live out Satan's ways. God created us; we are His creation, so He has a right to be jealous or indignant when we worship other things and do not acknowledge or obey Him, the one who created us. We should not be unfaithful to God by cheating on Him with other gods, just like a wife should not be unfaithful to her husband by cheating on him with another man. Worshiping other gods is called idolatry. God hates idolatry. God's first commandment says, *"Do not make idols of any kind, whether in the shape of birds or animals or fish. You must never bow down to them, for I, the Lord your God, am a jealous God who will not share your affection with any other god!..."* Deuteronomy 5:8-9

Purpose Point: Many years ago (and still often today) people created their own gods that were made from various materials such as gold, silver, ceramic, etc. Some people feel more comfortable worshiping a god they can see, rather than a god they cannot see. But one must realize that there is only one true living God. And that is the God who created the world. Although you cannot see Him, He is more alive and real than anything you can see. In fact, His mere existence is reflected in all the things we can see such as the beautiful sky, mighty oceans, rich green trees, and the sparkling stars in the midnight sky (Romans 1:20). God can be seen in everything He created. His mere existence is reflected in His creations like a face is reflected in shimmering water and a shadow is reflected on a wall. Fake gods have no creation, they themselves were created by idolatrous people. The one and only true living God is worthy of our affection and love – and only Jesus deserves our praise and worship.

It is important to know that anything that takes precedence and priority in your heart over God and consumes the majority of your affection, interest and time is your idol. For example, if you party and drink all the time, then partying and drinking is an idol. If you love to gamble and spend most of your time at the casinos, then gambling and the love of money is your idol. Engulfing yourself in social media, texting, internet, and TV for most of your day could also be considered an idol. God wants your love, affection, and time – He wants your heart. Some ways that we show God our affection and love is by praising and worshiping Him, praying and singing to Him, attending church, fulfilling and demonstrating our purpose, acknowledging Jesus throughout the day, reading the Bible, giving and helping others.

Jealousy derived from indignation will stem from love and what is right rather than from hate and selfish motives. God becomes jealous because of His great love for us.

"What do you think the Scriptures mean when they say that the Holy Spirit, whom God has placed within us, jealously longs for us to be faithful? He gives us more and more strength to stand against such evil desires. As the Scriptures say, God sets himself against the proud, but he shows favor to the humble. So humble yourselves before God..." James 4:5-7

"They made God angry by building alters to other gods; they made him jealous with their idols." Psalm 78:58

Purpose Point: Sometimes people may mistake indignation for jealousy. They may think that you do not like them because you are jealous of them, but the truth of the matter is you do not like them (their ways) because they are unfair, unjust, unfaithful, and untruthful. As princesses, we love to see right prevail just like our Father; consequently, we may become indignant when we see people being mistreated or when we are treated unfairly. But the battle is not ours, but the Lord's (2 Chronicles 20:15).

- (2) Jealousy derived from inner self

People who have jealousy in their heart derived from inner self will have hate and dislike in their hearts as well. Jealous people are known to be 'haters' when they act on that jealousy. The definition of the word 'haters' is found within the word itself – 'haters' are people who hate. They will hate you for no apparent reason at all, but it is usually due to what you have, how you look, and even your level of intelligence. Haters believe that they should have what you have and hate to see you succeed but love to see you fail. It drives them crazy to hear anything good about you and makes their day when they hear something bad about you. Additionally, they even hate being themselves and will love to be you. Yes, this is true, sometimes people hate you because they are not you. Their jealousy stems from their feelings of insecurity and lack ...motivated by the devil. Jealousy derived from inner self stems from hate – not love.

Again, this type of jealousy is extremely dangerous because it involves hate or a murderous heart. We know that hate is not of God – it is of the devil. When you become jealous and continually act out that jealousy by hating and doing evil things to others it shows that you do not belong to God. These actions demonstrate the characteristics of the devil. Devilish divas do exist.

"For jealousy and selfishness are not God's kind of wisdom. Such things are earthly, unspiritual, and motivated by the Devil. For wherever there is jealousy and selfish ambition, there you will find disorder and every kind of evil."
James 3:15-16

"If we are living now by the Holy Spirit, let us follow the Holy Spirit's leading in every part of our lives. Let us not become conceited, or irritate one another, or be jealous of one another." Galatians 5:25-26

Purpose Point: Some actions of jealousy include fighting, arguing, gossiping, mistreating others, lying, abuse, injustice, slander, defamation, rudeness, murder, etc.

Purpose Point: We all have haters and naysayers, but don't be one.

Purpose Point: God even has haters. Satan is his #1 HATER, in fact, he is the epitome of hate because all hate is derived from the devil. Remember, Satan was kicked out of heaven because he wanted to be like God. So, to sum up self-induced jealousy, it is basically wanting to be like someone else and wanting what that person has…or even wanting to be that person. Some people will do every kind of evil to get what you have and will attempt to make you unhappy in the process.

*"Their lives became full of every kind of wickedness, sin, greed, hate, envy, murder, fighting, deception, malicious behavior, and gossip. They are backstabbers, **haters of God**, insolent, proud and boastful…"* Romans 1:29-30

Purpose Point: Jealousy is often formed when people compare themselves to others. When you compare yourself to someone who appears to have more than you, you belittle yourself. Remember, we all have different purposes in life; do what God wants you to do and do not worry about what other people have, what they are doing or how they look.

"Be sure to do what you should, for then you will enjoy the personal satisfaction of having done your work well, and you won't need to compare yourself to anyone else. For we are each responsible for our own conduct." Galatians 6:4-5

Purpose Point: Jealousy brings dislike; therefore, there will be times when people will not like you for no apparent reason at all. You do not have to do anything to them; you can be just as kind and polite but for some 'strange' reason they will not like you, and you will not know why. But we know better – the reason, obviously, is jealousy! If you ever feel this way about a person, be honest with yourself and ask yourself, am I jealous? If so, repent and turn away from the spirit of jealousy!

Purpose Point: If they hated Jesus and was jealous of him for no reason, how much more will people hate you or be jealous of you – with or without cause.

Jesus said, *"This fulfills what is written in their Scriptures: 'They hated me without cause.'"* John 15:25

What God has for you, is for you!

Purpose Point: When a person is jealous it is usually because of three things:

1. They fear that their needs will not be met.
    - If you trust and believe God, He will meet your needs.
    "My God shall supply all your needs according to His riches in glory by Christ Jesus." Philippians 4:19 NKJV

2. They doubt or worry about their own worth and ability.
    - Remember, your price is far above rubies (Proverbs 31:10; Proverbs 3:15).
    - You can do all things through Christ who strengthens you (Philippians 4:13). However, whatever you do, do it for the right reason. Do not do it to compete with others for self-worth or attempt to make someone jealous of you.

3. They are not happy within themselves – (i.e. not happy with looks, abilities, status, or choices).

Essentially, people are jealous because they do not know who they are. They do not know that they were created in the image of God, made to be royalty, a child of the King – who has given them freely everything they need in this life and the next. They do not know that God is no respecter of persons, but He is a respecter of faith. When you come to know who you are in Christ and have faith to believe and obey, favor and blessings will follow you.

"...I see very clearly that God shows no favoritism. In every nation he accepts those who fear him and do what is right." Acts 10:34-35

"His divine power has given us everything we need for a godly life through our knowledge of him who called us by his own glory and goodness." 2 Peter 1:3 NIV

Purpose Point: Jealousy derived from indignation will stem from love, not hate. Jealousy derived from inner self will stem from hate, not love. Nevertheless, both types are influenced by the heart.

"You want what you don't have, so you scheme and kill to get it. You are jealous for what others have, and you can't possess it, so you fight and quarrel to take it away

from them. And yet the reason you don't have what you want is that you don't ask God for it. And even when you do ask, you don't get it because your whole motive is wrong – you want only what will give you pleasure." James 4:2-3

Purpose Point: God takes pleasure in giving His princesses good things. But sometimes He wants us to humble ourselves and ask Him for the things we want. We must be careful and ask for the right things for the right reason – with a right motive. For example, a woman asking God to make a man leave his wife for her is totally wrong and reflects an adulterous heart. Or, if a person asks God to bless them with a big house just so they can show it off and make others jealous, is also asking with the wrong motive. God will not give you anything that will please your sinful desires or selfish motives. And those who do receive the desires of their heart framed with malice, evil and selfish intentions, do not receive from God but from the enemy – the devil – which results in deception, and brings discontentment, degradation and/or destruction along with it.

Purpose Point: It pleases God when we do not ask for things with a selfish motive, but instead ask for things that will benefit others and bring God's will to pass in the earth. However, there is nothing wrong with asking God for things. He longs to bless you, but let it be for the enjoyment, edification and equipping of your personal growth (material or spiritual) and God's glory, and not to impress others or make them jealous.

I recall a story in the Bible where God asked a man named Solomon (son of David) what he wanted. His response was so selfless for the right reason.

"That night God appeared to Solomon in a dream and said, "What do you want?" Ask, I will give it to you!" Solomon replied to God, "You have been so faithful and kind to my father, David, and now you have made me king in his place. Now, Lord God, please keep your promise to David my father, for you have made me king over a people as numerous as the dust of the earth! Give me wisdom and knowledge to rule them properly, for who is able to govern this great nation of yours? God said to Solomon, "Because your greatest desire is to help your people, and you did not ask for personal wealth and honor or the death of your enemies or even long life, but rather you asked for wisdom and knowledge to properly govern my people, I will certainly give you the wisdom and knowledge you requested. And I will also give you riches, wealth, and honor such as no other king has ever had before you or will ever have again!"
2 Chronicles 1:7-12

Purpose Point: When you ask God for things unselfishly, with the right motive and the desire to help others or bring glory to God, God will give you what you ask for and so much more.

What do you do when people are jealous of you?

There is nothing you can do except pray for them. That person has to make the decision to work out some things within themselves – inside their heart. They obviously have some inner issues going on. I know it may be hard but try to be nice and not stoop down to their level. Overcome evil by doing good. If a person, however, is threatening or mistreating you, or causing you harm, then you may have to take the appropriate action for that situation, which may include involving an authority such as your parent, teacher, boss or law enforcement.

Purpose Point: Have you ever wondered why a person treats you differently from everyone else in a negative way? You may think it is showing favoritism or being inconsiderate or rude, but the real issue could be rooted in jealousy. The reason for jealousy is not always obvious.

Some people are jealous of your happiness; they will often get jealous or mad at you just because you are happy or successful. "Misery loves company." *Happiness is an annoying distraction to those who are not happy.*

Are you jealous of someone? If the answer is "yes", repent and realize that you are a rare ruby. God made you uniquely different and put a special gift inside of you.

Think about it; what sense would it make for an arm to be jealous of a foot or an eye to be jealous of an ear? They each serve a different purpose and produce a different result. We are all one body in Christ, each serving a different purpose and producing a different outcome. If we are to fulfill our purpose individually, we must work together as one body and not be jealous of one another. If the eyes did not provide vision, the feet could walk into a brick wall. God needs all of us to work together in harmony and get along. Don't be a hater!

"Yes, the body has many different parts, not just one part. If the foot says, "I am not a part of the body because I am not a hand," that does not make it any less a part of the body. And if the ear says, "I am not part of the body because I am only an ear and not an eye," would that make it any less a part of the body? Suppose the whole body were an eye – then how would you hear? Or if your whole body were just one big ear, how could you smell anything? But God made our bodies with many parts, and he has put each part just where he wants it. What a strange thing a body would be if it had only one part! Yes, there are many parts, but only one body. The eye can never say to the hand, "I don't need you." The head can't say to the feet, "I don't need you." In fact, some of the parts that seem weakest and least important are really the most necessary…This makes for harmony among the members, so that all the members care for each other equally." 1 Corinthians 12:14-25

"The human body has many parts, but the many parts make up only one body. So it is with the body of Christ." 1 Corinthians 12:12

"Now all of you together are Christ's body, and each one of you is a separate and necessary part of it." 1 Corinthians 12:27

Purpose Point: People who accept Jesus Christ as their Lord and Savior are all a part of the same body. We each have a different part to play and serve a different purpose. Some may be gifted to serve one purpose, and some may be gifted to serve another. And some people may seem very important, while others think of themselves as being insignificant. But according to scripture, the parts that seem weak and insignificant are really the most necessary. So do not be jealous of others; you have your own part to play. Let us all demonstrate our purpose, work together in harmony and care for each other equally. We all have the same evil enemy who seeks to destroy us every day; therefore, show each other support.

"Now there are different kinds of spiritual gifts, but it is the same Holy Spirit who is the source of them all. There are different kinds of services in the church, but it is the same Lord we are serving. There are different ways God works in our lives, but it is the same God who does the work through all of us. A spiritual gift is given to each of us as a means of helping the entire church. To one person the Spirit gives the ability to give wise advice; to another he gives the gift of special knowledge. The Spirit gives special faith to another, and to someone else he gives the power to heal the sick. He gives one person the power to perform miracles, and to another the ability to prophesy. He gives someone else the ability to know whether it is really the Spirit of God or another spirit that is speaking. Still another person is given the ability to speak in unknown languages, and another is given the ability to interpret what is being said. It is the one and only Holy Spirit who distributes these gifts. He alone decides which gift each person should have." 1 Corinthians 12:4-11

God is our creator; He created the physical characteristics of every individual and gave each person a special gift. Therefore, you cannot be jealous of another person because God made them a certain way or gave them a special gift. If you are, then you are basically saying that God does not know what He is doing and that He should have done things differently. You must remember that God made you special and has also given you a gift; you probably just have not tapped into it yet. We are all first in God's heart; God is no respecter of persons. He does not show favoritism. God established each person's gift long ago before that person was born. He will not change His mind and give you someone else's gift just because you are not happy with yours.

"For God does not show favoritism." Romans 2:11

"For God's gifts and his call can never be withdrawn." Romans 11:29

Purpose Point: If you are jealous of someone, it will surely show up or come out sooner or later.

"People with hate in their hearts may sound pleasant enough, but don't believe them. Though they pretend to be kind, their hearts are full of all kinds of evil. While their hatred may be concealed by trickery, it will finally come to light for all to see."
Proverbs 26:24-26

When you come to know God's purpose for you, there will be no room for jealousy. When you accept who you are and fully understand that God created us all unique… and gave us different gifts and talents, you will begin to embrace you. Consider the book of Exodus; God instructed Moses to build a Tabernacle (a special Holy place) for His priests to minister. This was a huge task to be completed which required many people to see it come to pass; therefore, Moses invited all people to bring offerings such as gold, silver, bronze, wood, yarn, and goat hair for cloth, to assist in building the Tabernacle. Everyone had unique talents and brought something different for this monumental cause.

"All the women who were skilled in sewing and spinning prepared blue, purple, and scarlet yarn, and fine linen cloth, and they brought them in. All the women who were willing used their skills to spin and weave the goat hair into cloth…every man and woman who wanted to help in the work the Lord had given them…brought their offerings to the Lord. And Moses told them, "The Lord has chosen Bezalel, son of Uri, grandson of Hur, of the tribe of Judah. The Lord has filled Bezalel with the Spirit of God, giving him great wisdom, intelligence, and skill in all kinds of crafts. He is able to create beautiful objects from gold, silver, and bronze. He is skilled in cutting and setting gemstones and in carving wood. In fact, he has every necessary skill…The Lord has given them special skills as jewelers, designers, weavers, and embroiders…They excel in all the crafts needed for the work…"
Exodus 35:25-35

   Everyone who assisted in building the tabernacle had a different skillset, a different purpose – and was willing to help. God gave some women the skill to spin and weave and gave others the skill to sew. He chose to give one man many special skills, while others were given select or few skills as jewelers, designers, weavers and embroiders. The people who had only one special skill could have easily become jealous with the man who was given many special skills from God, but instead they chose to work together in harmony. Like so, God has given each of His princesses a special skill(s), a gift, to assist in building His kingdom. Some princesses may have more skills than you, some may have less. Regardless, do not be jealous of another person. We should all be working together towards one goal led by one Spirit to serve one God with our collective skills and talents. **You will excel at the very task(s) God has called and gifted you to do when you step out and are willing to do it.**

"How wonderful it is, how pleasant, for God's people to live together in harmony! It is like the precious anointing oil…" Psalm 133:1-2 GNT

Purpose Point: Comparing yourself to others is meaningless. God made everyone different in their own way and gave each person special talents. When you compare yourself to others, you belittle God because you think God should have created you differently.

You also belittle yourself because you feel as though you are not enough and should be different.

Purpose Point: The scripture said, *"All women who were willing used their skills..."* Therefore, you should be willing to use the gift(s) that God has given you. Humble yourself, seek Him, and make yourself available to God so that your skills and gifts can be used.

Another biblical occurrence that comes to mind is…

After Jesus died and rose again, he appeared to his disciples several times. During the third occurrence, Jesus spoke specifically to one of his disciples, Peter. Jesus told Peter to follow him. As they walked along the beach, Peter looked back and saw another disciple. *"Peter asked Jesus, 'What about him, Lord?' Jesus replied, 'If I want him to remain alive until I return, what is that to you? You follow me.'"* John 21:21-22

In other words, Jesus was saying, *'Mind your own business; don't worry about him. I know the purpose and plans I have for him. You, focus on you, and follow me.'*

Purpose Point: Don't be concerned about what others are doing or what they have. Don't worry about someone having more than you or doing better than you. Focus on Jesus and follow him and let Jesus focus on others.

Purpose Point: Remember, as a princess you must take your place. Don't try to take someone else's place, rather be who God created you to be. When you try to take someone else's place while being envious and jealous you are out of order.

Purpose Point: Remember, God is no respecter of persons; what He did for one person He can do for You, as aligned with His will and purpose for your life. However, understand this: your life is not about you, but God's will and purpose (Romans 2:11; Luke 22:42; John 4:34).

There may be times when you find yourself wondering why someone has more than you, whether it be money, looks, or happiness; it may be because of their hard work, choices, genetics, diet/exercise, family ties, prayers or faith. Regardless, **be thankful for what you have because someone always has it worse.**

Purpose Point: When you compare yourself to others, it brings about stress and anxiety, and frames an inferior image of you that contributes to a low self-esteem. You can worry yourself crazy by constantly thinking about how someone looks better than you, or how someone has more than you. You discount yourself and God when you compare yourself to others. Love yourself and be happy with who you are and what you have. It is okay to strive to become better with the right motive, but do not try to change yourself or circumstances because you are trying to keep up or be like someone else. If you do, it can lead you down the wrong path to the wrong destiny. Be content with what you have in the moment.

Purpose Point: Contentment should not be confused with complacency. Contentment is being thankful or satisfied with what you have or accepting where you are for the moment while recognizing and living up to your full potential. Complacency, on the other hand, is being commonplace and satisfied with mediocrity – not recognizing or utilizing your God-given gifts, talents, skills, and abilities. Contentment *conquers* complaining, doubt, envy, jealousy, worry and fear. Complacency *cripples* your potential and God-given purpose. Change your thinking and renew your mind to achieve contentment and conquer complacency. Choose contentment over comparison; choose change over complacency. In other words, be content with where you are but do not stay stuck there – grow, go, and glow with God.

"... I have learned to be content whatever the circumstances. I know what it is to be in need, and I know what it is to have plenty. I have learned the secret of being content in any and every situation, whether well fed or hungry, whether living in plenty or in want. I can do all this through him who gives me strength." Philippians 4:11-13 NIV

"But godliness with contentment is great gain." 1 Timothy 6:6 NIV

Purpose Point: When you compare yourself to others, you dishonor God by forgetting or discrediting what He has done for you. When you criticize how you look and what you have, you are criticizing your Creator.

Purpose Point: God has patented you with purpose; therefore, you do not have the right to reinvent yourself. Don't infringe on the laws of God. You are copyright protected©. Choosing to make yourself a copy of someone else is strictly prohibited and goes against God's law. Your trade (talent/gift) is marked especially for you!

Jealousy vs. Envy

- Envy is the desire to have what someone else has, also known as to covet.
    - A person may envy the way a person looks, their possessions, job, talents, and gifts. In the 10th commandment, God tells us not to envy or covet others. *"Do not covet your neighbor's house. Do not covet your neighbor's wife...or anything else your neighbor owns."* Exodus 20:17
- Jealousy is a bitter feeling that someone has something that rightfully belongs to you – which can spark feelings of anger, rage, dislike, and hate.
- Envy can lead to jealousy. The words envy and jealousy are often used synonymously.

"Stop your anger! Turn from your rage! Do not envy others – it only leads to harm." Psalm 37:8

Purpose Point: You have no right to be envious or jealous of anyone, especially if you did not do what they did to get what they have. For example, you cannot be jealous of someone who has a big house and nice car if you never worked a day in your life or pursued an education. Jealousy and envy are two primary reasons why we have a world fraught with crime, violence, and wars – because some believe they should rightfully have what somebody else has worked hard for. As a result, they steal and murder to get it. If you work hard and prepare yourself with knowledge, you will have the potential of duplicating others who are successful. But do not get caught up with just having material things; get caught up with God and He will give you the desires of your heart. **Real success is living out your purpose and achieving your God-given destiny.**

Purpose Point: Some legitimate ways in which people obtain tangible things of value are prayer (asking God for it), education, wisdom, knowledge, and hard work.

Candid Clarification: There are many people who do not, or did not, have the same opportunities and options as others. It hurts to look at other people and see them have the very things you long for and were not given a fair chance in life to obtain (i.e. loving parents, a family, a home, transportation, money, a good education or even basic necessities such as food and clothing). God knows your story and situation. You may have had a rough start, or been recently faced with a tough situation, but God sees and feels your pain. Take the time now to pray and know that God is a restorer and redeemer of time. He can do exceedingly, abundantly above all that you can ask or think according to the power that works in you (Ephesians 3:20). Stay in faith; be encouraged.

13. <u>**A Princess is attentive.**</u> She is sensitive to the needs of others. She understands God's ways and the people around her. She knows their likes and dislikes – what makes them happy and what brings them displeasure. Her attention is drawn in their direction ready and waiting to meet their needs. When she sees people hurt or in need, she is ever ready to help. When she sees her husband in need, she fulfills that need; she fulfills the desires of God by serving and ministering to Him through prayer, worship, and praise. She fulfills the needs of her family with her unwavering support. She realizes that she was not born for herself, but for others. She sometimes stays up late doing things and thinking of ways to enrich the lives of the people around her and those aligned with her passion/calling. She is attentive in the marketplace, watching for bargains that could save her and her family money, and not buying everything that she sees or is on sale.

Proverbs 31 verse 18 and 20
"She watches for bargains; her lights burn late into the night."
"She extends a helping hand to the poor and opens her arms to the needy."

Proverbs 31 verse 11
"Her husband can trust her, and she will greatly enrich his life. She will not hinder him but help him all her life."

"Don't think only about your own affairs, but be interested in others, too, and what they are doing." Philippians 2:4

Purpose Point: Remember, standing means doing what is right by God's standards. When we continue to do what is right, we stand firm. And when we stand firm, we will stand with God forever. The Bible clearly describes the type of people who will stand firm:

- *"Those who lead blameless lives and do what is right, speaking the truth from sincere hearts.*
- *Those who refuse to slander others or harm their neighbors or speak evil of their friends.*
- *Those who despise persistent sinners* and honor the faithful followers of the Lord, and keep their promises even when it hurts.*

- *Those who do not charge interest on the money they lend, and who refuse to accept bribes to testify against the innocent.*

Such people will stand firm forever." Psalm 15:2-5

*Those who despise the sinful acts (not the person) of those who sin persistently without any desire to do what is right or any regard for right living.

In other words, people who: do what is right; speak God's truth with a genuine heart and do not lie; do not harm others by their words or actions; honor the faithful followers of God such as pastors, ministers and your brothers and sisters in the Lord; keep *dignified* promises even when they do not feel like it; do not charge interest on the money they lend; and refuse to accept bribes or money to hurt the innocent – will stand firm forever.

Purpose Point: When you continue to do what is right you stand firm – unmovable, unshakeable, and unwavering. There may be times when you stumble, but the key is to get back up and S.T.A.N.D. When you stop doing what is right you become out of order, out of place, and lose your firm footing.

The Princess Within

Minute Memoir: One day I was feeling extremely down and discouraged. As I was leaving work, I decided to stop at the store before heading home. I parked, got out the car, and proceeded to walk into the store; but as I was walking an elderly Caucasian gentleman with dark blue sunglasses rode passed me in his car as he was leaving the parking lot. He stopped and let down his window and asked me, *"Are you a pink princess?"*. Extremely dumbfounded by the oddity of his question, I responded, "I hope so". I did not know why he asked me that question. I was not dressed like a princess. I did not look like a princess. I had on blue jeans and a white and pink striped shirt. My shirt did not have "Princess" written on it; it was just a simple plain Polo shirt. But when the gentleman asked me that question, it immediately lifted my spirit. I felt as though this was God's way of encouraging me, reminding me of who I am. Out of all the questions the gentleman could have asked me, he asked was I a princess. At that moment when I didn't feel like a princess, when I didn't feel beautiful, valuable, or significant, a complete stranger saw the Princess within me.

Purpose Point: Regardless of how you feel, your beauty and value are intrinsic; others will see it, even when you do not.

Listen to your King!

*"My child never forget the things I have taught you. Store my commands in your **heart**, for they will give you a long and satisfying life. Never let **loyalty** and **kindness** get away from you! Wear them like a necklace; write them deep within your **heart**. Then you will find favor with both God and people, and you will gain a **good reputation**.* Proverbs 3:1-4

Daughters of a King:

To the tune of "Lilies." Of the Sons of Korah. A maskil. A wedding song.

"Kings' daughters are among your concubines. At your right side stands the queen, wearing jewelry of finest gold from Ophir! **Listen to me**, *O royal daughter; take to heart what I say. Forget your people and your homeland far away. For your royal husband delights in your beauty; honor him, for he is your lord. The princes of Tyre will shower you with gifts. People of great wealth will entreat your favor. The bride, a princess, waits within her chamber, dressed in a gown woven with gold. In her beautiful robes, she is led to the king, accompanied by her bridesmaids. What a joyful, enthusiastic procession as they enter the king's palace! Your sons will become kings like their father. You will make them rulers over many lands. I will bring honor to your name in every generation. Therefore, the nations will praise you forever and ever."* Psalm 45:9-17

In other words, this is what I believe God is saying to you in the above scripture:

'My daughters are among those who are gullible and vulnerable – and many respectable women. At your right side stands the queen wearing jewelry of the finest gold. I have predestined for her a life full of my best and blessings, the finest things in life. Listen to me, O royal daughter; take heart to what I say. Forget your past and friends from far away who do not mean you any good. For your royal Father delights in you, and so will your royal husband delight in your beauty. Honor me as Lord as you honor him. A godly prince will shower you with gifts. People of great riches will beseech you. You are a princess, waiting in your chamber, dressed in a spiritual gown woven in gold. In your beautiful robes, you are led to the king. How joyful and exciting it will be for you to enter the king's palace! Your sons will become kings like their Father. I will make them rulers in the earth and will bring honor to your name in every generation. People will praise you as you praise me.'

Purpose Point: Ultimately, this is the message for you:

Princesses please **STAND!** **S**et yourself apart, **T**ake your place, **A**ffirm your identity, **N**ullify your past and **D**emonstrate your purpose.

You are royalty, of great value – God's creation, His daughters. Know that you are a Princess, act as such, and mature into a Queen. Stand and walk in your destiny! For God has crowned you with glory and honor and has given you authority over all things. (Psalm 8:5-9).

STAND and walk in your delegated authority!!! Bow to the King…Jesus!

"Obey the king because you have vowed before God to do this. Don't try to avoid doing your duty, and don't take a stand with those who plot evil…" Ecclesiastes 8:2-3

"…how much more will those who receive God's abundant provision of grace and of the gift of righteousness **reign in life** *through the one man, Jesus Christ!"* Romans 5:17 NIV

Purpose Point: Remember, you are a **Predestined Priceless Precious Princess Possessing Powerful Purpose!** Try that for a tongue twister :>)

You are a part of God's kingdom—seated on the throne of His heart. *It is time to do some kingdom living! And the secret to Kingdom living is Kingdom thinking — change your thinking and change your life…change your mindset and move in majesty.*

Purpose Point: Don't allow fear, rejection and low self-esteem to paralyze you; don't use them as a crutch. You have the strength inside you to STAND on your own two feet.
Yes girl! You are strong enough to walk in worth.

Purpose Point: Refuse to keep the princess within you locked up in a jail cell in chains of bondage – hurt, rejection, low self-esteem, addictions, and abuse. Let her out by using Jesus Christ as the key. Unlock the cell—set her FREE! God has validated your value!

"For in that day, says the Lord Almighty, I will break the yoke from their necks and snap their chains…" Jeremiah 30:8

*"He redeems me from death and **crowns me with love and tender mercies**."* Psalm 103:4

**God's Majesty is greater than your Misery.
God's Royalty is stronger than any Rejection…**

**His Love reigns over all!
STAND in the truth of your experience and God's redemptive power. STAND in the Word of God; STAND for the Word of God and STAND on the Word of God.
By all means, S.T.A.N.D.**

"In your majesty ride forth victoriously in the cause of truth, humility and justice; let your right hand achieve awesome deeds." Psalm 45:4 NIV

**Those in Christ are Royalty…
Kings and Queens in the earth.**

"Fear not…for it is your Father's good pleasure to give you the kingdom." Luke 12:32 ESV

**As long as you have Christ,
you have an immortal crown.**

"To each there comes in their lifetime a special moment when they are figuratively tapped on the shoulder and offered the chance to do a very special thing, unique to them and fitted to their talents. What a tragedy if that moment finds them unprepared or unqualified for that which could have been their finest hour." - Winston Churchill

Chapter 6
Qualified Queen

*"...Who knows if perhaps you were made <u>**queen**</u> for just such a time as this?"* Esther 4:14

*"In this way, God <u>**qualified**</u> him as a perfect High Priest, and he became the source of eternal salvation for all those who obey him."* Hebrews 5:9

Purpose Point: Prepare yourself for a spiritual promotion – a new royal position! Enhance your qualifications through maturity and grow into a queen.

Know who you are
Understand your value, capability and purpose

Make life-long positive choices
Choose to do what is right...apply godly principles

When you think of a queen, you may think of a woman who rules next to or independent of her king. You may think of castles, soldiers, servants, and an abundance of riches. Living today as a princess or queen is a mindset that you must embrace as a child of God. Your castle is your home (family home/heavenly home); the kingdom (the totality of God...all that He is and all that He has) lives in you; your throne is the authority God gave you; your spiritual King is the God you serve – Jesus; and your natural king is the husband you marry. Your soldiers and servants are the angels of God; and your abundance of riches are wrapped in God's promises of salvation, love, wisdom, healing, peace, protection, favor, joy, and prosperity.

"But angels are only servants. They are spirits sent from God to care for those who will receive salvation." Hebrews 1:14

"...nor will they say, 'See here!' or 'See there!' For indeed, the kingdom of God is within you." Luke 17:21 NKJV

"I have given you authority...to overcome all the power of the enemy; nothing will harm you." Luke 10:19 NIV

*"...They stumble because they do not obey God's word, and so they meet the fate that was planned for them. **But you are not like that, for you are a chosen people. You are royal priests, a holy nation, God's very own possession**. As a result, you can show others the goodness of God, for he called you out of the darkness into his wonderful light. Once you had no identity as a people; now you are God's people. Once you received no mercy; now you have received God's mercy."* 1 Peter 2:8-10

Purpose Point: Being a queen is not about having the *things*, but about possessing the *traits* of godly royalty.

    A queen has the highest authority as a female in the kingdom. She strongly believes in duty first, self second. She is highly respected and honored – mature, kind, intelligent and wise. She handles herself with the utmost care and conducts herself in an orderly manner – as a lady with strength, courage, class, and dignity. She is guided by godly wisdom, grace, faith, modesty, elegance, and wise speech. She loves, serves, and defends her sovereign King. She is strong, beautiful, valuable, confident, caring, and contributes to the world around her. She rules in wisdom, possessing discernment and discretion in all matters. She walks by faith, and not by sight. She is a believer, an overcomer – victorious in all things.

    Consider Queen Esther, a faithful woman of God, who exemplified the core characteristics of a queen (Esther 1-10). Esther was teachable…receiving and applying godly instruction where it mattered most. She respected her king and risked her life to save her people. Her prevailing attitudes were, *"If it pleases my king…."*, and *"If I perish, I perish"* as she considered God and the welfare of others. What about you? Does your prevailing attitude involve pleasing God, your heavenly King and Father? Do you consider the well-being and souls of others despite your fears, insecurities, and selfish desires? This is what it means to be a true queen – godliness, faithfulness, wisdom, love, courage, and sacrifice.

    To progress to the role of a queen, you must get pass the past (by learning from it and allowing it to "refine you and not define you"), embrace the present, envision and prepare for the future. When you get pass the past, you can embrace your present as a princess, and envision and prepare for your future as a queen. Envision means to see something that does not yet exist in the natural…it involves faith.

    As a princess, you should imagine or see yourself in the future doing great things as a queen – going higher in God, growing in knowledge, and understanding, and teaching others. You should prepare yourself for the honorable task of a queen.

We should never stay stuck in a position or place, but we should grow and become better – learning better and then doing better and repeating it all over again. God does not want you to stay stagnated and stifled in your position as a princess. He wants you to grow and mature into a Queen – full grown in the Lord.

Purpose Point: Spiritual growth, like salvation, is not automatic. <u>You must choose</u> to grow up in the Lord.

Supporting Scriptures:

*"...until we come to such unity in our faith and knowledge of God's Son that we will be **mature** and **full grown in the Lord**, measuring up to the full stature of Christ. Then we will no longer be like children, forever changing our minds about what we believe because someone has told us something different or because someone has cleverly lied to us and made the lie sound like the truth."* Ephesians 4:13-14

*"So I....appeal to you to live a life worthy of the calling to which you have been called [that is, to **live a life that exhibits godly character, moral courage, personal integrity, and mature behavior** – a life that expresses gratitude to God for your salvation], with all humility [forsaking self-righteousness], and gentleness [maintaining self-control], with patience, bearing with one another in [unselfish] love."* Ephesians 4:1-2 AMP

*"Learn to be wise, and develop good judgment. Don't forget or turn away from my words. Don't turn your back on wisdom, for she will protect you. Love her, and she will guard you. Getting wisdom is the most important thing you can do! And whatever else you do, get good judgment. If you prize wisdom, she will exalt you. Embrace her and she will honor you; she will place a lovely wreath on your head; **she will present you with a beautiful crown.**"* Proverbs 4:5-9

Purpose Point: *You must bow before the Throne before you sit on a throne.* In other words, you must first believe, acknowledge the King (Jesus) and accept His authority and wisdom before you can acquire royalty status and reign in life.

<u>**Becoming Queen**</u>
As a baby, you grew and learned new things. You began to understand your surroundings and learned new concepts. Like so, as a princess you are in the baby stage, but as time goes on you should feed your spirit, grow, and develop by learning, understanding, and applying the principles of God. Once you are full-grown and mature in the Lord (following God's ways and living out His purpose) He qualifies you as a queen and places you on a throne of honor. The two most fundamental principles of becoming a queen are *obedience* and *wisdom*.

Obedience is learned from the things we experience and suffer. For example, if a child touches a hot iron after the parent says not to touch it, then when the child gets burned, he will probably never touch it again. Although his parent told him not to touch it, he learned to obey by getting burned, by feeling the heat – suffering. But sometimes suffering is not always a direct result of something wrong you did, sometimes it is allowed by God to achieve a greater purpose. Jesus learned obedience from the things he suffered, yet he never sinned.

The things that Jesus suffered were allowed by God so that Jesus could achieve his purpose in the earth; it was not because of something wrong he had done. *"So even though Jesus was God's Son, he learned obedience from the things he suffered. In this way, God **qualified** him as a perfect High Priest, and he became the source of eternal salvation for all those who obey him."* Hebrews 5:8-9 Not all people will suffer in life early on. Some will be born with a silver spoon in their mouth, so to speak, where their parents are rich, everything goes their way, and they have everything they ever wanted. In these cases, people are often spoiled and entitled, and have not had any real experiences to draw from to bring them closer to God. If this sounds like you, take initiative and do not wait until something bad happens to draw you closer to God. Start developing yourself spiritually today and move forward into maturity.

In addition to the principles of a princess, a queen:

- Believes and trusts God in all things – she perseveres (persist even when severe)
- Defends and *stands* for the Word of God
- Discerns matters and is spiritually aware
- Does not constantly change her mind about what she believes
- Does right without thinking twice (it is natural for her)
- Eats solid food (receives and understands the in-depth teachings of God's Word)
- Evaluates what is wise and beneficial for the kingdom, her family, and her destiny – seeks first the kingdom of God and all His righteousness
- Fellowships with other believers and attends church faithfully
- Has a devoted intimate relationship with God
- Is dedicated to the ministry – serves, gives, and helps others faithfully
- Is a doer of the Word – *preaches* and *practices* (*shares* God's Word and *sets the example*)
- Learns and grows from trails, tests, and troubles – analyzes the situation to discover lessons learned
- Manages her emotions effectively; she is not ruled by her feelings
- Manages her time and resources effectively (self-disciplined); she is not easily distracted and is a good steward of her time, treasures, and talents
- Obeys God in every area of her life; accepts constructive criticism
- Prays God's Word in every situation
- Strategizes for the greater God and the greater good
- Studies her Bible faithfully
- Takes care of her home faithfully – meets and exceeds the needs of her family (husband/children)
- Takes responsibility for her actions; she is willing to apologize sincerely and admit when she is wrong
- Tells and teaches others about Jesus; trains herself and others (discipline/disciple)
- Walks in purpose and aims to fulfill her God-given destiny
- Worships and praises God faithfully

Purpose Point: A princess may stumble while STANDing, but a Queen STANDS firm.

In summary, the qualifications of a queen essentially surround spiritual maturity and includes:

1. <u>**G**odly Wisdom</u> through studying and applying the Word of God
2. <u>**O**bedience</u> in every area of life – distinguishing right from wrong and doing what is right
3. <u>**D**emonstration of purpose</u> (faithfulness to God and serving others)

When you prove that you possess these qualifications by doing them, God will qualify you as a queen just like He qualified Jesus as a High Priest. You will then move forward on your journey from the position of a princess to the position of a queen. *"...Who knows if perhaps you were made queen for just such a time as this?"* Esther 4:14

"...What is more pleasing to the LORD: your burnt offerings and sacrifices or your obedience to his voice? Listen! **Obedience is far better than sacrifice**. *Listening to him is much better than offering the fat of rams."* 1 Samuel 15:22

PROVE YOURSELF

"Work hard so God can approve you. Be a good worker, one who does not need to be ashamed and who correctly explains the word of truth." 2 Timothy 2:15 NLT

"Study to show yourself approved unto God, *a workman that needs not to be ashamed, rightly dividing the word of truth."* 2 Timothy 2:15 KJV (2000 Bible)

"Remember how the Lord your God led you through the wilderness..., humbling you and testing you to **prove your character**, *and to find out whether or not you would really obey his commands. Yes, he humbled you by letting you go hungry and then feeding you with manna, a food previously unknown to you and your ancestors. He did it to teach you that people need more than bread for their life; real life comes by feeding on every word of the Lord..."* Deuteronomy 8:2-3

"...work hard to **prove that you really are among those God has called and chosen**. *Doing this, you will never stumble or fall away. And God will open wide the gates of heaven for you to enter into the eternal Kingdom of our Lord and Savior Jesus Christ."* 2 Peter 1:10-11

Purpose Point: Proving that you possess the qualifications of a queen should be done because of your love for God, and not to gain acceptance from Him or other people. God accepted you when you believed in Jesus. Proving yourself shouldn't be done in a way to show off as some self-righteous person. It's all about motive –what makes you do what you do. God wants to be the motive for everything you do. If He's not, He will know it because He knows every heart.

As a princess, you are in the infant or baby stage. You are still learning the simple things of God such as being born again and may have trouble understanding these simple truths. You are still in the process of becoming accustomed to God's ways; therefore, you might struggle with sin and sometimes live the world's way. You might still play both sides of the fence by sometimes doing godly things and other times engaging in worldly (ungodly) behaviors. You might waver back and forth in what you believe, even though you have accepted Jesus as your Lord and Savior. It may be difficult for you to understand the more in-depth teachings of the Bible because you are still learning the simple things. These simple and elementary truths are referred to as the "milk" of God's Word.

Paul, a servant of God, said: *"Dear brothers and sisters...I couldn't talk to you as I would to mature Christians. I had to talk as though you belonged to this world or as though you were infants in the Christian life. I had to feed you with milk and not with solid food, because you could not handle anything stronger. And you still aren't ready, for you are still controlled by your own sinful desires. You are jealous of one another and quarrel with each other. Doesn't that prove you are controlled by your own desires? You are acting like people who don't belong to the Lord."* 1 Corinthians 3:1-3

"So let us stop going over the basics of Christianity again and again. Let us go on instead and become mature in our understanding. Surely we don't need to start all over again with the importance of turning away from evil deeds and placing our faith in God. You don't need further instruction about baptisms, the laying on of hands, the resurrection of the dead, and eternal judgment." Hebrews 6:1-2

MEANINGFUL METAMORPHOSIS

Our goal as daughters and princesses in Christ should be to grow from an infant into an adult, from milk to solid food, from a princess to a queen. As a princess, you are an infant on milk, but as a queen you are an adult on solid food. We need to grow and be ready for everything God has for us, ready for solid food – spiritual sustenance. The main ingredient of spiritual solid food includes the in-depth teachings of God such as righteousness, being filled with the Holy Spirit, praying in tongues, understanding the fresh revelations and mysteries of God, and applying what you've learned through application and obedience. Don't be slow to learn; grow and mature into a queen – get your plates and forks ready to eat solid food by renewing your mind and ridding yourself of distractions.

"Anyone who lives on milk, being still an infant, is not acquainted with the teaching about righteousness." Hebrews 5:13 NIV

"Dear brothers and sisters, don't be childish in your understanding of these things. Be innocent as babies when it comes to evil, but be mature and wise in understanding matters of this kind..." 1 Corinthians 14:20

There are many people who have been attending church for over 20 years and are still learning the simple things of God – drinking milk through a bottle. This is totally unproductive and can limit your progress. It is just like being in kindergarten for 20 years and only knowing your ABC's and 123's. People who have been Christians for a long time should be queens, kings, and teachers themselves. They should have so much knowledge and wisdom of God that they are teaching others, instead of being taught the same old simple truths repeatedly.

You are responsible for your own personal growth and spiritual development. No one can force feed you. You must be hungry and want to eat – you must want to learn and grow.

Purpose Point: The level of teaching you receive is dependent on the person and place of teaching, but the level of understanding is dependent on you. For instance, you may attend a church where the pastor only serves milk with a bunch of hooting and hollering as a side snack.

If so, it is your responsibility to find a place that serves a full course meal – a pastor who teaches the meat of God's Word.

Minute Memoir: I remember after shortly graduating from high school, I left my church because I felt I needed more. I went to my pastor at the time and asserted to him respectfully that I was leaving because I needed something different that would help me to develop into the person God wanted me to be. I left and joined another church where I still attend today. My current pastor has been truly instrumental in my life by teaching me the meat of God's Word – helping me to know God and grow closer to Him. And for that I am eternally grateful. Changing churches was one of the best choices I made that altered my life for the better. However, this is not to say that my prior pastor was not a good pastor. He was a true man of God who taught the Word well, but I was greedy and hungry for more with an insatiable appetite for the knowledge of God.

It doesn't matter if you attended and grew up in a church for years, or if the church you currently attend has family ties; changing churches may be the catalyst for effective change to take place in your life. It is important for you to be in a place where you can be properly fed and grow spiritually – a place where you can be rooted, grounded, and spiritually challenged to excel in God. If unsure, pray and ask God for guidance. He will lead you. Begin to put away all the distractions and deterrents that will hinder spiritual progression and prevent you from wanting to learn and grow into a queen. Attend a Bible-based church regularly, study your Bible and ask God to bring wisdom, understanding, knowledge and revelation.

"There is so much more we would like to say about this. But you don't seem to listen, so it's hard to make you understand. You have been Christians a long time now, and you ought to be teaching others. Instead, you need someone to teach you again the basic things a beginner must learn about the Scriptures. You are like babies who drink only milk and cannot eat solid food. And a person who is living on milk isn't very far along in the Christian life and doesn't know much about doing what is right. **Solid food is for those who are mature, who have trained themselves to recognize the difference between right and wrong and then do what is right***."* Hebrews 5:11-14

Purpose Point: Feeding your spirit with God's Word (the Bible) is just as important as feeding your body. If you neglect to feed your spirit, you will weaken it; you will starve your soul and hinder your growth. Spiritual starvation results in depression, discouragement, hopelessness, sadness, fear, worry, confusion, and poor choices. Jesus said, *"It is written: 'Man shall not live on bread alone, but on every word that comes from the mouth of God.'"* Matthew 4:4 NIV

Purpose Point: People who do not grow and mature lack a desire or motivation for growth and change. They are stuck and complacent in their own way of doing things. It is not that they have a learning disability or are unable to learn, they simply choose not to. **God wants you to grow and go to another level in Him.**

Purpose Point: A queen overeats on God's Word; she can never get enough – she is fat with God's truth but is never spiritually constipated. As she *receives*, she *releases* faith, worship, and praise. She continuously feeds her heart with the Word of God and digests it slowly to receive the full nutrition and fruition of new knowledge and revelation. This is what keeps her strong, sane, and healthy. She does not have to be spoon fed like a baby in a highchair. She feeds herself on her throne and then teaches others how to feed themselves and grow gracefully.

Purpose Point: A queen rules her circumstances with her heart through God's Word and not with her head. When she feels herself getting weak or her circumstances getting tough, she feeds herself with more of God's Word and meditates on it day and night.

"Study this Book of Instruction continually. Meditate on it day and night so you will be sure to obey everything written in it. Only then will you prosper and succeed in all you do."
Joshua 1:8

"For if you wander beyond the teaching of Christ, you will not have fellowship with God. But if you continue in the teaching of Christ, you will have fellowship with both the Father and the Son. If someone comes to your meeting and does not teach the truth about Christ, don't invite him into your house or encourage him in any way. Anyone who encourages him becomes a partner in his evil work." 2 John 1:9-11

Purpose Point: Continuing in the teachings of the Bible and applying God's Word to your heart will make you wise and help you to make right decisions. To maximize your heart's beauty, you must gain wisdom.

"A woman who is beautiful but lacks discretion is like a gold ring in a pig's snout."
Proverbs 11:22

"A wise woman builds her house; a foolish woman tears hers down with her own hands."
Proverbs 14:1

Purpose Point: Contrary to popular opinion, knowledge is not power by itself. The acquisition and application of knowledge is power. For example, if you know something, but do not do it, use it, or apply it, is this power? The Bible says people perish for a lack of knowledge (Hosea 4:6). Sometimes we victimize ourselves by failing to acquire knowledge and apply it which leads to poor choices and unnecessary pain. When we grow in the knowledge of God and apply what we learn, we conserve ourselves and only then can help others.

As queens we should mentor, uplift and teach other women about the things of God and how to live godly. However, it is very important that you walk the walk, if you talk the talk. If you talk the talk (teach the Word of God) but do not walk the walk (obey the Word of God) then you bring shame to the Word of God and become a stumbling block – causing others to stumble and fall. *"And you yourself must be an example…by doing good deeds of every kind. Let everything you do reflect the integrity and seriousness of your teaching."* Titus 2:7

"These older women must train the younger women to love their husbands and their children, to live wisely and be pure, to take care of their homes, to do good, and to be submissive to their husbands. Then they will not bring shame on the word of God." Titus 2:4-5

Purpose Point: Many women tend to be jealous of other women and would rather see them ignorant and fail. They take on the mindset: 'I worked to get where I am without help and struggled through it, she can too' or 'I can't let her have more than me or go further than I have'. Anyone who thinks this way should repent and change their heart immediately. You should always love and pray for your fellow sisters in Christ; help them to know God and help them to grow in Him and in their personal lives. It is all about making a difference in someone else's life – building the kingdom. When you bless others, God will bless you.

Paul, a servant of God, stated: *"...We are only God's servants through whom you believed the Good News. Each of us did the work the Lord gave us. I planted the seed in your hearts, and Apollos watered it, but it was God who made it grow. It's not important who does the planting, or who does the watering. What's important is that God makes the seed grow. The one who plants and the one who waters work together with the same purpose. And both will be rewarded for their own hard work. For we are both God's workers. And you are God's field. You are God's building. Because of God's grace to me, I have laid the foundation like an expert builder. Now others are building on it. But whoever is building on this foundation must be very careful. For no one can lay any foundation other than the one we already have—Jesus Christ."*
1 Corinthians 3:5-11

Questionable Queen
It is important not to confuse the characteristics of a godly queen with the characteristics of an evil one. Many women who feed off control and power often operate in witchcraft – evil practices and egomania. They like to dominate as the QUEEN BEE controlling and manipulating those around them – those who they view as drones to do their work and meet their insatiable need for attention and praise. This type of person is known to have a Jezebel spirit. Jezebel was an evil queen discussed in the Bible who misused her royal power (1 Kings 18). As a princess developing into a queen, you absolutely <u>do not</u> want to take on a Jezebel spirit, as it is not of God, but of the devil.

Poetic Princess

"...How can there be peace as long as the idolatry and witchcraft of your mother, Jezebel, are all around us?" 2 Kings 9:22

The "J" is for Jezebel
The characteristics of Jezebel you just can't ignore…
She flexes her muscles to make others sore.
She has to be 'Ms. Know it all' because
she is afraid she just might fall.
She protects her ego from being bruised
because she's afraid she just might lose.
She walks and speaks with misused authority and a cocky head roll.
She is deceptive and always has to be in CONTROL.
She longs for reverence, compliments, accolades, and praise.
Her need for attention lingers on for days.
She doesn't like to be challenged and gets offended when you disagree.
She believes she is the one and only Queen Bee.
She wants to be the center of everything – always got to have her way.
She expects for you to read her mind, even when she does not say.
She doesn't realize that she is operating under a curse…
A form of self-idolatry because she always has to be first.
She may masquerade behind kindness…delegating through manipulation,

Appearing to be humble yet triggering your frustration.
She thrives off control and needs it to survive...
Pretending to be helpful, but it's all a disguise.
She loves power – every day and every hour.
She may give gifts and favors to get you under her wing
but it is just a way to control you, among other things.
For many she likes to be a beacon of light.
But at the end of the day she is just not right.
The wrongs of her rule she does not see.
Those who do not bow are perceived as the enemy.
Favoritism and phoniness with a pawn of deceit is the game she loves to play.
It is best for you to stay away.
You must kiss up to get and remain on her good side.
She is haughty, controlling, and full of pride.
She pretends to walk down the right path
but her behavior is that of witchcraft.
She must dictate and delegate everything and everyone down to the last bit...
Be cautious, be prayerful – use your wit.

A Jezebel spirit is often revealed in a position of power such as a boss or any position of authority (Proverbs 29:2; Proverbs 29:12; Proverbs 29:16) but can also manifest itself in friendships and associations (Proverbs 26:24-26).

*"Nearly all men can stand adversity,
but if you want to test a man's character, give him power."* - Abraham Lincoln

"A person with good sense is respected; a treacherous person walks a rocky road."
Proverbs 13:15

Purpose Point: It is easier to obey rules than it is to accept an unruly reign.

Purpose Point: When power or authority is granted it is important to do what is right and treat other people right. Abuse of power and misused authority are oppressive and stifles growth.

Purpose Point: On your journey to growth, many people will not want to see you grow and may try to discourage you along the way. The reason for their resistance could be jealousy, insecurity, fear, or unbelief. Nevertheless, do not give up. Stay planted in your growth and bloom! Ignore the negative voices and uproot yourself, if possible, from toxic environments.

Never Too Young to be Queen

Age is not a determining factor when applying or aiming for a queen's position. *'Young'* does not necessarily mean young age; it could also mean young or premature in understanding the things of God. For example, a woman who is 60 years old may only understand the basics of God's Word and may not fully obey which makes her a young infant. On the other hand, a woman who is 25 years of age who understands the in-depth teachings of God and obeys could be considered an elderly adult, spiritually. Again, never let anybody think less of you because you are young in age. If you understand God's Word and obey, you are spiritually old and mature, and are worthy to be queen. You can reduce the chances of people thinking less of you when you live according to God's standards and ways – fully grown in the Lord.

*"Teach these things and insist that everyone learn them. **<u>Don't let anyone think less of you because you are young.</u>** Be an example to all believers in what you teach, in the way you live, in your love, your faith and your purity."* 1 Timothy 4:11-12

*"The simpleton is clothed with folly, but **the wise person is crowned with knowledge**."* Proverbs 14:18

"A mocker seeks wisdom and never finds it, but knowledge comes easily to those with understanding. Stay away from fools, for you won't find knowledge there." Proverbs 14:6-7

Purpose Point: Sometimes, it is just about learning the right things to put you on the right path.

Purpose Point: Maturing involves putting away childish behaviors and ways of thinking. Your aim should be to mature and grow in God while humbling yourself before Him (child-like) but never exhibiting a childish nature by disobeying His commands or not wanting to learn.

Remember: "...don't be childish in your understanding of these things. Be innocent as babies when it comes to evil, but be mature and wise in understanding matters of this kind."
1 Corinthians 14:20

"It's like this: When I was a child, I spoke and thought and reasoned as a child does. But when I grew up, I put away childish things. Now we see things imperfectly as in a poor mirror, but then we will see everything with perfect clarity. All that I know now is partial and incomplete, but then I will know everything completely, just as God knows me now." 1 Corinth. 13:11-12

Have you ever heard the saying, *"I want to be like you when I grow up"*? Typically, when one hears this statement it is associated with some form of admiration of a person's fame, position, knowledge, success, or possessions. However, our aim should not be to be like people who are prominent, famous or rich, but our aim should be to be like people who are wise, godly, mature and are successful as a result or byproduct of right behaviors – to be like people who do not behave childishly, but Christ-like.

Germinating Gem - How to Grow in the Knowledge of God
- Learn about Jesus by going to church, reading the Bible, and praying (set aside daily time with God)
- Listen to good (godly) teaching and heed correction, i.e. word-based Christian programs – TV, radio, books, podcasts, godly counsel, etc.
  - *"If you reject criticism, you only harm yourself; but if you listen to correction, you grow in understanding."* Proverbs 15:32
  - *"If you ignore criticism, you will end in poverty and disgrace; if you accept criticism, you will be honored."* Proverbs 13:18
  - *"To learn, you must love discipline; it is stupid to hate correction."* Proverbs 12:1
- Learn from tests, trials, troubles, testimonies, and triumphs.

"Let your roots grow down into him, and let your lives be built on him. Then your faith will grow strong in the truth you were taught, and you will overflow with thankfulness." Colossians 2:7

"<u>As we know Jesus better, his divine power gives us everything we need for living a godly life.</u> He has called us to receive his own glory and goodness! And by that same mighty power, he has given us all his rich and wonderful promises. He has promised that you will escape the

decadence all around you caused by evil desires and that you will share in his divine nature. So make every effort to apply the benefits of theses promises to your life.

Then your faith will produce a life of moral excellence. A life of moral excellence leads to knowing God better. Knowing God leads to self-control. Self-control leads to patient endurance; and patient endurance leads to godliness. Godliness leads to love for other Christians, and finally you will grow to have genuine love for everyone. ***The more you grow like this, the more you will become productive and useful in your knowledge of our Lord Jesus Christ. But those who fail to develop these virtues are blind or, at least, very shortsighted.*** *They have already forgotten that God has cleansed them from their old life of sin.*

So, dear friends, work hard to prove that you really are among those God has called and chosen. Doing this, you will never stumble or fall away. And God will open wide the gates of heaven for you to enter into the eternal Kingdom of our Lord and Savior Jesus Christ."
2 Peter 1:3-11

Moral excellence is being able to discern or know right from wrong and do what is right. Knowing right from wrong and doing what is right leads to knowing God better. When we know God and His ways better, He empowers us to do more of the right things and helps us to control or stop ourselves when we think or desire to do wrong. Knowing God does not mean to know of God. When you truly know someone you know their will, their desires, what hurts them and what pleases them. It is the same with God; knowing Him means to know His will and His heart. It is this knowledge that helps us to control ourselves because we don't want to do anything to hurt or disappoint God. We want to please Him. When we want to please God, we grow more patient and can control ourselves when we are tempted to do wrong. This leads to godliness, and godliness leads to love for others – forgiving, praying, helping, and encouraging our brothers and sisters in the Lord because we are all one in Christ…princesses and queens, princes and kings growing in Him. **Queens don't Quit! Never stop learning and growing in God.**

*"…For we are joined together in his body by his strong sinews, and **we grow only as we get our nourishment and strength from God**." Colossians 2:19*

Purpose Point: Jesus grew in wisdom and so should we. Luke 2:52 says: *"Jesus grew in wisdom and in stature and in favor with God and all the people."* When we grow, we progress on the path that has been set before us and sustain our walk with God. But if we do not grow, we become very shortsighted as indicated in scripture and could eventually lose our way.

Life is an adventure – doing, learning, and growing!
Grow in knowledge, faith, obedience, and Christ-like character.

Purpose Point: God does not expect for you to be perfect, but He does expect for you to progress and strive for perfection through maturity – becoming better than you were yesterday and improving day by day.

"It takes courage to grow up and become who you really are." – E.E. Cummings

There comes a time when we all must S.T.A.N.D. and Grow Up.

Chapter 7
Faithful Father

*"The Lord is like a **father** to his children, tender and compassionate to those who fear him."* Psalm 103:13

*"Even if my mother and father abandon me, **the Lord will hold me close**."* Psalm 27:10

God said, *"...I looked forward to you calling me 'Father'..."* Jeremiah 3:19

Purpose Point: No matter your age or circumstance, you are always God's little princess and He is always your Father when you remain in His love. Daddy God is always there.
Jesus said, *"When you obey my commandments, you remain in my love, just as I obey my Father's commandments and remain in his love."* John 15:10

*"Understand, therefore, that the Lord your God is indeed God. He is the **faithful** God who keeps his covenant for a thousand generations and constantly loves those who love him and obey his commands."* Deuteronomy 7:9

Purpose Point: When you obey your Father's royal command(s) it makes you royalty.
"Yes indeed, it is good when you truly obey our Lord's royal command found in the scriptures..." James 2:8

Jesus said, *"...yet you still don't know who I am? Anyone who has seen me has seen the **Father**! So why are you asking me to show him to you?"* John 14:9

Sustain Relationship with God — Love God

Know who you are — Understand your value, capability and purpose

*"Forever, O Lord, your word stands firm in heaven. Your **faithfulness** extends to every generation, as enduring as the earth you created."* Psalm 119:89-90

Now that you have been adopted into a new family and have accepted Jesus as your Lord and Savior, you are a part of a new blood line. You have the blood of Jesus running through your veins. You are a new creature, a child of God; therefore, God is not only your Creator, but He is your Father. And as your Father, God will take care of you and meet your every need.

Remember, when you accept Jesus as your Lord and Savior, you take an oath to trust, believe and obey him. You become a part of his family – his sisters, which means God is your Father, and you are His daughter – His special princess and queen.

Jesus confirms this in scripture when he said, *"'Don't cling to me', Jesus said, 'for I haven't yet ascended to the Father. But go find my brothers and tell them, **'I am ascending to my Father and your Father, to my God and your God.'"*** John 20:17

As a child of God, you have so many benefits. God will protect you and keep you safe. He will never leave you or forsake you. He will strengthen, guide, and direct you. He will put you on a path of prosperity and ensure that you grow up into the person He called you to be. So whatever you may be going through in your life right now, whether it be living with unloving parents or being in an abusive relationship, God will deliver you. He will rescue you from all the hurt and pain. Just believe and know that a brighter day will soon come. God says: *"...Those who hope in me will not be disappointed."* Isaiah 49:23 NIV

Purpose Point: You may not be able to trust many people, but you can trust your heavenly Father; He will be faithful to you. See Him as the Father He is. Your biological father may have abandoned you, abused you or mistreated you, but your heavenly Father will never treat you this way. He sees your value; He knows you are precious, beautiful, and amazing. He will take care of you and heal your hurts. Trust Him to do it – you will not be disappointed.

God is a Father to everyone who believes in Him, particularly those whose fathers were absent and uninvolved in their life. None of God's children are fatherless or illegitimate. He is a Father to all who accept and believe in Him.

"Father to the fatherless, defender of widows – this is God, whose dwelling is holy. God places the lonely in families; he sets the prisoners free and gives them joy. But for rebels, there is only famine and distress." Psalm 68:5-6

Purpose Point: God longs for you to call Him Father. God said, *"...I looked forward to you calling me '**Father**'..."* Jeremiah 3:19

Minute Memoir: My relationship with my biological father was like a roller coaster – up and down, round and round…fast speeds going down and slow speeds during uphill battles. When I was a young child, he spoiled me rotten and gave me everything I wanted. I remember getting some of the most popular toys, such as the first Nintendo gaming system, Cabbage Patch dolls and a Cricket doll. The Cricket doll was a hard-plastic battery-operated doll that talked.

All the kids wanted it, and I was one of the few to have it. But despite his generosity, my father was very stern and strict. I was afraid of him because I knew he meant business if I ever did anything wrong. I remember one time when I was in kindergarten, and he picked me up after school. I did not say "Good Afternoon" to him – which was something he had taught me. He became extremely upset and threatened to stop the car to whoop me. This one incident, and several others, stayed stuck in my mind after all these years. I always thought that he would have been extremely cruel to whoop me over something small like that. But as I got older, I understood that he was simply trying to teach me good manners at an early age; he did the best he could.

There are many incidents that I remember when my father and I collided, where we intersected, and I got or almost got my butt whooped. Now that I am older, I know he did it because he loved me and wanted to train me the right way. However, there were many times that he went overboard with his strictness and rigid rules. But honestly, I wish he had been stricter but with a greater degree of compassion and instruction. I wish that amid the discipline and spankings he would have explained things to me in greater detail as to why I was being disciplined, and what consequences my actions could produce.

My father left me when I needed him the most. At age 14, a time when I was so rebellious, he asked me if I wanted him in or out my life. Being the teen that I was, I said, "I want you out of my life." After that, my father was never around and left me with my mother to deal with. I resented my father for years for leaving me. But as I grew closer to God, I decided to go to my father years later and apologized for being such a rebellious child. I also told him that I forgave him for walking out on me. Even though I told my father years earlier that I did not want him in my life, as a response to his question, I felt that the question should have never been presented to me. Parents do not walk out when times get tough; they stay and handle the situation to the best of their ability.

A father holds some of the most important moments in his child's life. And as I am writing this, I am thinking of some of those special moments, such as my father teaching me how to ride a bike, teaching me how to make banana pudding, and always taking me to the beauty shop to get my hair done. I will never forget those times. The role that a father has in his daughter's life is extremely significant, and very much necessary.

A big portion of the father's role involves fathers teaching their daughters how to be confident and making them feel like they are the most beautiful, valuable, and special person in the world. Fathers should make their daughters feel like a princess as we were created to be. As little girls we seek acceptance, validation, affirmation, approval, and love from our father. And when we do not receive those affections from our parents, we go looking to other male figures for it. We go looking for love in all the wrong and unfamiliar places. And that is when the trouble comes because girls become so desperate, so gullible, and so naïve that they allow the wrong people to take advantage of them. These wrong people or male figures know the girl is in need of something; they sense it and see it all over her face and exhibited in her behaviors. As a result, these wrong people use the palpable void, the deep hole in her heart, against her and for their benefit.

Minute Memoir: One day I got a phone call at work from one of my father's friends. She said, *"I haven't been able to reach your father for days."* I immediately left work and got a friend to take me to his apartment. When I arrived, I knocked on the door several times and there was no answer. I had a key, but I was afraid to use it, so I went to the property management office to see if they could open the door for me. Two maintenance guys arrived to open the door, and it was a tragic scene. My father sat dead on the couch and had appeared to be dead for a couple of days; rigor mortis (the stiffening of the body) had already set in. I was so shaken up and distraught. The little hope that I had in my heart of my relationship with my father being restored and rekindled had totally vanished forever. I felt so empty; his Chrissy (that is what he called me) felt so deprived. "What do I do now? – all is lost", I thought. My father had died from a massive heart attack. My heart had also been attacked with hurt, sorrow and hopelessness.

I talked to my father two weeks before he died. He called me just to see how I was doing. I specifically remember his last words to me during our conversation. He said: *"I'll keep in touch."* After he died, I hoped and prayed that these words were God's way of telling me that my father was in heaven and that we will see each other again. I felt that the mere fact that I was able to remember the last words he spoke to me two weeks before his death was meaningful and significant. Our relationship may have not been rekindled on earth, but there is still hope that our spirits will be rekindled in heaven. And his last words to me would finally prove true…he would have kept in touch.

I find myself sometimes still longing for an earthly father, still longing for the love embedded in this unique relationship; longing for a father's presence... longing for someone to talk to and go to for fatherly advice; and wishing that I had my father to walk me down the aisle on my wedding day. But despite the longings and unwavering desires, I must know that my heavenly Father wants and will fulfill this role. I must see God as both my earthly Father and my heavenly Father because He is well capable of fulfilling both roles. I must allow God to be Daddy God in my life and allow Him to fill the void in my heart that my father left—and so do you. All hope is not lost.

Purpose Point: God is faithful to His children. Everything He has promised, He will do it. But we must be patient and believe. God knows exactly how much we can bear, and He will never put anything more on us than we can handle or are able to stand.

I remember all the pain and torment I suffered in my teen years. The mental and physical abuse was extreme, but God gave me the strength to endure and eventually delivered me from the situation. I often wondered, "Where is God? Why won't He help me?" All the time God was there, just not in the way I thought He should be. Sometimes we don't know why certain things happen to us; we go around wondering "Why me?", but again, some things we suffer are for a greater purpose. We must remember that our current situation is only temporary, and that God's promises and deliverance will soon come.

The secret is to find some meaning, some purpose in what we suffer to maintain our joy. Choose not to allow what you suffer to be in vain, and do not allow your suffering to make you think that God does not care about you. Remember, God sometimes uses suffering to make us into the person he called us to be.

God's servant, David, said to Him: *"My suffering was good for me, for it taught me to pay attention to your decrees."* Psalm 119:71   Anything you suffer is valuable and can be used to help you, someone else, or even save someone else's life.

Keep doing your best in whatever situation you are in; keep obeying God's Word; keep praying; keep believing and keep hoping. And one day you will look up and say, *'Look how far God has brought me. He has changed my life. Look at what I have accomplished despite my circumstances and challenges.'* It is not a question of whether God will do what He says, will you?

Purpose Point: Your perception of God is so important. If you only see Him as a God in heaven, a cosmic force, who is not concerned with anything except punishing people for their sins, then you will not grow as a Christian and will not grow in God. You will feel as though God doesn't care about your circumstances and may even feel like God doesn't love you. You must see Him as the loving Father He is. You must get so connected with Him through prayer and worship that you become saturated with His love and His spirit of fatherhood. You must read your Bible to understand the ways of God and how much He really loves you. When you fully understand the extent of God's love for you, you will begin to see God as a real Father and begin to see yourself as His real daughter – precious and loved. You will be so confident in Him and will know without a doubt that your Father will take care of you.

Purpose Point: You must know that God loves you. Many of us tend to forget this fact and neglect to refuel our thoughts with the love of God. If you do not know that God loves you, then you will always be fearful, unhappy and feel as though you are alone or never enough. You will always feel a void or emptiness inside that no one can fill. Say to yourself, 'My Father loves me' and believe it. When you come to fully know that your heavenly Father loves you, you will not worry or fear anything or anyone because perfect love takes away all fear.

God's love for you is perfect, meaning it is unconditional, sacrificial, and eternal. But in order for this love to be perfected in your life, you must first believe that God loves you no matter what – trust Him and do not doubt in your heart.

"There is no fear in love. But perfect love drives out fear, because fear has to do with punishment. The one who fears is not made perfect in love." 1 John 4:18 NIV

"For God has not given us a spirit of fear and timidity, but of power, love, and self-discipline." 2 Timothy 1:7

Purpose Point: We show our heavenly Father that we love Him by *keeping* (obeying) His commandments, and our heavenly Father has already shown that He loves us by sacrificing His son Jesus for our sins and *keeping* His promises. We should love Him because He first loved us. Jesus said, *"If you love me, keep my commandments."* John 14:15 NIV

"For God so loved the world that he gave his only Son, so that everyone who believes in him will not perish but have eternal life." John 3:16

"So God has given us both His promise and his oath. These two things are unchangeable because it is impossible for God to lie...for we can hold on to his promise with confidence. This confidence is like a strong and trustworthy anchor for our souls..."
Hebrews 6:18-19

Purpose Point: Love is shown through faithfulness. **Love without sacrifice does not count.**

Purpose Point: When you continually and deliberately sin and disobey God, you lose your confidence in God and His promises because of self-induced guilt, condemnation, and rebellion (effects of sin). You may also lose confidence in the assurance of God's love for you. And when you lose that confidence you will become fearful, confused, discouraged, and unhappy. Therefore, obey your heavenly Father so that you can remain in fellowship with Him and perfected in His love for you.

Purpose Point: God deserves your love, obedience, and respect (reverence).

"...A son honors his father, and a servant respects his master. I am your father and master, but where are the honor and respect I deserve?..." Malachi 1:6

Purpose Point: We all have different fears in our lives, such as the fear of death, the fear of being alone, the fear of not being loved, the fear of rejection, the fear of sickness and disease, the fear of people, the fear of not having enough, the fear of being hurt and the fear of public speaking. Regardless of your fear, you do not have to fear because your heavenly Father is in control of everything and knows your end from your beginning. He is so consumed with you that He knows everything about you. He knows when you sit down or stand up; He knows your every thought. He knows what you are going to say even before you say it. You are so special to Him. David, the servant of God, understood how special he was to God and knew that God loved him dearly. He said:

"O Lord, you have examined my heart and know everything about me. You know when I sit down or stand up. You know my every thought when far away. You chart the path ahead of me and tell me where to stop and rest. Every moment you know where I am. You know what I am going to say even before I say it, Lord. You both precede and follow me. You place your hand of blessing on my head. Such knowledge is too wonderful for me, too great for me to know! I can never escape from your spirit! I can never get away from your presence! If I go up to heaven, you are there; if I go down to the place of the dead, you are there. If I ride the wings of the morning, if I dwell by the farthest oceans, even there your hand will guide me, and your strength will support me. I could ask the darkness to hide me and the light around me to become night – but even in darkness I cannot hide from you. To you the night shines as bright as day. Darkness and light are both alike to you.

You made all the delicate parts of my body and knit me together in my mother's womb. Thank you for making me so complex. Your workmanship is marvelous and how well I know it. You watched me as I was being formed in utter seclusion, as I was woven together in the dark of the womb. You saw me before I was born. Every day of my life was recorded in your book. Every moment was laid out before a single day had passed. How precious are your thoughts about me, O God! They are innumerable! I can't even count them; they outnumber the grains of sand! And when I wake up in the morning you are still with me!" – David, Psalm 139:1-18

So you see, God is with you always and knows everything about you. Everything that David spoke in the above scripture was given to him by God. God feels the exact same way about you. Your heavenly Father loves you more than you can ever know or comprehend. If you feel as though no one loves you, know that God loves you. You are so precious to Him. He created you for His own special purpose and knew you before you were born. God wants you to return that love by loving Him too and being faithful to Him.

Do you remember Israel – the group of people that God loves so much? Israel rejected God and did not love Him as God loved them. God was very hurt when Israel rejected Him and referred to Israel as a faithless wife.

God said, *"I thought to myself, 'I would love to treat you as my own children! I wanted nothing more than to give you this beautiful land – the finest inheritance in the world.* ***I looked forward to you calling me 'Father'****, and I thought you would never turn away from me again. But you have betrayed me, you people of Israel! You have been like a faithless wife who leaves her husband,' says the Lord."* Jeremiah 3:19-20

God looks forward to you calling Him Father and wants you to be faithful to Him as He is faithful to you. It makes Him so happy when you call Him Father and obey His commands. As a child of God, you are in a covenant relationship with Him which means that you both vow to love, respect, and honor each other. God will honor you by providing for you, protecting you and meeting your every need. And you should honor God by obeying His commands. God will be faithful to you, and you must also be faithful to Him. Don't be like Israel; don't reject or grieve your heavenly Father by disobeying His commands and worshiping other things or people in your life. Instead, be faithful to Him, as He is to you.

"Love the Lord, all you faithful ones! For the Lord protects those who are loyal to him..." Psalm 31:23

*"But be sure to fear the LORD and serve him **faithfully** with all your heart; consider what great things he has done for you."* 1 Samuel 12:24 NIV

*"So you must **remain faithful** to what you have been taught... If you do, you will continue to live in fellowship with the Son and with the Father. And in this fellowship we enjoy the eternal life he promised us."* 1 John 2:24-25

The covenant relationship that you and God have is so binding that you both become one – united together, like in marriage. If you have accepted and confessed Jesus as Lord then his spirit lives inside of you; therefore, you are never alone. He goes wherever you go and feels whatever you feel. When you hurt, God feels it too and will comfort you. When you are weak,

God will strengthen you. When you are in need, He will provide for you – YOUR HEAVENLY FATHER IS FAITHFUL!

"He is the Rock; his work is perfect. Everything he does is just and fair. He is a faithful God who does no wrong; how just and upright he is." Deuteronomy 32:4

"Understand, therefore, that the LORD your God is indeed God. He is the faithful God who keeps his covenant for a thousand generations and lavishes his unfailing love on those who love him and obey his commands." Deuteronomy 7:9

Purpose Point: God is so faithful that He is faithful even when you are not faithful. Some people may go back on their word or decide to disobey, but God remains faithful to His Word because God's Word is God and He cannot deny Himself.

"If we are unfaithful, he remains faithful, for he cannot deny himself." 2 Timothy 2:13

"In the beginning the Word already existed. He was with God, and he was God." John 1:1

Purpose Point: Your heavenly Father will be faithful in protecting you. He has designated angels to protect and watch over you wherever you go.

"For he orders his angels to protect you wherever you go. They will hold you with their hands to keep you from striking your foot against a stone." Psalm 91:11-12

You are extremely important to your heavenly Father. He wants you to minister to Him (worship Him). He wants you to help others and lead them to salvation. Don't ever think that you are not important or that no one loves you. You are God's highly valued special princess and He loves you more than you will ever know. He will be faithful to you. He will be true, but will you be faithful to Him?

Purpose Point: God wants us to be faithful not fickle. Being faithful means to be loyal and committed (constant). Being fickle or unfaithful means to be disloyal and not constant, ever changing. We can show our faithfulness to God by obeying His commands and worshiping Him only.

Purpose Point: Without God, your heavenly Father, you can do nothing, but with Him you can do everything.

Purpose Point: We have everything we need in our heavenly Father. He is a savior, giver, healer, provider, deliverer, comforter, teacher, counselor, peace maker and friend.

Purpose Point: God is a Father and a friend that speaks back to His children. I don't mean with a loud voice from heaven, but He speaks to you from within – after all, He is living in you if you have accepted Jesus as your Lord and Savior.

One night I asked my heavenly Father a silly question: "Lord, I wonder if you see women as being unclean when they are on their period (menstruation)?" At that time, I was menstruating. I know it sounds like a crazy thing to ask an Almighty God, but crazy things go through our mind from time to time. Less than 10 seconds later, my heavenly Father spoke to me from within and said: *"Sin is what makes you unclean; the blood cleanses you."* This is true for two reasons: For one, the menstrual cycle helps to cleanse the uterus (womb) of old uterine matter/lining; and two, the blood of Jesus cleanses us from our sins.

"But if we are living in the light of God's presence, just as Christ is, then we have fellowship with each other, and the blood of Jesus, his Son, cleanses us from every sin." 1 John 1:7

Purpose Point: God, our heavenly Father, will speak to you. And when He speaks, His words will always line up with the Bible, His Word.

Like Father, like Daughter

As a daughter of God, you should possess the characteristics of your Father and act like Him. Just like when children are born from their parents they look like their parents, talk like their parents, behave like their parents, and may even believe what their parents believe. Like so, we should behave like our heavenly Father. We should love one another because God is love; we should be kind, respectful, humble, and refrain from doing ungodly or worldly things because our Father is not ungodly or worldly.

"You should behave instead like God's very own children, adopted into his family – calling him 'Father', dear Father. For his Holy Spirit speaks to us deep in our hearts and tells us that we are God's children. **And since we are his children, we will share his treasures – for everything God gives to his Son, Christ, is ours, too.** *But if we are to share his glory, we must also share his suffering."* Romans 8:15-17

"...You are to live clean, innocent lives as children of God in a dark world full of crooked and perverse people. Let your lives shine brightly before them." Philippians 2:15

If you choose not to behave like your heavenly Father and choose not to obey Him, then this shows that God is really not your Father. If you truly want God to be your Father, you will need to perform a D.N.A. detoxification – **D**esist **N**egative **A**ttributes. Desist means to cease, refrain, or stop doing something. Negative behaviors or attributes may include lying, stealing, disobeying authority, cheating, gossiping, doing drugs, engaging in sexual immorality and perversion, etc. God's children should not participate in these types of activities. If you want God to be your Father, you must cease or stop doing the negative things and desist – try your best not to do them again. You must repent (turn away) and change your mindset as it relates to engaging in habitual sin. But remember, struggling with sin and enjoying it without the desire to change are two different things. God is a Father to those in Christ even amid a struggle.

Purpose Point: If you can resist, you can desist.

"So humble yourselves before God. Resist the devil, and he will flee from you. Draw close to God, and God will draw close to you..." James 4:7-8

The devil and your own evil desires tempt you to do wrong. If you can resist the devil and your evil desires, then you can stop doing the negative things and never do them again (desist). How do you resist? Make a conscious choice not to do wrong, pray and ask God to help you do what is right, and speak God's Word to that issue.

For example, if a thought or evil desire comes to your mind to disobey your parents, speak God's Word and say: *'It is written that children should obey their parents and as a result of my obedience I will live a long life'* (Ephesians 6:3). But you must know God's Word and what the Bible says before you can speak to an issue; therefore, it is so important to read your Bible and attend a Bible-teaching church.

Purpose Point: We need to **D**esist **N**egative **A**ttributes and **D**emonstrate **N**atural (God-given) **A**ttributes that are consistent with our new nature (the new nature and spiritual DNA we received when we were born again of the Spirit).

When people continue to do wrong, live the world's way and enjoy it without any conviction, this shows that they belong to the devil; hence, he is their father and not God.

*"Dear children, don't let anyone deceive you about this: When people do what is right, it is because they are **righteous**, even as Christ is righteous. But when people keep on sinning, it shows they belong to the Devil, who has been sinning since the beginning. But the Son of God came to destroy these works of the Devil.* ***Those who have been born into God's family do not sin, because God's life is in them. So they can't keep on sinning, because they have been born of God.****"* 1 John 3:7-9

"Jesus told them, "If God were your Father, you would love me, because I have come to you from God. I am not here on my own, but he sent me. Why can't you understand what I am saying? It's because you can't even hear me! For you are the children of your father the devil, and you love to do the evil things he does. He was a murderer from the beginning. He has always hated the truth, because there is no truth in him. When he lies, it is consistent with his character; for he is a liar and the father of lies." John 8:42-44

"We know that those who have become part of God's family do not make a practice of sinning, for God's Son holds them securely, and the evil one cannot get his hands on them. We know that we are children of God and that the world around us is under the power and control of the evil one. And we know that the Son of God has come, and he has given us understanding so that we can know the true God. And now we are in God because we are in his Son, Jesus Christ. He is the only true God, and he is eternal life." 1 John 5:18-20

"But they have acted corruptly toward him; when they act like that, are they really his children? They are a deceitful and twisted generation." Deuteronomy 32:5

"Dear children, keep away from anything that might take God's place in your hearts."
1 John 5:21

Purpose Point: When you constantly and deliberately sin, sin has taken God's place in your heart.

There may be times as a child of God when you mess up or go the wrong way. Remember, none of us are perfect; we may do wrong from time to time just like any other child. But it is when we continually and deliberately do wrong without any conviction that poses a serious problem. And when we do wrong, God may discipline or chastise us as any loving father would to encourage us to repent, cease and desist. He does this because He loves us and does not want us to go down a dangerous and destructive path that could lead to eternal death. It is through discipline that He trains us to live the right way.

"So you should realize that just as a parent disciplines a child, the Lord your God disciplines you to help you. So obey the commands of the Lord your God by walking in his ways and fearing him. For the Lord your God is bringing you into a good land..." Deuteronomy 8:5-7

"...My child, don't ignore it when the Lord disciplines you, and don't be discouraged when he corrects you. For the Lord disciplines those he loves, and he punishes those he accepts as his children. As you endure this divine discipline, remember that God is treating you as his own children. Whoever heard of a child who was never disciplined? **If God doesn't discipline you as he does all of his children, it means that you are illegitimate and are not really his children after all.** *Since we respect our earthly fathers who disciplined us, should we not all the more cheerfully submit to the discipline of our heavenly Father and live forever?"* Hebrews 12:5-9

"The LORD corrects those he loves, as parents correct a child of whom they are proud."
Proverbs 3:12 GWT

Suppose two women (unrelated) were in a grocery store shopping for groceries both with one child. The child of the first parent constantly screamed and knocked items off the shelves. The child of the second parent then starts knocking stuff off the shelves too after seeing the other child's behavior; however, this parent immediately spanks their child's hand and gives an abrupt scold. In this scenario, why did the second parent only discipline her child and not the other parent's child who was the first to misbehave? A stranger would not readily discipline another person's child, although they may want to. In the same manner, God does not discipline children who do not belong to Him because they are strangers to God. If God disciplines you, this is good – it proves that you are His child and that He knows you which means you are not illegitimate or a stranger. The child of the first parent is undisciplined (wild and unruly) and is allowed to continue in his ways. Consequently, his behaviors will inevitably lead to his detriment and destruction, as he grows up unrestrained.

"For our earthly fathers disciplined us for a few years, doing the best they knew how. **But God's discipline is always right and good for us** *because it means we will share in his holiness. No discipline is enjoyable while it is happening—it is painful! But afterward there will be a quiet harvest of right living for those who are trained in this way. So take a new grip with your tired hands and stand firm on your shaky legs. Mark out a straight path for your feet. Then those who follow you, though they are weak and lame, will not stumble and fall but will become strong."* Hebrews 12:10-13

Purpose Point: Discipline may hurt or be uncomfortable for a while, but it can produce lifelong rewards and save you from a dangerous and destructive path. Discipline could very well save your life – embrace it!

Oftentimes, when a child does wrong, their parent(s) spank and/or punish them, also known as chastising. Chastising is when you punish or discipline someone for a wrong they have done to teach and encourage them not to do it again. Chastising is usually applied as an act of love, or what some may call "tough love."

When you truly love someone, you will do whatever needs to be done to protect them from a destructive and dangerous path. And it is the parent's responsibility to do just that for their children – to teach them about what is wrong and what is right, and to discipline them when they choose to do what is wrong – to inflict "tough love" when necessary.

Minute Memoir: I wish my parents would have disciplined me more when I was younger. If they had, I believe my teen years may have not been as bad. I know as teenagers we want to be free to do whatever we want to do, but freedom without knowledge could be very dangerous. As a teenager, I had the freedom, but I did not have the knowledge – this essentially put me in bondage and on a dangerous path.

For instance, as a teen I did not know that there were over 25 sexual transmitted diseases out there that could consume me like fire. I did not know about the lions, tigers, and bears (perverted men, lustful boys, and wicked girls) that were waiting to devour me. And most importantly, I did not know about the evil enemy who had followed me since birth—who inspired and encouraged all these things in my life. I would have rather been spanked and locked up in my room than to have been out there with a pack of wolves fighting for my life.

"Zeal without knowledge is not good; a person who moves too quickly may go the wrong way." Proverbs 19:2

"You say, "I am allowed to do anything"— but not everything is good for you. You say, "I am allowed to do anything"— but not everything is beneficial." 1 Corinthians 10:23

Purpose Point: Do not despise God or your parents when they discipline you, as I am sure your parents are doing this because they love you. In fact, the Bible says, *"If you refuse to discipline your children, it proves you don't love them; if you love your children, you will be prompt to discipline them."* Proverbs 13:24

So you should not question your parent's love for you if they discipline you, as discipline actually proves that they love you. They simply do not want you to wander off and go down a dangerous and destructive path. Discipline gets us back on track and prevents us from traveling down the road of destruction and death.

"Only a fool despises a parent's discipline; whoever learns from correction is wise." Proverbs 15:5

"A wise child accepts a parent's discipline; a young mocker refuses to listen." Proverbs 13:1

"To learn, you must love discipline; it is stupid to hate correction." Proverbs 12:1

"My son, obey your father's commands, and don't neglect your mother's teaching. Keep their words always in your heart. Tie them around your neck. Wherever you walk, their counsel can lead you. When you sleep, they will protect you. When you wake up in the morning, they will advise you. For these commands and this teaching are a lamp to light the way ahead of you. The correction of discipline is the way to life. These commands and this teaching will keep you from the immoral woman [man], from the smooth tongue of an adulterous woman [man]." Proverbs 6:20-24

Purpose Point: You are a wise princess if you accept your parent's discipline, but when you reject it and do not listen, you are foolish. The Bible says it is stupid to hate discipline. If you hate discipline you will never learn what is true and right, and you will never develop into a queen – mature and fully grown in the Lord.

The Bible instructs parents to discipline their children. So when your parents justifiably discipline you, they are obeying the Word of God.

"Don't fail to correct your children. They won't die if you spank them. Physical discipline may well save them from death." Proverbs 23:13-14

"Discipline your children, and they will give you happiness and peace of mind. When people don't accept divine guidance, they run wild..." Proverbs 29:17-18

"...mere words are not enough – discipline is needed. For the words may be understood, but they are not heeded." Proverbs 29:19

"Discipline your children while there is hope. If you don't, you will ruin their lives." Proverbs 19:18

"To discipline and reprimand a child produces wisdom, but a mother is disgraced by an undisciplined child." Proverbs 29:15

"Train up a child in the way he should go; even when he is old he will not depart from it." Proverbs 22:6 ESV

"A servant who is pampered from childhood will later become a rebel." Proverbs 29:21

"It is painful to be the parent of a fool; there is no joy for the father of a rebel." Proverbs 17:21

Purpose Point: A Message for Parents: Parents should use discretion and godly wisdom when choosing to discipline a child. Sometimes physical discipline such as spanking may not always be necessary, and verbal insults such as calling a child out their name, cursing at them and diminishing their self-esteem are not effective or godly forms of discipline. Doing these things and spanking a child for everything he/she does wrong could ruin the relationship with the child and could bring about negative feelings of anger, bitterness, and resentment. *"Don't make your children angry by the way you treat them. Rather,* **bring them up with the discipline and instruction approved by the Lord.** *"* Ephesians 6:4

Purpose Point: Effective discipline involves instruction and guidance and not just punishment (physical and punitive). It is important for a disciplinarian to teach the *'why'* and the *'how'* rather than to only focus on the *'what'* (what they did wrong) and the *'whip'*.

Purpose Point: Do not disregard the experience of your parents. Your parents were young just like you and understand all the tricks and schemes that people play and even the tricks that you may try to play. As the saying goes, "The players change but the game remains the same." More than likely, your parents made mistakes when they were young, and they do not want you to repeat the same mistakes they made. So listen and learn from your parents to gain wisdom. Accept their discipline and obey them. In this way you will bring your earthly parents and your heavenly Father great joy. Remember, God says if you obey your parents you will have a long life.

"Listen to your father, who gave you life, and don't despise your mother's experience when she is old. Get the truth and don't ever sell it; also get wisdom, discipline, and discernment.

The father of godly children has cause for joy. What a pleasure it is to have wise children. So give your parents joy! May she who gave you birth be happy." Proverbs 23:22-25

"Children who mistreat their father or chase away their mother are a public disgrace and an embarrassment. If you stop listening to instruction, my child, you have turned your back on knowledge." Proverbs 19:26-27

Jesus obeyed his parents; therefore, so should you. The scripture states, *"Then he returned to Nazareth with them* [his parents] *and was obedient to them. And his mother stored all these things in her heart."* Luke 2:51

God disciplined David, his servant, for his wrongs, but David understood and said, *"I used to wander off until you disciplined me, but now I closely follow your word."* Psalm 119:67

"The suffering you sent was good for me, for it taught me to pay attention to your principles. Your law is more valuable to me than millions in gold and silver!" Psalm 119:71-72

"I know, O Lord, that your decisions are fair; you disciplined me because I needed it." Psalm 119:75

God disciplined Israel, but they later understood:

"I have heard Israel saying, 'You disciplined me severely, but I deserved it. I was like a calf that needed to be trained for the yoke and plow. Turn me again to you and restore me, for you alone are the Lord my God. I turned away from God, but then I was sorry. I kicked myself for my stupidity! I was thoroughly ashamed of all I did in my younger days.'" Jeremiah 31:18-19

Purpose Point: Discipline teaches, instructs, trains, and directs. Receive it!

God is a forgiving God and continues to love us even after we do wrong…

"'Is not Israel still my son, my darling, child?' asks the Lord. 'I had to punish him, but I still love him. I long for him and surely will have mercy on him.'" Jeremiah 31:20

Purpose Point: Discipline not only means punishment; it also involves self-control or self-discipline. Not only should you willingly accept discipline or punishment for a wrong that has been done, but you should also discipline or control yourself to do what is right, refrain from doing wrong and be productive. Train yourself for disciplined thought, disciplined speech, and disciplined action.

Discipline yourself to read and obey God's Word, make good grades in school, respect your parents and authority and refrain from negative behaviors. When you discipline yourself or practice self-control you behave in accordance with a rule or standard that has been set.

Purpose Point: God has empowered and equipped you with discipline. *"For God has not given us a spirit of fear and timidity, but of power, love, and **self-discipline**."* 2 Timothy 1:7

*"But the Holy Spirit produces this kind of fruit in our lives: love, joy, peace, patience, kindness, goodness, faithfulness, gentleness, and **self-control**. There is no law against these things!"* Galatians 5:22-23

Purpose Point: Disciplining yourself keeps you from discipline as punishment. Self-discipline is the best discipline. Self-control is the best control measure (Proverbs 26:28).

"But if we were more discerning with regard to ourselves, we would not come under such judgment. Nevertheless, when we are judged in this way by the Lord, we are being disciplined so that we will not be finally condemned with the world." 1 Corinthians 11:31-32 NIV

"But if we judged ourselves truly, we would not be judged." 1 Corinthians 11:31 ESV

Purpose Point: Judging self is not condemning self; it simply means to self-evaluate to self-correct (course correct) as necessary. *All discipline (proper punishment, correction, instruction, and self-control) will direct you to your destiny and determine your destination.*

Benefits of Discipline*: Discipline keeps you on the right course, validates right behavior, rebukes and rejects wrong behavior, maintains order, advances justice, saves you from destruction and is indicative of love and the law. *"An open rebuke is better than hidden love!"* Proverbs 27:5 Self-discipline minimizes distractions, keeps you on the right track, increases productivity, and engenders success. *Righteous (approved) discipline according to Ephesians 6:4.

Purpose Point: Anyone who disciplines themselves or others show that they really care.

So girls, regardless of what is going on in your life right now; regardless if your biological father left you or was never there, God loves you and will never mistreat you. He will always be with you. God is all you need. He will be everything and anything you want and need Him to be – a father, brother, friend, counselor, comforter, teacher, tutor, mentor, healer, helper, savior, deliverer, and provider. He will be there… He will be faithful! Trust Him with your life. He got your back!

"…For God has said, 'I will never fail you. I will never abandon you'. So we can say with confidence, 'The LORD is my helper, so I will have no fear. What can mere people do to me?" Hebrews 13:5-6

As God is faithful to you, He desires for you to be faithful to Him. *"Oh, love the LORD, all you His saints! For the LORD preserves the faithful, and fully repays the proud person."* Psalm 31:23 NKJV

Purpose Point: See and know God as your heavenly Father. Embrace His love; embrace His discipline; embrace His faithfulness. YOUR FATHER IS FAITHFUL AND HIS FAITHFUL LOVE ENDURES FOREVER!!!

*"Give thanks to the Lord, for he is good! His **faithful** love endures forever.
Give thanks to the God of gods. His **faithful** love endures forever.
Give thanks to the Lord of lords. His **faithful** love endures forever.
Give thanks to him who alone does mighty miracles. His **faithful** love endures forever.
Give thanks to him who made the heavens so skillfully. His **faithful** love endures forever.
Give thanks to him who placed the earth on the water. His **faithful** love endures forever.
Give thanks to him who made the heavenly lights. His **faithful** love endures forever.
the sun to rule the day – His **faithful** love endures forever, and the moon and stars to rule the night. His **faithful** love endures forever… Give thanks to him who led his people through the wilderness. His **faithful** love endures forever…
He remembered our utter weakness. His **faithful** love endures forever.
He saved us from our enemies. His **faithful** love endures forever.
He gives food to every living thing. His **faithful** love endures forever.
Give thanks to the God of heaven. His **faithful** love endures forever."* – Psalm 136

Chapter 8
Evil Enemy

"My prayer is not that you take them out of the world but that you protect them from the evil one." – Jesus, John 17:15 NIV

What or who is red and often depicted as having big horns with a pitchfork? The answer is obvious, right? The devil. In many instances, how something or someone looks is not as important as their capability – what they are capable of. The devil may not look the part as the world portrays but he certainly represents the part of pure evil in the world.

The devil is real; he is not just a villain that people made up in a story book, or a scary Halloween costume. He is far from fantasy; he is very much reality. He is your evil enemy and he wants to kill and destroy you. *"Be careful! Watch out for attacks from the Devil, your great enemy. He prowls around like a roaring lion, looking for some victim to devour."* 1 Peter 5:8

The devil, also known as Satan or Lucifer, has been around for a very long time…before the beginning of the world. Initially, he was an angel in heaven, but God kicked him out because the devil became very jealous and wanted to be like God. God was so angry with the devil that He cursed him to eternal fiery damnation. There were also other angels who were kicked out of heaven with Satan. Satan and these angels are known as fallen angels as they have fallen from heaven and the grace of God.

Make life-long positive choices
Choose to do what is right…apply godly principles

Know who you are
Understand your value, capability and purpose

"How you are fallen from heaven, O shining star, son of the morning! You have been thrown down on earth, you who destroyed the nations of the world. For you said to yourself, 'I will ascend to heaven and set my throne above God's stars.

I will preside on the mountain of the gods far away in the north. I will climb to the highest heaven and be like the Most High.' But instead, you will be brought down to the place of the dead, down to its lowest depths...Like a corpse trampled underfoot, you will be dumped into a mass grave with those killed in battle. You will descend to a pit." Isaiah 14:12-15 & 19

"...there was a war in heaven. Michael and the angels under his command fought the dragon and his angels. And the dragon lost the battle and was forced out of heaven. This great dragon – the ancient serpent called the Devil, or Satan, the one deceiving the whole world – was thrown down to the earth with all his angels." Revelations 12:7

Satan is the leader of the fallen angels, also known as demons. Demons are evil spirits that can manifest themselves through people and things. They can inhabit the bodies of people, possessing their souls, if granted access.

Demons are given legal access to our life, body and mind when we live an ungodly life and when people do not break curses that may have been formed over their generation and blood line as a result of what their ancestors or parents did in the past. The only way to defeat Satan and his demons is with Jesus Christ and the Word of God. Accepting Jesus as your Lord and Savior and obeying his commandments protects you from the evil tactics of Satan – the devil.

You may wonder why Satan hates you so much. He hates you (and me) because he hates God. We are God's very special children and the devil does not like that. He wants to hurt God through hurting us and deceiving us to live out his ways by doing evil and wicked things. He has bad plans for you and has already devised tricks and schemes to destroy you. He will try to accomplish this by working through people, working through your circumstances, and working through you. He works through people by getting them to harm, hurt, tempt, and offend you. When this happens, you may develop negative feelings such as hate, bitterness, resentment, discouragement, and lust. You may then choose to act out these feelings while disobeying God. For example, Satan may work through your friends by getting them to tempt or persuade you to steal. This of course goes against God's command that says, "you must not steal" (Exodus 20:15). Satan will try really hard to work through people to get you to go against the commands of God, and to discourage you from believing and obeying Him. Satan also works through your circumstances by using them to make you feel angry, sad, depressed, worried, hopeless, and fearful. He knows that if he can get you to have these feelings you will not value life, fulfill your purpose or succeed in building the kingdom of God. He works through you by putting thoughts, ideas, and suggestions in your mind to get you to disobey and doubt God.

The devil has been following you since birth – watching your every move and orchestrating situations where he can destroy you. But God protects us. He is much stronger and greater than the devil. The devil's plan cannot work or replace God's plan for us unless we allow it.

Purpose Point: If you add a "D" to the beginning of the word "evil," what do you get? Devil. That's right, the devil is so evil that the word "evil" is found within his name. The devil is evil in its purest form; there is nothing good in him or about him.

Let's see what other words we can scramble or make up with the letters found in 'DEVIL':

- **Lie** – The devil is full of **lies** (deception), there is no truth in him.

    Jesus said the devil, *"...was a murderer from the beginning. He has always hated the truth, because there is no truth in him. When he lies, it is consistent with his character; for he is a liar and the father of lies."* John 8:44

    The devil works to *deceive* you into thinking that something is right when it is really wrong and that something is the truth when it is really a **lie**. He is wily and crafty in cooking up ways to trick you. The Bible even says that he "masquerades as an angel of light" to deceive us into believing his **lies**, meaning that he often *disguises* himself as being a person or minister of God so that we can be more receptive to believing his **lies**. *"...Even Satan can disguise himself as an angel of light. So it is no wonder his servants can also do it by pretending to be godly ministers. In the end they will get every bit of punishment their wicked deeds deserve."* 2 Corinthians 11:14-15

    Purpose Point: A way to distinguish if a person is really a minister of God is to compare what they are saying to the Word of God, the Bible, and to observe their fruit (behaviors/results). If what they are teaching or preaching agrees with the Bible, then this person could be a true minister of God. It is important, therefore, to read and study your Bible for yourself, so that you can know if a person's words agree with God's words. Unless you read the Bible, you will not know what is in it. And if you do not read God's Word, you will be easily deceived. Good Bible-based teachers will give scripture references to back up what they are saying and will live a life consistent with God's Word and will.

    "Dear friends, do not believe everyone who claims to speak by the Spirit. You must test them to see if the spirit they have comes from God. For there are many false prophets in the world. This is how we know if they have the Spirit of God: If a person claiming to be a prophet acknowledges that Jesus Christ came in a real body, that person has the Spirit of God. But if someone claims to be a prophet and does not acknowledge the truth about Jesus, that person is not from God. Such a person has the spirit of the Antichrist, which you heard is coming into the world and indeed is already here. But you belong to God, my dear children. You have already won a victory over those people, because the Spirit who lives in you is greater than the spirit who lives in the world. Those people belong to this world, so they speak from the world's viewpoint, and the world listens to them. But we belong to God, and those who know God listen to us. If they do not belong to God, they do not listen to us. That is how we know if someone has the **Spirit of truth or the spirit of deception**.*"* 1 John 4:1-6

    "Beware of false prophets who come disguised as harmless sheep but are really vicious wolves. <u>You can identify them by their fruit, that is, by the way they act...</u>" Matthew 7:15-16

- **Die** – The devil's main objective is to kill and destroy you. He wants you to **die** without knowing God so that you can die with him for eternity. He also wants you to die early so you cannot fulfill your purpose. The Devil (a thief) loves death and hates life.

Jesus said, *"The thief's purpose is to steal and kill and destroy. My purpose is to give them a rich and satisfying life."* John 10:10

- **Vile** – the word "vile" means morally bad; wicked and extremely unpleasant. The devil definitely fits this description; nevertheless, there is no adjective in any dictionary that could describe the magnitude of his wickedness.

- **Lived** (devil spelled backwards) – The Devil is not fantasy, but very much reality. He **lives** on earth; however, his remaining time on earth is very short-**lived**.

"...But terror will come on the earth and the sea. For the Devil has come down to you in great anger, and he knows that he has little time." Revelations 12:12

Purpose Point: The devil and his demons are evil spirits. You cannot see them; however, you can see their characteristics through other people, movies, music, and media. The breadth of his wickedness is mainstream. For instance, horror movies and music promoting death, sex, violence, witchcraft and lies are infested with the devil's characteristics – evil, death and destruction.

Why did God create Satan?

Like all angels, God originally created Satan (whose name was Lucifer at the time) to worship and serve Him. But Lucifer was not happy with worshiping and serving God; he instead wanted to be like God and be worshiped.

God's original intent for Satan was not for wickedness, but for worship. When Satan wanted to be like God and rebelled against Him, he was kicked out of heaven and went from being an angel of God to an enemy of God – operating as the devil. And since the devil was the first being to disobey God, he became the author and creator of sin. Therefore, sin and evil came because of the devil's decision to go against God. And because Adam and Eve, the first humans on earth, also decided to disobey God, sin and evil spread throughout the world and the entire human race.

The scripture says in Romans 6:23, "the wages of sin is death." Therefore, when we sin or disobey God the punishment for it is death. But God loved us so much that He sent His son Jesus to die for us so that we could receive forgiveness of sins and obtain eternal life. Without a sacrifice, the shedding of blood, there would be no forgiveness of sins – Hebrews 9:22. That's why Jesus had to die so that his blood could be shed for us and he could be made the ultimate sacrifice.

Fighting Satan and his demons

"Put on all of God's armor so that you will be able to stand firm against all strategies and tricks of the Devil. For we are not fighting against people made of flesh and blood, but against

the evil rulers and authorities of the unseen world, against those mighty powers of darkness who rule this world, and against wicked spirits in the heavenly realms." Ephesians 6:11-12

The world is the devil's domain; he rules this evil world which is why you see and hear more bad than good, more hate than love, more lies than truth. The above scripture mentions that wicked spirits are in heavenly realms; however, this does not mean that wicked spirits are in heaven. There are spiritual realms, a spiritual atmosphere (the spirit world), where intense spiritual activity occurs. Evil spirits also manifest themselves on earth and encourage demonic activity – possessing and persuading people to do the devil's work.

"Once you were dead because of your disobedience and your many sins. You used to live in sin, just like the rest of the world, obeying the devil—the commander of the powers in the unseen world. He is the spirit at work in the hearts of those who refuse to obey God. All of us used to live that way, following the passionate desires and inclinations of our sinful nature. By our very nature we were subject to God's anger, just like everyone else. But God is so rich in mercy, and he loved us so much, that even though we were dead because of our sins, he gave us life when he raised Christ from the dead. (It is only by God's grace that you have been saved!)" Ephesians 2:1-5

Technically, we do not fight against people and situations; we fight against the devil and his demons because it is the devil who works through people and situations to try to destroy us. We cannot see the devil or his demons as they are a part of the unseen spiritual realm. However, we can see the manifestations of his work – confusion, chaos, corruption, and crime. The only way to fight the unseen powers of darkness and evil (the devil) is with the unseen powers of light and righteousness (God). We do not possess the power to fight what is unseen alone, this is like going into battle with a blindfold on. We must use the spiritual weapons that God gave us – His mighty armor.

Purpose Point: The devil is powerful, only if we allow him to be. God, on the other hand, is all powerful and does not leave us defenseless against Satan. By yourself, you have no chance to defeat Satan but with God Satan is powerless against you and is already defeated. Greater is He (God) that is in you, than he (devil) that is in the world (1 John 4:4).

"Look, I have given you authority over all the power of the enemy…Nothing will injure you." Luke 10:19

How to fight the devil:

– STAND your ground! - Put on God's armor and resist the devil.

> *"…Therefore, put on every piece of God's armor so you will be able to resist the enemy in the time of evil. Then after the battle you will still be standing firm. Stand your ground, putting on the belt of truth and the body armor of God's righteousness. For shoes, put on the peace that comes from the Good News so that you will be fully prepared. In addition to all of these, hold up the shield of faith to stop the fiery arrows of the devil. Put on salvation as your helmet, and take the sword of the Spirit, which is the word of God. Pray in the Spirit at all times and on every occasion. Stay alert and be persistent in your prayers for all believers everywhere."* Ephesians 6:13-18

"Take a firm stand against him, and be strong in your faith..." I Peter 5:9

"...Resist the Devil, and he will flee from you." James 4:7

- **Put on the sturdy belt of truth** – Remember, there can only be one truth in everything. For example, disobeying your parents is a lie; the truth is that you should obey your parents as stated in God's Word, the Bible. When you believe God's Word as the truth and obey it by faith, you have successfully put on your belt of truth. **Don't believe Satan's lies!**

"Stand your ground, putting on the sturdy belt of truth and the body armor of God's righteousness." Ephesians 6:14

- **Put on the body armor of God's righteousness** – Righteousness is being in right standing with God. When you repent of your sins, accept Jesus as your Lord and Savior, you are in right standing with Him – you are righteous. Once you have done this, you have successfully put on your body armor. Even when you mess up, you are still the righteousness of God; simply repent (turn away from the sin), confess it to God, and ask for forgiveness.

"Keep watch and pray, so that you will not give in to temptation. For the spirit is willing, but the body is weak!" Matthew 26:41

- **Put on your shoes of peace** – The peace of God comes from the good news of salvation and eternal life – our hope of glory. With this good news, you should trust God as your savior, protector, provider, and deliverer. When you fully trust God, you obtain a supernatural peace that surpasses all understanding. The things that you were once afraid of or worried about seem to almost disappear when you fully believe and trust God.

Minute Memoir: For a long time, I felt like there was no hope for me. But when I learned of the good news about Jesus dying for me and wanting to change my life for the better, I began to regain hope and an inner peace entered my heart. Trusting and believing God will eliminate the fears of evil in your life and will disarm the devil from tormenting your mind. When you trust and believe God, you have successfully put on your shoes of peace. Don't allow Satan to bombard your mind with fear, worry, and hopelessness. Trust God. Lean on His promises to activate peace in your heart.

"For shoes, put on the peace that comes from the Good News, so that you will be fully prepared." Ephesians 6:15

"You will keep in perfect peace all who trust in you, all whose thoughts are fixed on you!" Isaiah 26:3

Purpose Point: The Good News is the message of Christ that announces the truth about Jesus Christ dying for your sins, adopting you into his royal family, filling you with his Holy Spirit, giving you a new spirit and saving you from hell and eternal death. The Good News also teaches God's promises of prosperity, healing, and deliverance which helps to foster faith, hope, peace, perseverance, and endurance.

– **Take hold to the shield of faith** – The devil will try to attack your mind with fear and worry. He will try to make you believe that something bad is going to happen or that the bad you are currently experiencing will never change. He will try to make you believe that no one, including God, really loves you. He'll even try to make you feel bad about yourself as if you are not worthy, important, or beautiful; he'll encourage you to feel condemned, guilty, worthless, and shameful. But despite his tactics, stand strong and use your shield of faith against him – remember and declare who you are.

Whatever the devil tries to attack your mind with, just believe, think, and say the opposite. For example, if he whispers in your mind that you are a nobody, believe by faith that you are a somebody. Say or declare *"I am somebody...I am a child of the most High God. My heavenly Father loves me and with Him I will do mighty things."*

Moreover, the devil may whisper in your ear negative words of defeat such as, 'Your life is just too messed up, there is no hope for you; things will never get better.' This is when you must use your shield of faith and believe and say the opposite, *'Nothing is impossible with God. God said he has good plans for me, to give me a future and a hope. He will work out his plans for my life. If I trust him, he will give me the desires of my heart. He will keep his promise'* (Luke 1:37; Jeremiah 29:11; Psalm 138:8; Psalm 37:4; Hebrews 10:23).

Use God's Words to fight Satan. The faith-filled statements mentioned above are all from the Word of God, the Bible. But again, in order for you to say God's words you must first know God's Word. Read, study, and refer to your Bible daily.

"In every battle you will need faith as your shield to stop the fiery arrows aimed at you by Satan." Ephesians 6:16

"Take a firm stand against him, and be strong in your faith. Remember that Christians all over the world are going through the same kind of suffering you are. In his kindness God called you to his eternal glory by means of Jesus Christ. After you have suffered a little while, he will restore, support, and strengthen you, and he will place you on a firm foundation." 1 Peter 5: 9 –10

"What is faith? It is the confident assurance that what we hope for is going to happen. It is the evidence of things we cannot yet see." Hebrews 11:1

"...a righteous person will live by faith." Hebrews 10:38

"Without wavering, let us hold tightly to the hope we say we have, for God can be trusted to keep his promise." Hebrews 10:23

Any and all thoughts that you have that makes you feel sad, depressed, lonely, hurt or defeated are not of God, but of the devil. Remember, there can only be one truth to anything…whatever the devil tells you is a lie, so the opposite of that must be the truth. The devil tells us lies and tries to make us feel bad and do bad things because he wants us to carry out his plans for our life, his will. He knows that if we carry out his plans, we cannot carry out God's plans.

Overcome the devil's lies and fear tactics with faith! Try not to be fearful, depressed, sad or distressed when the devil tells you a lie...see it for what it is. Use the shield of faith and believe God's truth. The shield of faith can block anything that comes from the devil. Faith is the opposite of fear, and God's truth is the opposite of the devil's lies. Don't give in to fear and lies, instead overcome fear with faith! Use your shield!

How to obtain faith: Faith comes by hearing and listening to the Word of God. You must hear God's Word to obtain faith. Some ways to hear God's Word include attending a bible-based church, reading and meditating on scriptures in your Bible, and watching and listening to Christian networks and music. Hearing the testimony of others or how God has helped others also increases your faith. Fear comes the same way as faith – by hearing…hearing and believing the lies of the devil. *"So faith comes from hearing, that is, hearing the Good News about Christ."* Romans 10:17

- **Put on salvation as your helmet.** You must be saved to defeat the devil. When you accept Jesus as your Lord and Savior, you have received the gift of salvation where the Lord has saved you from your sins. It was through the death of Jesus, the shedding of his blood, that you are saved. When you allow Jesus to save you, you have successfully put on your helmet of salvation. The enemy cannot touch you when the blood of Jesus is on your life. However, to be truly effective, you must be assured or confident in the salvation Jesus provides. Faith, obedience, and trust in God gives you the confidence you need.

"Put on salvation as your helmet, and take the sword of the Spirit, which is the word of God." Ephesians 6:17

- **Take the sWord of spirit (the Word of God).** The Word of God will sever and stop all Satan's schemes, lies, plans, and tricks. If used properly, it is capable of decapitating Satan's head – stopping him dead in his tracks. Satan tried to tempt Jesus, but Jesus used his **sWord** (the scriptures/God's Word) against Satan and successfully defeated him.

"Then Jesus was led out into the wilderness by the Holy Spirit to be tempted there by the Devil. For forty days and forty nights he ate nothing and became very hungry. Then the Devil came and said to him, 'If you are the Son of God, change these two stones into loaves of bread.' But Jesus told him, 'No! The Scriptures say, 'People need more than bread for their life; they must feed on every word of God.' Then the Devil took him to Jerusalem to the highest point of the Temple, and said, 'If you are the Son of God, jump off! For the Scriptures say, 'He orders his angels to protect you. And they will hold you with their hands to keep you from striking your foot on a stone.'

Jesus responded, 'The Scriptures also say, 'Do not test the Lord your God.' Next the Devil took him to the peak of a very high mountain and showed him the nations of the world and all their glory. I will give it all to you', he said, 'if you will only kneel down and worship me.' 'Get out of here, Satan,' Jesus told him. 'For the Scriptures say, You must worship the Lord your God; serve only him.' Then the Devil went away, and the angels came and cared for Jesus." Matthew 4:1-11

- **Pray at all times and on every occasion.** Prayer is what connects you to God. It is through prayer that you speak to God and God speaks back to you from within. No matter what you are going through, good or bad, you should always pray. Your prayer should include the following points:

    - thank God for who He is and what He has done; worship Him
    - pray that God's plans will come to pass on earth as it is in heaven
    - pray that God will meet your needs daily
    - ask God to help you with anything that concerns you or others
    - confess any known sins and ask God to forgive your sins - choose to forgive others
    - ask God to help you avoid temptation and deliver you from evil

The last point of asking God for help in avoiding temptation and being delivered from evil is more related to the devil. When you pray this type of prayer, you welcome God to work in your life and protect you from the evil one and his temptations.

Jesus said, *"When you pray, don't babble on and on as people of other religions do. They think their prayers are answered merely by repeating their words again and again. Don't be like them, for your Father knows exactly what you need even before you ask him! Pray like this: Our Father in heaven, may your name be honored. May your Kingdom come soon. May your will be done here on earth, just as it is in heaven. Give us our food for today and forgive our sins, just as we have forgiven those who have sinned against us. And don't let us yield to temptation, but deliver us from the evil one."* Matthew 6:7-13

- **Stay alert and be persistent in your prayers.** When you think you are standing strong, you could fall. When you think everything is going well, something could take an unexpected turn. Stay alert, be watchful and keep praying! The enemy is watching you like a lion, so do not get too lax in praying – stay alert.

    "If you think you are standing strong, be careful, for you, too, may fall into the same sin." 1 Corinthians 10:12

"Be careful! Watch out for attacks from the Devil, your great enemy! He prowls around like a roaring lion, looking for some victim to devour." 1 Peter 5:8

- **Wear your crown of confidence!** Another important factor of your armor is your crown which is like the belt of truth. Your crown is the unwavering belief that you are special, valuable, and precious to God. It reflects a high level of self-esteem, confidence, and assurance (faith). Knowing who you are, your value, whose you are and why you were created without doubting also helps you to defeat Satan. Being confident in yourself makes it difficult for Satan to lie and trick you about your identity. When you know the truth, it is hard to believe a lie. A crown is worn on the head which is the protector of the mind and the very place that Satan will try to attack you – your mind. He will attempt to bombard your mind with fear, hopelessness, confusion and despair; however, when you wear your crown and walk in confidence knowing that God is with you and that He loves you, Satan is disarmed. Remember, if you have accepted Christ, you are a child of the Most High God, a daughter of God, an heiress to the throne. Your price is far above rubies. You were created to worship and praise God, to love and to be loved, to help your natural king (your husband), to procreate life through divine order and to help others to know Jesus. Satan will try to trick you into believing that you are insignificant and worthless. He pulled this same trick on Jesus by trying to get him to question his identity, the person God created him to be.

*"Then the Devil took him to Jerusalem to the highest point of the Temple, and said, **'If you are the Son of God**, jump off! For the Scriptures say, He orders his angels to protect you. And they will hold you with their hands to keep you from striking your foot on a stone.' Jesus responded, 'The Scriptures also say, Do not test the Lord your God.'"* Matthew 4:5-7

The devil is extremely deceptive; he knows the Bible and will state a truth in an attempt to get you to neglect and disregard all others. The devil will also try to get you to question your identity and may send thoughts to your mind that say, *'If you are a daughter and princess of God, then why don't you have this, why doesn't God answer your prayer, why did this happen?'* You must know God's Word (rightly dividing the Word of truth – 2 Timothy 2:15) and *know your Worth* to fight the devil effectively.

- **Use the name of Jesus.** Demons tremble when they hear the name of Jesus. When you think the devil is attacking you, then by faith speak God's Word against the devil out loud and use the authority of Jesus Christ. For example, if the devil is trying to attack you through other people, then during your prayer time say aloud, *'Satan, by the authority of the name of Jesus I rebuke you and command you to cease operating in <u>insert person's name here</u> to try to hurt me. The blood of Jesus is against you. I render all your works, tricks, and schemes to be ineffective and inoperative in my life. No weapon formed against me will prosper, and every tongue that rises against me will be condemned'* (Isaiah 54:17).

The disciples of Jesus said to him, 'Lord, even the demons obey us when we use your name!' 'Yes', he told them, 'I saw Satan falling from heaven as a flash of lightning! And I have given you authority over all the power of the enemy…" Luke 10:17-19

Purpose Point: Only by the blood of Jesus are we able to defeat Satan. When you accept Jesus as your Savior and confess with your mouth that he is Lord and that he died for your sins, God gives you His special armor and favor. Without Jesus, you are doomed without any armor or protection and cannot successfully fight the devil. God is the only one who can protect you – not your parents, police, family, or friends.

"...And they have defeated him because of the blood of the Lamb and because of their testimony." Revelations 12:11

"But the Lord is faithful; he will make you strong and guard you from the evil one."
2 Thessalonians 3:3

Princesses Prepare for Battle! The devil (Satan) is your enemy, and he wants to destroy you. Fight the enemy with God's armor and the Word of God. Resist the devil and he will flee! The battle is not yours, but it is the Lord's (2 Chronicles 20:15: 1 Samuel 17:47). God has already won the battle, but you must still fight to live the good life God has planned for you! "Fight the good fight of the faith. Take hold of the eternal life to which you were called when you made your good confession in the presence of many witnesses." 1 Timothy 6:12 NIV

Purpose Point: The enemy can only destroy you if you allow him. When you choose to do wrong and violate the principles and commands of God, you open the door to the devil and give him access to work in your life.

"Don't give the devil any opportunity to work. Thieves must quit stealing and, instead, they must work hard. They should do something good with their hands so that they'll have something to share with those in need." Ephesians 4:27-28 GW

There are four (4) entry points or open doors that give the devil quick access to your life:
1. Habitual sin/disobedience – Galatians 5:19-21; Hebrews 10:26
2. Idolatry/worshiping false gods – Exodus 20:3-6
3. Participating in witchcraft and the occult – Deuteronomy 8:10-13; Isaiah 28:15
4. Speaking negative words about yourself and others – Proverbs 13:3; Proverbs 18:21

Engaging in the above activities will give the devil vast opportunity to disrupt and destroy your life. Stay close to God to abide in His love and protection.

"We know that God's children do not make a practice of sinning, for God's Son holds them securely, and the evil one cannot touch them." 1 John 5:18

The Spirit of God that lives in you is greater than Satan himself. *"...You have already won your fight...because the Spirit who lives in you is greater than the spirit who lives in the world."* 1 John 4:4

"I called on the LORD, who is worthy of praise, and he saved me from my enemies."
Psalm 18:3

Satan - the Tempter, Accuser, Adversary, Deceiver, Snake, Dragon

Satan is the author of temptation. The moment you give your life to Jesus, the devil will try to tempt you to backslide or go back to living an ungodly life. He will try to draw you back to your past and make you want to do worldly and ungodly things. He will use your weaknesses and struggles against you, placing them strategically on your path for you to stumble. People tend to think it is God who does the tempting, but this is absolutely not true. God does not tempt us to do wrong. *"And remember, no one who wants to do wrong should ever say, 'God is tempting me.' God is never tempted to do wrong, and he never tempts anyone else either. Temptation comes from the lure of our own evil desires. These evil desires lead to evil actions, and evil actions lead to death. So don't be misled... Whatever is good and perfect comes to us from God above..."* James 1:13-17

Moreover, the devil encourages your sinful desires, wicked/lustful thoughts, and selfish motives. He will put evil thoughts, ideas, and suggestions in your mind to stimulate what may already be in your heart. God may allow the devil to tempt you so that you can either prove yourself or see your faults for the purpose of growing and becoming better and stronger. Again, God does not do the tempting. Temptation is like a test – it tests your faith, morals (character/integrity) and values. It reveals your mind frame, the thoughts, and intentions of your heart, in a difficult or uncomfortable situation.

For example, in school you are given various tests, and these tests prove your knowledge on a particular subject. The test allows you to prove yourself, and the graded test gives you the opportunity to become better by allowing you to see the questions that were missed so that you can learn from your mistakes and pass the final exam. Like so, God allows tests to be given so you can prove your knowledge and faith in various areas and prove your commitment to God and others. Realizing the mistakes that you made during the test gives you the opportunity to do better in the future. And seeing the problems that you got correct motivates you to keep getting them right when you see them again. We should not be "defined by our past but refined by it." Remember, God doesn't want us to stay stuck where we are. He wants us to grow and become better day by day. Being tempted and tested helps us to see the things in us that are not of God such as pride, hate, greed, rebellion, and unforgiveness. Seeing these things allows you to work on problem areas and become better in the process. And passing the test(s) and seeing the positive outcome(s), encourages and empowers you to keep doing better in the future. Therefore, passing a test doesn't mean you won't see the material again, it only means that you are prepared (knowledgeable) and ready – provided that you don't forget or lose faith in what you learned. But not passing a test ensures you'll see it again, but will you be ready?

Purpose Point: God can change your evil thoughts if you allow Him. Open your heart to God and refuse to behave like the world. Although it is difficult to completely rid yourself of every wrong thought and every ounce of temptation, you have the power to reject wrong thinking and negative behaviors. God has given you the power to control your thoughts by faith and to make ungodly thoughts obey.

For instance, God said, cast down every thought that is not of Him and bring it under the subjection to the mind of Christ. What does this mean? **Refuse to think about the wrong**

thoughts and stop its power. How do you stop thinking about wrong thoughts? Cast them down and say something that is contrary to that thought. For example, if you are thinking about engaging in a wrong behavior such as having intimate relations with a boy you just met, say out loud in your private time: *'I will not yield my body to sexual immorality. My body is a temple. God bought me with a high price and wants me to honor by body. God lives in me. I cast down every wrong thought that is not of Christ.'* Keep saying it until that thought leaves your mind, and if it returns, say it again. In this way, you are arresting that wrong thought, stopping its power, holding it captive, and making it obey Christ.

"Casting down imaginations, and every high thing that [exalts] itself against the knowledge of God, and bringing into captivity every thought to the obedience of Christ."
2 Corinthians 10:5 KJV

"Don't copy the behavior and customs of this world, but let God transform you into a new person by changing the way you think..." Romans 12:2

Additionally, to stop wrong thoughts, believe what is opposite of that wrong thought and think about something else, something good. For example, if you think hate, think love instead; if you think loss, think hope. *"...Fix your thoughts on what is true and honorable and right. Think about things that are pure and lovely and admirable. Think about things that are excellent and worthy of praise. Keep putting into practice all you learned from me and heard from me and saw me doing, and the God of peace will be with you."* Philippians 4:8-9

Adam and Eve...Apple and Evil – The Ultimate Temptation

Adam and Eve were the first humans on earth who Satan accused and tempted. Remember, Satan is the accuser of us all. What does it mean to accuse someone? When you accuse someone, you charge them with an offense; you assert or claim that someone did something wrong which would imply punishment or misfortune to the person accused. Accusing someone also means to criticize, condemn, and prejudge harshly, often before the person even makes a mistake. For instance, before Satan tempted Adam and Eve, he probably went to God and accused them of being wicked. He most likely said something to the effect to God, 'They will not obey you; they too desire to be like you and know all things. They will surely betray you like I did. Your precious humans may be made in your image, but they are all evil just like me.' The Bible does not give this scenario per say, but it does tell of Satan's accusing behavior in the book of Job (Job 1:6-12). God allowed Adam and Eve to be tempted by the devil, and they failed the test – opening the door for evil, sin and death to enter the world.

"...the Lord planted a garden in Eden, in the east, and there he placed the man he [Adam] had created. And the Lord God planted all sorts of trees in the garden – beautiful trees that produced delicious fruit. At the center of the garden he placed the tree of life and the tree of knowledge of good and evil... The Lord God placed the man in the Garden of Eden to tend and care for it. But the Lord gave him this warning: 'You may freely eat any fruit in the garden except fruit from the tree of the knowledge of good and evil. If you eat from its fruit, you will surely die. And the Lord God said, "It is not good for the man to be alone...the Lord God made a woman (Eve)..." Satan later approached Eve as a snake (serpent) while she was alone. *"...he asked the woman. 'Did God really say you must not eat any of the fruit in the garden?'*

'Of course, we may eat', the woman told him. 'It's only the fruit from the tree at the center of the garden that we are not allowed to eat. God says we must not eat it or even touch it, or we will die.' 'You won't die!' the serpent hissed. 'God knows that your eyes will be opened when you eat it. You will become just like God, knowing everything, both good and evil.' The woman was convinced. The fruit looked so fresh and delicious, and it would make her so wise! So she ate some of the fruit. She also gave some to her husband, who was with her. Then he ate it, too. At that moment, their eyes were opened, and they suddenly felt shame at their nakedness. So they strung fig leaves together around their hips to cover themselves...Then the Lord asked the woman, 'How could you do such a thing?' 'The serpent tricked me,' she replied, 'That's why I ate it..." Genesis 2:8-9; Genesis 2:15-22; Genesis 3:1-7; Genesis 3:13

The first humans on earth, Adam and Eve, were given a choice from God. God gave them a commandment and they chose not to obey it. As a result of not choosing God, they were sentenced to death along with their future generations. Since they were the first humans with a sinful nature, their sinful bloodline contaminated the entire human race because all humans would be born from their bloodline, thus all humans would sin and die. So, you see, the choices that you make not only affect you, but it also affects others. Despite Adam and Eve's sin, God sent His son Jesus Christ to save us from eternal death and offer eternal life to anyone who accepts and obeys him.

"When Adam sinned, sin entered the entire human race. Adam's sin brought death, so death spread to everyone, for everyone sinned...For this one man, Adam, brought death to many through his sin. But this other man, Jesus Christ, brought forgiveness to many through God's bountiful gift. And the result of God's gracious gift is very different from the result of that one man's sin. For Adam's sin led to condemnation, but we have the free gift of being accepted by God, even though we are guilty of many sins. The sin of this one man, Adam, caused death to rule over us, but all who receive God's wonderful, gracious gift of righteousness will live in triumph over sin and death through one man, Jesus Christ...Because one person disobeyed God, many people became sinners. But because one other person obeyed God, many people will be made right in God's sight. So just as sin ruled over all people and brought them to death, now God's wonderful kindness rules instead, giving us right standing with God and resulting in eternal life through Jesus Christ our Lord. Well then, should we keep on sinning so that God can show us more and more kindness and forgiveness? Of course not! Since we have died to sin, how can we continue to live in it? Or have you forgotten that when we became Christians and were baptized to become one with Christ Jesus, we died with him? For we died and were buried with Christ by baptism..." Romans 5:12; Romans 5:15-17; Romans 5:19-21; Romans 6:1-4

Purpose Point: It was through Adam and Eve's disobedience to God that all humans were sentenced to eternal death. And it was through Jesus' obedience that this judgment was reversed, and all humans were given the option of eternal life. It is important to note that through Adam and Eve's disobedience eternal death was automatic to everyone; however, eternal life through Jesus Christ is <u>not</u> automatic. We must confess Jesus as Lord, turn away from living a sinful life (repent) and obey God to receive the gift of salvation and eternal life. Jesus did not die for us so that we could keep sinning; he died so that we could have the power to overcome sin through him and obey God by doing good.

When you are baptized, the act of going under water is symbolic of your old sinful spirit dying (being buried) with Jesus. Conversely, coming out of the water is symbolic of your new godly spirit becoming alive similarly to the rising of Jesus from the dead. The new spirit, the spirit of God, comes to live in you and gives you the desire to obey Him. This is not to say that you will never mess up, or never sin, but you should have a desire to want to change your sinful ways and make steps by faith to eliminate sin from your life. When you mess up, you should feel some conviction or remorse and know that you are wrong; you should then confess it to God, ask for forgiveness and repent or turn away from that sin.

What can we learn from Adam and Eve's wrong choice?

1. Don't listen to Satan; he is wily, crafty and tricky.

"The snake tricked me," she replied... Genesis 3:13

2. Don't chase after things just to make yourself look good; this could make you disobey and dishonor God. Furthermore, what may look good, may not be good for you. In other words, everything that looks good, is not good and not God.

"...The woman was convinced. The fruit looked so fresh and delicious, and it would make her so wise!" Genesis 3:6

3. Obey and believe God even when people or the devil try to make you believe something else.

"But the Lord God gave him this warning: 'You may freely eat any fruit in the garden except fruit from the tree of the knowledge of good and evil...'" Genesis 2:16

"Satan ... asked the woman, 'Did God really say you must not eat any of the fruit in the garden?' 'Of course, we may eat it, the woman told him. 'It's only the fruit from the tree at the center of the garden that we are not allowed to eat. God says we must not eat it or even touch it, or we will die.' 'You won't die!' the serpent hissed." Genesis 3:1-4

4. Don't try to cover up your sins and hide from God; confess it to God, repent and ask for forgiveness. God already knows what you have done, so there is no need to hide your faults or conceal your mistakes.

"...So they strung fig leaves together around their hips to cover themselves." Genesis 3:7

"Nothing in all creation is hidden from God. Everything is naked and exposed before his eyes, and he is the one to whom we are accountable." Hebrews 4:13

5. When we sin, the people around us could duplicate what we do, bringing disaster upon everyone and future generations to come. Your poor choices cannot only have a negative impact on you but on others as well. The entire world became sick with sin the moment Adam and Eve ate the forbidden fruit... *"The woman was convinced. The fruit looked so fresh and delicious, and it would make her so wise! So she ate some of the fruit. She also gave some to her husband, who was with her."* Genesis 3:6

6. The wages of sin is death.

"But the Lord gave this warning: 'You may freely eat any fruit in the garden except fruit from the tree of the knowledge of good and evil. If you eat from this fruit, you will surely die.'"
Genesis 2:16

"For the wages of sin is death, but the free gift of God is eternal life through Christ Jesus our Lord." Romans 6:23

7. It is better to know God than to chase after knowledge itself. God is the source of all wisdom and knowledge; therefore, to know Him is to have access to the knowledge you seek.

"... 'You won't die!' the serpent hissed. God knows that your eyes will be opened when you eat it. You will become just like God, knowing everything, both good and evil.' The woman was convinced. She saw that the tree was beautiful and its fruit looked delicious, and she wanted the wisdom it would give her..." Genesis 3:4-6

8. Shame is not a part of God's plan for you. Sin brings about shame; repent and be free.

"...Then he ate it too. At that moment, their eyes were opened, and they suddenly felt shame at their nakedness..." Genesis 3:6-7

9. Satan will attack you when you are most vulnerable – when you are alone. Satan approached Eve in the absence of Adam. Therefore, it is best to surround yourself with godly people and seek godly counsel so that they can hold you accountable and guide you in making the right decision(s). But always go to God first in prayer (Matthew 6:33; Ephesians 6:18).

"The godly offer good counsel; they teach right from wrong. They have made God's law their own, so they will never slip from his path." Psalm 37:30-31

10. God's words are always true, anything else is a lie. Remember, there is only one truth, but many lies. The lies that Satan told Eve were: (1) you will not die (2) you will be just like God (3) and Satan implied that God did not really say that she couldn't eat from the forbidden tree – he made Eve doubt. But the ONE truth – as God explicitly told them in the beginning was that if you eat from the forbidden tree, you will surely die. When you choose God's truth over the devil's lies, *you live*. But when you choose the devil's lies over God's truth, *you lose*.

Purpose Point: Recognizing the tricks and tactics of the enemy and knowing God's truth makes us mature in Christ and positions us to resist Satan.

Purpose Point: Because of sin and the devil, life can be hard – full of pain and sorrow. But Jesus said, *"I have told you all this so that you may have peace in me. Here on earth you will have many trials and sorrows. But take heart, because I have overcome the world."* John 16:33 Additionally, Jesus prayed to God, *"I'm not asking you to take them out of the world, but to keep them safe from the evil one."* John 17:15

Many wonder why God placed the forbidden tree in the garden. I believe that the reason behind this was to give Adam and Eve a choice. Remember, God does not force himself on anyone. He gives us a choice between good or evil, God or Satan. When we do not choose God or choose to disobey Him, we side with Satan, the snake. God will tell you what choice to make and will even tell you the consequences of not making that choice, but He will not force you to make His choice. If God had not put the tree of knowledge of good and evil in the garden, then Adam and Eve would have been forced to choose God. How would you feel if your family, friends, or husband always forced you to do something…forced you to do what they wanted you to do? What if they never allowed you to make your own decisions or do the things that you wanted to do. Would you feel as though they really loved you? Probably not.

Purpose Point: God is love. He loves us so much that He allows us to make our own choices. He will tell you which choice to make and explain the benefits of the right choice and the consequences of the wrong choice, but He will never force you to make the right choice because of His great love for you.

Purpose Point: It hurts God when we do not choose Him…when we fail the test AND give up. God does not want us to hide from Him when we fail. He wants us to confess our wrongs, turn away from doing wrong, and try again. If we do this, He is faithful and just to forgive us and to cleanse us from all unrighteousness.

The devil not only accused and tempted Adam and Eve, but the Bible also tells us about other people he tempted and accused, including God's servant, Job. God allowed Satan to test Job's faithfulness to God amid great sorrow and tribulation. Job lost his children, livestock, servants, and health almost simultaneously. He was tempted and encouraged to curse God and die.

"One day the angels came to present themselves before the Lord, and **Satan the Accuser** *came with them. 'Where have you come from?' the Lord asked Satan. And Satan answered the Lord, 'I have been going back and forth across the earth watching everything that's going on.' Then the Lord asked Satan, 'Have you noticed my servant Job? He is the finest man in all the earth – a man of complete integrity. He fears God and will have nothing to do with evil.' Satan replied to the Lord, 'Yes, Job fears God, but not without good reason! You have always protected him and his home and his property from harm. You have made him prosperous in everything he does. Look how rich he is! But take away everything he has, and he will surely curse you to your face!' 'All right, you may test him', the Lord said to Satan. 'Do whatever you want with everything he possesses, but don't harm him physically.' So Satan left the Lord's presence."* Job 1:6-12

Job's '…wife said to him, 'Are you still trying to maintain your integrity? Curse God and die.' But Job replied, 'You talk like a godless woman. Should we accept only good things from the hand of God and never anything bad?' So in all of this, Job said nothing wrong." Job 2:9-10

Job later complained and questioned the wisdom of God, but he repented and took back everything he said.

"Then Job replied to the Lord: 'I know that you can do anything, and no one can stop you. You ask, 'Who is this that questions my wisdom with such ignorance?' It is I. And I was talking about things I did not understand, things far too wonderful for me…I take back everything I said, and I sit in dust and ashes to show my repentance'…the Lord blessed Job in the second half of his life even more than in the beginning…" Job 42:2-3; Job 42:6; Job 42:12

Purpose Point: Sometimes God will allow bad things to happen in our life for reasons He only knows. We cannot become angry with God and question His wisdom. Try to trust God no matter what happens in your life – good or bad. I know it might be difficult in times of trouble and loss, but believe God is in control and He will not allow you to be tempted or tried more than you can handle.

Candid Clarification: It was Satan who took away Job's possessions and attacked his health; God only allowed it. The Lord is the giver of life.

Another sign of Satan being an accuser is in Zechariah 3:1: *"...The Accuser, Satan, was there at the angel's right hand, making accusations against Jeshua."*

Jesus defeated Satan. He canceled all charges against you. So even when you feel the accusations from self, other people, or the devil, know that you are not condemned in Jesus' name. *"You were dead because of your sins and because your sinful nature was not yet cut away. Then God made you alive with Christ, for he forgave all our sins. He canceled the record of the charges against us and took it away by nailing it to the cross. In this way, he disarmed the spiritual rulers and authorities. He shamed them publicly by his victory over them on the cross. So don't let anyone condemn you for what you eat or drink, or for not celebrating certain holy days or new moon ceremonies or Sabbaths."* Colossians 2:13-16

Why does the devil tempt you?

The devil tempts you because he wants you to believe that Jesus has not saved you and that you are not worthy of salvation. He also wants to persuade God into believing that you do not honor and love Him. The devil accuses us 24/7 of being unloving, ungodly, and disobedient towards God.

Imagine a courtroom and you were the person on trial. God is the judge, and the devil is the prosecutor going before God accusing you of horrible things. He wants God, the judge, to sentence you to death for eternity. In order for the devil to prove his case, he will tempt you to do wrong so that he can say to God: 'I told you so – she is guilty!' Although the devil's plan for temptation is to prove to God how bad we are, God's plan in allowing the temptation is for us to prove to God our love and faithfulness for Him and to learn from our mistakes so that we can grow more in Him and like Him – becoming better and more confident in the process. The devil may think that he is working for the bad in your life by tempting you, but God can use him to produce something good.

"And we know that God causes everything to work together for the good of those who love God and are called according to his purpose for them." Romans 8:28

Passing the devil's tests (temptations) puts us in a position to graduate in God, to grow from a princess to a queen. If the devil never tempted, then how could we prove ourselves...how could we graduate in God and know what we are capable of? There is no way one could graduate from any school without first passing exams. And for a person to pass a test there must first be a test. The devil is the tempter, the tester of evil, but God grades the test. He determines whether you passed or failed because God knows your heart. The devil only knows the lies he has whispered in your ear and the situations he has orchestrated in your life. So let's work to make an "A" on the test and prove to God our great love and honor for Him...prove the devil's accusations to be wrong! But if you fail the test, confess to God that you failed and do better the next time – do not condemn yourself. God will teach you how to pass the next exam successfully with faith, fortitude, and fervor. *"...For the Accuser has been thrown down to earth – the one who accused our brothers and sisters...day and night."* Revelations 12:10

But regardless of what the devil tries to do and no matter how much he accuses us, *"Who dares accuse us whom God has chosen for his own? Will God? No! He is the one who has given us right standing with himself. Who then will condemn us? Will Christ Jesus? No, for he is the one who died for us and was raised to life for us and is sitting at the place of highest honor next to God, pleading for us."* Romans 8:33-34   Therefore, if God or Jesus does not accuse or condemn us, we stand unaccused, not condemned, and possess right standing with God.

<u>Whenever you are faced with a test, remember:</u>
- Tests are necessary and temporary. *"...the testing of your faith produces perseverance."* James 1:3 NIV
- Tests prove character, credibility (trustworthiness) and capability. For instance, you would not trust a doctor to perform surgery on you if he were never tested in medical school. Consumers would not trust or purchase products that have not been tested, tried, and proven. Moreover, no product should ever try to fix itself. If you fail a test, go back to your manufacturer (God), open your heart (repent) and allow Him to repair you. Supporting Scripture: *"Remember how the Lord your God led you through the wilderness..., humbling you and testing you to prove your character, and to find out whether or not you would really obey his commands.* Deuteronomy 8:2
- One key to succeeding is that when you fail, you get back up and prepare yourself for the retake so you can pass to the next level.
- Expect and embrace the tests. Expect a battle but know it has already been won.
- The enemy sends temptations and trails for our bad, but God works them out for our good. Supporting Scripture: *"You intended to harm me, but God intended it for good to accomplish what is now being done, the saving of many lives."* Genesis 50:20 NIV
- Tests (passed or failed) provide us with a <u>testi</u>mony for the benefit of self and others. For example, if you fail a test and learn from it, you can advise others of the tricks and consequences to dissuade them from repeating the same behavior(s) and going down a similar path. And if you pass the test, you can encourage and tutor (disciple) others during their test and show them how to pass it as well, using the Word of God and its principles as the answer guide. You also benefit from lessons learned.
- God is glorified when we pass the tests. But even when we do not pass, the moment we choose to humble ourselves and learn from our failures, we become better because of them and God will still get the glory and make adjustments to put us on top. However, we save ourselves a lot of time and trouble when we pass the test the first time.

Purpose Point: If God allows a test, He knows that you are well capable of passing it. Everybody goes through similar tests; there is no test that is new to mankind, so don't ever think or feel like you are alone. God is good. He will not allow you to be tested or tempted beyond what you can handle. He will show you a way to get out of the temptation if you trust and obey Him; he'll show you how to win and not give in or give up. *"But remember that the temptations that come into your life are no different from what others experience. And God is faithful. He will keep the temptation from being so strong that you can't stand up against it. When you are tempted, he will show you a way out so that you will not give in to it."* 1 Corinthians 10:13; *"History merely repeats itself. It has all been done before. Nothing under the sun is truly new..."* Ecclesiastes 1:9-10

Purpose Point: When we accept Jesus as our Lord and Savior, confess our wrongs and turn away from doing bad things, we are deemed not guilty when we make a mistake or fail the test.

"So now there is no condemnation for those who belong to Christ Jesus. And because you belong to him, the power of the life-giving Spirit has freed you from the power of sin that leads to death." Romans 8:1

Purpose Point: Failing tests does not make you a failure. You are a winner as long as you have Christ, and when you keep trying and getting back up with a new attitude to achieve.

"They may trip seven times, but each time they will rise again..." Proverbs 24:16

Purpose Point: Satan works very hard to deceive and trick you. He tries to make you believe something is right when it is really wrong. He also tries to make you think something is true when it is really a lie. The devil has been successful in deceiving millions of people for years and years to come from all around the world. The only way to overcome his deceptions is to know the Truth – God's Word and apply it. For example, if I had known God's Word about not having sex before marriage and that my body was a temple of God, I would have had a better chance of overcoming Satan's lie that sex was okay before marriage with no consequences to endure.

"This great dragon, the ancient serpent called the Devil, or Satan, the one deceiving the whole world – was thrown down to the earth with all his angels." Revelations 12:9

Candid Clarification: All tests are not the same and temptations are different from standard tests. The type of tests God sends is when He tests your heart…when He tests you to do what is right. For example, God may test you to see if you will give to your church. There is nothing wrong with giving to a good and godly cause, right? In fact, God says we should tithe and give to our church (Malachi 3:10), and if we give it will be given back to us (Luke 6:38). Satan, on the other hand, tempts you to do what is wrong; he tempts you with evil. For example, he may tempt you to bully a girl because you are jealous of her. Doing so, would be wrong.

An old proverb asserts, *"Satan tempts us to make us worse. God tests us to make us better."*

So remember, *"Keep watch and pray, so that you will not give in to temptation. For the spirit is willing, but the body is weak!"* Matthew 26:41

"If you think you are standing strong, be careful not to fall." 1 Corinthians 10:12

Jesus said, *"Pray that you will not give in to temptation."* Luke 22:40

When we pass tests and overcome temptations, God is proud and releases more provision. The following scripture tells of a parable relating to a master who tested his servant. The servant passed the test, and the master was so happy. This is how God feels when we pass tests...

"The master was full of praise. 'Well done, my good and faithful servant. You have been faithful in handling this small amount, so now I will give you many more responsibilities. Let's celebrate together!" Matthew 25:21

---

*"God blesses those who patiently endure testing and temptation. Afterward they will receive the **crown of life** that God has promised to those who love him."* James 1:12
*"The devil…will test you…But if you remain faithful…I will give you the **crown of life**."* Rev 2:10

Satan and the Woman

"Then I witnessed in heaven an event of great significance. I saw a woman clothed with sun, with the moon beneath her feet, and a crown of twelve stars on her head. She was pregnant, and she cried out in pain of labor as she awaited her delivery. Suddenly, I witnessed in heaven another significant event. I saw a large red dragon with seven heads and ten horns, with seven crowns on his heads. His tail dragged down one-third of the stars, which he threw to the earth. He stood before the woman as she was about to give birth to her child, ready to devour the baby as soon as it was born. She gave birth to a boy who was to rule all nations with an iron rod. And the child was snatched away from the dragon and was caught up to God and to his throne. And the woman fled into the wilderness, where God had prepared a place to give her care..." Revelations 12:1-6

Although the above passage speaks in allegorical terms, Satan has a special interest in women. He especially hates women because he knows that it is through a woman that human life is formed. God uses women to procreate. Of course, a man (his seed) is needed to achieve this outcome, but it is in the woman's womb that a baby develops and grows. It is the woman who God uses to help manufacture the product and it is God who creates the blueprint and establishes the power for the product to grow, develop, function, and live. A precious baby is the product, purpose, and plan of God.

The Bible states in Malachi 2:15 that God wants godly children from the marriage union. Satan knows that every baby who is born has a God-given purpose on this earth. And of course, a part of their purpose would be to worship and praise God, build the kingdom of God by teaching others about Jesus and encouraging them to live out God's ways instead of the ways of the devil and the world. When people acknowledge God and advocate for Him, it hurts the devil's kingdom and reduces the number of people who worship and serve Satan, thus minimizing his power in the earth. So to prevent this from happening, the devil will try his best to attack women so that they cannot produce a godly seed (baby). He will also try his best to recruit women to live out his ways so that their children can live out his ways too.

Purpose Point: The more people who live out the devil's ways, the greater his power on earth. The less people to live out the devil's ways, the lesser his power on earth. The devil needs people to manifest his power and presence in the earth.

Purpose Point: The devil hates life. He does not want to take a chance of a baby being born because when the baby gets older and matures into an adult, he or she could decide to follow God and damage the devil's kingdom. On the flip side, the baby could grow up and decide to follow the devil and attempt to damage God's kingdom. But since Satan does not know which side the child will choose when he/she gets older, he would rather just kill all babies rather than take a chance. His fear and high levels of anxiety comes from the birth of Jesus. Jesus was once a baby and was formed in his mother's womb. The devil also tried to kill Jesus when he was an infant, but the devil could not find him, so he sent soldiers to kill all the babies in the land. Rather than take a chance of not killing Jesus, the godly seed (child), he decided to kill all babies who were two years old and under. But God was in control, and He still is. He protected Jesus from the enemy and will protect you too. It is because of Jesus (godly seed) that the devil is defeated, and his kingdom is doomed.

"Jesus was born in a town of Bethlehem in Judea, during the reign of King Herod. About that time some wise men from eastern lands arrived in Jerusalem asking, 'Where is the newborn king of the Jews? We have seen his stars as it rose, and we have come to worship him.' Herod was deeply disturbed by their question, as was all of Jerusalem... Matthew 2:1-3 *"...an angel of the Lord appeared to Joseph in a dream. 'Get up and flee to Egypt with the child and his mother, the angel said. 'Stay there until I tell you to return, because Herod is going to try to kill the child.'* Matthew 2:13 *"...Herod was furious...He sent soldiers to kill all the boys in and around Bethlehem who were two years old and under..."* Matthew 2:16

It was established long ago that women are an enemy of the devil. The devil hates all people, men and women, but he has immense hate for women. As princesses of God, this is why we must be extremely cautious and careful. We must use God's armor to successfully fight the devil, as he desperately wants to kill and destroy you. Additionally, he wants to kill and destroy your children or future children so they will not grow up to be a child of God – a kingdom builder. He will try to kill babies in the womb or as soon as they are born and will even try to encourage mothers and fathers to kill their own babies through abortion and/or murder. Recently, there have been several stories in the news about mothers who have killed their own children. In numerous reports, the accused mothers stated: *"The devil told me to kill my baby."*

After Satan was successful in encouraging Eve to sin, God became furious. He said to Satan, *"'**From now on, you and the woman will be enemies, and your offspring and her offspring will be enemies.** He will crush your head, and you will strike his heel.' Then he said to the woman, 'You will bear children with intense pain and suffering...'"* Genesis 3:15-16

Purpose Point: Painful childbirth among all women came as a result of Adam and Eve's sin. Women experience painful contractions and labor because Adam and Eve disobeyed God. Someone will always be affected by the choice(s) you make, whether good or bad.

The devil also declared war against the woman and her children…

"And when the dragon realized that he had been thrown down to the earth, he pursued the woman who had given birth to the child. But she was given two wings like those of a great eagle. This allowed her to fly to a place prepared for her in the wilderness, where she would be cared for and protected from the dragon for a time, times, and half a time. Then the dragon tried to drown the woman with a flood of water that flowed from its mouth. But the earth helped her by opening its mouth and swallowing the river that gushed out from the mouth of the dragon. **Then the dragon became very angry at the woman, and he declared war against the rest of her children – all who keep God's commandments and confess that they belong to Jesus.***"* Revelations 12:13-17

So, you see, women and their children are enemies of the devil (also known as the dragon). The devil especially hates women because they serve as the vessel and incubator for life. And since boys who later grow up to be men are born from a woman, they are enemies of the devil too. The devil has declared war against the woman and her children – all who obey God and confess Jesus as Lord. But God will protect both the woman and her children. He will help you to avoid the devil's tricks, schemes, and attacks. God will guide, support, and defend you. He will lead you to a place where He can care for you and safeguard you from evil. He will not allow you to drown in fear, depression, and worry. Remember, the battle is not yours or the woman's; but the battle is God's because He created the woman. He will fight for you – only stand, take your place/position, pray and resist!

"...This is what the Lord says: Do not be afraid! Don't be discouraged by this mighty army, for the battle is not yours, but God's..." 2 Chronicles 20:15 *"But you will not even need to fight.* **Take your positions; then stand** *still and watch the Lord's victory! He is with you..."* 2 Chronicles 20:17

"So humble yourselves before God. Resist the Devil, and he will flee from you. Draw close to God, and God will draw close to you..." James 4:7

Purpose Point/Minute Memoir: If Satan does not get you in the womb, he will attempt to quickly take you to the tomb (grave), without knowing God. I can recall two significant incidents when Satan tried to kill me. First, he tried to kill me in the womb by suggesting to my father that he advise my mother to get an abortion. Secondly, he encouraged my abusive ex-boyfriend to abuse me physically and emotionally, pushing me closer to death's door… pushing me closer to the tomb. But God protected me. He is in control…not Satan and not an abusive maniac.

Purpose Point: Don't give the devil the opportunity to destroy you and your children. When you disobey God and fail to accept Jesus as your Lord and Savior, you allow the devil to work in your life. Don't allow him to trick you; don't believe his lies! When I was a teenager, I believed the devil's lie that teen sex was okay. This opened the door for the devil to work through my ex-boyfriend. If I never decided to have sex at such an early age, my ex-boyfriend probably would have never entered or remained in my life.

Purpose Point: If we allow Satan to kill our babies, our world dies with them, and God's heritage dies too.

"Children are indeed a heritage from the Lord, and the fruit of the womb is His reward." Psalm 127:3 BSB

What did God mean when He stated the following to Satan? *"From now on, you and the woman will be enemies, and your offspring and her offspring will be enemies. He will crush your head, and you will strike [bruise] his heel."* Genesis 3:15

In the Bible, God often uses metaphors or a figure of speech to describe things. In this instance he used the word "head" to describe the part of the kingdom with the most power (authority) or the ruler of the kingdom. For example, Satan is the head or ruler of the kingdom of darkness and evil. Jesus is the head or ruler of the kingdom of light and righteousness. The body of Satan's kingdom is his demons and followers – the people who worship him and live out his ways. The body of Jesus is his angels and church – the people who worship God and live out

His ways. The scripture asserts that the offspring of the woman will crush Satan's head; this offspring is Jesus Christ who was born from a woman. When Jesus died on the cross, he crushed the head of the kingdom of darkness, Satan himself. He destroyed Satan's power over death once and for all.

The scripture also says that Satan will bruise the heel of Jesus. I believe that this means that Satan will bruise the body of Jesus, the church. We can see this happening today where Satan has caused so much division and inconsistencies in the church. The heel is farthest from the head than any other part of the body. This tells us that Satan's power is far from touching the head of the kingdom of God, Jesus Christ, and reveals how limited Satan's power really is. Satan can only bruise or afflict injury on the church, but God is a healer and can restore the church back to health…healing and curing every wound with the miracle antidote – the Blood of Jesus. Jesus, on the other hand, is a crusher – a destroyer. He has completely crushed and destroyed the devil's kingdom with no hope of it ever being restored. For example, if you only cut the tail of a snake it still lives. But if you crush his head, instant death! Thank God for Jesus, the Head Crusher!

Purpose Point: In terms of power, everything flows from the head down to the other parts. For example, the owner/CEO of a company may have the most power; this power then flows down to the Executive Directors, managers, and supervisors.

Moreover, I believe God spoke metaphorically because he did not want to release too much information to the devil. God already had a backup plan just in case mankind decided to sin. In fact, God already knew that mankind would sin…he had everything already planned out before time. If the devil would have known about God's backup plan, Jesus Christ, the devil would have never encouraged people to crucify Jesus.

Jesus said, *"…You are permitted to understand the secret of the Kingdom of God. But I use parables for everything I say to outsiders, so that the Scriptures might be fulfilled: When they see what I do, they will learn nothing. When they hear what I say, they will not understand. Otherwise, they will turn to me and be forgiven."* Mark 4:11-12

Purpose Point: It was God's plan for Jesus to die. It hurt God, but God knew it had to be done. God gave His only son, Jesus, so that the world could receive forgiveness for their sins (past, present, and future). God required Jesus to die and shed his blood for us because without the shedding of blood there would be no forgiveness of sins. When Jesus died and rose after death, he destroyed the devil's evil works. He took away the keys of death from the devil and evicted its power. As a result, we now have the option to live forever, if we believe and obey Jesus. Before Jesus, we did not have the option of eternal life. But because Jesus sacrificed himself for us, we can receive the gift of salvation which includes eternal life, peace, deliverance, prosperity, joy, healing, favor, love, wisdom, hope and so much more.

"For God so loved the world that he gave his only Son, so that everyone who believes in him will not perish but have eternal life. God did not send his Son into the world to condemn it, but to save it." John 3:16-17

"But he [Jesus] was wounded and crushed for our sins. He was beaten that we might have peace. He was whipped, and we were healed." Isaiah 53:5

"Because God's children are human beings – made of flesh and blood – Jesus also became flesh and blood by being born in human form. For only as a human being could he die, and only by dying could he break the power of the Devil, who had the power over death. Only in this way could he deliver those who have lived all their lives as slaves to the fear of dying." Hebrews 2:14-15

The devil worked through the Roman soldiers and used them to beat, wound, torture, and kill Jesus. He knew that Jesus was the son of God, so he wanted to kill him because he did not want the world to know the truth about God. Jesus boldly went around preaching and teaching the gospel. If people did not know the truth about God or the ways of God, then that meant people would continue to worship or live out Satan's ways and consequently increase his power in the earth. But the devil not only worked through the Roman soldiers to kill Jesus, he also worked through Jesus' friend, Judas. Satan encouraged Judas to betray Jesus by turning him over to the Roman soldiers so they could kill him.

"It was time for supper, and the Devil had already enticed Judas...to carry out his plan to betray Jesus." John 13:2

Purpose Point: The devil may even try to work through people that are closest to you, such as your friends. Although you never really know who a person is or what they will one day do, it is important to choose your friends carefully. And remember, just because someone says they are your friend doesn't mean they really are. People pretend and act well. Jealousy, envy, and betrayal often live next door—in those closest to you. In every relationship, heed the warning signs, lean on the wisdom of God, and the discernment of the Holy Spirit.

Although the devil is often referred to as a snake (serpent), the Bible tells us that we must be wise as snakes and innocent as doves. In other words, you must be just as smart as Satan in terms of your dealings with people and situations. For instance, you should be *cautious* but not cunning, *strategic* but not sly, *discerning* but not deceptive, *magnanimous* but not malevolent, manipulative, or mischievous. You should not behave like snakes but instead be wise enough to see their slithering attacks and vicious venom. We defeat Satan by knowing God's Word and doing it God's way!

Remember this: Be wise as a snake and innocent as a dove, but those who are as snakes (cunning, sly, deceptive, duplicitous, manipulative, and mischievous) be wise not to deal with them.

Jesus said, *"I am sending you like lambs into a pack of wolves. So be as wise as snakes and as innocent as doves."* Matthew 10:16 CEV

Purpose Point: It is wise to recognize evil and wrongdoing, but you are not innocent if you take part in it – if you try to defeat evil with evil. Be wise to recognize wickedness, tricks, schemes, persecution, temptation, and deception for what it is, and maintain your innocence by handling it the right way. Pray, seek godly counsel, and refer to God's Word for guidance.

Remember, you must watch, pray and be vigilant! Don't be fearful but be prepared in your faith and equipped with wisdom. You must warfare in prayer like it matters because it does (see Powerful Prayer chapter). You must put on your armor, the spiritual armor of God, to fight Satan. Jesus has already defeated Satan. The war has already been won, but as long as we are on earth, we must be strong for the battle and stand to fight. Victory belongs to us.

"Dear children, don't let anyone deceive you about this: When people do what is right, it is because they are righteous, even as Christ is righteous. But when people keep on sinning, it shows they belong to the Devil, who has been sinning since the beginning. ***But the Son of God came to destroy these works of the Devil.****"* 1 John 3:7-8

Purpose Point: What you see is not your enemy! The girl who doesn't like you, the family member who abandoned or abused you, the person who often mistreats you and the friend who betrayed you, are not your enemy. The devil and his evil spirits are. He works through people to destroy and discourage you through offenses, confusion, jealously, strife, violence, assaults, and attacks (virtual, verbal and/or physical). He uses your weaknesses against you and will often attack you in areas of insecurity and lack. For instance, if you've always felt left out, the devil will orchestrate situations to continually make you feel that way – or if you tend to feel unwanted, he will create situations to make you feel unloved.

"For we are not fighting against people made of flesh and blood, but against the evil rulers and authorities of the unseen world, against those mighty powers of darkness who rule the world, and against wicked spirits in the heavenly realms." Ephesians 6:12

Purpose Point: As you have learned, there was a snake in the Garden of Eden, the most glorious place of them all; how much more will you find snakes on your Perfect Path? As you walk down the Perfect Path of life (the Princess' Pathway) there will be snakes that will come in the form of lying, deceptive, hateful, jealous, wicked, and two-faced people who are influenced by the devil to disrupt and destroy your life. Be wise, be cautious, and do not get caught in their venomous trap.

Why didn't God just destroy Satan?

In writing, I wondered why God didn't just destroy Satan and his angels rather than kick them out of heaven. I believe that God didn't destroy Satan because he saw a purpose for him.

God may have wanted to use Satan to provide a choice for people. Remember, love does not force itself on anyone, and God loves us beyond measure; however, He does not force us to accept, love or believe in Him. He gives us a choice between good and evil, right and wrong. And since God cannot sin or promote sin in any way, I believe He used Satan to provide the alternative choice – evil and wrong. Remember, sin is simply doing what God told you not to do. When you choose God's truth and do what is good and right, you choose God/Jesus – life; but when you choose Satan's lies and do what is evil and wrong, you choose Satan – death.

God vs. Satan (the devil)

God's *Character*istics	Satan's *Character*istics
God is love, faith, good, kindness, humility, joy, hope, peace, health, prosperity, and eternal life. • God is all powerful, all knowing and everywhere. He is sovereign, omnipotent, and omnipresent. • God lives and rules forever. • God is the author and finisher of our faith.	Satan is hate, fear, evil, wickedness, deception, pride, selfishness, despair, confusion, chaos, and eternal death. • Satan's power is limited. He does not know everything, nor can he be everywhere. • Satan will be destroyed forever in the lake of fire. • Satan is the author of sin.

God's plans for you	Satan's plans for you
"For I know the plans I have for you", says the Lord. "They are plans for good and not for disaster, to give you a future and a hope." Jeremiah 29:11	Satan's plans for you are to kill, steal, and destroy you. John 10:10

Whose side would you rather be on…someone who loves and cares for you, or someone who hates and wants to destroy you?

We make choices every day and these choices are either good or bad – there is nothing in between. Our culture, parents, people around us, books, music and TV all teach us what is right and wrong – which is why Satan especially works through these channels to deceive us or make us think something is right when it is really wrong. For example, today's secular television and music teaches us to believe that promiscuous and perverted sex, violence, and drugs are okay, when in fact they are not. This is why it is so important to guard your gates – mind, eye, and ear and refrain from watching or listening to anything that will draw you away from God. Rather than allowing music, TV, and your friends to teach you how to live, you should instead allow the Bible to teach you. This will ensure that you make the right decisions. If you let the world teach you, then you will make the wrong decisions and choose Satan.

The Bible is the truth; it will not lie to you about what is right and wrong. Anything or anybody who teaches something different from what the Bible says is telling a lie. Therefore, when considering what is right and wrong you should allow the Bible to be your guide and anyone who teaches according to the Bible.

Moral principles of good and right are established and defined in the Word of God (the Bible) and are manifested in your conscience. Your God-given conscience teaches you right from wrong and compels you to do what is right. God is the one who promotes His ways and commands through your conscience (a sense of knowing) while the devil promotes his ways through your mind and emotions.

Satan attempts to counteract a person's good conscience by placing evil thoughts, ideas and suggestions into the person's mind. When the person is in the process of making a choice between doing what's right and doing what's wrong their conscience is really fighting with their mind. You are ultimately the one to make the final choice; you are the one to end the battle and decide who wins…if you make the right choice your conscience has won the battle and if you make the wrong choice then your mind along with negative thinking, feelings and emotions have won. This is why it is often said, **"You are your own worst enemy."** It is you who has the last say so; it is you who makes the choice – not God and not the devil. So don't ever go around saying the devil made me do it, or blame God for the consequences of a wrong choice. I hear many pastors give the answer to the proverbial question, "Why does God send people to hell?" Their answer: "People send themselves to hell by the choices they make."

"We have met the enemy and he is us." Pogo (comic character), Author, Walt Kelly

Many people operate without a conscience, and these people perform some of the most evil and atrocious acts. For example, serial killers and rapists obviously have no conscience; they have no morals, no values, no heart. They do not feel guilty for what they have done, and some even believe that their evil acts are right or justified. Were they born this way? I believe everyone is born with a conscience. There will be an inclination for doing wrong because of our sinful nature, but we are all given a conscience. Remember, our conscience compels us to do what is right; however, it does not mean we will always choose to do what is right. At some point in a person's life, when they begin to do wrong, they will most likely feel some sense of conviction to the extent that they believe that what they are doing is wrong or could be wrong. But when that person continually performs a wrong act, ignoring and denying their conscience, then it will come to a point where God will give them over to a reprobate or wicked mind because their conscience has deteriorated. Your conscience is your moral compass that guides you to salvation. This moral compass was built in you when you were born to oppose your sinful nature. It is the parents' responsibility to not only nurture a child but to nurture their conscience by teaching them right from wrong so they can readily accept Jesus when they reach a level of understanding or the *age of accountability*. It is the conscience that produces godly sorrow which leads to repentance unto salvation (2 Corinthians 7:10). When a child or an adult continually rejects or violates their conscience, they lose their way and the way of salvation because their moral compass is broken. 1 Timothy 1:19 AMP states: *"keeping your faith [leaning completely on God with absolute trust and confidence in His guidance] and having a good conscience; for some [people] have rejected [their moral compass] and have made a shipwreck of their faith."* Sometimes unfortunate life experiences such as abuse and neglect could defile or override a person's good conscience by making them into a person they would not have otherwise become. For example, when someone is abused as a child they could possibly grow up and abuse others too. In the beginning they may feel as though what they are doing is wrong but may keep doing it anyway and later come to believe that what they are doing is right because it was done to them. In this case, their conscience has been defiled through unfortunate life experiences. When your evil deeds continue to overpower your good conscience, your conscience weakens and dies.

It is important to know that when you deny your conscience, you deny God. It is through your conscience that God works in you and guides you in the right direction. But when you ignore Him continually, by ignoring your conscience, God could cease His work in you and give you over to a reprobate or depraved mind. The word reprobate is defined as morally corrupt (without morals). It is a dangerous thing to be without a good conscience – and even more dangerous to be without God because you will not only be a danger to others, but you'll be in danger of eternal damnation. Not having a good conscience is evident of not having God, and evident of having the devil work through you. People without a conscience live lives full of every kind of evil.

"When they refused to acknowledge God, he abandoned them to their evil minds and let them do things that should never be done. Their lives became full of every kind of wickedness, sin, greed, hate, envy, murder, fighting, deception, malicious behavior, and gossip. They are backstabbers, haters of God, insolent, proud, and boastful. They are forever inventing new ways of sinning and are disobedient to their parents. They refuse to understand, break their promises, and are heartless and unforgiving. They are fully aware of God's death penalty for those who do these things, yet they go right ahead and do them anyway. And, worse yet, they encourage others to do them, too." Romans 1:28-32

Purpose Point: A good conscience can only lead you; it cannot save you. Only your faith in Jesus Christ can save you. When you do not listen to your conscience, you are refusing to acknowledge God's work in you. Your conscience is what compels you to do what is right. And when you are born again (get rid of the old sinful nature and accept your new nature in Christ on top of having a good conscience) you become exceedingly powerful and precious to God.

Purpose Point: A person can regain their good conscience and reconcile with God by repenting or turning away from their sins and asking God for forgiveness. It is hard to do good when you have habitually done evil.

However, confessing your sins to God, turning away from them, and inviting God to work in your life will empower and strengthen you to start doing what is right. God is so powerful – His redemptive saving power has turned many murderers into ministers and many crooks into Christ followers. He will help a person regardless of what they have done, but they must first humble themselves, pray and stop committing evil acts (repent).

"Then if my people who are called by my name will humble themselves and pray and seek my face and turn from their wicked ways, I will hear from heaven and will forgive their sins and heal their land." 2 Chronicles 7:14

"...if wicked people turn from their wickedness, obey the law, and do what is just and right, they will save their lives. They will live because they thought it over and decided to turn from their sins. Such people will not die." Ezekiel 18:27-28

Fast Fact: The word conscious, pronounced [kon-shuh ns], is a homonym because it can be spelled two different ways and mean two different things but have the same sound.
- "Conscience" is the ability to know right from wrong, as discussed.
- "Conscious" means to be fully aware or sensitive to something.

God wants you to be conscious of your conscience, fully aware of your ability to know right from wrong and hear His voice.

"Blessed are those who have a tender conscience, but the stubborn are headed for serious trouble." Proverbs 28:14

Purpose Point: Satan's main entrance point is through your mind. Guard your gates with all diligence.

Purpose Point: Satan's primary goal is to keep you from fulfilling your destiny. He achieves this goal by getting you to follow his evil ways and turn away from God.

The devil can only defeat and destroy you, if you allow him, by consistently making the wrong choices and rejecting Jesus – giving the devil access to your life. Satan is not greater than God and he is not greater than you because the Spirit of God lives in you (if you have accepted Jesus as your Lord and Savior). When you have and obey Jesus, the devil cannot win.

If you do not have Jesus, then you will surely lose and be destroyed forever with Satan. Jesus is the only way to God and eternal life (John 14:6). God will soon destroy Satan and all his demons, and anyone who worships him and lives out his ways will be destroyed for eternity with him. Make your choice today and choose to accept Jesus as your Lord and Savior to prevent yourself from being destroyed. This is what God is saying to you: *"This command I am giving you today is not too difficult for you to understand or perform. It is not up in heaven, so distant that you must ask, 'Who will go to heaven and bring it down so we can hear and obey it?' It is not beyond the sea, so far away that you must ask, 'Who will cross the sea to bring it to us so we can hear and obey it?' The message is very close at hand; it is on your lips and in your heart so that you can obey it. Now listen! Today I am giving you a choice between prosperity and disaster, between life and death. I have commanded you today to love the Lord your God and to keep his commands, laws, and regulations by walking in his ways. If you do this, you will live and become a great nation, and the Lord your God will bless you...But if your heart turns*

away and you refuse to listen, and if you are drawn away to serve and worship other gods, then I warn you now that you will certainly be destroyed. You will not live a long, good life...Today I have given you the choice between life and death, between blessings and curses. ***I call on heaven and earth to witness the choice you make. Oh, that you would choose life, that you and your descendants might live! Choose to love the Lord your God and to obey him and commit yourself to him, for he is your life. Then you will live long...***"
Deuteronomy 30:11-20

So God is giving you a choice, and He is so good that He even tells you which choice to make, but He absolutely will not force you to make the right choice. He said, **"Oh, that you would choose life."** Choosing life and blessings means choosing to love God with all your heart, accept Jesus as your Lord and Savior, and obey His commands. Only in this way will you have eternal life and live forever because *"...Christ redeemed us from the curse of the law by becoming a curse for us..."* Galatians 3:13 NIV   But if you don't choose Jesus, you are choosing death and curses and will be destroyed forever with Satan and all his demons.

Purpose Point: Ultimately, you only have two choices (two paths) in life....

1. God/Jesus, life, and blessings
2. Satan, death, and curses

Most of the decisions that you will make will be derived from these two core choices. You can only choose one, there is no in between. Heaven and earth are both witnesses to the choice you make. The way you live on earth will reveal your choice; and not making it to heaven will reveal your end result – eternal damnation and separation from God.

Purpose Point: If you choose Satan and live out the world's ways, you become a child of Satan. Satan's kingdom will be destroyed and all his children.

"This is what the Lord Almighty says: I, myself, have risen against him! I will destroy his children and his children's children, so they will never sit on his throne." Isaiah 14:22

Purpose Point: Satan is after your influence! He wants you to make wrong decisions so that you can encourage others either directly or indirectly to make wrong decisions too.

*"...They are fully aware of God's death penalty for those who do these things, yet they go right ahead and do them anyway. **And, worse yet, they encourage others to do them, too.**"*
Romans 1:32

Curses and Blessings
Purpose Point: Did you know that curses can be disguised as blessings? Something that someone perceives to be a blessing could actually be their curse. For example, many rich people who are cruel, greedy, and arrogant may think that their money is a blessing from God. Although they may believe this, they remain cruel to people and use their money to support a lavish and sinful lifestyle. They refuse to help the poor and needy, and instead use their money

on sex, drugs, alcohol, gambling, houses, cars, clothes, jewelry, trips, etc. But their money cannot buy them happiness and peace...it instead drives them deeper into unhappiness, and may lead to mental illness, drug overdose or even suicide – dying without ever knowing God. Money, the thing that was perceived to be a blessing, turned out to be their curse.

Purpose Point: People who are not on top of the world, so to speak, in terms of being rich learn to cope when life gets hard. But oftentimes when rich people feel unhappiness, they feel like there is no hope and are unable to cope because they think if money can't make me happy or give me peace, what will. God can and He will when you choose to believe in Him.

Purpose Point: Blessings are not characterized by value or prestige but are defined by the sender, recipient and the Word of God. Even Satan can manipulate situations to make people rich and famous. The reason behind this would be so that they can use their power, fame, and money to influence others to be like them – ungodly. If the sender is not God then it is not a blessing, or if the sender is God and the recipient does not acknowledge or recognize God as providing the blessing then the blessing has not been truly manifested in that person's life. God blesses us so that we can bless others. If we do not realize our blessing, then how can we truly be a blessing to others?

"And it is a good thing to receive wealth from God and the good health to enjoy it..." Ecclesiastes 5:19   All true blessings flow from "The Blessing" – Jesus.

Purpose Point: The blessing of the Lord makes a person rich; not just in terms of money, but in other areas such as health, wisdom, joy, and peace of mind (true prosperity). Nothing bad comes from or happens as a result of receiving God's blessings – He adds no trouble with it. *"The blessing of the Lord makes a person rich, and he adds no sorrow with it."* Proverbs 10:22

Satan Soul Selling

What does it mean to sell or surrender your soul to the devil? Many people do it every day. Soul selling involves giving up your soul to the devil in exchange for wealth/money, fame, happiness, acceptance and/or power. For example, a woman who wants to become a top paying actress receives a phone call from her agent about a special audition for a lead role that pays $10,000,000. The woman auditions and later receives a call from the movie director. The director tells her that he will give her the lead role if she has sex with him and five of his friends. He also requests that she become a part of their religious cult and profess to their satanic god. The woman agreed to do everything in exchange for the lead role and $10M. She soon acted in the movie and received the money and fame promised to her. She continued to worship the satanic god to receive more lead roles. One day she died in a car crash and went to hell for eternity.

This woman could be described as someone who sold her soul to the devil. Performing sinful acts in exchange for money, wealth, fame, possessions, recognition, acceptance, or power is considered as selling your soul to Satan. Some people do it unconsciously not fully knowing what they are doing, and some people deliberately and explicitly choose to worship Satan in exchange for possessions. Simply put, Satan soul surrendering involves: making a decision to follow your sinful desires, choosing to do wrong without a conscience or conviction, failing to acknowledge or accept Jesus no matter the consequences, worshiping self, people or things (idolatry), and using your gifts and talents perversely while polluting yourself and the world.

"I gave them over to worthless decrees and regulations that would not lead to life. I let them pollute themselves with the very gifts I had given them..." Ezekiel 20:25-26

Purpose Point: Riches and possessions may provide a lavish lifestyle – so short, so swift, but they cannot buy or provide a lavish eternity – which lasts forever. It is not about what you have acquired, accomplished, or achieved, but it is about knowing Jesus as your Lord and Savior. Don't be in awe of a person's gifts, talents, possessions, and accomplishments – pray that they know God.

Purpose Point: There is nothing wrong with being rich; however, there is something wrong with not knowing God and accepting Jesus as your Lord and Savior.

Purpose Point: Satan wants your worship, and he will tempt you to get it. When Satan tempted Jesus, he promised to give him all the kingdoms, if Jesus would bow down to worship him.

"Next the devil took him to the peak of a very high mountain and showed him all the kingdoms of the world and their glory. 'I will give it all to you,' he said, 'if you will kneel down and worship me.' 'Get out of here, Satan,' Jesus told him. 'For the Scriptures say, "You must worship the Lord your God and serve only him." Then the devil went away, and angels came and took care of Jesus." Matthew 4:8-11

Purpose Point: To *resist* Satan you must *recognize* him and his tactics. To *defeat* him, you must *discover, declare,* and *decree* God's Word.

Purpose Point: If you live to please your sinful desires, you will lose your chance of eternal life in heaven and will experience hell as a result. But if you live to please God and help others, you will find true life on earth and in heaven. Jesus said, *"If you try to keep your life for yourself, you will lose it. But if you give up your life for my sake ...you will find true life. And how do you benefit if you gain the whole world but lose your own soul...?"* Mark 8:35-36

Purpose Point: When you love sin, you love Satan. When you hate sin, you love God.

Are you a sheep or goat?

Jesus (the Son) will return to earth one day to gather all of God's children both dead in the grave and alive on earth to take them to heaven. He will later destroy Satan, his demons and all his children completely and irrevocably. The children of God are referred to as sheep and the children of the devil are referred to as goats. *"But when the Son of Man comes in his glory, and all the angels with him, then he will sit upon his glorious throne. All the nations will be gathered in his presence, and he will separate them...sheep from the goats. He will place the sheep at his right hand and the goats at his left. Then the King will say to those on the right, 'Come, you who are blessed by my Father, inherit the Kingdom prepared for you from the foundation of the world...Then the King will turn to those on the left and say, 'Away with you, you cursed ones, into eternal fire prepared for the Devil and his demons...And they will go away into eternal punishment, but the righteous will go into eternal life."* Matthew 25:31-46

"Not everyone who calls out to me, 'Lord! Lord!' will enter the Kingdom of Heaven. Only those who actually do the will of my Father in heaven will enter. On judgment day many will say to me, 'Lord! Lord! We prophesied in your name and cast out demons in your name and performed many miracles in your name.' But I will reply, 'I never knew you. Get away from me, you who break God's laws.'" Matthew 7:21-23

Jesus said, *"I am the good shepherd; I know my own sheep, and they know me, just as my Father knows me and I know the Father. And I lay down my life for the sheep."*
John 10:14-15

Purpose Point: You cannot fool Jesus. Jesus knows who the real children of God are. When Jesus died on the cross, he died so that the children of God could live forever. He laid his life down for his sheep so they could have a good life on earth and live for eternity.

Purpose Point: Remember, Satan is your accuser and adversary. He brings adversaries and enemies of the soul such as fear, confusion, despair, hopelessness, depression, worry, pride, lust, discouragement, insecurities/low self-esteem, bitterness, resentment, hate, unbelief, etc. Satan's goal is to accuse and annihilate you. The Lord Jesus, however, has prayed for you that your faith does not fail. Jesus constantly intercedes in prayer on your behalf because he loves you and destroys all your enemies.

"And in your steadfast love you will cut off my enemies, and you will destroy all the adversaries of my soul, for I am your servant." Psalm 143:12 ESV

Jesus said, *"...Satan has asked to sift each of you like wheat. But I have pleaded in prayer for you... that your faith should not fail. So when you have repented and turned to me again, strengthen your brothers...Pray that you will not give in to temptation."* Luke 22:31-32 & 40

"Therefore he is able, once and forever, to save those who come to God through him. He lives forever to intercede with God on their behalf." Hebrews 7:25

Purpose Point: Jesus does not want you to make the wrong choice because he knows there will be consequences. Understand that not making a choice means making a choice. If you do not make a choice to accept Jesus as your Lord and Savior, then you have ultimately chosen Satan and his kingdom.

Whose kingdom will you live in forever, which path will you take?
Will you choose to side with your evil enemy and be destroyed for eternity? Or will you choose to side with Jesus and live forever? The choice is yours – *"Oh, that you would choose life."*

"In the path of righteousness is life, and in its pathway there is no death." Proverbs 12:28 ESV

If you would like to accept Jesus as your Lord and Savior, pray the following prayer:

> *Lord Jesus, I confess that you are the Son of God. I believe that you died for my sins and was raised from the dead. I turn to you and trust you to help me to turn from my sins. I give my life to you. Cleanse me and make me anew. Come into my heart and live in me. I accept you as my Lord and Savior.*
>
> If you have prayed this prayer, you are saved and have become one of God's special children. Rejoice! Now love God with all your heart, obey His Word and resist the evil enemy.
>
> And remember, nothing, not even Satan and his demons, can ever separate you from God's love.
>
> *"And I am convinced that nothing can ever separate us from God's love. Neither death nor life, neither angels nor demons, neither our fears for today nor our worries about tomorrow — not even the powers of hell can separate us from God's love."* Romans 8:38

Chapter 9
Perfect Path - Princess' Pathway
(Highway of Holiness...Righteous & Royal Road)

There are many experiences that lead us to our destiny; but there is only one right path and one wrong path. When you start the journey of life, your choices will take you there.

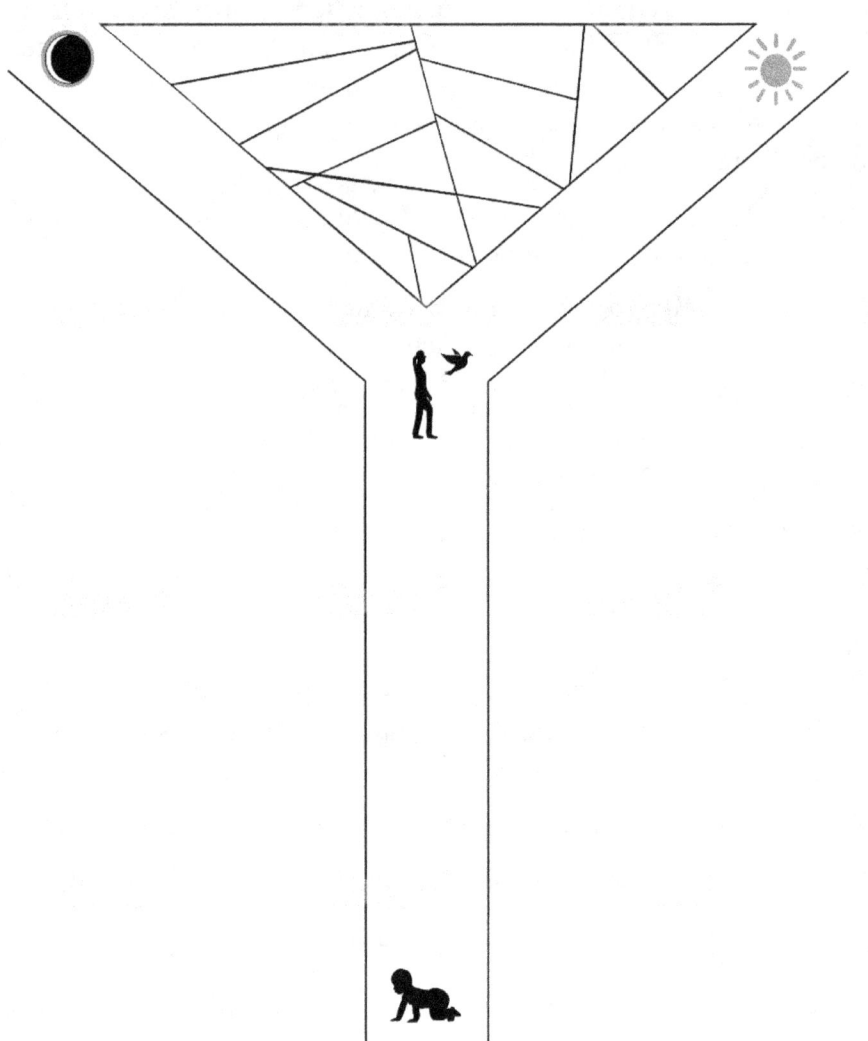

"Trust in the Lord with all your heart; do not depend on your own understanding. **Seek his will in all you do, and he will show you which path to take."** Proverbs 3:5-6

"Let those who are wise understand these things. Let those with discernment listen carefully. **The paths of the Lord are true and right, and righteous people live by walking in them..."** Hosea 14:9

"In the path of righteousness is life, and in its pathway there is no death." Proverbs 12:28 ESV

Perfect Path

Imagine yourself standing in the forest with two roads or pathways before you. You are lost and not sure which way to go. The road on your right is known to be the Highway of Holiness and the road on your left is known to be the Rocky Road. Suddenly, a gentleman walks up to you and offers to give you directions. He explains the differences between the two roads and its end destination in hopes of you choosing the best path and going in the right direction. He starts off by first explaining the Highway of Holiness – the Righteous/Royal Road…

The Highway of Holiness is right; it is the Perfect Path – the right way to go. On this path you will find life, salvation, blessings, happiness, favor, peace, joy, love, protection, strength, deliverance, healing, prosperity and so much more. Your heavenly Father, the one who created you, can be found on this path and will walk closely beside you along your journey in life. When you face the most difficult times, He will be right there by your side helping you to find your way. He will guide and direct your steps and will even strengthen or carry you when you feel yourself getting weary and discouraged by the challenges of life.

*"And a main road will go through that once deserted land. It will be named the **Highway of Holiness**. Evil-hearted people will never travel on it. It will be only for those who walk in God's ways; fools will never walk there. Lions will not lurk along its course, and there will be no other dangers. Only the redeemed will follow it."* Isaiah 35:8-9

The Perfect Path scenario makes me think about one of my favorite poems, "Footprints".
— *Mary Stevenson, 1936*

An excerpt from this poem reads:

"You promised me Lord, that if I followed you, you would walk with me always. But I have noticed that during the most trying periods of my life there has only been one set of footprints in the sand. Why, when I needed you most, have you not been there for me?" The Lord replied, "The years when you have seen only one set of footprints, my child, is when I carried you."

One of God's servants, Job, said, *"You put my feet in stocks. You watch all my paths. You trace all my footprints."* Job 13:27

Purpose Point: God is not only present in the end; He is present throughout your journey.

Purpose Point: When you walk down the Perfect Path of life, you will always have a supernatural presence with you supporting and guiding your steps. This presence is so great that it has the power to ease your worries, minimize your problems, and calm your fears. This divine presence will strengthen you to endure and overcome every obstacle in your life. Even if you are on the verge of death, you will not be afraid because you will know God is with you.

> Make life-long positive choices
> Choose to do what is right…apply godly principles

> Sustain Relationship with God
> Love God

"The Lord is my shepherd; I have everything I need. He lets me rest in green meadows; he leads me beside peaceful streams. He renews my strength. ***He guides me along right paths****,*

bringing honor to his name. Even when I walk through the dark valley of death, I will not be afraid, for you [God] are close beside me..." Psalm 23:1-4

The Highway of Holiness is God's perfect path and perfect will for your life. God created you to walk down this perfect path with Him. On the Righteous Road you will discover your specific God-given purpose and grow from a true princess into a qualified queen. But it is important to know that very few people walk down the righteous road. So as you walk down this perfect path, it will not be easy – people will talk about you, you may lose friends or suffer persecution, you may feel sad and alone, but your journey and destination will be exceedingly satisfying and joyous. And even if you feel alone; you are never alone…you have the Creator of the universe, your heavenly Father walking beside you.

God is faithful – He will provide for you. He will protect and guide you as you walk down the perfect path of life.

The Perfect Path is the Princess's Pathway…the path of light and life.
The Princess's Pathway is the Road to Righteousness and Royalty – the narrow gate.

"The way of the righteous is like the first gleam of dawn, which shines ever brighter until the full light of day. But the way of the wicked is like total darkness. They have no idea what they are stumbling over." Proverbs 4:18-19

"You can enter God's Kingdom only through the narrow gate. The highway to hell is broad, and its gate is wide for the many who choose that way." Matthew 7:13

"Make every effort to enter through the narrow door, because many, I tell you, will try to enter and will not be able to." Luke 13:24 NIV

"For the LORD watches over the path of the godly, but the path of the wicked leads to destruction." Psalm 1:6

Now you may ask, what does it mean to walk down the Perfect Path?
Walking down the perfect path or righteous road means walking with God – obeying His commands, worshiping Him, meditating on His Word, praying, and spending time with Him. It means to S.T.A.N.D….to <u>S</u>et yourself apart from the world, <u>T</u>ake your place, <u>A</u>ffirm your identity, <u>N</u>ullify your past and <u>D</u>emonstrate your purpose. It means doing the things that you were created to do, such as loving God, loving yourself and others, serving Jesus and helping others to know Jesus. It means reverencing and honoring God by living a life that is pleasing to Him – a life that will bring Him glory. In other words, living in such a way, that people praise and worship God, and draw closer to Him, because you allowed Him to work through you. *"Those who follow the right path fear the Lord; those who take the wrong path despise him."* Proverbs 14:2

We are all given two paths in life – the Perfect Path (good) or the Rocky Road (evil)…we are all free to choose which path we will take. Just like you cannot drive down two different roads at the same time, you cannot walk down two separate paths simultaneously either. You must choose which path in life to take. When you S.T.A.N.D., you are paving a bright future down the perfect path of life.

Purpose Point: It is important to lead and not follow. But if you do follow, *"…follow the steps of good men [women] instead, and stay on the paths of the righteous."* Proverbs 2:20

"Dear friend, don't let this bad example influence you. Follow only what is good. Remember that those who do good prove that they are God's children, and those who do evil prove that they do not know God." 3 John 1:11

Moreover, when you see others going down the wrong path it is okay to help them get on the right path; however, be careful not to allow their ways to influence you.

"Dear friends, if a Christian is overcome by some sin, you who are godly should gently and humbly help that person back onto the right path. And be careful not to fall into the same temptation yourself." Galatians 6:1

Purpose Point: It is easier to pull someone down than it is to lift someone up. If you try to help others to do what is right, but they refuse to listen and choose to continue in their ways, it may be best to walk away from that friendship or association because their wrong behavior could very well influence you and take you off the right path. You can always pray for them while "social distancing" yourself from the relationship. Allow God to lead you on the best course of action.

"Do not be deceived: "Bad company ruins good morals." 1 Corinthians 15:33 ESV

Purpose Point: When God's hand is on your life, He will protect you, support you and widen your path to keep you from slipping and being subdued by the hardships of life.

"You have given me your shield of victory. Your right hand supports me; your help has made me great. You have made a wide path for my feet to keep them from slipping." Psalm 18:35-36

Purpose Point: Pray and ask God to help you to walk and remain on the Perfect Path of life. This path was created and is centered around God's commands – His Word.

David, a servant of God, stated: *"You made me; you created me. Now give me the sense to follow your commands."* Psalm 119:73 *"Make me walk along the path of your commands, for that is where my happiness is found."* Psalm 119:35 *"Your word is a lamp for my feet and a light for my path."* Psalm 119:105

Purpose Point: Be careful not to rush into things or make quick decisions to do what others are doing. If you do, it can lead you the wrong way.

"Zeal without knowledge is not good; a person who moves too quickly may go the wrong way." Proverbs 19:2

Purpose Point: The key to S.T.A.N.Ding is to under***stand***. It is important to understand the two paths of life, the consequences and results of each, and the commands of God. Knowing and applying these principles will help you to stand and walk on the right path. Don't be a fool who despises understanding and godly wisdom.

"Wisdom is the principal thing; therefore get wisdom: and with all your getting get understanding." Proverbs 4:7 AKJV

"Fools have no interest in understanding; they only want to air their own opinions." Proverbs 18:2

To love oneself is to acquire wisdom and understand the truth of God.

"To acquire wisdom is to love oneself; people who cherish understanding will prosper." Proverbs 19:8

"Cry out for insight and understanding. Search for them as you would for lost money or hidden treasure. Then you will understand what it means to fear the Lord, and you will gain knowledge of God." Proverbs 2:3-5

"Your commandments give me understanding; no wonder I hate every false way of life." Psalm 119:104

"Wisdom will save you from evil people, from those whose speech is corrupt. These people turn from right ways to walk down dark and evil paths. They rejoice in doing wrong, and they enjoy evil as it turns things upside down. What they do is crooked, and their ways are wrong." Proverbs 2:12-15

"For the Lord grants wisdom! From his mouth come knowledge and understanding. He grants a treasure of good sense to the godly. He is their shield, protecting those who walk with integrity. He guards the paths of justice and protects those who are faithful to him." Proverbs 2:6-8

"How can we understand the road we travel? It is the Lord who directs our steps." Proverbs 20:24

"The person who strays from common sense will end up in the company of the dead." Proverbs 21:16

Purpose Point: Walking down the Perfect Path means that you truly understand <u>the way to life</u>. If you stray from understanding, you could end up on the Rocky Road – the place of eternal death. When people do not believe in Jesus and obey his statutes, they walk the path of sin and are essentially dead spiritually, although they are alive on earth. They are a dead man or woman walking, so to speak. Where there is sin there is spiritual death because the wages of sin is death. Sadly, if people do not turn away from their sins (repent) and accept Jesus, when they die a physical death on earth, their final destination will be eternal death and darkness.

"For the wages of sin is death, but the free gift of God is eternal life through Christ Jesus our Lord." Romans 6:23

Jesus said, *"I am <u>the way</u>, the truth, and <u>the life</u>. No one can come to the Father except through me."* John 14:6

Purpose Point: When you choose to walk the Perfect Path (the Righteous Road), spiritual death is behind you and eternal life is within you and ahead of you, as promised through Jesus' sacrifice. But when you walk the Rocky Road, spiritual death is in front of you, all around you and within you – perpetually present and imminent.

Remember: *"In the path of righteousness is life, and in its pathway there is no death."* Proverbs 12:28 ESV

"Once you were dead because of your disobedience and your many sins. You used to live in sin, just like the rest of the world, obeying the devil — the commander of the powers in the unseen world. He is the spirit at work in the hearts of those who refuse to obey God. All of us used to live that way, following the passionate desires and inclinations of our sinful nature. By our very nature we were subject to God's anger, just like everyone else. But God is so rich in mercy, and he loved us so much, that even though we were dead because of our sins, he gave us life when he raised Christ from the dead. (It is only by God's grace that you have been saved!) For he raised us from the dead along with Christ and seated us with him in the heavenly realms because we are united with Christ Jesus. So God can point to us in all future ages as examples of the incredible wealth of his grace and kindness toward us, as shown in all he has done for us who are united with Christ Jesus.

God saved you by his grace when you believed. And you can't take credit for this; it is a gift from God. Salvation is not a reward for the good things we have done, so none of us can boast about it. For we are God's masterpiece. He has created us anew in Christ Jesus, so we can do the good things he planned for us long ago." Ephesians 2:1-10

Purpose Point: Many people believe that the Rocky Road is the right way to go because of what TV, music, family, friends, and their culture have taught them. Do not be deceived…the Rocky Road is absolutely the wrong way! When you come to understand the commands of God and His will for your life, you will know which path to take – the path that ends in eternal life. That's why it is important to lead and not follow (using God's Word as your guide) because following someone who thinks they are on the right path could very well be on the wrong path that ends in eternal death.

"There is a path before each person that seems right, but it ends in death." Proverbs 14:12

"Whoever walks with the wise will become wise; whoever walks with fools will suffer harm." Proverbs 13:20

Purpose Point: Walking down the perfect path will birth the process of perfection in you. Having a desire to please God as you walk through life will motivate you to become better and better.

*"Joyful are people of integrity, who follow the instructions of the Lord. Joyful are those who obey his laws and search for him with all their hearts. They do not compromise with evil, and **they walk only in his paths.**"* Psalm 119:1-3

Purpose Point: When we give our life to Jesus our life is no longer our own. Therefore, we should trust in Jesus to direct our steps and help us to find our way. Regardless of your experiences, God's Word (His instructions and directions) will guide you to your destiny…to the right place.

"LORD, I know that people's lives are not their own; it is not for them to direct their steps." Jeremiah 10:23 NIV

"You make known to me the path of life; you will fill me with joy in your presence, with eternal pleasures at your right hand." Psalm 16:11 NIV

Purpose Point: The Perfect Path leads to eternal life. At the end of this road or at the end of your physical life (death), you will ascend to heaven and live forever.

Purpose Point: How you finish is more important than how you start. Many of us started on the Rocky Road of life. But thank God we are able to switch paths because of what Jesus did for us. He gave us an option for a better way when there was not one. He opened the pathway to life – the Perfect Path to destiny.

"Finishing is better than starting. Patience is better than pride." Ecclesiastes 7:8
"By his death, Jesus opened a new and life-giving way..." Hebrews 10:20

Minute Memoir: During the early part of my adolescent years I unknowingly chose the Rocky Road. And as a result, I experienced abuse, abandonment, low self-esteem, heartache, trauma, and hopelessness. Choosing the Highway to Holiness later in life revolutionized my life for the better. There is a huge difference in how I started versus where I am now. Walking on the Perfect Path of life has brought me a sense of value as well as happiness, confidence, peace, joy, love, faith, wisdom, health, and prosperity. God's way works!!! I am living proof that it does, and many others would agree. You cannot go wrong when you choose the Perfect Path of life – God's way.

"Make me walk along the path of your commands, for that is where my happiness is found." Psalm 119:35

Purpose Point: God has a vested interest in you choosing the right path because He knows if you choose His way, you will be protected and happy, and He will be glorified. When you live a life for God and choose to do what is right in His sight, people will begin to see the God in you which could very well influence them to seek a similar path, thus bringing glory to His kingdom and marvelous name.

"He makes me lie down in green pastures, he leads me beside quiet waters, he refreshes my soul. ***He guides me along the right paths for his name's sake.*** *Even though I walk through the darkest valley, I will fear no evil, for you are with me; your rod and your staff, they comfort me."* Psalm 23:2-4 NIV

Action Activity: Pray and meditate on the following scriptures:

"Show me the right path, O LORD; point out the road for me to follow.
Lead me by your truth and teach me, for you are the God who saves me.
All day long I put my hope in you.
Remember, O LORD, your compassion and unfailing love,
which you have shown from long ages past.
Do not remember the rebellious sins of my youth.
Remember me in the light of your unfailing love, for you are merciful, O LORD.
The LORD is good and does what is right;
he shows the proper path to those who go astray.
He leads the humble in doing right, teaching them his way. *The LORD leads with unfailing love and faithfulness all who keep his covenant and obey his demands.*

For the honor of your name, O LORD, forgive my many, many sins. ***Who are those who fear the LORD? He will show them the path they should choose. They will live in prosperity, and their children will inherit the land.***
The LORD is a friend to those who fear him.
He teaches them his covenant.
My eyes are always on the LORD,
for he rescues me from the traps of my enemies."
Psalm 25:4-15

Now, let's discuss the Rocky Road – the path of darkness and death.

*"A person with good sense is respected; a treacherous person walks a **rocky road**."*
Proverbs 13:15

The Rocky Road (wide/broad gate) goes in a totally different direction from the Perfect Path. On the Rocky Road you will find eternal death, destruction, torment, wickedness, evil, fear, confusion, unhappiness, hopelessness, and despair. The devil and his demons can be found on this path; they control it. There is no light on this road because it is headed in the wrong direction; only pure darkness and gloom which makes it easy for you to fall into traps of danger and destruction.

"The wicked walk into a net. They fall into a pit that's been dug in the path. A trap grabs them by the heel. A noose tightens around them. A snare lies hidden in the ground. A rope lies coiled on their path. Terrors surround the wicked and trouble them at every step. Their vigor is depleted by hunger, and calamity waits for them to stumble." Job 18:8-12

Candid Clarification: Just because you experience negative emotions such as fear, confusion, unhappiness, and hopelessness does not mean that you have chosen or are walking on the Rocky Road. It simply means that these emotions emerge from a dark direction and are blown onto your pathway...attempting to blow you off course But we, princesses of God, stand strong like a mighty tree firmly rooted and grounded (Colossians 2:7). Conversely, when you live on the Rocky Road or on a path of continual disobedience, negative emotions and ungodly behaviors are your way of life; they emerge and remain on your path because you have decided to walk the wrong way.

Purpose Point: You cannot grow and glow in the dark or on the Rocky Road. The Perfect Path, however, is illuminated with light because it leads you in the right direction. You can only grow and glow on this pathway.

Now you may ask, what does it mean to walk down the Rocky Road?

Walking down the Rocky Road means to live the world's way – to live a life of immorality, perversion, evil and wickedness. It means to obey the devil and engage in sinful acts such as idolatry, malice (hurting others), sexual immorality, cheating, lying, stealing, killing, etc.

Purpose Point: The Rocky Road leads to eternal death (eternal separation from God). At the end of this road and at the end of physical life (death), one will descend to hell and will suffer forever in the lake of fire. *"Don't do as the wicked do, and don't follow the path of evildoers. Don't even think about it; don't go that way. Turn away and keep moving. For evil people can't sleep until they've done their evil deed for the day. They can't rest until they've caused someone to stumble. They eat the food of wickedness and drink the wine of violence!"* Proverbs 4:14-17

Purpose Point: Your perception and beliefs will lead you to your destination. The way you see things or your perspective of life (worldview) will determine which way you choose to go.

Purpose Point: Refuse to walk on the path of evil – the Rocky Road. Instead, be obedient to God's Word so that you may live forever. David, a servant of God, said in Psalm 119:101: *"I have refused to walk on any evil path, so that I may remain obedient to your word."* Let's adopt this same attitude which will keep us from behaving like an immoral woman.

"Wisdom will save you from the immoral woman, from the flattery of the adulterous woman. She has abandoned her husband and ignores the covenant she made before God. Entering her house leads to death; it is the road to hell. The man who visits her is doomed. He will never reach the path of life. Follow the steps of a good man instead, and stay on the paths of the righteous." Proverbs 2:16-20

Purpose Point: The way you act determines your track.

Purpose Point: Don't test the Rocky Road just to see what it is like. If you do, you may never find your way out of its dark and gloomy path.

God is powerful and mighty, but He will not force you to choose the Perfect Path. God instead allows or permits you to choose your own path. When a person chooses to walk down the rocky road of life, she is walking in her own will – not supported or sanctioned by God. He allows her to do whatever she wants to do, despite the negative consequences, because it is her choice. On the other hand, when a person chooses to walk down the perfect path – the path that God has chosen for her, this person is walking in God's *perfect will*.

Purpose Point: One way to find out God's perfect will for your life is to read and study His Word – the Bible. His Word is His will. Obeying God's commands and directions – which are listed all throughout the Bible – puts you on the perfect path of life. God will also guide and speak to you inwardly to reveal His perfect will for your life. Additionally, attending a Bible-based church will impart wisdom and guidance.

Purpose Point: God's perfect will and perfect path will take you to your divine destiny.

Purpose Point: Your purpose is the reason why you were created; your destiny is doing what you were created to do.

What is the perfect will of God for your life?
God's perfect will for your life is for you to live out your purpose by doing the things you were created to do. Remember, your essential purposes in life are to love God, love your neighbor as yourself, help others, and help others to know Jesus

Purpose Point: When you live your life by trying to fit in with everyone else you are rejecting God's perfect will. But when you live your life as a princess by doing what you were created to do, you are living in God's perfect will.

Purpose Point: People who choose evil have chosen to walk down the rocky road or the wrong path. Sometimes people suffer because of the bad choices others make, and sometimes a person suffers because of the bad choices they make. **Continuing to make bad choices will inevitably put you on the wrong path and others around you may suffer as "collateral damage".**

Text Term: Collateral damage – unintended harm afflicted on others because of someone else's choice(s).

Purpose Point: Walking down the perfect path does not necessarily mean your life will be perfect or that you will live a perfect life; no one has ever lived a perfect life, except Jesus. *"All of us have strayed away like sheep. We have left God's paths to follow our own..."* **Isaiah 53:6**

Imperfections will always be present on the perfect path and will come in the form of roadblocks, pitfalls, wilderness experiences, missteps, and mistakes – all will try to trip you up and get you off course. When this happens, you must seek God and trust Him as you continue on the right path.

Moreover, when you choose to walk down the perfect path, you strive to be more and more like Jesus every day in terms of your love walk with God and others. Jesus said, *"If you love only those who love you, what reward is there for that? Even corrupt tax collectors do that much. If you are kind only to your friends, how are you different from anyone else? Even pagans do that.* ***But you are to be perfect, even as your Father in heaven is perfect.****"*
Matthew 5:46-48

Therefore, being perfect means realizing your potential for progression and choosing to mature in Christ…choosing to live out His ways to the best of your ability with the help of God.

Purpose Point: No one is perfect, only God/Jesus are. But we can delight in His perfections as He works to make us perfect (Philippians 1:6).

"The one thing I ask of the LORD — the thing I seek most— is to live in the house of the LORD all the days of my life, ***delighting in the LORD's perfections*** *and meditating in his Temple."*
Psalm 27:4

Remember, God's greatest commandment is that we love Him, ourselves and other people (respecting, honoring, forgiving, and being kind). When we love, this shows that we have God living in us. *"…God is love, and all who live in love live in God, and God lives in them. And as we live in God, our love grows more* ***perfect****…"* 1 John 4:16-17

Psalms 119:96 asserts that God's commands have no limits, but perfection does. *"Even perfection has its limits, but your commands have no limit."*

Additionally, not only should we strive to grow perfect in our love towards God, ourselves, and others, but we should also strive for God's love to be perfected in us. We do this by choosing the perfect path and trusting God as we journey through life.

"Such love has no fear because perfect love expels all fear. If we are afraid, it is for fear of judgment, and this shows that his love has not been perfected in us." 1 John 4:18

Purpose Point: God wants you to know without a doubt His great love for you. Trust and believe God loves you; you have nothing to fear in life or death. God has your back! He will never leave you or forsake you. When you are afraid or fearful in life, this shows that you do not truly believe that God loves you.

Since God has your back, don't turn your back on Him and look the other way – choosing to go down the Rocky Road. Jesus sacrificed himself for you; he died so that you could live.

"...We turned our backs on him and looked the other way when he went by. He was despised, and we did not care. Yet it was our weaknesses he carried; it was our sorrows that weighed him down. And we thought his troubles were a punishment from God for his own sins! But he was wounded and crushed for our sins. He was beaten that we might have peace. He was whipped, and we were healed!" Isaiah 53:3-5

Purpose Point: God's love for you is already perfect, but when you do not believe this or doubt Him it shows that His love has not been perfected in you. God has already proven His love for you by sending His Son, Jesus, to die for your sins. And we show God that we love Him by keeping His commandments. You may mess up or stumble along the way, starting down the wrong road, but the key is to dust yourself off, get back up and continue on the perfect pathway.

"...This is what the Lord says: When people fall down, don't they get up again? When they start down the wrong road and discover their mistake, don't they turn back? Then why do these people keep going along their self-destructive path, refusing to turn back, even though I have warned them? I listen to their conversations, and what do I hear? Is anyone sorry for sin? Does anyone say, "What a terrible thing I have done?" No! All are running down the path of sin as swiftly as a horse rushing into battle!" Jeremiah 8:4-6

"If someone says, "I love God," but hates another Christian, that person is a liar; for if we don't love people we can see, how can we love God, whom we have not seen? And God himself has commanded that we must love not only him but our Christian brothers and sisters, too." 1 John 4:20–21

Purpose Point: Just like there are many stages of life, there are also many passageways (sub-pathways) or stages of the Perfect Path and the Rocky Road. Some passageways of the Perfect Path are the paths to sanctification, marriage, deliverance, knowledge/wisdom, and ministry/calling. And some sub-pathways of the Rocky Road are the paths to idolatry, lust/immortality, murder, and greed.

Another way to look at the Perfect Path and the Rocky Road are as two different *free*ways with many different exits (an alternative route to the same end destination) – free to go whichever way you choose. You can veer off or avoid a sub-pathway (exit) and still remain on the same course or main road/thoroughfare. For instance, many people choose Christ (the Perfect Path) but do not choose to walk in their ministry and calling (a sub-pathway). Not doing so, does not negate their salvation or their walk on the Perfect Path, it simply means that they have chosen complacency in Christ rather than fulfilling the calling and commission Christ desires (Matthew 28:16-20). It is all about who you allow in the driver seat of your life. Will you allow Jesus to drive you to your destiny or will *you* choose to settle where you are? Or will you make the fatal choice and allow Satan to drive you to destruction?

Life is fast, and as we walk down the road of our chosen path, we will have many different experiences that will take us in many different directions with many exits along the way (see Figure 2 SEKM model). It is important to know that if you trust God and seek His perfect will, the perfect path for your life, He will direct your paths and guide you based on His purpose and will for you. He will help you to avoid the dead ends and danger zones. He will order your steps to take you in the right direction. *"Trust in the Lord with all your heart; do not depend on your own understanding. Seek his will in all you do, and he will direct your paths."* Proverbs 3:5-6

"The steps of a good man are ordered by the Lord...He delights in his way." Psalm 37:23 NKJV
"We can make our plans, but the LORD determines our steps" Proverbs 16:9
"In him we were also chosen, having been predestined according to the plan of him who works out everything in conformity with the purpose of his will..." Ephesians 1:11 NIV

Purpose Point: Ultimately, there are two pathways in life, the Perfect Path and Rocky Road with its respective sub-pathways. And essentially, you have two God-given callings – a call to salvation and a call to your vocational ministry comprised of your gifts, talents, passions, and purpose. Your calling is the way in which God wants you to use your gifts for His glory.

On the Perfect Path, every Christian should grow and mature to take the appropriate sub-pathway to their calling or ministry. This path (journey) will not be the same for all Christians because God has given each of us different gifts, talents, assignments, and callings. He gave us all a different purpose and a different destiny to walk into, all the while leading to the same end destination. That's why your story may not be my story; your experiences may not match my experiences…but in the end our faith in God will lead us to our heavenly home – one God, one Savior, one eternal destiny.

Purpose Point: Some people deliberately set traps for those who decide to walk down the Perfect Path in an effort to make them fail and fall. Watch and pray as you travel through life. *"The proud have set a trap to catch me; they have stretched out a net; they have placed traps all along the way."* Psalm 140:5 Moreover, do not be foolish and set a trap for yourself. When you value life and value God, you will not engage in dangerous activities such as sexual immorality, negative peer pressure, gangs, alcohol, drugs, or criminal behaviors. *"The deceitful walk a thorny, treacherous road; whoever values life will stay away."* Proverbs 22:5

Purpose Point: If you find your perfect path getting dark and gloomy from life's problems and trials and you begin to experience an emotional eclipse, God's Word will serve as light or a lamp to your feet and will guide you through moments of despair. *"Your word is a lamp for my feet and a light for my path."* Psalm 119:105

Purpose Point: Taking short-cuts and detours in life gets you nowhere. Stay on the path God has chosen for you; allow Him to guide you on the best pathway for your life and lead you down the passageways and sub-pathways He has marked for your journey according to His will for you. Trust the process and persevere. It is only when you choose to cross over to the other side (the Rocky Road) that you lose your way and separate yourself from God.

Purpose Point: God will put up road signs and warning signals to keep you on the perfect path. DO NOT neglect the road signs and flashing signals God has placed before you.

- Road signs and warning signals include:
    - The Bible, which explicitly explains "the truth" and the consequences of sin.
    - Parents and other people God has placed on your path to inform you of potential danger zones, bumps ahead, pitfalls, roadblocks, and dead ends.
    - Your conscience…listen to that small inner voice in your mind that compels you to do right; do not ignore the prompting and guidance of the Spirit.

"Do not do as the wicked do or follow the path of evildoers. Avoid their haunts. **Turn away and go somewhere else..."** Proverbs 4:14-15

"The way of the righteous is like the first gleam of dawn, which shines ever brighter until the full light day. But the way of the wicked is like complete darkness. Those who follow it have no idea what they are stumbling over." Proverbs 4:18-19

Again, refuse to walk on the path of evil – the Rocky Road. Instead, be obedient to God's Word because you love Him and want to live forever with Him. Choose the Highway of Holiness – the Perfect Path; live in God's perfect will! Your attitude should be: Lord, *"Let me hear of your unfailing love each morning, for I am trusting you. Show me where to walk, for I give myself to you."* Psalm 143:8

God is saying to you...

"My child, if sinners entice you, turn your back on them! They may say, "Come and join us. Let's hide and kill someone! Let's ambush the innocent! Let's swallow them alive as the grave swallows its victims. Though they are in the prime of their life, they will go down into the pit of death… ***Don't go along with them, my child! Stay far away from their paths.*** *They rush to commit crimes. They hurry to commit murder. When a bird sees a trap being set, it stays away. But not these people! They set an ambush for themselves; they booby-trap their own lives! Such is the fate of all who are greedy for gain. It ends up robbing them of life."*
Proverbs 1:10-19

"My child, listen to me and do as I say, and you will have a long, good life. ***I will teach you wisdom's ways and lead you in straight paths. If you live a life guided by wisdom, you won't limp or stumble as you run. Carry out my instructions; don't forsake them. Guard them, for they will lead you to a fulfilled life."*** Proverbs 4:10-13

"Look straight ahead, and fix your eyes on what lies before you. ***Mark out a straight path for your feet; then stick to the path and stay safe.*** *Don't get sidetracked; keep your feet from following evil."* Proverbs 4:25

Purpose Point: When you choose to walk down the Rocky Road, you walk into a *maze* – a labyrinth – replete with many twists, turns and short-cuts that only lead you back to destruction no matter which way you go. However, when you walk down the Perfect Path, a straight pathway, you will be a*maze*d at the joy and abundance you will find.

Purpose Point: The Lord goes before you as you walk down your perfect pathway preparing the way for opportunities, favor, blessings and promises—all aligned with His purpose and will for your life.

"The LORD himself goes before you and will be with you; he will never leave you nor forsake you. Do not be afraid; do not be discouraged." Deuteronomy 31:8 NIV

If you ever go the wrong way in life, turn away (repent), turn around and proceed in the right direction. *Keep your eye on the prize and your foot on the path. God has paved a pathway for you and has called you into purpose for such a time as this. With joy and gratitude, embrace the pathway He has set before you. Walk on it continually and consistently with wisdom, worship, and willingness of heart embedded in every step. God is with you always, even until the end of the world. "The world and its desires pass away, but whoever does the will of God lives forever."*
1 John 2:17 NIV

The Rocky Road robs you of life. The Perfect Path leads you to life!
Oh, that you would choose life!

Purpose Point: All roads and paths <u>do not</u> lead to Jesus. There is only one way.
Jesus stated, "I am the way and the truth and the life. No one comes to the Father except through me." John 14:6 NIV

The Proverbs' Perspective – Comparison and Contrast of the two Paths   Traveler - the person who chooses the path.

Righteous Road...Highway of Holiness - "The Princess's Pathway" (Perfect Path)	Rocky Road - Path of Perdition (Destruction)	Supporting Scriptures
Open highway; straight and safe path - narrow gate...narrow way - Matthew 7:13	Dead end; feet follow evil; a crooked path - wide gate...broad way	Proverbs 15:19; Proverbs 4:26-27; Proverbs 21:8
Leads upward	Leads downward to the grave	Proverbs 16:24
Leads away from evil...leads to God - eternal life	Leads to evil...leads away from God - eternal separation	Proverbs 16:17
The way of righteousness - begins and ends with life	This way seems right, but it is wrong and ends in death	Proverbs 16:25; Proverbs 12:15; Proverbs 14:12
The path to life; it will never intersect with the paths of death	The path of death; it will never reach the path to life	Proverbs 2:19; Proverbs 12:28; Proverbs 11:19
Led by the steps of a good man - follow him/her as they follow Christ	Led by the steps of the wicked - avoid these people	Proverbs 2:20; Proverbs 28:10; Proverbs 14:7
Stay on this path; do not veer off	Stay far away from this path	Proverbs 1:15; Proverbs 15:21
The traveler lives God's way - the way of the godly leads to life	The traveler lives their own way - the way of the world leads to death and darkness	Proverbs 1:31; Proverbs 12:15; Proverbs 12:28; Proverbs 16:2
The traveler seeks to obey God; their steps are ordered by the Lord - Psalm 37:23	The traveler rushes to commit sin and evil	Proverbs 1:16-18; Proverbs 16:9
Guarded by God as He protects those who walks this safe way	No protection or guard rails - this way is dangerous and deadly	Proverbs 2:8; Proverbs 3:23-26; Proverbs 25:28
The traveler walks with integrity; remains prudent, cautious and avoids danger	The traveler (fool) walks with a heart of evil and deception; plunges ahead recklessly	Proverbs 2:7; Proverbs 9:9; Proverbs 14:16; Proverbs 20:7; Proverbs 22:3; Proverbs 14:8
Wisdom and the fear (reverence) of the Lord guides you down this path of life	Fools despise wisdom and God, and are guided down this rocky way	Proverbs 3:17; Proverbs 1:7; Proverbs 14:2; Proverbs 19:23; Proverbs 22:4; Proverbs 16:6
The path of a virtuous woman	The path of an immoral and adulterous woman	Proverbs 5, 7 and 31; Proverbs 16:17; Proverbs 14:1
Total light; "shines ever brighter until the full light of day". God's Word is a lamp unto your feet and a light on your path - Psalm 119:105	Total darkness; the traveler has no idea what she is stumbling over and is blinded by lies and sin	Proverbs 4:18-19; Proverbs 13:9; Proverbs 6:23
The traveler confesses and repents when she falls down or slips up in sin	The traveler is held captive by their own sins	Proverbs 5:22; Proverbs 28:13
The traveler is accepted and beloved by God and knows where she is going	The traveler is lost	Proverbs 5:23; Proverbs 14:8; Proverbs 14:22
Corrective discipline and humility leads this way - the way to life	Rebellion and pride paved this road - the way to death and darkness	Proverbs 6:23; Proverbs 10:17; Proverbs 18:12; Proverbs 16:18; Proverbs 3:12; Proverbs 11:2
Blessings and rewards chase the godly on this path	Trouble and destruction chase sinners	Proverbs 13:21
God is pleased with those who pursue the way of godliness	The Lord detests the way of the wicked	Proverbs 15:9; Proverbs 15:26; Proverbs 16:26

"For the Lord sees clearly what a man does, examining every path he takes." Proverbs 5:21; *"Search me, O God, and know my heart...*
Point out anything in me that offends you, and lead me along the path of everlasting life." Psalm 139:23-24

Chapter 10
Powerful Prayer

Prayer Warriors are built to last...

"Listen closely to my prayer, O Lord; hear my urgent cry." Psalm 86:6

**Prayer is a privilege, not a pain.
It should be desired and never drudged.**

"God looks down from heaven on the entire human race; he looks to see if there is even one with real understanding, one who seeks for God." Psalm 53:2

"My heart has heard you say, 'Come and talk with me.' And my heart responds, 'LORD, I am coming.'" Psalm 27:8

    What is prayer? Simply put, prayer is seeking God, talking to Him and listening for a response. Prayer is a privilege, an honor afforded to us by God. As such, it is not required that we bring sacrifices, pay a fee, or see a priest to pray to the Creator of the universe. We can go to Him directly from the heart, anytime and anywhere. How awesome is this! Prayer is the ultimate source of communication between God and the human race. It was designed to be two-sided; however, oftentimes people pray one-sided prayers with no real understanding…only thinking about me, myself, and I. Their prayers focus on statements such as: 'Lord, I need this…please do this… give me this.'

One-sided prayers are often selfish and include:

- Prayers that are not in accordance with God's will.
- Prayers that only focus on your desires/wants and needs, and no one else.
- Prayers that do not involve some form of thanksgiving, praise, or worship towards God.
- Prayers that are full of complaining, criticizing, griping, and grumbling.
- Prayers that involve the wrong motives.

Additionally, one-sided prayers do not allot time for God to respond. Praying to God should be like talking to a friend, where you talk, listen (expect a response), and both of you convey information. You may not hear God respond immediately or in an audible voice. He may instead respond in a quiet, still voice deep in your spirit or through His Word – the Bible. He may also respond through a pastor, friend, or Christian media/resource such as TV programs, podcasts, music, or books. For example, some people may pray to God for an answer to their problems and may later hear their answer during a sermon or discover the solution while reading their Bible.

Purpose Point: All of God's children have the ability to hear Him.

The below scriptures refer to Jesus (who is one with God) as our good shepherd, and God's children as the sheep who hear His voice.

"The gatekeeper opens the gate for him, **and the sheep hear his voice and come to him**...*"* John 10:3

"I am the good shepherd. The good shepherd lays down his life for the sheep." John 10:11

*"**My sheep recognize my voice;** I know them, and they follow me. I give them eternal life, and they will never perish..."* John 10:27-28 *"The Father and I are one."* John 10:30

*"...**Today you must listen to his voice**. Don't harden your hearts against him as Israel did..."* Hebrews 3:7-8

Purpose Point: You should have a heart to obey when you hear God's voice. Otherwise, you will just be taking an idle walk through life that could lead you in the opposite direction – down the rocky road. Know that God will never tell you anything wrong and His voice will always line up with His Word – the Bible. Any voice that does not line up with God's Word is not of God. Therefore, it is important for you to know God's Word by reading your Bible and attending a Bible-based church so you can recognize the lies and deceptions of the enemy.

Purpose Point: Sometimes, the most opportune time to hear God is in silence. Several books that I have read recommend at least two fifteen-minute breaks of complete quiet time a day – where there is nothing but pure and utter silence.

One book reads, *"Silence will speak more to you in a day than the world of voices can teach you in a lifetime. Find silence. Find solitude – and having discovered her riches, bind her to your heart."* – Frances J. Roberts, Come Away My Beloved

It is important to discern and listen for God's voice to discover your answer, so you can:

- Make the right decision.
- Find comfort and direction.
- Know God's will for your life – your purpose and destiny.
- Know how to help others.

When you do and know these things, you become positioned to please God, carry out your purpose and experience His marvelous promises.

Purpose Point: Prayer is a gift from God. Think about how awesome it is to be able to talk to the Creator of the universe. Prayer empowers us to stand strong and tall in the spiritual realm, defeat evil and bring about restoration, reconciliation and a release from God.

Essentially, the three (3) core expectations of prayer are:

1. *Restoration* – the restoration of healing, health, wholeness, and loss of resources and assets.

2. *Reconciliation* – reconciling woman/man back to God (salvation and deliverance); reconciling or repairing relationships – woman/man back to family, friends and/or acquaintances through love and forgiveness. And sometimes we need to reconcile with self (forgive and love yourself).

3. *Release* – the release of blessings, wisdom, knowledge, revelation, provision, promotion, money, favor, abilities, justice, and other desires of the heart.

Purpose Point: Although prayer involves bringing your requests to God, the most important aspect of prayer is ministering to God – spending time with Him, communing with Him, praising Him, worshiping Him, and acknowledging Him for who He is. This in turn provides God the opportunity to minister to you and meet your needs.

Many people dread praying, and view it as some boring, tiresome, and dreadful act demanded by God. This thinking is definitely the wrong attitude towards prayer and could limit what God wants to do in your life. We must be grateful for prayer and realize that it is a privilege and not a pain, something that is meant to add to our life, and not take away from it. The way we view and understand prayer stems from the way we view and understand God. When people get caught up in the rituals and rules, they are unable to embrace a true relationship with God. For example, some people believe that you must pray so many times a day for so many minutes or hours, such as three (3) times a day for an hour. Additionally, some believe that since they have made mistakes or continue to make mistakes they cannot pray or are not worthy to pray – or they believe that someone else must pray for them.

When people feel like they have broken the rituals and the rules or cannot abide by them, they give up on prayer because they lack **I. Clarity, II. Confidence, and III. Commitment**.

When you lack these three things, prayer becomes a dread rather than a delight, thus ineffective, dull, null, and void in a person's life. But when you have a true relationship with God, you are not governed by rules – you talk to God at every opportunity, whether it is for three minutes or three hours, when you mess up or don't always do what is right. You pray while you are in the car (eyes open if driving), in the shower, on the treadmill, in bed, at school, on the job or anywhere you feel the unction or urge to. In fact, my beloved pastor, facetiously exclaimed that some of his best talks with God were on the toilet.

Purpose Point: Although not required, praying on your knees and/or hands lifted exemplifies honor, reverence and surrender to God. Praying spontaneously can include praying privately or publicly, aloud, or silently in your heart and mind.

I. CLARITY

People who are unfamiliar or new to prayer have many questions and desire clarity, mostly about prayer ***posture, place, position, and partnership,*** amongst other things.

A. Posture/Pose (physical body) and Place (location)

Is there a certain posture your body should be in when you pray, such as kneeled (on your knees), hands clasped together and held closely to your mouth?

Where should you pray…in a closet, in a church, at the altar, on the side of your bed?

God is specific in His command for you to pray, *"Keep alert and pray. Otherwise temptation will overpower you. For though the spirit is willing enough, the body is weak!"* Matthew 26:41; however, God does not set specific guidelines on where you should pray and how you should pray as it relates to a standard place and posture.

In fact, Jesus said true worship (the highest form of prayer) should be done in spirit and truth. In other words, it is not a matter of where you pray but your heart's attitude. We are a three-part being – spirit, soul, and body. Therefore, when you pray, you should open your heart (soul) and spirit to God to the extent that you are completely broken, sincere and honest before Him – all the while declaring your love, reverence, and the truth of His Word and character (i.e. Lord, I love you. You are the Creator of all things; the King of kings and the Lord of lords….). It is not so much about the place – it is about the position (condition) of your heart.

"Jesus replied, 'Believe me, dear woman, the time is coming when it will no longer matter whether you worship the Father on this mountain or in Jerusalem. You Samaritans know very little about the one you worship, while we Jews know all about him, for salvation comes through the Jews. **But the time is coming—indeed it's here now—when true worshipers will worship the Father in spirit and in truth.** *The Father is looking for those who will worship him that way. For God is Spirit, so those who worship him must worship in spirit and in truth.'"*
John 4:21-24

Purpose Point: The Spirit of God lives in you if you have accepted Jesus Christ as your Lord and Savior. Therefore, the Spirit goes wherever you go. He is in you and with you always.

Purpose Point: God sets restrictions, but He operates with no limits.

"For he is sent by God. He speaks God's words, for God gives him the Spirit without limit."
John 3:34

God is a God of no limits; there is no limit to what He can do, how much He can do, when He can do it and where He can do it. And since we serve a no limit God, He does not put limits on us when it comes to certain things; therefore, you can pray with your hands lifted, clasped, closed, holding the phone, or even holding the steering wheel (with your eyes open and you intently focused on driving, of course). You can pray while standing up, sitting up, kneeling, or laying down...in the closet, in the car, in the church, in the corner or on the couch. However, we should always honor God in prayer and create an atmosphere where He is comfortable to dwell, and not dishonor Him by praying in idol postures, or even idol places of worship.

An idol is a false god or anything or anyone worshiped outside of the true living God and His son Jesus Christ. Idol places are locations where false gods are worshiped and idol postures are positions in which they are worshipped. For example, Buddhists often pray in a worship posture commonly practiced or portrayed by an idol god, Buddha. This prayer posture is often rehearsed in a sitting position with legs folded with the sole of one foot turned upward in a locked position, and hands placed together (turned upward) and placed in the front center of the chest (see Figure B). Since this prayer posture reverences an idol god, we as Christians should not emulate or practice this stance when praying to the one and only true living God...our Lord and Savior Jesus Christ.

Below are some idol postures of worship and prayer that you should avoid as a Christian since these postures were conceived and perverted to worship and honor false gods.

Figure A   Figure B   Figure C

"Do not make idols or set up an image or a sacred stone for yourselves, and do not place a carved stone in your land to bow down before it. I am the LORD your God."
Leviticus 26:1 NIV

It is important to know that an idol can be anything or anyone that takes priority in your heart over God. Therefore, your possessions can be an idol as well as social media, the internet, TV, sororities/fraternities, friends/boyfriend, money, shopping, car, house, fame, etc. – these can all be established as idols in your heart. Of course, you won't literally bow down to worship these things, but you may instead worship them with your time, efforts and money, while denying God your time, tithes and talents which were all given to you for His glory.

"Son of man, these leaders have set up idols in their hearts. They have embraced things that lead them into sin. Why should I let them ask me anything? Give them this message from the Sovereign Lord: I, the Lord, will punish the people of Israel who set up idols in their hearts so they fall into sin and then come to a prophet asking for help. I will do this to capture the minds and hearts of all my people who have turned from me to worship their detestable idols." Ezekiel 14:3-5

Purpose Point: Any form of idolatry can hinder your prayers. Idols block you from receiving the blessings of God.

"...stay away from idols! I am the one who answers your prayers and cares for you. I am like a tree that is always green; all your fruit comes from me." Hosea 14:8

"...You must acknowledge no God but me, for there is no other savior." Hosea 13:4

Purpose Point: Another key component of prayer is to establish in your heart (mind) and words spoken *'who you are praying to'*. Many pray generic prayers, unspecific, to encompass idol gods — the universe, sun, moon, stars, mother nature, angels, animals or whomever the world worships relative to their faith. There is only ONE true God — one true faith, the God of the Holy Bible (the God that lives) and His Son Jesus Christ. Be specific when you pray and pray in Jesus' name.

"But when you ask him, be sure that your faith is in God alone. Do not waver, for a person with divided loyalty is as unsettled as a wave of the sea that is blown and tossed by the wind. Such people should not expect to receive anything from the Lord. Their loyalty is divided between God and the world, and they are unstable in everything they do." James 1:6-8

B. Position (inner heart/motives)

What is the position of your heart? What are your motives or reasons for praying? Do you hold unforgiveness against someone?

The position of your heart is by far the most important aspect of praying when it comes to getting your prayers answered. Again, when I speak of your heart, I am not speaking of the organ in your chest that pumps blood, but rather the condition of your mind, matters and motives. Your motive is why you do what you do, but as it relates to prayer, it is the reason why you make your request to God, or the real reason for your petition.

Your heart can be situated in many different positions such as a position of hate, strife, unforgiveness, selfishness, envy, jealousy, deceit, disobedience, idolatry, lust, greed, pride, arrogance, evil and unbelief which all produce wrong motives. To the contrary, your heart can be positioned in a more positive place such as love, respect, kindness, compassion, peace, faithfulness, servitude, obedience, and meekness which all produce right motives. When your heart is not positioned properly it can hinder your progress with God and block your prayers.

Therefore, to assume a position of success, one's heart must be aligned with the fruit of God's Spirit—love, joy, peace, patience, kindness, goodness, faithfulness, gentleness, and self-control (Galatians 5:22-23). In this case, when your heart is properly positioned, your motives will be rightfully aligned.

"The human heart is most deceitful and desperately wicked. Who really knows how bad it is? But I know! I, the Lord, search all hearts and examine secret motives. I give all people their due rewards, according to what their actions deserve." Jeremiah 17:9-10

"...You want what you don't have, so you scheme ad kill to get it. You are jealous for what others have, and you can't possess it, so you fight and quarrel to take it away from them. ***And yet the reason you don't have what you want is that you don't ask God for it. And even when you do ask, you don't get it because your whole motive is wrong – you want only what will give you pleasure.****"* James 4:1-3

"The Lord's searchlight penetrates the human spirit, exposing every hidden motive." Proverbs 20:27

Purpose Point: For your prayers to be effective, you must approach prayer with an open and sincere heart, considering your motives and God's will for your life.

Now let's test your knowledge of wrong motives:

I. Consider a person who prays to God for a new car:

A. She wants a new car because she wants to make her classmates and co-workers jealous.

B. She wants a new car because her existing car is 15 years old and keeps breaking down.

Which scenario do you think involves the wrong motive?

Answer: Scenario (A) involves the wrong motive. A person whose prayers are self-centered and intended to bring harm, danger, discord, temptation or mischief to another person or group are not prayers God supports.

II. Consider a person who desires to be married and prays for a husband:

A. She wants to marry because she desires to please God, be free from sexual sin and serve as a help meet (wife) to a godly/single man.

B. She wants to marry because all her friends are married, and she feels left out.

Which scenario do you think involves the wrong motive?

Answer: Scenario (B) involves the wrong motive. Our decisions should not be based on what somebody else has or does. Marriage is a big step and one should evaluate themselves and be honest about where they are in terms of being truly ready to submit to and serve another.

III. <u>Consider a person who prays for an increase in their finances:</u>

A. She wants more money to take care of the basic needs of her family (e.g. food, shelter, healthcare, etc.).

B. She wants more money to gamble and shop with.

Which scenario do you think involves the wrong motive?

Answer: Scenario (B) involves the wrong motive. God promises to supply all our needs according to His riches and glory by Christ Jesus (Philippians 4:19). Gambling and excessive shopping are not considered needs in God's book.

Purpose Point: With God, it is not so much what you ask for, but why you ask for it. Remember, people look at the outward appearance, but God looks at the heart.

"...Don't judge by his appearance or height.... The Lord doesn't make decisions the way you do! People judge by outward appearance, but the Lord looks at a person's thoughts and intentions." 1 Samuel 16:7

Purpose Point: You can never fool God; He alone knows the true motives of every heart.

Purpose Point: Motives are a critical factor in every aspect of life…why do people do what they do or say what they say? Motives are the bedrock of human behavior. Establishing a motive is a critical component for law enforcement when solving crimes, as well as for general investigations, psychology, counseling, coaching, social work, strategic planning, human resources management, marketing/consumer behavior, economics, sales, research, and relationships overall. If motives are critical in these instances, how much more with God?

C. Partnership (covenant/commitment)

Is God obligated to answer your prayer? Do you have a right to pray? Can you get your prayers answered on your own or do you need someone else to pray for you and with you?

Recently, I heard someone say, *"Religion is popular, but relationship is personal."* When you accept Jesus as your Lord and Savior, God sees you as His special child and longs for you to develop a personal relationship with Him. He does not want you to be bogged down with rituals and religion, but He instead wants you to know Him, His ways, and walk in them.

"Oh, that we might know the Lord! Let us press on to know him..." Hosea 6:3

"I want you to show love, not offer sacrifices. I want you to know me more than I want burnt offerings." Hosea 6:6

As a daughter of God – His princess, you can come to your Father on your own, without your brothers and sisters in Christ tagging along. You have the right to pray, and the right to get your prayers answered because you are the righteousness of God through Christ Jesus. Although God encourages you to pray with others (Matthew 18:19-20), your faith, prayer, and fervency are sufficient to capture God's heart and His ear. Your sincerity can get a prayer through and a prayer answered.

"For God made Christ, who never sinned, to be the offering for our sin, so that we could be made right with God through Christ." 2 Corinthians 5:21

Jesus said, *"At that time you won't need to ask me for anything.* ***The truth is, you can go directly to the Father and ask him, and he will grant your request because you use my name."*** John 16:23

"Confess your sins to each other and pray for each other so that you may be healed. ***The earnest prayer of a righteous person has great power and produces wonderful results."*** James 5:16

Jesus said, all it takes is faith the size of a mustard seed (about the size of a pen tip). Mustard seeds are considered the smallest of the seeds and can produce a large mustard plant (tree); hence, it only takes a little faith to produce a big blessing (Mark 4:30-32).

"You didn't have enough faith," Jesus told them. I assure you, even if you had faith as small as a mustard seed you could say to this mountain, 'Move from here to there', and it would move. Nothing would be impossible." Matthew 17:20

David, a psalmist and servant of God, prayed to God often and put his faith to work. When he prayed it was private and personal; he didn't wait on the pastor, elders, or his friends. Repeatedly in the scriptures he indicates how personal his prayers really were by exclaiming, "**I** Will Pray…**My** prayers…**I** believe…the Lord Answered **Me**."

David wrote:

"I love the Lord because he hears and answers MY prayers. Because he bends down and listens, I WILL PRAY as long as I have breath!" Psalm 116:1-2

"I BELIEVED in you, so I PRAYED, "I am deeply troubled, Lord."" Psalm 116:10

"In my distress I PRAYED to the Lord, and the Lord ANSWERED ME and rescued me." Psalm 118:5

"I thank you for answering MY PRAYER and saving me." Psalm 118:21

"When I PRAY, YOU ANSWER ME; you encourage me by giving me the strength I need." Psalm 138:3

"The Lord has heard MY PLEA; the Lord will answer MY PRAYER." Psalm 6:9

Purpose Point: You can pray privately or corporately, alone or with other people. Either way, God answers prayer because He is obligated to His ***partnership of promises***.

*"Elijah was as human as we are, and yet when **he prayed earnestly** that no rain would fall, none fell for the next three and a half years! Then he prayed for rain, and down it poured. The grass turned green, and the crops began to grow again."* James 5:17-18

Jesus said, *"But if you stay joined to me and my words remain in you, you may ask any request you like, and it will be granted!"* John 15:7

"Are any among you suffering? They should keep on praying about it. And those who have reason to be thankful should continually sing praises to the Lord. Are any among you sick? They should call for the elders of the church and have them pray over them, anointing them with oil in the name of the Lord. And their prayer offered in faith will heal the sick, and the Lord will make them well. And anyone who has committed sins will be forgiven." James 5:13-15

"I also tell you this: If two of you agree down here on earth concerning anything you ask, my Father in heaven will do it for you. For where two or three gather together because they are mine, I am there among them." Matthew 18:19-20

Moreover, God is in covenant with His children. When you accept Jesus as your Lord and Savior, you become covenant partners with Him which means He has your back, and you should have His back as well. God is committed to you during the good times and the bad times, through the ups and the downs; therefore, you should also remain committed to Him during your happy moments and during your trials, tests and sufferings.

*"...these trials will make you **partners with Christ** in his suffering, and afterward you will have the wonderful joy of sharing his glory when it is displayed to all the world."*
1 Peter 4:13

***"He always stands by his covenant – the commitment he made** to a thousand generations."*
Psalm 105:8

Purpose Point: Remember, when you accept Christ as your Lord and Savior, he comes to live in you – what greater commitment than that! This partnership is so great, that denying you would be like denying himself.

"If we are unfaithful, he remains faithful, for he cannot deny himself." 2 Timothy 2:13

"The Spirit of God, who raised Jesus from the dead, lives in you. And just as God raised Christ Jesus from the dead, he will give life to your mortal bodies by the same Spirit living within you." Romans 8:11

Purpose Point: When your heart is in proper position, in the right place with the right motives, the Lord is open to your prayers. He is committed to hearing and answering you.

"The eyes of the Lord watch over those who do right, and his ears are open to their prayers. But the Lord turns his face against those who do evil." 1 Peter 3:12

- ➢ **Point of Clarification – Prayer Uncertainty and Unworthiness**

Purpose Point: When people make mistakes and feel like they cannot live by religious rules and rituals, they subconsciously condemn themselves or suffer discontent and disbelief about praying.

Therefore, it is important to understand that you are the righteousness of God through Christ Jesus which means your good works, long prayers, and good deeds will not make you right with God. Jesus made you right with God when you accepted and believed in Him. So no matter how much or how long you pray, or the mistakes you have made, God still sees you the same because of what Christ did for you. God will not turn His face against you when you turn to Him. **No one can gauge the grace of God.** He is sovereign and without measure.

"For God made Christ, who never sinned, to be the offering for our sin, so that we could be made right with God through Christ." 2 Corinthians 5:21

*"...For they don't understand God's way of making people right with himself. Instead, they are clinging to their own way of getting right with God by trying to keep the law. They won't go along with God's way. For Christ has accomplished the whole purpose of the law. **All who believe in him are made right with God.**"* Romans 10:3-4

Candid Clarification: When Christ made you right with God (Romans 3:22-25), this did not give you a free ticket to sin or do wrong and neglect praying. Knowing the mere fact that Christ made you right with God without any effort on your part should compel you to do right, pray and praise Him even the more. Only when we have faith do we truly aim to obey God (Romans 3:31).

Purpose Point: Praying does not make you righteous, but righteous people pray. Your good deeds do not make you righteous, but righteous people do good deeds; they aim to make the right decisions and do what is pleasing in God's sight.

You must believe that you are right with God because of what Jesus did for you. Although good deeds should be done as an act of faith because faith without good deeds is dead, good deeds do not make you right with God. It is knowing and having faith that you are right with God that should produce good deeds. And when you do good deeds as a result of your faith in God, He is greatly pleased!

"What good is it, dear brothers and sisters, if you say you have faith but don't show it by your actions? Can that kind of faith save anyone? Suppose you see a brother or sister who has no food or clothing, and you say, "Good-bye and have a good day; stay warm and eat well" – but you don't give that person any food or clothing. What good does that do? So you see, faith by itself isn't enough. Unless it produces good deeds, it is dead and useless...You say you have faith, for you believe that there is one God. Good for you! Even the demons believe this, and they tremble in terror. How foolish! Can't you see that faith without good deeds is useless?" James 2:14-20

"Do those things that will show that you have turned from your sins." Matthew 3:8 GNT

Powerful Prayer

Purpose Point: Never feel unworthy to pray. If you mess up, do wrong, or don't pray as often as you should, do not condemn yourself. If you do, you will feel uncomfortable about praying and lack confidence and faith to believe.

Purpose Point: God wants you to be convicted, not condemned. Conviction is when you realize and understand what you have done wrong and take steps to correct the problem. Therefore, the moment you realize that you have done wrong, repent and try your best to do better. Don't put yourself down, or feel as though you can't pray, are not worthy to pray or that God will not hear your prayers because of your mistake(s). God loves you unconditionally.

Purpose Point: You were made right with God when you accepted Jesus as your Lord and Savior; however, there is a process to getting your heart right before Him.

A disciple of Jesus, Peter, pointed out in the following scripture a man's heart that needed to be changed. Peter advised him to turn and pray. *"...Peter replied, 'May your money perish with you for thinking God's gift can be bought! You can have no part in this, **for your heart is not right before God**. Turn from your wickedness and pray to the Lord...for I can see that you are full of bitter jealousy and are held captive by sin.'"* Acts 8:20-23

Purpose Point: If you are struggling with a sin and have a desire to turn from that sin, continue to pray and trust God for deliverance. His power will save you and bring you out if you don't give up.

"So now there is no condemnation for those who belong to Christ Jesus. For the power of the life-giving Spirit has freed you through Christ Jesus from the power of sin that leads to death." Romans 8:1-2

Remember, when you accepted Christ, he made you right with him. So condemnation and shame have no place in you.

"Who dares accuse us whom God has chosen for his own? Will God? No! He is the one who has given us right standing with himself. Who then will condemn us? Will Christ Jesus? No, for he is the one who died for us and was raised to life for us and is sitting at the place of highest honor next to God, pleading for us." Romans 8:33-34

> **No matter what you have done, you can always go to God in prayer with a heavy heart, guilty conscience, broken spirit, or joyful praise. He listens, He hears, and He will deliver and answer you.**

Purpose Point: To ensure effectiveness in your prayers, get your heart right. Confess your sins to God and be honest about your struggles. Confess your faults to others (someone you trust) so they can pray for you (James 5:16). Get an *accountability partner,* someone who will keep your business confidential while encouraging you to continue on the right path.

"But if we are living in the light of God's presence, just as Christ is, then we have fellowship with each other, and the blood of Jesus, his Son, cleanses us from every sin. If we say we have

no sin, we are only fooling ourselves and refusing to accept the truth. But if we confess our sins to him, he is faithful and just to forgive us and to cleanse us from every wrong. If we claim we have not sinned, we are calling God a liar and showing that his word has no place in our hearts." 1 John 1:7-10

"Confess your sins to each other and pray for each other so that you may be healed. The earnest prayer of a righteous person has great power and produces wonderful results."
James 5:16

"People who cover over their sins will not prosper. But if they confess and forsake them, they will receive mercy." Proverbs 28:13

Candid Clarification: Oftentimes people allow sin to draw them away from God because of self-imposed guilt, condemnation, and willful disobedience – which all hold you back and weigh you down. *"My guilt overwhelms me – it is a burden too heavy for me to bear."*
Psalm 38:4

Simply repent and turn to God.

"For the kind of sorrow God wants us to experience leads us away from sin and results in salvation. There's no regret for that kind of sorrow. But worldly sorrow, which lacks repentance, results in spiritual death." 2 Corinthians 7:10

"For his unfailing love toward those who fear him is as great as the height of the heavens above the earth. He has removed our sins as far from us as the east is from the west. The LORD is like a father to his children, tender and compassionate to those who fear him. For he knows how weak we are; he remembers we are only dust. Our days on earth are like grass; like wildflowers, we bloom and die. The wind blows, and we are gone — as though we had never been here. But the love of the LORD remains forever with those who fear him. His salvation extends to the children's children of those who are faithful to his covenant, of those who obey his commandments!" Psalm 103:11-18

Why aren't my prayers answered?

Without a convicted, repentant, forgiving, and contrite heart, sin can hinder your prayers and stop God from working in your life. For example, unforgiveness, idolatry, pride, unbelief, disobedience, evil works, strife, and jealousy are just a few things that can hinder your prayers.

Consider the following scriptures:

"Listen! The Lord is not too weak to save you, and he is not becoming deaf. He can hear you when you call. But there is a problem – your sins have cut you off from God. Because of your sin, he has turned away and will not listen anymore. Your hands are the hands of murderers, and your fingers are filthy with sin. Your mouth is full of lies, and your lips are tainted with corruption. No one cares about being fair and honest. Their lawsuits are based on lies. They spend their time plotting evil deeds and then doing them. They spend their time and energy

spinning evil plans that end up in deadly actions. They cheat and shortchange everyone. Nothing they do is productive; all their activity is filled with sin. Violence is their trademark. Their feet run to do evil, and they rush to commit murder. They think only about sinning. Wherever they go, misery and destruction follow them. They do not know what true peace is or what it means to be just and good. They continually do wrong, and those who follow them cannot experience a moment's peace. It is because of all this evil that deliverance is far from us..."
Isaiah 59:1-9

"Then Jesus said to the disciples, "Have faith in God. I assure you that you can say to this mountain, 'May God lift you up and throw you into the sea', and your command will be obeyed. All that's required is that you really believe and do not doubt in your heart. Listen to me! You can pray for anything, and if you believe, you will have it. **But when you are praying, first forgive anyone you are holding a grudge against, so that your Father in heaven will forgive your sins, too.**" Mark 11:22-25

"Son of man, **these leaders have set up idols in their hearts**. *They have embraced things that lead them into sin.* **Why should I let them ask me anything…?**" Ezekiel 14:3

"In the same way, you husbands must give honor to your wives. Treat her with understanding as you live together. She may be weaker than you are, but she is your equal partner in God's gift of new life. **If you don't treat her as you should, your prayers will not be heard.**"
I Peter 3:7

"The eyes of the Lord watch over those who do right, and his ears are open to their prayers. **But the Lord turns his face against those who do evil.**" 1 Peter 3:12

David, a servant of God, understood the importance of repentance – a contrite heart. He said, **"If I had not confessed the sin in my heart, the Lord would not have listened. But God did listen! He paid attention to my prayer. Praise God**, *who did not ignore my prayer or withdraw his unfailing love from me."* Psalm 66:18-20

Purpose Point: In terms of getting your prayers answered, 80% of your prayers are dependent on your relationship with God because He knows every heart and you have to believe in God first to pray; and 20% of your prayers are dependent on your relationship with people. In other words, your relationship with God can be great, but if you are holding unforgiveness against others and refuse to forgive, then your prayers can go unanswered…and maybe your relationship with God is not so great after all.

"And without faith it is impossible to please God, because anyone who comes to him must believe that he exists and that he rewards those who earnestly seek him."
Hebrews 11:6 NIV

"If someone says, "I love God," but hates another Christian, that person is a liar; for if we don't love people we can see, how can we love God, whom we have not seen? And God himself has commanded that we must love not only him but our Christian brothers and sisters, too."
1 John 4:20

"…If you want a happy life and good days, keep your tongue from speaking evil, and keep your lips from telling lies. Turn away from evil and do good. **Work hard at living in peace with others**." 1 Peter 3:10-11

"Blessed are those who have a tender conscience, but the stubborn are headed for serious trouble." Proverbs 28:14

Purpose Point: No matter what you have done, when you *recognize your wrong*, and go to God in prayer with a *heart of repentance* (a turning away from doing wrong) or a *will to obey* amid a struggle, He will not despise or turn His ear from you. His grace will cover you. It is God's will that no man perishes.

"The sacrifice you want is a broken spirit. A broken and repentant heart, O God, you will not despise." Psalm 51:17

"...He does not want anyone to perish, so he is giving more time for everyone to repent." 2 Peter 3:9

God does, however, despise the prayers of those who reject his Word and His ways.

"The prayers of a person who ignores the law is despised." Proverbs 28:9

David exemplified a true heart of repentance, conviction, and brokenness. His prayer was sincere – an act of surrender.

David wrote:

"Have mercy on me, O God, because of your unfailing love. Because of your great compassion, blot out the stain of my sins. Wash me clean from my guilt. Purify me from my sin. For I recognize my shameful deeds – they haunt me day and night. Against you, and you alone, have I sinned; I have done what is evil in your sight. You will be proved right in what you say, and your judgment against me is just. For I was born a sinner – yes, from the moment my mother conceived me. But you desire honesty from the heart, so you can teach me to be wise in my inmost being. Purify me from my sins, and I will be clean; wash me, and I will be whiter than snow. Oh, give me back my joy again; you have broken me – now let me rejoice. Don't keep looking at my sins. Remove the stain of my guilt. Create in me a clean heart, O God. Renew a right spirit within me. Do not banish me from your presence, and don't take your Holy Spirit from me. **Restore to me again the joy of your salvation and make me willing to obey you.** *Then I will teach your ways to sinners, and they will return to you."* Psalm 51:1-13

Purpose Point: Although David prayed and requested in the above scripture that God's Holy Spirit not be taken away, when you truly accept Jesus as Lord and Savior His Holy Spirit lives in you permanently. He will never leave or be taken away no matter your mistakes or slip ups – you are sealed and secure through Christ and your continued belief in Him (Ephesians 1:13).

Purpose Point: Pour out your heart to God. Humble yourself before Him. God longs for you to have an encounter with Him – an experience that will bring you both closer.

"Draw close to God, and God will draw close to you..." James 4:8

Purpose Point: Again, no matter what you have done, prayers that are open-hearted and sincere are more inclined to capture God's ear. God values honesty, humility, and sincerity.

Take this biblical story for example: *"Then Jesus told this story to some who had great confidence in their own righteousness and scorned everyone else: "Two men went to the Temple to pray. One was a Pharisee, and the other was a despised tax collector. The Pharisee stood by himself and prayed this prayer: 'I thank you, God, that I am not like other people—cheaters, sinners, adulterers. I'm certainly not like that tax collector! I fast twice a week, and I give you a tenth of my income.' But the tax collector stood at a distance and dared not even lift his eyes to heaven as he prayed. Instead, he beat his chest in sorrow, saying, 'O God, be merciful to me, for I am a sinner.' I tell you, this sinner, not the Pharisee, returned home justified before God. For those who exalt themselves will be humbled, and those who humble themselves will be exalted."* Luke 18:9-14

Purpose Point: Yes, God wants you to pray and take time to spend with Him, but He does not want you to feel condemned about not doing so – and He does not want you to come to Him with an arrogant, haughty, and entitled attitude. He may convict you in your spirit when you don't set aside time for Him or when you approach Him with the wrong attitude/motive, but only to change your heart towards Him. God loves you so much. He wants you to enjoy spending quiet time with Him daily and have a sincere heart for prayer, repentance, and obedience.

Purpose Point: Prayers are not answered for two main reasons: (1) A person's heart is not right or positioned properly before God (Psalm 66:18); (2) he/she does not ask (James 4:2-3). However, don't confuse delays with denials if these two qualifications are met (your heart is right and you ask). God's *timing* is perfect and his *teachings* in the process are profound. Always surrender to God's will for your life for His glory (i.e. Lord, not my will be done, but your will be done – Luke 22:42).

> **Point of Clarification - Prayer and Pain**

Have you ever been so burdened and stricken down with depression, despair, discouragement, and devastation that you did not want to pray? You felt like you just wanted to fly away to be free from all the storms of life – your pain, problems, and responsibilities. I know I have. This scripture describes it best, *"Oh, how I wish I had wings like a dove; then I would fly away and rest! I would fly far away to the quiet wilderness. How quickly I would escape – far away from this wild storm..."* Psalm 55:6-8

Like wings, prayer is what takes you away from your troubles – it is your way of escape. Prayer brings rest to your spirit, peace in your heart and hope for your soul. Prayer is what strengthens you and gets you through. Hide yourself in prayer, the secret place, to escape from the troubles of this world – rest in the palaces of prayer. Supporting Scripture: *"Rescue me from my enemies, LORD; I run to you to hide me."* Psalm 143:9 Never neglect or give up on prayer, no matter how things seem. Even if you just pray a few words, *"Lord help me...", "Lord give me strength...", "Jesus have mercy on me!"* (Luke 19:38). God will meet you where you are. **Don't allow your pain to stop you from praying.** Cry out to God in prayer through every circumstance...and praise Him through it all. *"I cry out to the Lord; I plead for the Lord's mercy. I pour out my complaints before him and tell him all my troubles. For I am overwhelmed, and you know the way I should turn..."* Psalm 142:1-3

"Listen to my prayer, O God. Do not ignore my cry for help! Please listen and answer me, for I am overwhelmed by my troubles." Psalm 55:1-2

"Give your burdens to the Lord, and he will take care of you. He will not permit the godly to slip and fall." Psalm 55:22

Purpose Point: Circumstances, crises, chaos, conflicts, changes, challenges, and confrontations will force you to your knees. For instance, I never knew how to pray until tribulation hit my life. In fact, I didn't really start to read and study my Bible until devastation struck. Don't wait until a crisis hits to pray and study God's Word. Prepare yourself now! Learn to pray, attend church, get filled with His Word, obtain wisdom and knowledge, make godly connections, and cultivate godly friendships.

One of my favorite acronyms is P.U.S.H. – Pray Until Something Happens. To the contrary, you not only have to pray before it happens or until it happens, but you must also pray when it happens, and after it happens. You must P.U.S.H. and persevere in life to get everything God has for you. And even when you get it, continue to cover yourself and the manifested desire(s) in prayer to protect it. Push your way through…never let up! Fight with faith! Never stop praying!

Purpose Point: Remember, one misconception to prayer is that you have to pray a long time for your prayers to work. This is not entirely true. You can start off praying in small increments, and gradually work your way up to longer prayers, but it is not required. The key is persistency in your prayers – a never give up faith-filled attitude.

The key to *"Praying Until Something Happens"* is to praise and thank your way through. You may pray for something once as a means to make a formal request to God, but after you ask, the scripture says that you should apply your faith and believe that you have received, and begin to thank Him continuously for it.

"Don't worry about anything; instead, pray about everything. Tell God what you need, and thank him for all he has done. If you do this, you will experience God's peace, which is far more wonderful than the human mind can understand. His peace will guard your hearts and minds as you live in Christ Jesus." Philippians 4:6-7

If you have truly believed that you have received when you pray, why would you ask God again and again for it? For example, if you ask your parents for a car and they buy you the car you desire, would you keep asking and asking for the same car that you already have? No, you would be thanking your parents for it. In the same manner, when you initially make your prayer request to God, believe that God has already done it for you; then for every subsequent prayer thank Him and praise Him for the very thing(s) you prayed for. This is how faith works – you believe you have received even though you don't see it.

"Faith is the confidence that what we hope for will actually happen; it gives us assurance about things we cannot see." Hebrews 11:1

> **Point of Clarification - Praying for People**

- When someone crosses your mind, especially someone you haven't seen or heard from in a while, immediately pray for them. Don't wait. Additionally, if you know there is something you should pray for, or you know of a person you should pray for, pray as soon as possible before you forget. Incorporate prayer throughout your day. For example, you could pray on your lunch break, in the car or just silently in your heart.

- When you have to deal with or work with someone who is difficult or hard to get along with, pray for them. Pray for your enemies. *"Pray for the happiness of those who curse you. Pray for those who hurt you."* Luke 6:28

- When you get hurt or offended by someone, pray for them; this will help you to avoid and overcome bitterness and unforgiveness. Remember, God said do not get even with someone who hurts you, but instead pay them back with a blessing. The greatest blessing is praying genuinely and whole heartedly about the person, as well as exhibiting heartfelt emotion through tangible acts of kindness towards him/her. *"Don't repay evil for evil. Don't retaliate when people say unkind things about you. Instead, pay them back with a blessing. That is what God wants you to do, and he will bless you for it."* 1 Peter 3:9

- If you tell someone you are going to pray for them, really do it. Don't speak sympathetic cliches such as, "I will pray for you" or "I am praying for them" just because you think it is the right thing to say (unless you really mean it from the heart). Furthermore, don't simply write on the sympathy card, text, email or post, *"You are in my thoughts and prayers."* Really mean it and do it. Be a person of integrity. Say what you mean and mean what you say.

- Seize every opportunity to pray for others. If someone is down or discouraged, ask if you could pray for them or with them. Intercessory prayer is the most selfless and sacrificial prayer you could give. Jesus said, *"I also tell you this: If two of you agree down here on earth concerning anything you ask, my Father in heaven will do it for you. For where two or three gather together because they are mine, I am there among them."* Matthew 18:19 But remember, *don't pry, pray!* You don't have to know it all or know everything about the situation to pray for someone. God knows it all.

- Are you worried about someone, perhaps a friend or family member who is in trouble, unsaved, living the wrong way or has lost their way? Did you know that you can aid in their salvation, protection, recovery, deliverance, repentance, and success by praying for them and standing in the gap? For example, when a person is out of fellowship or separated from God, there is a gap between God and him/her. As indicated in the diagram below, point A represents God, and point B represents the person who is lost. The space or distance between point A and B is the gap. Interceding and praying on the person's behalf fills the gap and builds a connection for God to work in their life. There is no distance in prayer. Prayer can reach anyone, anywhere, anytime no matter how far away or spiritually distant from God.

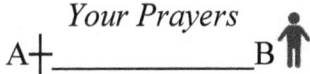

Purpose Point: Stand in the gap for your loved ones and others. Pray Acts 26:18 or this prayer: *Lord help* (insert person's name here) *– protect him, guide him, and direct him. Open his eyes and turn him from darkness to light, and from the power of Satan to you so that he may receive forgiveness of sins. Draw his heart closer to you. Give him the desire to change and do your will, and a desire to know you, serve you, and attend church. I come against anything or anyone that will keep him from serving you and fulfilling his purpose. Nothing is too hard for you, oh God. It is your will that no man perish. Thank you for saving and helping* (insert person's name here). *By faith, I call it done. In Jesus name, I pray. Amen"*

Pray continuously for the person and believe that God will bring him out and bring him through. Don't give up. Your prayers could very well save their life. Never underestimate the power of prayer. Remember, *"...The earnest prayer of a righteous person has great power and produces wonderful results."* James 5:16

"I looked for someone who might rebuild the wall of righteousness that guards the land.
I searched for someone to stand in the gap *in the wall so I wouldn't have to destroy the land, but I found no one."* Ezekiel 22:30

Purpose Point: If you fail to pray and stand in the gap for a person, their life could be destroyed because of their sins and poor choices. But their life could be saved because of your choice to pray. Pray for someone other than yourself.

> ### Point of Clarification - Mystery or not....

Have you ever heard the adage, *"God works in mysterious ways"*? Did you know that God reveals mysteries and secrets by granting knowledge to His children through prayer, divine wisdom, visions, and dreams?

Supporting Scriptures:

*"**But there is a God in heaven who reveals secrets**, and he has shown King Nebuchadnezzar what will happen in the future. Now I tell you your dream and the visions you saw as you lay on your bed."* Daniel 2:28

*"Then he explained to them, "**You have been permitted to understand the secrets of the Kingdom of Heaven**, but others have not. To those who are open to my teaching, more understanding will be given, and they will have an abundance of knowledge. But to those who are not listening, even what they have will be taken away from them."* Matthew 13:11-12

"No, the wisdom we speak of is the mystery of God—his plan that was previously hidden, even though he made it for our ultimate glory before the world began. But the rulers of this world have not understood it; if they had, they would not have crucified our glorious Lord...But it was to us that God revealed these things by his Spirit. **For his Spirit searches out everything and shows us God's deep secrets.** *No one can know a person's thoughts except that person's own spirit, and no one can know God's thoughts except God's own Spirit. And we have received God's Spirit (not the world's spirit), so we can know the wonderful things God has freely given us."* 1 Corinthians 2:7-12

God says, *"Call to Me and I will answer you, and **I will tell you great and mighty things, which you do not know.**"* Jeremiah 33:3 NASB

Purpose Point: Unanswered questions leads to unsolved mysteries and unresolved issues. Knowledge brings answers, and truth engenders revelation.

➢ Point of Clarification - Praying in Tongues

God's Holy Spirit lives in you and empowers you to live a Christian life. His Spirit reveals mysteries and enables you to pray perfectly. Essentially, there are two types of prayer: (1) praying with understanding in your respective language and (2) praying without understanding in tongues through the Holy Spirit.

The Holy Spirit is an essential part of the Trinity, the triune God or the three-part being of God – (1) God the Father, (2) God the Son (3) and God the Holy Spirit.

As stated in scripture, *"...the Holy Spirit fell upon all who had heard the message. The Jewish believers who came with Peter were amazed that the gift of the Holy Spirit had been poured out upon the Gentiles, too. And there could be no doubt about it, for they heard them speaking in tongues and praising God."* Acts 10:44-46

Sometimes we do not always know what to pray for. We know we should pray but are unsure about what to say and how to say it. This is where the Holy Spirit comes in, enabling us to pray in tongues – the ultimate prayer language – the perfect prayer, even though we may not understand what we are saying.

"And the Holy Spirit helps us in our weakness. For example, we don't know what God wants us to pray for. But the Holy Spirit prays for us with groanings that cannot be expressed in words. And the Father who knows all hearts knows what the Spirit is saying, for the Spirit pleads for us believers in harmony with God's own will. And we know that God causes everything to work together for the good of those who love God and are called according to his purpose for them." Romans 8:26-28

Purpose Point: Praying in the Holy Spirit is praying in your heavenly prayer language – the perfect will of God. Therefore, when you pray in the Holy Spirit, you don't have to worry or question if you are praying God's will or if God hears you.

Purpose Point: Second to the gift of salvation, the gift of the Holy Spirit is by far the best gift God gives. The Holy Spirit is a comforter, counselor, helper, and friend who is always with you. Essentially, the only requirement for receiving the Holy Spirit is to be saved. However, being filled with the Holy Spirit with the evidence of speaking in tongues requires additional steps. The Word of God says, *"...Each of you must repent of your sins and turn to God, and be baptized in the name of Jesus Christ for the forgiveness of your sins. Then you will receive the gift of the Holy Spirit."* Acts 2:38

How to receive and be filled with the Holy Spirit:
1. Confess with your mouth that Jesus is Lord and accept him as your Lord and Savior.
2. Believe in your heart that God raised Jesus from the dead (Romans 10:9).
3. Get baptized in the name of the Father, the Son, and the Holy Spirit (Matthew 28:19).
4. Receive prayer and the laying of the hands by a pastor, minister or elder of the church who believes in the gift of the Holy Spirit.
5. As the minister directs you, begin speaking. Let words flow from the depths of your belly as the Holy Spirit gives you utterance.

Jesus said, *"...you will receive power when the Holy Spirit comes on you; and you will be my witnesses..."* Acts 1:8 NIV

"And everyone present was filled with the Holy Spirit and began speaking in other languages, as the Holy Spirit gave them this ability." Acts 2:4

"Now when the apostles at Jerusalem heard that Samaria had received the word of God, they sent to them Peter and John, who came down and prayed for them that they might receive the Holy Spirit, for he had not yet fallen on them, but they had only been baptized in the name of the Lord Jesus. Then they laid their hands on them and they received the Holy Spirit." Acts 8:14-17 ESV

Purpose Point: Whichever Christian prayer language you choose, have confidence and faith in it. And most importantly, have confidence and faith in God. If you don't trust God or know God, you won't trust your prayers, regardless of the prayer type you choose.

Jesus said, *"But when the Father sends the Advocate as my representative—that is, the Holy Spirit—he will teach you everything and will remind you of everything I have told you."* John 14:26

"But you, dear friends, must build each other up in your most holy faith, pray in the power of the Holy Spirit..." Jude 1:20

Purpose Point: The Holy Spirit is a person (God); He has feelings just like you. *"And do not bring sorrow to God's Holy Spirit by the way you live. Remember, he has identified you as his own, guaranteeing that you will be saved on the day of redemption."* Ephesians 4:30

> **Point of Clarification – Miracle Maker**

Purpose Point: Praying for a miracle is not out of date. God still answers prayer by responding through miracles. God can do the impossible; nothing is too hard for Him despite what the doctors and experts say. He can cause the blind to see and the sick to be healed. He can save us from close calls (narrow escapes) and rescue us from dangerous situations. He can work through people to bring miracles or make "creative miracles" happen supernaturally through His mighty power. Note that a creative miracle is a sudden appearance or manifestation of something that did not previously exist, such as restored sight to the blind instantaneously.

If you are alive and breathing with a roof over your head, you are living a miracle. In fact, you are a miracle. Miracles are sometimes about perspective. For example, to a homeless person a miracle may be getting a hot meal or having a place to call home. The church volunteers may be the miracle to that homeless person as they prepare and serve him hot meals. Look for opportunities to be someone's miracle so that God can get the glory.

Jesus said, *"This is to my Father's glory, that you bear much fruit, showing yourselves to be my disciples."* John 15:8   See Galatians 5:22-23 to learn the fruit of God's Spirit which produces fruitful and favorable results in our lives and the lives of others.

Moreover, we may never know the miracles that God grants us every day; or how much He protects us. We may never know how He protected us from an accident that occurred minutes before or after, or how He protects us from lighting strikes, natural disasters, slips and falls, or a perpetuator who suddenly changed his mind about afflicting harm. God does the impossible in our lives every day. He can birth miracles from your mistakes, misfortunes, troubles, and trials. His miracles through His complete sovereignty are relative, relevant, and right on time.

"For he will order his angels to protect you wherever you go." Psalm 91:11

"For the angel of the LORD is a guard; he surrounds and defends all who fear him." Psalm 34:7

"There are different ways God works in our lives, but it is the same God who does the work through all of us...The Spirit gives special faith to another, and to someone he gives the power to heal the sick. He gives one person the power to perform miracles, and to another the gift to prophesy..." 1 Corinthians 12:6-10

"The LORD has established His throne in the heavens, and His sovereignty rules over all. Bless the LORD, you His angels, mighty in strength, who perform His word, obeying the voice of His word! Bless the LORD, all you His hosts, you who serve Him, doing His will. Bless the LORD, all you works of His, in all places of His dominion; Bless the LORD, O my soul!" Psalm 103:19-22 NASB

"Jesus went through all the towns and villages, teaching in their synagogues, proclaiming the good news of the kingdom and healing every disease and sickness." Matthew 9:35 NIV

Purpose Point: God is known for doing the impossible; assist Him in His efforts and be a miracle to someone. Miracles can happen anytime and anywhere; miracles happen in and through you. You are God sent and a godsend – a blessing and blessed.

➢ Point of Clarification - Prayer Prohibition

We live in a world today where prayer is no longer supported or allowed in some places and only considered appropriate in some instances such as during emergency or catastrophic events. In the early 1960s, state-sponsored prayer and the reading of the Bible were prohibited from public schools. In 1980, courts ruled to remove the Ten Commandments from public schools. Prior to this, it was common practice to pray corporately at school; however, now in most places outside of church, it is uncommon, unpopular, and even against the law to pray. The world now deems prayer to be "politically incorrect".

Purpose Point: The government (world) may pass laws and policies, but the law of God stands firm and supersedes man-made laws and ideologies. What is biblically correct is far more important than what is so called "politically correct". In fact, anything or anyone that speaks contrary to the Bible is inherently incorrect, unstable, and misguided, no matter what he/she claims to be.

"Their loyalty is divided between God and the world, and they are unstable in everything they do." James 1:8

"...We must obey God rather than any human authority." Acts 5:29

"The church must be reminded that it is not the master or the servant of the state, but rather the conscience of the state. It must be the guide and the critic of the state, and never its tool. If the church does not recapture its prophetic zeal, it will become an irrelevant social club without moral or spiritual authority." — Martin Luther King, Jr.

The world seeks to devalue the Christian Bible and eradicate Christian prayer, but we cannot allow them to take prayer and God's Word away from our hearts and home. Although the world downplays and undermines prayer, we cannot decrease or undercut prayer from our daily lives. **Prayer is paramount**, and without it chaos at its max would rule in our lives and the world as we know it. We have only been granted the protection, freedoms, and peace of mind on our homeland and in our homes because of the many prayers that have been prayed on behalf of the nation.

Without prayer, the world would be in a state of utter horror. When people turn away from God and prayer, engage in idol worship and wicked living, the health of the world soon deteriorates (as it is now) and the risk of chaos, crime and conflict grows exponentially, becomes imminent, and increasingly evident. Therefore, we must always pray.

I recently heard someone assert on the radio that the nation has enough prayer and that prayer is not lacking from our world. He was implying that something else should be done to fix the problem. I firmly disagree; you can NEVER have enough prayer – there is no such thing as too much prayer. In some cases, prayer should not be the only response, but it should be the main response; and in other cases, all you can do is pray. However, the real issue could be the lack of people who choose not to humble their hearts before God and seek Him. Many people pray, but very few humble themselves. It is only when people humble themselves (seek His face and turn from their wicked ways) AND pray, that our world can become a much better place.

It is important to know that just because you pray, does not mean you've humbled yourself. Many people pray in reactive mode, only when devastation strikes; they pray out of fear and torment, but they still want to continue in their own ways rather than turning away from them.

"Then if my people who are called by my name will humble themselves and pray and seek my face and turn from their wicked ways, I will hear from heaven and will forgive their sins and heal their land. I will listen to every prayer made in this place..." 2 Chronicles 7:14-15

"Now, therefore, thus says the Lord of hosts: Consider your ways." Haggai 1:5 ESV

Sin, hatred, rebellion, and disobedience *infects* our land, metastasizing devastation, division, and defilement; only repentance and prayer can *cure* it.

"So do not defile the land and give it a reason to vomit you out, as it will vomit out the people who live there now...So obey my instructions, and do not defile yourselves by committing any of these detestable practices that were committed by the people who lived in the land before you. I am the Lord your God." Leviticus 18:28-30

"Surely his salvation is near to those who honor him; our land will be filled with his glory." Psalm 85:9

Purpose Point: Pray for the government leaders of our nation such as the President, congressmen, judges, senators, governors, mayors, and all elected/appointed officials (1 Timothy 2:1-3). Vote for those who believe in doing what is right and possess Christian morals, convictions, and values. *"When there is moral rot within a nation, its government topples easily. But with wise and knowledgeable leaders, there is stability."* Proverbs 28:2

"When the godly are in authority, the people rejoice. But when the wicked are in power, they groan." Proverbs 29:2

> **Point of Clarification: Be careful what you ask for**

It is important when you pray to seek God in the situation for wisdom and study His Word to understand His will for your life. This will help to ensure that your desires line up with His desires and His will.

"If you need wisdom – if you want to know what God wants you to do – ask him, and he will gladly tell you. He will not resent your asking. But when you ask him, be sure that you really expect him to answer, for a doubtful mind is as unsettled as a wave of the sea that is driven and tossed by the wind. People like that should not expect to receive anything from the Lord. They can't make up their minds. They waver back and forth in everything they do." James 1:5-8

Sometimes, we pray for the things we <u>think</u> we want, but God knows we are not truly ready for them. He knows that the timing is not right or the very thing you desire is not right for you. Seeking understanding and trusting in the wisdom of God will help you to avoid a lot of mistakes and misfortune. For example, some girls think that they want a baby out of wedlock and without an established career, until they have to take care of the child. Some girls think they want to be with a boy forever until he starts cheating on them or abusing them. Some people think that they want the job and position/title of their dreams until they are completely worn out by all the hours they work which takes away from family and leisure time.

When you put your desires over God's desires, your desires could run wrong and wild. You might just receive the very thing you asked for, but with a dose of disappointment, devastation, and despair to go along with it.

"In the wilderness, their desires ran wild, testing God's patience in that dry land. So he gave them what they asked for, but he sent a plague along with it." Psalm 106:14-15

Purpose Point: I encourage you to trust God (His infinite wisdom) and know that His ways are always better than your ways.

"My thoughts are completely different from yours," says the Lord. And my ways are far beyond anything you could imagine. For just as the heavens are higher than the earth, so are my ways higher than your ways and my thoughts higher than your thoughts." Isaiah 55:8-9

> **Point of Clarification: New Level, New Devil**

Purpose Point: Sometimes when God wants to promote you, take you to a new level, and move you to a specific purpose, you may not experience a *friend or favor*, but a *foe*. You may not be greeted with a *treat*, but with a *trial* and/or *test*.

Take God's servant, David, for example. When God wanted to promote David, He allowed him to cross paths with Goliath, a Philistine giant who seemed too enormous for him to conquer. But God gave him the strength, wit, and fortitude to defeat him. David remained confident despite what it looked like – a giant over 9ft tall of mighty stature against a little boy with a sling shot. Throughout life you will have giants – problems that seem too big to overcome, but like David you can conquer the giants in your life if you just stay focused, confident, prayerful, and keep God first.

David had unwavering confidence in God and said, *"The Lord who saved me from the claws of the lion and the bear will save me from this Philistine! ..."* 1 Samuel 17:37

Purpose Point: Look at past victories to gain confidence for new challenges to generate new victories.

"David shouted in reply, "You come to me with a sword, spear, and javelin, but I come to you in the name of the Lord Almighty..." 1 Samuel 17:45

Purpose Point: Lean on and trust in God's mighty power and name, not your own.

"So David triumphed over the Philistine giant with only a stone and sling. And since he had no sword, he ran over and pulled Goliath's sword from its sheath. David used it to kill the giant and cut off his head." 1 Samuel 17:50-51

Purpose Point: When faced with challenges, sometimes we must refer back to what God has already done in our life and how He brought us through to gain confidence to overcome. Negative people and situations (devils and demons) may come to you with opposition and aggression but you must respond in the name of the Lord Almighty and use your s*Word* – the Word of God.

Purpose Point: Challenges can either cripple you or catapult you to your destiny.

Purpose Point: Everything is not meant to be prayed away, instead pray for strength and wisdom to endure and overcome. Oftentimes, who we become in the process is greater than who we currently are.

Purpose Point: With blessings and promotions come greater responsibilities and increased challenges. *"...From everyone who has been given much, much will be demanded; and from the one who has been entrusted with much, much more will be asked."* Luke 12:48 NIV

Purpose Point: Sometimes fear and anxiety creeps in when you are thinking about going to a higher level in God or a new level in life, such as accepting a new job, stepping out in your career, business, or ministry, embracing new relationships, and starting new endeavors.

I have learned that taking the following attitude in prayer helps to ease the burden of worry and indecision.

"Lord, if it is for me, bring it to pass; if not, block it. I will do my best and trust you with the rest." Remember, God goes before you and prepares the way. Do not fear or be discouraged. God is with you (Deuteronomy 31:8).

II. CONFIDENCE

When we pray, the Word of God says that we should come confidently and boldly before Him. We should not act as cowardly slaves but as humble princesses of God knowing that our Father is open to listen to our prayers and longs for His daughters to come to Him. You are a part of God's very own household – a princess of His castle. As the scripture states: *"...And we are God's household, if we keep up our courage and remain confident in our hope in Christ."* Hebrews 3:6

Therefore, you have a right to approach God with confidence and assurance. You have a right to remind Him of His promises. For example, if you need a car to get to work and school, pray: *"Lord, you said, you would supply all of my needs according to the riches of your glory in Christ Jesus, according to Philippians 4:19. I need a car. Thank you for providing me with the transportation I need."*

"So let us come boldly to the throne of our gracious God. There we will receive his mercy, and we will find grace to help us when we need it most." Hebrews 4:16

Purpose Point: Go boldly to God's throne in prayer and pray bold prayers. God is a big God and wants to do big things for you!

I think about the confidence and boldness men of God like Jabez and Hezekiah had when they prayed. Jabez outright asked God to bless him and enlarge his territory. Hezekiah prayed to God while on the verge of dying and reminded God of how faithful he had been to Him, and God granted him 15 more years to live. We may not always get the same answer, but a request is better than no request at all. When you pray boldly and confidently to God, you are in essence acknowledging the mighty power of God, a compliment to His sovereignty. Remember, oftentimes we have not because we ask not.

"There was a man named Jabez who was more honorable than any of his brothers. His mother named him Jabez because his birth had been so painful. He was the one who prayed to the God of Israel, "Oh, that you would bless me and expand my territory! Please be with me in all that I do, and keep me from all trouble and pain!" And God granted him his request."
1 Chronicles 4:9-10

"Hezekiah turned his face to the wall and prayed to the Lord, "Remember, Lord, how I have walked before you faithfully and with wholehearted devotion and have done what is good in your eyes." And Hezekiah wept bitterly. Then the word of the Lord came to Isaiah: "Go and tell Hezekiah, 'This is what the Lord...says, I have heard your prayer and seen your tears; I will add fifteen years to your life." Isaiah 38:2-5 NIV

"Now all glory to God, who is able, through his mighty power at work within us, to accomplish infinitely more than we might ask or think." Ephesians 3:20

Confidence is the by-product of your ever-increasing faith. You must believe, trust God, and have confidence in your prayers to increase its effectiveness. Faith and believing are essential for confidence. If you don't trust or believe in something or someone, how can you have confidence and assurance in their abilities?

*"So, you see, it is impossible to please God without **faith**. Anyone who wants to come to him must **believe** that there is a God and that he rewards those who sincerely seek him."*
Hebrews 11:6

*"Even strong young lions sometimes go hungry, but those who **trust in the LORD** will lack no good thing."* Psalm 34:10

"...Anyone who believes in him will not be disappointed..." Romans 10:11

Wow, **God is so confident within Himself** that He said that whoever believes in Him will not be disappointed. You must gain this kind of confidence when you pray and know that God will not disappoint you. And in order to build your confidence you must build your faith by meditating and hearing the promises of God. Hearing the Word of God increases your faith and increases your confidence.

"...faith comes by hearing, and hearing the Word of God." Romans 10:17 NKJV

"So you see, it isn't enough just to have faith. Faith that doesn't show itself by good deeds is no faith at all – it is dead and useless." James 2:17

*"...But if we look forward to something we don't have yet, **we must wait patiently and confidently**. And the Holy Spirit helps us in our distress..."* Romans 8:25-26

Purpose Point: Confidence <u>requires</u> patience. What you are believing God for may not manifest right away, but confident trust is being assured that it will come in this world and/or the next.

"Do not throw away this confident trust in the Lord, no matter what happens. *Remember the great reward it brings you! Patient endurance is what you need now, so you will continue to do God's will. Then you will receive all that he has promised."* Hebrews 10:35-36

"Yet I am confident I will see the LORD's goodness while I am here in the land of the living. Wait patiently for the LORD. Be brave and courageous. Yes, wait patiently for the LORD."
Psalm 27:13-14

Purpose Point: Praying in faith is praying in confidence. Believing that you will see the Lord's goodness in your situation and believing that God will respond despite your past and present, and trusting that He knows your future. The prayer of faith will heal the sick, save the lost and change your life.

Purpose Point: When you are confident, you are secure in God's love, promises and protection. And you are convinced that anything is possible with God.

*"**And I am convinced** that nothing can ever separate us from his love. Death can't, and life can't. The angels can't, and the demons can't. Our fears for today, our worries for tomorrow, and even the powers of hell can't keep God's love away..."* Romans 8:38

Jesus said, *"...Humanly speaking, it is impossible. But with God everything is possible."* Matthew 19:26

"And we can be confident that he will listen to us whenever we ask him for anything in line with his will. *And if we know he is listening when we make our requests, we can be sure that he will give us what we ask for."* 1 John 5:14

So what is God's will?

His will is His Word and His Word is His will. Read your Bible and you will discover His will – His desires, commands, character, promises and decrees.

Purpose Point: The opposite of an *attitude of self* is an *attitude of surrender*. When you surrender yourself to God, His will becomes your will, and His desires become your desires. Your prayers will then line up with His will for your life. Therefore, if God says that He will give you the desires of your heart, we can conclude that **God does answer some selfish prayers**, particularly those that are aligned with His will AND with the right motive.

*"Trust in the LORD and do good. Then you will live safely in the land and prosper. **Take delight in the LORD, and he will give you your heart's desires.** Commit everything you do to the LORD. Trust him, and he will help you."* Psalm 37:3-5

In reading your Bible, you will discover that salvation, healing/health, marriage, joy, peace, prosperity, provision, faith, love, giving, abundance, long life, wisdom, knowledge, and so much more are all in God's will. However, you must learn how to rightfully divide or handle the Word of truth when studying your Bible to determine God's will for your life. For example, the Bible says that it is better to marry than to burn with lust, but the Bible also says do not be unequally yoked (don't marry an unbeliever). So although marriage is God's will, marrying someone who is not a believer of Christ and who has not accepted Jesus as their Lord and Savior, is not. See supporting scriptures below.

"Do your best to present yourself to God as one approved, a worker who does not need to be ashamed and who correctly handles the word of truth." 2 Timothy 2:15 NIV

"But if they cannot control themselves, they should go head and marry. It is better to marry than to burn with lust." 1 Corinthians 7:9

"Do not team up with those who are unbelievers. How can goodness be a partner with wickedness? How can light live with darkness? What harmony can there be between Christ and the Devil. How can a believer be a partner with an unbeliever...?" 2 Corinthians 6:14-15

Purpose Point: When you know God's will, you can develop confidence and assurance when you pray. Confidence is assurance, the surety that God is able and faithful to His promises. Confidence comes when you are convinced that God is who He says He is, and that He can do what He says He can do.

Confidence is knowing that HE CAN and HE WILL.

*"They do not fear bad news; **they confidently trust the Lord** to care for them."* Psalm 112:7

*"The Lord has heard my plea; **the Lord will** answer my prayer."* Psalm 6:9

*"Take delight in the Lord, and **he will** give you your heart's desires."* Psalm 37:4

*"Give your burdens to the Lord, and **he will** take care of you. **He will** not permit the godly to slip and fall."* Psalm 55:22

*"**And this same God** who takes care of me **will supply** all your needs from his glorious riches, which have been given to us in Christ Jesus."* Philippians 4:19

*"And we can be confident that **he will listen** to us whenever we ask him for anything in line with his will. And if we know he is listening when we make our requests, we can be sure that **he will** give us what we ask for."* 1 John 5:14

Purpose Point: Confidence is also displayed when you know that you can do and endure anything through Him despite your weaknesses. Your confidence should not be in yourself or others but in God and what Christ did for you.

*"Not that I was ever in need, for I have learned how to get along happily whether I have much or little. I know how to live on almost nothing or with everything. I have learned the secret of living in every situation, whether it is with a full stomach or empty, with plenty or little. **For I can do everything with the help of Christ who gives me the strength I need.**"* Philippians 4:11-13

The Lord said, *"...My grace is sufficient for you, for my power is made perfect in weakness."* Paul, a servant of God, concluded that, *'Therefore I will boast all the more gladly about my weaknesses, so that Christ's power may rest on me.'"* 2 Corinthians 12:9 NIV

Purpose Point: Furthermore, confidence is not depending on what others can do, or even what you can do, but what God can do.

"...We put no confidence in human effort. Instead, we boast about what Christ Jesus has done for us." Philippians 3:3

"It is better to trust in the Lord than to put confidence in man. It is better to trust in the Lord than to put confidence in princes." Psalm 118:8-9 NJKV

There are times when we are not sure what God's will is as it relates to certain situations in our lives. Consequently, we lose confidence. But remember, His Word is His will. Find a promise in His Word and stand on it – believe that promise(s). For example, if you need healing in your body, find some healing scriptures (e.g. Jeremiah 30:17; Isaiah 53:4-5) in the Bible and meditate on those scriptures; pray God's Word as a way to remind Him of His promise. For example, *"Lord, you said in your Word that you will restore health and cure to me. Thank you for healing me."* During times of suffering, pain and tragedy, no child of God wants to believe that these things are His will. Confusion and despair kicks in and you want to believe that things will get better but the pain and suffering that you see and feel overshadows any ounce of faith. Sometimes, when you do not know what to pray for – or when you lose faith and grow numb to hope, just pray in tongues – your heavenly prayer language, or simply pray: *"Lord, help me, let your will be done."* **We can choose the right pathway but the seasons we experience and the roads we travel on that path is not always up to us. Trust God and His will for your life, no matter how difficult.**

"Father, if you are willing, please take this cup of suffering away from me. Yet I want your will to be done, not mine." Luke 22:42

Moreover, it is important to know that God never fails, regardless of sickness, death, lack and tragedy. Victory is yours when you trust and have confidence in Him. It won't be easy to remain confident in God when pain, loss, disappointment, devastation and suffering seem to prevail, but in the end all pain is temporary. A brighter day will soon come either in this world or the next – heaven is our eternal home and there will be nothing missing, nothing broken, nothing loss – no pain, no sickness, no despair, only glory forever and ever with God and our saved loved ones.

Purpose Point: It takes a high level of maturity to be confident in Christ, especially when things are bad all around us. If you are only focused on the outward appearance, external circumstances, and material things, it will be difficult to trust the eternal source, Jesus Christ, when bad things happen in your life. You must have faith and begin to focus on Jesus for peace to be released. The Bible says Jesus will, *"...keep in perfect peace all who trust in you, whose thoughts are fixed on you! Trust in the Lord always, for the Lord God is the eternal Rock."* Isaiah 26:3-4

Purpose Point: When bad things happen in your life, you must be mature enough to keep your trust in God, maintain the faith and your confidence. You must be the queen He has qualified you for and mature enough to pray/believe His Word, i.e. *"No weapon formed against me will prosper; every tongue that rises against me will be condemned"* (Isaiah 54:17) while accepting *"Lord, let your will be done"*. No matter what happens, you will always win with God by your side even when it seems as though you have failed or the circumstances around you have faltered. Greater is He (God) that is in you than anything or anyone in the world (1 John 4:4).

Purpose Point: Keeping the faith and having confidence at all times, even in the most difficult seasons of life, can be challenging. But you must trust God and refuse to blame Him.
*"...asking God, the glorious Father of our Lord Jesus Christ, to give you spiritual wisdom and insight so that you might grow in your knowledge of God. **I pray that your hearts will be flooded with light <u>so that you can understand the confident hope he has given</u> to those he called—his holy people who are his rich and glorious inheritance.** I also pray that you will*

understand the incredible greatness of God's power for us who believe him. This is the same mighty power that raised Christ from the dead and seated him in the place of honor at God's right hand in the heavenly realms. Now he is far above any ruler or authority or power or leader or anything else—not only in this world but also in the world to come. God has put all things under the authority of Christ and has made him head over all things for the benefit of the church. And the church is his body; it is made full and complete by Christ, who fills all things everywhere with himself." Ephesians 1:17-23

III. COMMITMENT

Commitment is constant communication with God. It's communicating with God through the good times and bad times, praising and thanking Him when you are happy and when you are sad, and setting aside time daily for Him despite your busy schedule.

Commitment is continuing in the faith even when things are not going well in your life…in times of pain, lack, sickness, and sorrow. Even in these times, you should love God and not blame Him; praise Him, and not persecute Him; commit to Him and not contend with Him. It would be unfaithful of you to only love God when things are going well and give up on Him when things get tough. You must be COMMITTED as He is committed—love Him and keep praying no matter what. *"Are any among you suffering?* **They should keep on praying about it***. And those who have reason to be thankful should* **continually** *sing praises to the Lord."* James 5:13

Purpose Point: Commitment is remaining faithful. Just like a husband and wife should remain committed to each other and their vows (i.e. I'll be true to you through good times and bad times, for better or worse through sickness and in heath until death do us part), we should also remain committed to God and His ways.

God remains committed to you, even when you do wrong. When you fall short or do not always obey, God still loves you, grants you mercy, gives you grace and remains faithful to you, despite you being unfaithful to Him. If He can do it for you and me, let's do it for Him…let's remain committed…let's remain faithful.

"If we are unfaithful, he remains faithful, for he cannot deny himself." 2 Timothy 2:13

Point of Clarification: God Knows and Understands

Many may argue that God is not faithful or committed. They may say things like, "If God is faithful, why would he make me sick…why won't he heal me or my loved one…why did he allow this tragedy to happen...why should I be committed to God, when he does not seem to be committed to me?"

I do not profess to have the answer for everything but what I do know is that God loves His children and will not harm or inflict ill will towards us, just like you would not harm or inflict ill will towards the people you love. The devil is the author of sickness, disease, confusion, fear, evil, destruction, despair, and turmoil (John 10:10). God is good (Mark 10:18).

Trust in the fact that God knows the end from the beginning, and that His thoughts are higher than your thoughts and His ways are higher than your ways (Isaiah 55:9; Isaiah 46:10).

We must trust God to do it His way – in His perfect timing…trusting that He sees the *pitfalls, problems, and possibilities* that we cannot.

For example, God may see the possibility of someone becoming saved and profoundly changed because of someone's untimely death. Another example would be a woman who is crazy in love with a man and wants to marry him; however, God sees the secret areas of his life that he hides and conceals – the lust, cheating, anger, and deceit. As a result, God blocks the woman from marrying him by allowing him to reject her or exposing his lies. The woman may in turn become angry with God and blame Him for her unhappiness. Behind the scenes God knew the devastating outcome and only wanted to protect her. So, you see, it is important to trust God; we may never know the 'Why' but we can absolutely trust in the 'Who' (God), who knows the 'What' – who knows all things.

Purpose Point: Blaming and resenting God should never be an option.

Purpose Point: Rejection is sometimes your protection – a denial to protect you from a trial, and a "No" to protect you from the things you just don't kNOw. Additionally, prayers delayed are not always prayers denied.

Minute Memoir: As I look back over my life, I see the full effect of God's faithfulness. Both the big and little things that I prayed for years ago have all come to past in my life. While going through it, it seemed as though it took forever, but eventually God gave me everything I asked for. He will do the same for you if you stay committed to the faith! Furthermore, when you look at past victories it gives you faith for the future. When you learn from your mistakes, you are more equipped to handle future challenges; and when you overcome a trial it makes you stronger and grows you up. His timing is always perfect and profound as promised.

Commitment is praying continually, remaining in constant communication with God consistently.

"Pray at all times and on every occasion in the power of the Holy Spirit. Stay alert and be persistent in your prayers for all Christians everywhere." Ephesians 6:18

"Don't worry about anything; instead, pray about everything. Tell God what you need, and thank him for all he has done. If you do this, you will experience God's peace, which is far more wonderful than the human mind can understand. His peace will guard your hearts and minds as you live in Christ Jesus." Philippians 4:6-7

Purpose Point: A committed person is a constant person. A person who is constantly constant is patient, persistent, and perseveres perpetually.

*"…**But I am in constant prayer** against the wicked and their deeds…"* Psalm 141:5

*"But I will call on God, and the Lord will rescue me. **Morning, noon, and night I plead aloud** in my distress, and the Lord hears my voice. He rescues me and keeps me safe from the battle*

waged against me, even though many still oppose me. God, who is king forever, will hear me and will humble them." Psalm 55:16-19

*"Lord, we love to obey your laws; our heart's desire is to glorify your name. **All night long I search for you; earnestly I seek for God.**"* Isaiah 26:8-9

- A committed person has a continual, constant, and consistent communing with God.

    *"Search for the Lord and for his strength, **continually seek him.**"* Psalm 105:4

- A committed person lives a life of fellowship through a quality relationship with God.

- A committed person keeps on praying, keeps on believing by faith, keeps on worshiping and praising God, and keeps on seeking Him. This is what makes prayer truly effective.

"Keep on asking, and you will be given what you ask for. Keep on looking, and you will find. Keep on knocking, and the door will be opened. For everyone who asks, receives. Everyone who seeks, finds. And the door is opened to everyone who knocks. You parents—if your children ask for a loaf of bread, do you give them a stone instead? Or if they ask for a fish, do you give them a snake? Of course not! If you sinful people know how to give good gifts to your children, how much more will your heavenly Father give good gifts to those who ask him."
Matthew 7:7-11

Fasting & Prayer – Consecrating your spirit, soul, and body

What does it mean to fast? Essentially, fasting is denying your body food or restraining from certain foods. The purpose of fasting involves maximizing your senses to hear from God and improving your level of spirituality by seeking God and devoting more time for Him. Doing this, amplifies your ability to hear from God and feel His presence.

Many people view fasting as a strict diet that involves denying your body food for the purposes of detoxifying, losing weight or preparing for a medical procedure; however, the true meaning and sole motive for fasting should be to deny your body so that you can draw closer to God. Fasting without any spiritual component is simply dieting or food prohibition.

The key to fasting is to deny yourself something that you like; to deny yourself the things you enjoy and spend most of your time doing. When you deny yourself, you deny the distractions and deterrents in your life. Doing this, frees up your mind and unclogs your ears of all the interferences, indulgences and interests that often stifle your spiritual growth and your relationship with God. Fasting is about real sacrifice, truly giving up something that causes you discontent and discomfort to draw closer to God. Whenever you fast, God wants to know that you are really doing it for Him, and not just to achieve a selfish, superficial, or side benefit. The weight loss, detoxification, refreshing, and spiritual awakening are simply byproducts of the immense desire to connect with God on a new level and in a new way – to love on Him and to grow in Him. Evaluate your motives and fast with the right heart.

The Lord says, *"...when you fasted and mourned in the summer and in early autumn, was it really for me that you were fasting? And even now in your holy festivals, aren't you eating and drinking just to please yourselves?"* Zechariah 7:5-6

Additionally, many believe that fasting only involves giving up food, however, fasting involves so much more. A person can also fast from TV, social media, gaming, hobbies, hanging out with friends, shopping, or anything of pleasure that they spend most of their time doing. However, a sincere and effective fast will involve both, giving up food as well as those things you spend most of your time doing so you can fully engulf yourself in prayer, setting a flame to God's heart. If you only fast from food, for example, but still spend most of your day watching TV and talking on the phone without praying, then this is not a sincere or effective fast, but more of a diet instead. Shut it off, shut it down, shut it out, and seclude yourself with God.

"...They come to the Temple every day and seem delighted to hear my laws. You would almost think this was a righteous nation that would never abandon its God. They love to make a show of coming to me and asking me to take action on their behalf. 'We have fasted before you!' they say. Why aren't you impressed? We have done much penance, and you don't even notice it!' I will tell you why! **It's because you are living for yourselves even while you are fasting***..."* Isaiah 58:2-3

Purpose Point: Fasting must be sincere, deliberate, and intentional. You must set your day and set your mind to deny yourself and spend time with God. If you approach fasting half-heartedly, you will lose heart and veer off.

Purpose Point: Fasting should always be coupled with prayer. **You can pray and not fast, but you should never fast and not pray.** Some issues in your life can only be tackled or overcome with prayer AND fasting.

"But this kind of demon won't leave unless you have prayed and fasted." Matthew 17:21

Food fasts can be *partial* where you only eat certain foods or *full fasts* where you do not eat any food.

Jesus did a full fast for 40 days and nights; he ate nothing. But it is important to note that everyone should be led by the Spirit because not everyone is called to endure lengthy full fasts as Jesus was.

"Then <u>Jesus was led</u> out into the wilderness by the Holy Spirit to be tempted there by the Devil. For forty days and forty nights he ate nothing and became very hungry. Then the Devil came and said to him, 'If you are the Son of God, change these stones into loaves of bread.' But Jesus told him, 'No! The Scriptures say, People need more than bread for their life; they must feed on every word of God.'" Matthew 4:1-4

Purpose Point: Oftentimes, when you are not anointed, led, or called to do something, you won't possess the wit or strength to do it, or the ability to follow-through. You will grow incompetent, impatient, and frustrated through the process.

Purpose Point: Fasting is not easy. When you become tempted to quit, lose faith, lose hope or tempted to eat that piece of chicken, declare the Word of God and stand on His promises like Jesus did when he fasted and was tempted. Stay committed to fasting and prayer and believe that it will catapult you to your breakthrough. And if you fail while fasting by eating something you should not eat, repent and get back on track.

Now let's discuss the partial fast. The most popular partial fast is a 21-day (3 week) Daniel Fast where only fruits, vegetables, nuts, legumes, whole grains, and water are allowed.

"When this vision came to me, I, Daniel, had been in mourning for three weeks. All that time I had eaten no rich food or meat, had drunk no wine, and had used no fragrance oils."
Daniel 10:2-3

Below is the Daniel fast list which tells you what you can eat and what you should not eat while on the Daniel Fast.

Important: If you have a medical condition, consult your doctor before beginning any food fast.

The Daniel Fast Food List

Foods to Eat on the Daniel Fast

- **All fruit** – fresh, frozen, dried, juiced, or canned
- **All vegetables** – fresh, frozen, dried, juiced, or canned
- **All whole grains** – amaranth, barley, brown rice, oats, quinoa, millet, and whole wheat
- **All nuts & seeds** – almonds, cashews, macadamia nuts, peanuts, pecans, pine nuts, walnuts, pumpkin seeds, sesame seeds, and sunflower seeds; unsweetened almond milk. Nut butters are also included such as peanut and almond butter
- **All legumes** – canned or dried; black beans, black eyed peas, cannellini beans, garbanzo beans (chickpeas), great northern beans, kidney beans, lentils, pinto beans, and split peas
- **All quality oils** – avocado, coconut, grapeseed, olive, peanut, sesame, and walnut
- **Beverages** – distilled water, filtered water, and spring water
- **Other** – unsweetened almond milk, coconut milk, rice milk, or soymilk; herbs, spices, salt, pepper, seasonings, soy products, vinegar and tofu

Foods to Avoid on the Daniel Fast

- **All meat & animal products** – Poultry, pork, fish, and beef - chicken, turkey, bacon, buffalo, eggs, lamb, duck
- **All dairy products** – butter, cheese, cream, milk, and yogurt
- **All sweeteners** – sugar, nectar, artificial sweeteners, brown rice syrup, cane juice, honey, molasses, raw sugar, syrups, and stevia
- **All leavened bread & yeast** – baked goods and Ezekiel bread (if it contains yeast and honey)

- **All refined & processed food products** – artificial flavorings, chemicals, food additives, preservatives, white flour, and white rice
- **All deep-fried foods** – corn chips, French fries, and potato chips
- **All solid fats** – lard, margarine, and shortening
- **Beverages** – alcohol, carbonated drinks, coffee, energy drinks, herbal tea

Source: https://ultimatedanielfast.com/ultimate-daniel-fast-food-guidelines/

Read the food labels to determine ingredients.

Purpose Point: Search the internet to discover Daniel Fast recipes to help you create healthy, robust, and nutritious meals.

Be confident in the fact that God hears…God answers.

"And the man said to me, "O Daniel, greatly loved of God, listen carefully to what I have to say to you. Stand up, for I have been sent to you…then he said …Since the first day you began to pray for understanding and to humble yourself before your God, your request has been heard in heaven. I have come in answer to your prayer." Daniel 10:11-12

Additional Prayer and Fasting Tips:

1. Don't announce to everyone that you are fasting just to be recognized and looked highly upon. A fast should only be between you and God.

"And when you fast, don't make it obvious, as the hypocrites do, who try to look pale and disheveled so people will admire them for their fasting. I assure you, that is the only reward they will ever get. But when you fast, comb your hair and wash your face. Then no one will suspect you are fasting, except your Father, who knows what you do in secret. And your Father, who knows all secrets, will reward you." Matthew 6:16-18

2. Avoid negative influences and behaviors

Engaging in negative behaviors and mistreating others during fasting and prayer will get you nowhere. The purpose of fasting is to propel you into your purpose and destiny by receiving divine guidance and direction from God; and to empower and equip you to deny the negative urges, thoughts, behaviors, and habits. Yield to the fruit of the Spirit – love, peace, meekness, patience, gentleness, faithfulness, and self-control.

"What good is fasting when you keep on fighting and quarrelling? This kind of fasting will never get you anywhere with me." Isaiah 58:4

Purpose Point: Fasting involves humbling your heart before God. The Bible also refers to fasting as doing what is right, helping others and maintaining self-control (Isaiah 58:5-8).

In other words, you can fast all day long – many days and many nights, but if you treat people badly, fasting will not work for you.

As a result of fasting (with a humble heart and a gracious spirit) the Bible says:

"Then your salvation will come like the dawn, and your wounds will quickly heal. Your godliness will lead you forward, and the glory of the Lord will protect you from behind. Then when you call, the Lord will answer. 'Yes, I am here,' he will quickly reply." Isaiah 58:8-9

Purpose Point: When you truly commit yourself to fasting it will strengthen you to break old habits and give you the power to refrain from negative behaviors.

3. Keep a journal, pray specifically

Purpose Point: Although your primary goal of fasting is to get closer to God and enhance your ability to hear from Him, keep a journal of what you are believing God for and pray specifically about those things during the fast. Preferably, write down your requests (Habakkuk 2:2) and make a mental note.

In the space below, write down the things you are believing God for that are aligned with His will (e.g. healing for you or others, the salvation of a loved one, making a better grade, getting accepted into college, receiving a promotion or getting a job, financial increase, etc.).

_____
_____
_____
_____
_____
_____

4. Consider making fasting a lifestyle, something you do regularly to seek and grow closer to God. For example, you may choose to fast one day a week —or on some days you may fast lunch and instead pray and study your Bible during your lunch time. You may also choose to seek God early before fasting breakfast. Be flexible with fasting yet committed to the process.

5. Seek God early

Purpose Point: It is truly an honor to God when we put Him first and seek Him early before the start of our day. Even if you are not fasting, God is pleased when you acknowledge Him before beginning your day. Seeking God first shows that He is priority in your life.

"Listen to my voice in the morning, Lord. **Each morning I bring my requests to you and wait expectantly.**" Psalm 5:3

*"I pray with all my heart; answer me, Lord! I will obey your principles. I cry out to you; save me, that I may obey your decrees. **I rise early, before the sun is up**; I cry out for help and put my hope in your words. I stay awake through the night, thinking about your promise. In your faithful love, O Lord, hear my cry; in your justice, save my life."* Psalm 119:145-149

*"So don't worry about having enough food or drink or clothing. Your heavenly Father already knows all your needs, and he will give you all you need from day to day if you live for him and **make the Kingdom of God your primary concern.**"* Matthew 6:32-33

*"**But seek first his kingdom and his righteousness**, and all these things will be given to you as well. Therefore do not worry about tomorrow, for tomorrow will worry about itself. Each day has enough trouble of its own."* Matthew 6:33-34 NIV

Purpose Point: Rather than bringing requests to God each morning, sometimes a simple, *"Good Morning, Lord...I love you"* will do.

6. Commit to studying God's Word. Be persistent in discovering His will for your life and draw from His strength. Feed on His Word by allowing it to penetrate your heart and listen as God speaks to you through His Word. Focus! Rather than thinking about food, hunger after God instead – His will, ways, and wisdom. When you become truly serious about seeking God and hearing from Him, the hunger pains will eventually dissipate.

Consider Jesus and his attitude about food. *"Meanwhile his disciples urged him, 'Rabbi, eat something.' But he said to them, 'I have food to eat that you know nothing about.' Then his disciples said to each other, 'Could someone have brought him food?' 'My food,' said Jesus, 'is to do the will of him who sent me and to finish his work.'"* John 4:31-34 NIV

Purpose Point: Food is important for sustenance and nourishment, but God's Word and the Bread of Life is essential for salvation.

"Jesus replied, 'I am the bread of life.'" John 6:35

REMEMBER:
If you have a medical condition,
consult your doctor before beginning any food fast.
Never go beyond what you are called or led to do or overdo partial or full food fasts that are not conducive to your health. Drink plenty of water while fasting.

THE LORD'S PRAYER
*A Model Prayer Guide – HOW TO PRAY

Jesus said, 1. Pray like this 2. Our Father 3. in heaven, 4. May your name be honored 5. May your kingdom come soon, May your will be done here on earth, just as it is in heaven. 6. Give us our food for today. 7. And forgive us our sins, just as we have forgiven those who have sinned against us. 8. And don't let us yield to temptation, but deliver us from the evil one: 9. For yours is the kingdom and the power, and the glory, forever. 10. Amen." Matthew 6:9-13

1. Pray like this: – Jesus provides an essential guide for prayer which explains how we should approach God when we pray. He also gives important aspects to include in our prayers. Many pray the Lord's Prayer verbatim, word for word, which is okay, but this prayer can also be used as a personal guide for adapting our prayers to the Lord's prayer in a similar manner.

Essentially, your prayers should include: Greeting your great God with love, honor and admiration (thanksgiving/worship); acknowledging God for who He is and lifting up His kingdom (praise); yielding to His will for your life and to His will for the world (surrender); seeking provision, forgiveness and protection (requests), and celebrating His kingdom (praise) – for thine is the kingdom and the power and the glory forever.

Therefore, the majestic formula for prayer is:

Thanksgiving + Worship + Praise + Surrender + Requests + Praise = Prayer

So, you see, *'Requests'* are just a small fraction of the formula. Prayer is comprised mostly of Thanksgiving, Worship, and Praise. Therefore, your prayers should begin with thanksgiving and worship, and end with praise with a little extra praise in between. *'Requests'* should only make up a small portion of your prayer(s).

In this way, you are loving God for who He is, and not just for what He can do. When you seek God's kingdom first, everything else – the requests, the desires of your heart, will be added to you (Matthew 6:33) if they are aligned with His will and the promises found in His Word. For example, if someone lives in a bad neighborhood and they pray to God for protection, it is God's will to protect them because His Word, the Bible, promises that "no weapon formed against you will prosper" (Isaiah 54:17) and that He gives His angels charge over you (Psalm 91:11).

On the other hand, if you pray that you get a "B" in class when you know that you've missed several assignments because you refused or forgot to complete the work, then this is probably too far-fetched. The Bible says, *"God cannot be mocked. A man reaps what he sows."* Galatians 6:7 Therefore, if you sow missed assignments and poor performance, you will reap bad grades.

2. <u>Our Father (Praise/Thanksgiving)</u> – During this portion of the prayer, release all your worries, fears, disappointments and hurts to God. Embrace the love of God. Envision your heavenly Father sitting on His throne in front of you, full of love and compassion. Remember, a father's job is to protect his family and meet their needs.

When you pray, begin by acknowledging God for who He is to you…Abba, Father, Daddy God i.e. **"Heavenly Father I come to you in prayer…."**

Purpose Point: Perceiving and visualizing God as your loving Father instead of some distant, condemning, angry, cosmic, and supernatural being gives you a sense of confidence and boldness when you pray.

"So you have not received a spirit that makes you fearful slaves. Instead, you received God's Spirit when he adopted you as his own children. **Now we call him, "Abba, Father."***
Romans 8:15

*"...He prayed that, if it were possible, the awful hour awaiting him might pass him by. **'Abba, Father'**, **he said, 'everything is possible for you.** Please take this cup of suffering away from me. Yet I want your will, not mine."* Mark 14:35-36

"In his goodness he chose to make us his own children by giving us his true word. And we, out of all creation, became his choice possession." James 1:18

"Cast your cares on the LORD and he will sustain you; he will never let the righteous be shaken." Psalm 55:22 NIV

"Enter his gates with thanksgiving; go into his courts with praise. Give thanks to him and bless his name. For the Lord is good..." Psalm 100:4-5

*Examples of Thanksgiving and Powerful Praise:

1. Father, I thank you; you are the everlasting God, the Creator of the world.
2. Father, I am grateful for everything you have done, and continue to do.
3. Father, I lift you up and magnify your name.
4. You are an awesome God.
5. You are King of kings and Lord of lords, the Alpha, and the Omega.
6. You are the beginning and the end - and everything in between.
7. Lord, I bless your glorious name forever.
8. I honor you my sovereign King.
9. Nothing is too hard for you.
10. Mighty are your works.
11. You are the great "I AM", the God of Abraham, Isaac, and Jacob.
12. The Lord Almighty, the Creator of all things, reigns forever.
13. You are my Lord and Savior; thank you for dying on the cross for my sins.
14. Lord, use me for your glory. I give my life to you, the Great God.
15. You are my everything, the delight of my heart.
16. Nothing or no one is greater than you; all dominion, glory, and praise belongs to you forever.

Purpose Point: The greatest thanks you can give God is to live as you should.

"As I learn your righteous regulations, I will thank you by living as I should! I will obey your decrees. Please don't give up on me." Psalm 119:7-8

*Examples of Words of Worship:

1. *"You are worthy, our Lord and God, to receive glory and honor and power, for you created all things, and by your will they were created and have their being."* Revelations 4:11 NIV

2. You are my everything…the mere breath that I breathe. I cannot do anything without you.
3. *"Holy, holy, holy are you the Lord God Almighty, the one who was, and is, and is to come."* (Revelation 4:8)
4. I worship you in spirit and in truth.
5. Lord, I Love you; you are the beat of my heart.
6. You are the one and only true and living God.
7. Lord, I am desperate for you; I long for you. I can't live without you. You are my everything.

Purpose Point: The greatest expression of worship is obedience.

3. <u>Which art in heaven</u> **(Praise/Worship)** – Acknowledge God for where He is, the heavenly realm of glory (His home), realizing that all blessings come from heaven (i.e. *"Heavenly Father **which art in Heaven** I come to you in prayer; you are an awesome God. Father, thank you for everything. Your throne and kingdom reigns forever. Mighty are your works. You are king of Kings and lord of Lords. I exalt your name. Lord you mean so much to me, I am nothing without you…"*)

Supporting Scripture: *"Whatever is good and perfect comes to us from God above, who created all heaven's lights…"* James 1:17

4. <u>Hallowed be thy name</u> **(Praise/Worship)** – Give respect to God's name, honoring His holiness and sovereignty. Praise God for who He is (i.e. ***I praise your Holy name, Yahweh, Jehovah, the Great I AM,*** *the God of Abraham, Isaac and Jacob…"*)

Supporting Scriptures: God said, *"'I AM THE ONE WHO ALWAYS IS.' Just tell them, 'I AM has sent me to you.' God also said, 'Tell them, 'THE LORD, the God of your ancestors – the God of Abraham, the God of Isaac, and the God of Jacob – has sent me to you.' This will be my name forever; it has always been my name, and it will be used throughout all generations.'"* Exodus 3:14-15

"The Lord says, 'I will rescue those who love me. I will protect those who trust in my name. When they call on me, I will answer. I will be with them in trouble…'" Psalm 91:14-15

"As your name deserves, O God, you will be praised to the ends of the earth…" Psalm 48:10

5. <u>Thy kingdom come, thy will be done on earth as it is in heaven</u> **(Surrender)** - Pray that God's will prevail over your will and the will of your loved ones. Pray that His will be done in all things – overshadowing and overcoming everything that works in contrary to His will (i.e. *"There is nothing too hard for you, and nothing shall be impossible with you. May your will reign on earth as it is in heaven. May your will reign in my life and the lives of my loved ones. May my selfish desires decrease so that your will and desires can increase in me. Let your light shine across the world and use me as a vessel to bring your will to past. Save, deliver and set free. I call in souls from the north, south, east and west. For it is your will that no man perish."*

Supporting Scripture: *"Father, if you are willing, please take this cup of suffering away from me. **Yet I want your will to be done, not mine.**"* Luke 22:42

6. <u>Give us this day our daily bread</u> **(Requests)** – Pray to God for your special needs and provision, while declaring and decreeing His promises (i.e. *"Lord, I pray for wisdom, favor, protection and direction. I ask Lord, that you bless me with a good paying job to support myself and family* (need/motive). **"You said"** *in your word that you shall supply all of my needs according to your riches and glory by Christ Jesus* (promise) *Philippians 4:19. Thank you for meeting my every need, and guiding me to the job that you have for me* (aligning your need to His will).

Purpose Point: Trust God daily to meet your needs.

Supporting Scripture: *"So don't worry about having enough food or drink or clothing. Why be like the pagans who are so deeply concerned about these things? Your heavenly Father already knows all your needs, and he will give you all you need from day to day if you live for him and make the Kingdom of God your primary concern. So don't worry about tomorrow, for tomorrow will bring its own worries. Today's trouble is enough for today."* Matthew 6:31-34

Discover, Declare, Decree daily

a) Discover – Discover God's promises and purposes through daily reading of His Word – the Bible.

b) Declare – Declare God's promises and what He says about you (affirm who you are in Christ)–speak it by faith, in an enthusiastic and confident manner. Remind God of what He promised you *(i.e. Lord you said that by your stripes I am healed.)* Isaiah 53:4-5.
Pray the promise – pray God's Word. Take authority over the devil; speak the Word and promises of God against the enemy when he comes against you.

c) Decree – Make a royal command that is backed by the authority of God's Word – make it law, the final say, in your life.

"I tell you the truth, whatever you forbid on earth will be forbidden in heaven, and whatever you permit on earth will be permitted in heaven." Matthew 18:18

"May all the kings of the earth praise you, LORD, when they hear what you have decreed." Psalm 138:4 NIV

(c2) Detail (write) – Whenever a law is established or decreed it is written to cement its power. Therefore, write the vision down and make it plain (Habakkuk 2:2). Jot down, highlight and detail scriptures and affirmations that reflect the promises of God for your particular need – and meditate on them daily (make it personal). Use index (note) cards or 'stick it notes' to record and remind yourself of God's Word. Be specific and keep a journal of your decrees, affirmations, challenges, goals, prayer requests, successes, and testimonies – which serves as a reference for how God brought you through and reminds you of His promises and answered prayer. Additionally, when God speaks to you or reveals Himself to you through dreams, visions, or His still small voice, write that down as well.

DISCOVER God's goodness, THINK positive thoughts, WRITE your vision down (decrees, goals, desires, and dreams) and SPEAK your victories into existence!
You have already won, simply declare it!
Discover, Declare and Decree…all in the name of Jesus.

Supporting Scripture: *"Then Jesus told her, 'I Am the Messiah!'"* John 4:26

Jesus declared who he was. You must also declare who you are!

Declarations of Who You Are in Christ:

1. I am valuable – my price is far above rubies; God bought me with a high price. I am worth waiting for. 1 Corinthians 6:20; Proverbs 31:10
2. I am fearfully and wonderfully made. Psalm 139:14
3. I am not abandoned or rejected; the Lord accepts me and holds me close. Psalm 27:10
4. I am an heir – a princess/queen. Galatians 3:29; Romans 8:17
5. My body is the temple of God. I am a new person in Christ. 1 Corinthians 6:19; 2 Cor. 5:17
6. I am saved in Christ, born again, sealed by God's Holy Spirit and possess eternal life. Roman 10:9, John 3:3-5. Ephesians 1:13; I John 5:11-13; John 3:16
7. Heaven will be my home when I die. 2 Corinthians 5: 1; John 12:1-3
8. God has set me apart from the world and He will protect me. Deuteronomy 7:6; Psalm 91
9. God loves me. He is my heavenly father. John 3:16; Romans 8:15
10. Nothing can separate me from God's love. Romans 8:31-39
11. I do not have to be ashamed; I am free from condemnation. Romans 8:1; John 3:18
12. God listens to me when I pray. 1 John 5: 14-15
13. God has great plans for me. Jeremiah 29:11
14. God has given me the power to overcome the enemy. Luke 10:19
15. God has given me His promises and blessings. Roman 8:32; 2 Peter 1:4
16. I have the Holy Spirit dwelling in me to help, guide, and lead me. Romans 8:14; Romans 8:9; I am redeemed from the curse of the law. Galatians 3:13
17. I can overcome anything because greater is He that is in me. 1 John 5:4-5; 1 John 4:4
18. I do not have to be controlled by any sin or habit. Romans 6:14
19. I have the commands of God written on my heart to obey them. Romans 2:15
20. I can do all things through Christ. Philippians 4:13
21. I am healed by the stripes of Jesus. Isaiah 53:5
22. No weapon formed against me will prosper. Isaiah 54:17
23. I have the power to get wealth. Deuteronomy 8:18

7. Forgive us our sins as we forgive others **(Requests)**– Ask God for forgiveness from all your sins - known and unknown. Forgive those who have wronged you. Pray for them (i.e. ***"Lord I confess my sin of (insert sin)****. I turn away from it and ask that you forgive me and cleanse me of all my sins, known and unknown. I choose to forgive (insert name) because she really hurt and offended me today. Empower me to hold true to this forgiveness; take this hurt away from my heart and help me to love her as you do. Bless her oh God; draw her heart closer to you*

and meet her every need. Create in me a clean heart, oh God, and renew a right spirit within me.")

Supporting Scripture: *"Listen to me! You can pray for anything, and if you believe, you will have it.* ***But when you are praying, first forgive anyone you are holding a grudge against, so that your Father in heaven will forgive your sins, too****."* Mark 11:24-25

8. <u>And lead us not in temptation but deliver us from evil</u> **(Requests)** – Pray for the safety, deliverance and protection of you, your family, church, nation, and the world. **Plead the blood of Jesus** over your possessions – family, home, car, finances, job, health, etc. Take authority over Satan; resist him so that he can flee from you. Dispatch your angels to protect you and fight on your behalf against evil (e.g. *Lord, I thank you for your protection. I plead the blood of Jesus, a hedge of protection, over my life, health, family, home, cars, and every road traveled. I plead the blood of Jesus over my job and over all things you have given me in this life. Where I am weak, you are strong. Thank you for empowering me to resist the devil; therefore, he must flee. I dispatch my ministering angels to do battle on my behalf and on behalf of my family, church, community, city, and nation. I pray that this world will humble themselves, seek you and pray, and turn from their wicked ways so that the world can be healed and delivered from all manner of evil.)*

Supporting Scripture: *"So humble yourselves before God. Resist the Devil, and he will flee from you."* James 4:7

<u>Winning in Warfare</u>

As we learned earlier, because we have an evil enemy God has equipped us with His armor to engage in spiritual warfare. We cannot fight the evil enemy with physical weapons or fight him with our hands, but we must instead fight him with the Word of God. The evil enemy seeks to steal what God has for us and works 24-7 to block God's blessings from operating in our lives. Therefore, we must STAND and fight the evil enemy when he sticks out his ugly head, and even when he tries to hide. We must do our best to be prepared at all times because we never know when the evil enemy will strike. The difference between regular prayers and spiritual warfare is that with spiritual warfare you are taking your authority over the enemy. Rather than speaking to God, you speak directly to Satan using God's Word (e.g. *Satan, you cannot have my family; the Blood of Jesus is against you. I command you to take your hands off my brother. For God's Word says that with long life God will satisfy him. You cannot take him before his time. I command you to loose him now! I break, sever, cancel, and eradicate your works from operating in his life. Go now, in the name of Jesus!"*

Here is how to Warfare spiritually:

- Praise and worship God to invoke His presence.
- Repent or turn away from sin – you cannot fight Satan on his turf.

- Speak the name of Jesus and plead the blood of Jesus over your life and your loved ones. Satan is defeated by the blood of Jesus.
- Put on your armor as discussed in the 'Evil Enemy' chapter, according to Ephesians 6:10-18.
- Commission your angels for assistance.
- Speak and declare God's Word against Satan using your God-given authority.
- Pray in the Holy Spirit and team up with Him.

Purpose Point: Spiritual warfare requires spiritual maturity. A princess prays, but a Queen declares, decrees, and exercises her God-given authority.

Jesus said, *"Look, I have given you authority over all the power of the enemy...Nothing will injure you."* Luke 10:19

9. For thine is the kingdom and the power and the glory forever **(Praise)** – Praise God for His mighty power. Declare His victory. Thank God again for who He is and what He has done. **Nothing is too hard for Him, and nothing is impossible with Him. Pray, trust, and believe.**

Supporting Scriptures: *"I am the Lord, the God of all the people of the world. Is anything too hard for me?"* Jeremiah 32:27

"For nothing is impossible with God." Luke 1:37

Reference: "The Lord's Daily Prayer Guide" by A. R. Williams 2005*

10. Amen ("so be it") – When we pray to the Father we should always end with the name of Jesus (i.e. *"In Jesus name I pray, Amen."*). Note: Since Jesus himself prayed the Lord's Prayer to the Father, he did not end his prayer with his own name, but we should.

Supporting Scripture: *"At that time you won't need to ask me for anything. The truth is, you can go directly to the Father and ask him, and he will grant your request because you use my name....**Ask, using my name, and you will receive, and you will have abundant joy.**"*
John 16: 23-24

In addition to your personal prayers, below are the Top 8 Kingdom Prayers to pray:

1. *Prayer of Praise, Sustainability, and Stability* – The Lord's Prayer (Matthew 6:9-15)
2. *Prayer of Expansion* – The Prayer of Jabez (1 Chronicles 4:10)
3. *Prayer of Obedience* – The Ten Commandments (Pray: Lord, help me to put you first; help me not to steal; help me not to kill; help me not to covet…) – Exodus 20:2-17
4. *Prayer of Provision* – Psalm 23
5. *Prayer of Protection* – Psalm 91
6. *Prayer for Spiritual Wisdom* – Ephesians 1:17-20
7. *Prayer for Help and Guidance* – Psalm 143

8. *Prayer of Salvation* (MVP or the Most Valuable Prayer) – Remember, Romans 10:9, as you demonstrate your purpose as God's special princess to lead others to Christ. When doing so, one question to ask the person is: *"If you died tonight, where would you go?"* and then lead them into the following prayer, if they are unsure about whether or not they will go to Heaven. Request that they repeat the following after you:

"Dear God, I need you. I confess that Jesus is Lord. Thank you, Jesus, for dying for my sins and loving me. I believe you rose from the dead and are alive today interceding on my behalf. I turn from my sins and choose to live for you. Come into my heart; I make you my Lord and Savior."

After they have prayed this prayer, praise God and encourage them to become a part of a Bible-based church. In summary,

Persevere in prayer (*PER*sist even when *SEVERE*)

Receive and Reclaim what is yours – God's promises; **R**epent as necessary

Acknowledge God for who He is through thanksgiving, praise, and worship, and not just for what He can do

Yield to the Will of God (surrender, trust, and rest in His love for you)

Purpose Point: A princess is not wimpy or pitiful; she is confident, bold, and powerful with her prayers.

Purpose Point: Always pray and ask in Jesus name. Amen.

*"**You didn't choose me. I chose you. I appointed you to go and produce lasting fruit**, so that the Father will give you whatever you ask for, using my name."* John 15:16

**God is with you always; when you want to feel Him near,
He is only a prayer away.**

Take a break and go have a chat, conversation, and confrontation with Jesus.
"The lions may grow weak and hungry, but those who seek the LORD lack no good thing." Psalm 34:10 NIV

"Let all that I am praise the Lord; with my whole heart, I will praise his holy name. Let all that I am praise the Lord; may I never forget the good things he does for me. He forgives all my sins and heals all my diseases. He redeems me from death and crowns me with love and tender mercies. He fills my life with good things. My youth is renewed like the eagle's!" Psalm 103:1-5

*"Let me hear Your lovingkindness in the morning, for I trust in You. **Teach me the way in which I should walk, for I lift up my soul to You.** Rescue me, O Lord, from my enemies; I take refuge in You. Teach me to do Your will [so that I may please You], for You are my God; **Let Your good Spirit lead me on level ground**. Save my life, O Lord, for Your name's sake; In Your righteousness bring my life out of trouble. In your lovingkindness, silence and destroy my enemies..."* Psalm 143:8-12 AMP
*"**The end of all things is at hand; therefore be self-controlled and sober-minded for the sake of your prayers.**"* 1 Peter 4:7 ESV

Chapter 11
Endless End

Congratulations…you have made it to the end of this book. To every beginning there is an end. Nothing in this world will last forever. There will come a time when your life will end, and the world will end. There will come a time when laughter, fun, pain, sorrow, and suffering on earth will all end…a time when the end will end only to begin again and last forever without end – endless...never-ending.

When you die on earth your life has ended, but there will be an afterlife – life after death. If you die in Christ or die having been saved, then your life will begin again in heaven and will last forever. But if you die without Christ, not having been saved, your life (as death) will begin again in hell and will last forever – endless. Although you have made it to the end of this book, there are two important books that you should be concerned about because your life depends on it.

Book #1: The *Book of the Law* (the Bible – Word of God) is your instruction manual for life. You should study this book faithfully to gain wisdom, knowledge, understanding and purpose. Then you will know how to live your life on earth according to God's standards and will, as God's precious princess. *"Keep this Book of the Law always on your lips; meditate on it day and night, so that you may be careful to do everything written in it. Then you will be prosperous and successful."* Joshua 1:8 NIV Consider the Bible not only as the Book of the Law, but the Book *to* Life—which with proper usage secures your place on the page in the Book *of* Life.

Book #2: The *Book of Life* is God's personal journal of human record keeping. It lists the names of all people who have accepted Jesus, and whose life will begin again in heaven. *"Anyone whose name was not found written in the book of life was thrown into the lake of fire."* Revelations 20:15 NIV

Companion books to the Book of Life are the *books of behaviors and deeds* of every person who lives/lived on earth. Every day of your life is recorded in these books (Psalm 139:16).

When you die on earth, you will soon face judgment from Jesus and God. You will have to stand before them in the spirit realm as they judge you (2 Corinthians 5:10). To assist God with judgment, He will open His Book(s) to see if your name is written in it and judge you according to your works. If your name is not written in the Book of Life, then you will be sentenced to death in hell, and eventually the lake of fire, forever. This is the second death which will last endlessly. Revelations 20:12-14 reads, *"I saw the dead, both great and small, standing before God's throne. And the books were opened, including the Book of Life. And the dead were judged according to what they have done, as recorded in the books…all were judged according to their deeds… The lake of fire is the second death."*

Secure Salvation

Sustain Relationship with God
Love God

Purpose Point: The first death is when a person dies on earth (Hebrews 9:27). The second death is when a person transitions from hell to the lake of fire.

"But cowards who turn away from me, and unbelievers, and the corrupt, and murderers and the immoral, and those who practice witchcraft, and idol worshipers, and all liars – their doom is in the lake that burns with fire and sulfur. This is the second death." Revelations 21:8

Purpose Point: Not every Christian will die physically, but every Christian will be transformed. I know this sounds untrue, but some people will not experience physical death, the first or second death. When Jesus returns to earth, he will have come to rapture or take all of God's children with him back to heaven – those who are still living on earth and have accepted Him. They will be transformed, will live forever, and therefore will not experience physical death.

"But let me tell you a wonderful secret God has revealed to us. Not all of us will die, but we will all be transformed. It will happen in a moment, in the blink of an eye, when the last trumpet is blown. For when the trumpet sounds, the Christians who have died will be raised with transformed bodies. And then we who are living will be transformed so that we will never die. For our perishable earthly bodies must be transformed into heavenly bodies that will never die. When this happens – when our perishable earthly bodies have been transformed into heavenly bodies that will never die – then at last the Scriptures will come true: "Death is swallowed up in victory. O death, where is your victory? O death, where is your sting?" For sin is the sting that results in death...How we thank God, who gives us victory over sin and death through Jesus Christ our Lord! So, my dear brothers and sisters, be strong and steady, always enthusiastic about the Lord's work, for you know that nothing you do for the Lord is ever useless." 1 Corinthians 15:51-58

Purpose Point: No one knows when Jesus will return to earth. If you are alive on earth when he returns and have not yet accepted him as your Lord and Savior, then Jesus will not take you to heaven with him. You will remain on earth during a time of intense chaos, destruction, tribulation, pain, and suffering...nothing like it is today. The world will be different in the worst possible way. The devil will manifest himself as the Anti-Christ and will control and afflict everyone who remains. Evil will rule the world with no good in it. So, if you want to be saved from hell on earth and hell itself, you <u>must</u> make your decision soon before it is too late. You must make your decision today because you are not promised tomorrow. Jesus will come back soon; it could be tomorrow, next week or 20 years from now, will you be ready?

"...he will come with his mighty angels, in flaming fire, bringing judgment on those who don't know God and on those who refuse to obey the Good News of our Lord Jesus. They will be punished with everlasting destruction, forever separated from the Lord and from his glorious power when he comes..." 2 Thessalonians 1:7-10

Purpose Point: One way that we show that we have accepted Jesus is when we love one another. Remember, when you accept Jesus you become adopted into his family, where God becomes your father and others who have accepted Jesus become your brothers and sisters in Christ. Remember, your brothers and sisters are not just your biological siblings, but your true brothers and sisters are the people who have accepted Jesus Christ as their Lord. Jesus expects us to love our brothers and sisters and look after them. When we do, it is just like we are loving and helping Jesus. God's greatest commandment is for you to love God with all your heart and mind, and to love your neighbor as yourself. Your brothers, sisters, and the people you encounter are your neighbors; therefore, your neighbor is not necessarily someone who lives next door to you. Your love walk (how you treat God, yourself and others) are recorded in His books. Accepting Jesus and living for Him seals and separates you as His child (sheep).

"But when the Son of Man [Jesus] comes in his glory, and all the angels with him, then he will sit upon his glorious throne. All nations will be gathered in his presence, and he will separate the people as a shepherd separates the sheep from the goats. He will place the sheep at his right hand and the goats at his left. Then the King will say to those on his right, 'Come, you who are blessed by my Father, **inherit the Kingdom prepared for you from the creation of the world...***when you did it to one of the least of these my brothers and sisters, you were doing it to me!"* Matthew 25:31-40

"One day an expert religious law stood up to test Jesus by asking him this question: **'Teacher, what must I do to receive eternal life?'** *Jesus replied, 'What does the law of Moses say? How do you read it?' The man answered,* **'You must love the Lord your God will all your heart, all your soul, all your strength, and all your mind. And, 'Love your neighbor as yourself.'** *'Right', Jesus told him. 'Do this and you will live!'"* Luke 10:25-28

Candid Clarification: With all the scams, schemes, scandals, sin, and sinister agendas in our world today, understand that you can't help, trust or be neighborly to everyone. You can love people from a distance by choosing to do them no harm while protecting yourself from harm and potential danger. Trust God to lead you as it relates to people and pray for *a discerning spirit.*

You have the power to control your final destination, your final end. If you want your final end to be in heaven, you must make the decision (if you haven't already) to confess and accept Jesus as your Lord and Savior. If you do not make this decision, then your final end will automatically be in hell, the lake of fire, with the devil and his demons. This is not a joke; this is not a story that someone made up. **Heaven and Hell are real!** You must know that Jesus is the only way and the only truth; no one can enter heaven without him.

"Jesus told him, 'I am the way, the truth, and the life. No one can come to the Father except through me..." John 14:6

"And this is what God has testified: He has given us eternal life, and this life is in his Son. So whoever has God's Son has life; whoever does not have his Son does not have life." 1 John 5:11-12

"...It is by the name of Jesus Christ of Nazareth, whom you crucified but whom God raised from the dead, that this man stands before you healed...Salvation is found in no one else, for there is no other name under heaven given to mankind by which we must be saved." Acts 4:10-12 NIV

"Whoever believes in the Son has eternal life, but whoever rejects the Son will not see life, for God's wrath remains on them." John 3:36 NIV; *"Whoever believes in him is not condemned, but whoever does not believe stands condemned already because they have not believed in the name of God's one and only Son."* John 3:18 NIV

You must make the decision on earth while living to accept and obey Jesus because once you die it will be too late. Your final destination will inevitably be eternal damnation in hell… irreversible, irrevocable, final…endless. Allow Jesus to save you from eternal death by confessing and accepting him today. See the Prayer of Salvation at the end of this chapter.

Purpose Point: In hell people will be torrefied and terrified with pain and suffering. The devil and everyone who ends up there will be tormented day and night forever with nowhere to escape – forever separated from God.

"Then the Devil, who betrayed them, was thrown into the lake of fire that burns with sulfur, joining the beast and the false prophet. There they will be tormented day and night forever and ever." Revelations 20:10

Purpose Point: Hell is both terrifying and torrefying.

Text Term: Torrefy – to experience intense heat and fire
Text Term: Terrify – to fill with terror

Purpose Point: People who are alive but have not yet accepted Jesus still have an opportunity to accept Jesus and receive eternal life as long as they live. However, if a person dies without accepting and obeying Jesus, the person will have no chance of being saved – it will be too late. Their eternal destination and final end would be finalized in hell and the lake of fire forever with no turning back. They will be forever separated from God and will no longer have the opportunity to accept Jesus.

Jesus told this story in the Bible:

"Jesus said, "There was a certain rich man who was splendidly clothed and who lived each day in luxury. At his door lay a diseased beggar named Lazarus. As Lazarus lay there longing for scraps from the rich man's table, the dogs would come and lick his open sores. Finally, the beggar died and was carried by the angels to be with Abraham. The rich man also died and was buried, and his soul went to the place of the dead. There, in torment, he saw Lazarus in the far distance with Abraham. The rich man shouted, 'Father Abraham, have some pity! Send Lazarus over here to dip the tip of his finger with water and cool my tongue, because I am in anguish in these flames.' But Abraham said to him, 'Son, remember that during your lifetime you had everything you wanted, and Lazarus had nothing. So now he is here being comforted, and you are in anguish. And besides, there is great chasm separating us. Anyone who wanted to cross over to you from here is stopped at its edge, and no one there can cross over to us.' Then the rich man said, 'Please, Father Abraham, send him to my father's home. For I have five brothers, and I want him to warn them about this place of torment so they won't have to come here when they die.' But Abraham said, 'Moses and the prophets have warned them. Your brothers can read their writings anytime they want to.' The rich man replied, 'No, Father Abraham! But if someone is sent to them from the dead, then they will turn from their sin.' But Abraham said, 'If they won't listen to Moses and the prophets, they won't listen even if someone rises from the dead.'" Luke 16:19-31

Purpose Point: So you see it will be too late to turn back once you die physically without accepting Jesus. You will be tormented in fire and flames forever. You will feel and be consciously aware of the pain, suffering, and past mistakes. You will wish and cry out for someone to help you, but help will not come – there will be no one to aid your rescue. You will regret not accepting Jesus and not listening to the warning messages that God sent you through His pastors, ministers, teachers, and prophets. You will wish that you could go and tell your loved ones who are still living to repent or turn away from their sins and accept Jesus, but you will not be able to do so. You will burn forever with no escape and no help from anyone – not even God.

It is a TERRIBLE thing to be eternally separated from God.

Purpose Point: Death is not the end; it is merely a change or transition to our beginning – a beginning that will never end. After Jesus died, he rose again three days later, and entered eternal paradise. Simply put, death is a vehicle that will take you to your final and eternal destination – Heaven or Hell. Death is the beginning of forever.

Purpose Point: People who have been perceived to have nothing on earth and looked at as last will be first and have everything in heaven, far away from evil peoples' grasp. In the place of torment, many will be pleading and begging, asking for help and rescue. But they will hear the words reverberate, *"I never knew you."*

"Not everyone who says to me, 'Lord, Lord,' will enter the kingdom of heaven..."
"Then I will tell them plainly, 'I never knew you. Away from me, you evildoers!'"
Matthew 7:21; 7:23 NIV

The weeds will burn, but the good seeds will live

*"Then, leaving the crowds outside, Jesus went into the house. His disciples said, 'Please explain the story of the weeds in the field.' 'All right,' he said. 'I, the Son of Man, am the farmer who plants the good seed. The field is the world, and the good seed represents the people of the Kingdom. The weeds are the people who belong to the evil one. The enemy who planted the weeds among the wheat is the Devil. The harvest is the **end of the world**, and the harvesters are the angels. Just as weeds are separated out and burned, so it will be at the **end of the world**. I, the Son of Man, will send my angels, and they will remove from my Kingdom everything that causes sin and all who do evil, and they will throw them into the furnace and burn them. There will be weeping and gnashing of teeth. Then the godly will shine like the sun in their Father's Kingdom. **Anyone who is willing to hear should listen and understand!**"*
Matthew 13:36-43

No one knows when their time on earth will expire; no one knows when they will die. You could die tomorrow; you could die today; you could die right now while reading this book...God forbid.

My point is, don't gamble with your life; don't gamble with your final destination. Time is of the essence; the clock is ticking; your time is winding down. Make the decision to live for Christ – to love, honor and obey him.

Choose to walk in your princesshood down the perfect path of life and mature into a queen. Make the decision to S.T.A.N.D. – **S**et yourself apart, **T**ake your place, **A**ffirm your identity, **N**ullify your past and **D**emonstrate your purpose.

Make the decision to have your endless end in heaven surrounded by God – His love, peace, joy, and glory. In Heaven, there will be no more sickness, no more pain, no more shame, no more fear, no more worry, no more crying, no more struggling…no more!

But in hell there will be fear, pain, burning, gnashing of teeth, and suffering forevermore.

Believing with Benefits

Abraham was very special to God and once lived on earth. He was one of the first few people to really believe by faith and obey God. As a result, God made him the father of many nations and the father of faith (Genesis 17:1-6). We receive the blessings of Abraham when we believe.

"Understand, then, that those who have faith are children of Abraham. Scripture foresaw that God would justify the Gentiles by faith, and announced the gospel in advance to Abraham: "All nations will be blessed through you." So those who rely on faith are blessed along with Abraham, the man of faith." Galatians 3:7-9 NIV

Purpose Point: When we choose to believe and obey God, we will experience blessings on earth and rewards in heaven.

"Physical training is good, but training for godliness is much better, promising benefits in this life and in the life to come." 1 Timothy 4:8

Purpose Point: God gives us hope from now to eternity.

"For the Lord himself will come down from heaven with a commanding shout, with the voice of the archangel, and with the trumpet call of God. First, the Christians who have died will rise from their graves." 1 Thessalonians 4:16

"…as it is written, "What no eye has seen, what no ear has heard, and what no human mind has conceived — the things God has prepared for those who love him —"
1 Corinthians 2:9 NIV

Jesus has prepared a *royal Kingdom* – the perfect Palace and Paradise for you (Luke 23:43). *"Nothing impure will ever enter it, nor will anyone who does what is shameful or deceitful, but only those whose names are written in the Lamb's book of life."* Revelations 21:27 NIV

Jesus said, *"Let not your hearts be troubled. Believe in God; believe also in me. In my Father's house are many rooms. If it were not so, would I have told you that I go to prepare a place for you? And if I go and prepare a place for you, I will come again and will take you to myself, that where I am you may be also. **And you know the way to where I am going.**"* John 14:1-4 ESV
Jesus is the way — the narrow gate. The Princess's Pathway is the right way to go.

Accept Jesus with the Right Motive
Most of the time fear and trouble lead people to God, particularly the fear of going to hell. Although this may be what leads a person to God, don't let it be your only motive for choosing

Him and accepting Jesus. You should love God because He first loved you. You should be grateful to Him for all He has done. You should accept Jesus as your Lord and Savior because of who He is, and not just for what He can do in your life and the life to come.

God loves you unconditionally and He wants you to love Him the same in return. He has demonstrated His love for you by sending His only son Jesus to die for your sins and to give you the gift of eternal life – accept it, rejoice and be thankful!

Purpose Point: Many people make the mistake to believe that since they are young, they have plenty of time to repent and accept Jesus. Young people die every day. There are more young people dying from accidents, violence, sickness, and disease than ever before. There is no such thing as old folks' disease(s) anymore; young people are getting the same diseases and dying early. None of us are promised tomorrow, not even young people.

Death has no age limit. So don't think that you can have fun and live wildly without possibly experiencing death, and then decide later to accept and serve Jesus when you are older; there may not be a later.

Life and death both have a way of sneaking up on you with a big, scary, and sometimes deadly surprise. You could be asleep one minute and wake up in hell the next minute. *Again, don't gamble with your final destination; it is not worth it.* If you do, you could lose, and be lost in hell and the lake of fire forever. When it comes to determining your eternal destination, there will be a Judge, but there will be no trial, no jury of your peers, no 5 to 20 year sentence, no bailout, no bond, no get out of jail free card, no appeal, no acquittal, no advocacy, no life line, no rescue, no calls for help, no second chance, no escape plan, no plan B and no exceptions; if you die without Jesus, there will be no hope for you.

"For we must all stand before Christ to be judged. We will each receive whatever we deserve for the good or evil we have done in this earthly body." 2 Corinthians 5:10

"Don't you realize how kind, tolerant, and patient God is with you? Or don't you care? Can't you see how kind he has been in giving you time to turn from your sin? But no, you won't listen. So you are storing up terrible punishment for yourself because of your stubbornness in refusing to turn from your sin. For there is going to come a day of judgment when God, the just judge of all the world, will judge all people according to what they have done. He will give eternal life to those who persist in doing what is good, seeking after the glory and honor and immortality that God offers. But he will pour out his anger and wrath on those who live for themselves, who refuse to obey the truth and practice evil deeds. There will be trouble and calamity for everyone who keeps on sinning..." Romans 2:4-9

Purpose Point: The mass majority of us will travel the road of physical death but the difference is some people will experience eternal life afterwards and some will experience eternal separation from God (eternal death) in a conscious state with terror and torment amid fire. Physical **death is not the end**; you will live on somewhere (Heaven or Hell). Your choices will decide.

If you still have not yet accepted Jesus as your Lord and Savior, pray the prayer below. Choose eternal life by accepting and obeying Jesus. The Lord knows all hearts and both heaven and earth will be witnesses to the choice you make. Once you accept Jesus, God will transform you from the inside out and give you the desire to obey Him. Draw closer to God and He will draw closer to you (James 4:8).

"This day I call the heavens and the earth as witnesses against you that I have set before you life and death, blessings and curses. **Now choose life, so that you and your children may live and that you may love the Lord your God, listen to his voice, and hold fast to him.** *For the Lord is your life, and he will give you many years in the land he swore to give to your fathers, Abraham, Isaac and Jacob."* Deuteronomy 30:19-20 NIV

Prayer of Salvation – *"Dear God, I need you. I confess that Jesus is Lord. Thank you, Jesus, for dying for my sins and loving me. I believe you rose from the dead and are alive today interceding on my behalf. I repent of my sins and choose to live for you. Come into my heart; I make you my Lord and Savior."*

If you have prayed this prayer, you are saved from eternal death and have become one of God's very own – His princess. Rejoice! Now love God with all your heart as He works in you.

"For if you confess with your mouth that Jesus is Lord and believe in your heart that God raised him from the dead, you will be saved. For it is by believing in your heart that you are made right with God, and it is by confessing with your mouth that you are saved. As the Scriptures tell us, 'Anyone who believes in him will not be disappointed.'"
Romans 10:9-11

"The end of the world is coming soon. Therefore, be earnest and disciplined in your prayers. Most important of all, continue to show deep love for each other, for love covers a multitude of sins...God has given gifts to each of you from his great variety of spiritual gifts. Manage them well so that God's generosity can flow through you. Are you called to be a speaker? Then speak as though God himself were speaking through you. Are you called to help others? Do it with all the strength and energy that God supplies. Then God will be given glory in everything through Jesus Christ. All glory and power belong to him forever and ever. Amen."
1 Peter 4:7-11

"How frail is humanity! How short is life, and how full of trouble! Like a flower, we blossom for a moment and then wither. Like a shadow of a passing cloud, we quickly disappear."
Job 14:1-2

"Yes, and I ask you, my true companion, help **these women since they have contended** *at my side* **in the cause of the gospel...whose names are in the book of life**.*"* Philippians 4:3 NIV

Purpose Point: The moment you accept and believe in Jesus, is the moment you have eternal life and are well on your way. And because you reverence him by obeying God's Word, contending for the gospel, and demonstrating your purpose, you can be assured that your name is written in the Book of Life.

Purpose Point: Your life has meaning, value, and purpose. What you do in life and how you live your life matters.

I love happy endings. What about you? I pray that you choose the path to Life – commemorated in the Book of Life with a happy ending guaranteed. **Let Jesus be your endless end.**

Poetic Princess

The Burning Bed
This is not it; it is not the end.
Life is only the beginning, my friend.
Wake up! Wake up! Listen to my voice.
Oh, how I pray, that you'll make the right choice.
God has been sounding the alarm…
In an effort to keep you away from harm.
He says, this thing is real; open your eyes and see!
Life is not how things will forever be.
Get out from under the sheets of unbelief – the selfish and sinful bed.
Or you could very soon be joining the dead.
"I am burning, I am burning" I hear people yell,
But sadly, there is no escape from hell.
Always in torment and under attack,
With no hope of turning back.
Someone says, *"I have everything, I am the true diva!"*
But in the blink of an eye she could burn like fiery fever.
Listen to your alarm; don't hit snooze.
If you wait until later, you just might lose.
People who are hateful, selfish, unforgiving and think that they are first…
Will be begging for someone to quench their thirst.
The time is now; wake up and S.T.A.N.D. my predestined princess.
I want all of you, and nothing less.
Accept my calling, hear my voice, and be led.
Or you could die forever in your burning bed.

"When the watchman sees the enemy coming, he sounds the alarm to warn the people. Then if those who hear the alarm refuse to take action, it is their own fault if they die. They heard the alarm but ignored it, so the responsibility is theirs. If they had listened to the warning, they could have saved their lives." Ezekiel 33:3-5

S.T.A.N.D. to win…let Heaven be your endless end!

"…but the one who stands firm to the end will be saved." Matthew 24:13 NIV

"Be on guard! Be alert! You do not know when that time will come." Mark 13:33 NIV

*Repent… "Turn to God and change the way you think and act, because **the kingdom of heaven is near.**"* Matthew 3:2 GW

Last chances may be the last, but they are not the end. Understand the urgency and remember this Prayer of Salvation (the Most Valuable Prayer) for you, your family and those you seek to help: *"Dear God, I need you. I confess that Jesus is Lord. Thank you, Jesus, for dying for my sins and loving me. I believe you rose from the dead and are alive today interceding on my behalf. I repent of my sins and choose to live for you. Come into my heart; I make you my Lord and Savior."*

The End…

www.ingramcontent.com/pod-product-compliance
Lightning Source LLC
Chambersburg PA
CBHW080239170426
43192CB00014BA/2501